SHAKESPEARE AS A MAN OF ACTION

The uncontested, provable "facts" about William Shakespeare, the Elizabethan poet, actor, playwright, and gentleman, could be recorded on a single page of this book. In spite of the earnest researches of three centuries of scholarship, he remains a noncommittal figure, like his bust in the Stratford church, solid, dimensional, but a person without a personality. Aside from the record of his professional successes and of a few fleeting appearances on other public occasions, his "biography" is based on inferences drawn from his works.

It would be amusing, and perhaps a little chastening, to assemble a gallery of portraits based on the various "biographies" of Shakespeare. Depending on the artist's point of view, his subject would be drawn as the misogynist, the theologian, the psychologist, the shamefaced actor, the man of affairs. Nor would these portraits be totally inaccurate. For the first significant "fact" about Shakespeare is that he began his career as an actor, as a man who must, in his time, play many parts.

This fact is doubly significant, for the biographer and for the playreader. The notions about Shakespeare's character and personality have not been drawn from essays and discourses, or from prefaces and digressive first-person monologues in novels; they have been laboriously pieced together from dramatic dialogue and lyric poetry (the sonnets). And in both dramatic dialogue and lyric poetry, the artist speaks not as himself, but as whatever character he elects or is compelled to assume at the moment. The ability to portray an emotion he does not feel, apparently to lose his own personality in that of his character, is generally recognized as the basic requirement for the successful actor; it is too easily forgotten that this is also the basic requirement for the successful playwright. And Shakespeare was a successful actor who became a successful playwright.

So, for example, as Polonius, he can rattle off a baker's dozen of moral commonplaces with such conviction that three centuries later the speech is quoted as a golden text for the guidance of youth, quite ignoring the fact that throughout the play of *Hamlet* Polonius is held up to ridicule as an intruding fool, weak in his wits. So Iago, the malignant hypocrite of *Othello,* uses a pious speech about the preciousness of his "good name" to throw his victims off guard; and the speech has been remembered as proverbial wisdom, rather than as the dramatic irony it is.

Perhaps the most striking instance of this kind of uncritical innocence may be found in the misreadings of *I Henry IV.* Toward the end of this history play, the chief comic character, Sir John Falstaff, soliloquizes about the motives for his cowardly behavior on the battlefield. The essence of his defense is that "he who fights and runs away will live to fight another day." Particularly in the period of reaction and disillusion which follows any war, such a realistic attitude toward the meaninglessness of honor to the dead hero has natural appeal; there is great temptation to see Falstaff as the hero of the play, as the rational man. But to see only this is to ignore another attitude toward honor represented in the play, with equal conviction, by the character of Hotspur. The tendency of any producer is to cast as Hotspur his most romantically attractive player, and it is a tendency the reader will find it difficult to resist. Hotspur's wife recalls after his death that

> *by his light*
> *Did all the chivalry of England move*
> *To do brave acts.*

We behold him cutting his way through court intrigues, maintaining his rights, even against the king, inspiring his outnumbered warriors, fighting and making love, all with a directness and singleness of purpose that might well persuade us that the pursuit of honor is the sole duty of man.

Yet it is just at this point that we must remind ourselves that Falstaff and Hotspur are actors in a play and not lecturers on a platform or preachers in a pulpit. Whatever they say must be understood in the context of the action. Falstaff is a mightily persuasive rascal, but his rational conclusions about the vanity of honor must be recognized as the words of a man who is bent on corrupting the heir-apparent to the throne, on robbing the king's representatives, on ruthlessly directing his wretched draftees into the thick of the fight while he prudently goes into hiding. And Hotspur's romantic idealism must be recognized as the philosophy of a man who will quarrel over the tenth part of a hair, who is in open rebellion against his king, who is rash, proud, and self-centered. When Falstaff or Hotspur speak of honor they do not speak for Shakespeare, and the point of the play does not lie in one or the other of their speeches.

As a playwright, Shakespeare must be able to assume in turn each of the roles of which he is the first creator, to speak each of the speeches in turn with the same sense of compulsion he will demand from his actors, the second creators. The point of a play, then, will not lie in any one speech or any one character, but in their relationships within the whole. The "point" of a play lies in its action.

2

To the fact that Shakespeare was an actor-playwright must be added the "fact" that he was a highly successful playwright. His reputation did not come, as students must sometimes be persuaded, from the bibliographical and textual researches of musty scholars, or from the solitary meditations of critics in their libraries, or lovers of poetry in perfumèd bowers. It is true that part of Shakespeare's Elizabethan reputation depended on his "sugared sonnets" and two erotic narrative poems, but these were fashionable exercises undertaken (as far as we can be certain) early in his career, and intended for an audience comparable to that of the "little magazines" of the twentieth century.

For reasons that we can only surmise, the major part of his work both in quantity and importance was written for the audience of the public theaters, what we would today call the commercial theater, of which Broadway is both a generic and qualitative designation. If the occasion demanded he could write special pieces for the court or for the so-called private theaters, largely attended by the upper classes. But he began his career as a member of Burbage's theatrical troupe, catering to a widely diversified audience of gallants and apprentices, merchants and nobles, and he learned early the art of theatrical action which governed his technique as a playwright, regardless of the small modifications demanded by particular theaters or particular audiences. To re-enter the portrait gallery, we have seen various images of Shakespeare the Poet, Shakespeare the Actor, and Shakespeare the Playwright, but he was primarily and predominantly, in the theatrical sense of the term, a Man of *Action*.

3

In the Elizabethan theater action assumed a special importance. Although a detailed knowledge of that theater and its methods of production is not of first importance in beginning to understand Shakespeare, some knowledge of its peculiar nature will clarify the design of his plays and, perhaps, justify the emphasis that is placed upon an analysis of their action. Shakespeare's theater was unencumbered by scenery. The main acting area was an enormous platform, extending into the audience area, with no proscenium frame and no front curtain to separate the actors from the spectators. Entrance to this platform was by doors on either side, at the rear. Between these doors, in the center of the back, there seems to have been a small alcove— the inner stage—which could be shut off by a draw curtain. Above the inner stage was another small room—the upper stage —flanked on either side by large windows. All these locations— platform, inner and upper stages, and windows—might be used as acting areas, permitting great flexibility, and a constant flow of movement. Since there was no scenery to be shifted, the action was practically continuous from beginning to end, and there was nothing upon the stage—barring an essential property, such as a throne or a bed—to distract the attention of the audience from the actor and what he was doing.

This raises the question of the division of the printed texts into acts and scenes. For the most part the act divisions have been inserted by later editors. There seem to have been no intermissions between the acts in Elizabethan performances, and in general the editorial divisions have been made with an eye to the conventions of classical drama rather than the inner form of the Elizabethan. That is to say, most of the act divisions ignore the essential structure of the action; they come at places where a knowing dramatist would be unlikely to dismiss his audience even for a moment. The scene divisions, on the other hand, make better sense. The Elizabethan audience would be aware of them as the stage was momentarily empty after the exit of one group of characters and before the entrance of a new group. But of scene change, in our sense of shifting settings, there was none. The location of scenes (*"Another part of the forest"*) is again editorial contribution.

Indeed Shakespeare is often careful to leave the actual setting of a given scene indefinite. There is no mention of place in the opening scenes of *I Henry IV*. We are presented first with a king and his counsellors, then with Hal and Falstaff, then with the counsellors again. The focus is on what occurs, on the action, not on where it occurs, the place. The proper description of I.1 would be *A council meeting,* which is vastly different from its usual editorial identification as *A room in the palace.* On the other hand, when the place of the action is vital to an understanding of its significance, or will carry some additional meaning for the spectator, specific reference will be made in the dialogue. The action in Act II, Scene 3, of *Much Ado about Nothing* depends upon an arbor from which a plot may be overheard. No arbor was actually used on the stage, but the place was nevertheless insistently suggested to the audience in the dialogue. At the beginning of the scene, Benedick directs his servant boy to fetch a book from his chamber and to "Bring it hither to me in the orchard." A moment later, as the conspirators approach, he steps behind a pillar of the stage, announcing "I will hide me in the arbor"—and thus easily is the stage "set" for the ensuing comedy.

Thus the seeing of an Elizabethan play was in a special and exclusive sense the seeing of an action. The theater and the production were so contrived that the focus was always upon the actor and his movement. Anyone familiar with the tradition of the theater that preceded Shakespeare's—the classical drama of Greece and Rome—or of our own "realistic" theater, will not fail to mark both the quantity and kind of Shakespearean action: battles, murder, and sudden death; shipwrecks, marchings, duels, tempests and torturing. Nor did the absence of scenery diminish the realism of the action. Theatrical records give evidence of the splendor of the costuming, of the attention to details of spectacular processions and battles, even of bladders of red wine worn under clothing to provide blood for dueling scenes. The actors, too, were trained as athletes and the fighting must have been lifelike and glittering indeed to hold the attention of audiences to whom street brawls were commonplace sights. And all was performed at break-neck pace, for the running time of these plays was in the neighborhood of two hours (a heavily cut version of any of them runs three hours in the modern theater), using any or all of the available acting areas. Shakespearean drama is a vivid and bustling picture of life, framed (as one of his fellows put it with significant emphasis) in lively *action*.

4

There are many ways for the modern reader to approach the problem of understanding Shakespeare. Working from the basis of narrative art in general, he may begin with an analysis of the verse, the verbal art, the imagery. From the basis of social and historical background, he may begin with a study of the ideas in relation to the moral and philosophical principles of the Renaissance. But these, as has been implied, are only contributory to Shakespeare's art in his chosen profession of playwright. An analysis of the action is the first and in many ways the simplest approach to the study of a drama. When that has been completed, the functions of characterization, dialogue, and cultural framework should be studied to discover how they enforce or modify the basic design. For though a play, to be successful with its immediate audience, must be simple on at least one level, it can be (and in the case of Shakespeare invariably is) infinitely complex.

An analysis of the action does not mean a summary of the plot. It is not a report of what happens. It is a description of the design—the order in which the action is presented. For instance, *I Henry IV* tells two stories, either of which might do for an evening's entertainment. A report of the action might state that in one plot King Henry's plans for a pilgrimage are interrupted by a rebellion of his nobles. They are led by Hotspur, who has taken offense at a summary order of the king's and who is an easy tool in the hands of his scheming uncle. Hotspur assembles a number of dissidents and plans to meet the king at Shrewsbury. However, caution and sickness deprive him of much of his expected support, and he is defeated by a combination of superior numbers, skillful generalship, and the swordplay of Prince Hal. The secondary action centers on Falstaff, a dissolute nobleman, who is a drinking companion of the Prince of Wales, who takes part in a highway robbery, abuses the king's press, and covers himself with fraudulent glory on the battlefield.

Such might be a brief description of what happens in *I Henry IV*. But it is inaccurate in more than its omissions. It does not take into consideration the design, the order of events, and it is the order of events that determines the effect of the play. From the summary, for instance, it would be difficult to see how the two stories are fitted together except by the circumstance that certain characters appear in both. Consider, however, the design in performance:

I.1. The opening scene is a kind of prologue. The king and his nobles in all the splendor of a state occasion, solemnly conferring on matters of grave importance—the Pilgrimage to the Holy Land, rebellions in progress, the kingdom threatened. But the scene establishes more; it establishes the two major problems confronting the king, the defection of his nobles, and the dissoluteness of the heir to the throne, whom his father sadly contrasts to the high-minded and dutiful Hotspur.

I.2. As the royal group makes its stately exit through one of the doors, the roistering, mountainous figure of Falstaff appears through the other, followed by Prince Hal. In the ensuing scene, we see in action the ignoble behavior of the Prince of Wales, to which King Henry had referred in the "prologue," and later, as Poins enters, we hear the three men lay a plot to rob the king's treasury. The scene ends with Hal's soliloquy as he declares his readiness to "pay the debt [he] never promised," a speech that prepares us for his future actions.

I.3. The third scene restores the noble group and dramatizes the second of King Henry's problems—the defection of his nobles. After his angry exit, the Percies come together to lay a plot to rob the king of his power, beginning the second line of action in the play, and establishing *an exact parallel* to the action in Falstaff's story.

Thus in the first three scenes Shakespeare has *selected* only three out of all the possible events in the two stories and has *arranged* them in such a way as to suggest at once an organic relationship between the Hotspur and the Falstaff actions. The rest of the play dramatizes the consequences of the two scenes of plotting in Act One, and resolves the problems which confront the king in the opening scene. *I Henry IV* might be described as a driving movement between the point of departure in the king's council chamber to the point of arrival at Shrewsbury, a kind of giant stride in five-act boots. In the theater, the audience is perhaps scarcely aware of anything except the major all-encompassing stride. But the reader, with the command of unlimited repetitions in his own hands, should be aware that the major movement is composed of many smaller steps. That is to say, the content of each individual scene within the whole is an action in itself and may be tagged by a verb which characterizes that action. For example, here is a possible way of describing the individual scenes which make up a portion of the Falstaff story:

I.2. Falstaff *demonstrates* his attraction for Hal; *plots* to rob the king.

II.1. Minor members of the gang *set up* the robbery.

II.2. Falstaff and his gang *rob* the travelers; Hal and Poins *rob* the thieves.

II.4. Hal and Poins *force* Falstaff to reveal his failure, and so on.

These component actions might be summarized in some such formula as:
Falstaff plots to rob the king's treasury and is thwarted by Prince Hal.
If the component actions of the Hotspur story are similarly "verbalized," a summary statement might take this form:
Hotspur plots to rob the king of his power and is thwarted by Prince Hal.

Arranged thus geometrically, the constant elements of the two stories are the king and his son, while Falstaff and Hotspur, the variable elements, are equated and contrasted. Both are rebels against established order and authority, both are defeated by Hal as he justifies his behavior to the audience and regains the confidence of his father. This analysis of the action demonstrates that the focus of *I Henry IV* is actually upon the Prince of Wales and his progress from man-about-town to man of honor.

Honor has been much discussed in the dialogue of this play, and it is in their declarations upon the subject that Hotspur and Falstaff are most plainly contrasted and likened. For the romantic idealist and the realist are both fundamentally egocentric. Hotspur seeks glory for himself, at whatever cost to others; Falstaff seeks ease for himself, at whatever cost to others. And against these two Hal is constantly measured, in the development of the action, in the worried confession of his father, in the sneers of the Percies and the promptings of the gang at the Boar's Head Tavern.

The design, the structure, of the action can be summarized in terms of Hal's position in the two stories. The play is not primarily concerned with two rebellions or plots, but with the defeat of two rebellious men and the ways of life (as made overt in their definitions of honor) for which they stand. The climactic moment of the action thus arrives in Act V, Scene 4, where Hal stands on the stage between the corpse of Hotspur and the sham corpse of Falstaff. Over each Hal speaks a eulogy, a few words of praise for Hotspur's courage and spirit, for Falstaff's fellowship; but also a few words of shrewd analysis, pointing up their shortcomings, Hotspur's "ill-weaved ambition," Falstaff's exclusive concern with gratification of worldly desires. And having spoken these words, Hal departs, symbolically rejecting both philosophies and assuming the debt of social responsibility which his birth and position held out to him. The theme of the play, then, as implied by the design of the action and reinforced by the juxtaposition of characters and overt statements in the dialogue, is the education of a prince (and by extension, any young man), Hal's discovery of the true rule of honor by which a man must live in society.

5

Only one other play in this volume, *King Lear,* employs the fully developed double-plot structure of *I Henry IV*. But in all the plays the design of the action, the contrasts and comparisons, the juxtapositions of smaller actions in successive scenes, reveals the meaning of the whole play.

Lear occupies in the Elizabethan drama a position similar to *Oedipus Rex* in classical Greek drama. It represents the ultimate perfection of the form; it becomes the ideal play. Shakespeare, in reworking the "history" of a legendary king of prehistoric Britain, carefully added a subplot so detailed that it could constitute a play in itself, but paralleling in an amazing and significant way the action of his main plot. It has often been said that the Lear story is too tremendous to be realized on a stage or to be comprehended by an average spectator; the colossal figure of the hero, at war with himself, with his society, with the universal forces of nature, and his paradoxical act of finding reason in madness are thought to construct an image of life beyond the grasp of mere humanity.

The Earl of Gloucester, however, is recognizably human. Sensual, superstitious, and self-indulgent, his actions are governed by passion, not reason. He is, therefore, the easy victim of his illegitimate son—significant word, illegitimate!—who is not swayed by pleasant vices. The irony in Gloucester's story is reasonably obvious. Because he is blind to the nature of his bastard son, he wrongs his legitimate heir, and falls prey to the forces of evil in the primitive world of the drama. By these forces he is actually blinded, in a scene of deliberate and detailed horror. This action is, of course, symbolic, a dramatization of the double meaning of the word *blind.* Yet it is apparent that the shock of the torture, the putting out of his eyes, is great enough to bring him for the first time to an understanding, a vision, of the true state of affairs. The physical action clearly interprets the paradox of the man who sees clearly only after he has been blinded.

There is plenty of physical action in the Lear story, of course, but the center of the action is in the mind of the king and hence does not yield its meaning as directly to the spectator. However, the Gloucester story serves as a constant commentary or interpretation. Lear, like Gloucester, is blind to the true characters of his children. Edmund is illegitimate, Regan and Goneril are unnatural; they dupe their father by flattery, Edmund by playing on his credulousness. As the physical torture of Gloucester opens his mind's eyes, so the unnatural behavior of his daughters, the assaults upon his pride of place and person, and his symbolic warfare with the elements drive Lear into a madness in which he realizes the true order of things. Both Gloucester and Lear are saved by filial devotion, and both, having found the truth through trial and torture, escape from their tragic education into death.

Thus the fully developed double plot provides perhaps the richest revelation of Shakespeare's tragic vision. Not only does the parallel action of Gloucester interpret and humanize the story of Lear, the psychological action and spiritual conflict of Lear magnify the more domestic experiences of Gloucester. Indeed, the term *double plot* is hardly sufficient to indicate the nature of the structure of this play; it would be more accurate to describe it as *complementary plotting*.

Before realizing the full significance of the action of a tragedy like *Hamlet,* it is perhaps necessary to understand the kind of tragedy to which it belongs. *Hamlet* began as a revenge play, a type as popular and as familiar to Elizabethans as the western film is in our own popular theater. Its basic ingredients were the commission of a crime (murder) by one so highly placed as to be beyond the reach of ordinary justice and the imposition of the duty of revenge on a relative of the victim. It becomes immediately apparent that the play of *Hamlet* is concerned with two interrelated revengers. Of these, Laertes is the more conventional. Learning of his father's death, he at once returns to Denmark prepared to hack his way through all obstacles until he reaches the murderer and willing to employ any stratagem, any unfair means, to gain his end.

Laertes is set against Hamlet, who is not only a Dane and the Prince of Denmark, but a scholar and a Christian. *Hamlet* is a complex and, in many ways, mysterious play, but approached strictly from the nature of its action its basic intention is plain. Hamlet's dilemma is not "to be or not to be," but to revenge or not to revenge. Must he act according to the code accepted by his society, or should he follow his instincts as a philosopher and Christian student? The greater part of the play is devoted to examining the conflict within the hero, and, if the solution is finally forced upon him by the conniving of Laertes and Claudius, the question is still alive. Those who have died by Hamlet's agency, all but one, have died without just cause. The Ghost sententiously advised Hamlet to leave the judgment of Gertrude to Heaven; the play's action would seem to reiterate that vengeance is the Lord's. And the insistence upon the domestic nature of the tragedy, the emphasis upon the family relationships of father, mother, son, daughter, brother, sweetheart, rather than, say, on king and advisors, involves the spectator sympathetically in the action.

Even a modern audience will recognize the action of Fortinbras as political retribution. The Elizabethans were prepared to justify the revenge of Laertes as a convention, as part of the social code. Beside these men stands Hamlet, who does not subscribe to the code with a whole heart and who acts in accord with it only at moments when his emotion dominates his reason. The secondary actions of the play thus comment on, and are illuminated by, the main situation of Hamlet's dilemma.

The necessity for such analysis of the action of serious plays will be conceded by most readers and theater-goers. They are reluctant to consider anything more about comedy than its function as an "entertainment." *Entertainment,* however, is almost as elusive a word as *tragedy* and *comedy.* A sympathetic response to Shakespeare's art—as an entertainer—should be based not merely upon our spontaneous laughter, but upon an inquiry into what we are laughing about. There is plenty of obvious comedy in *Much Ado about Nothing,* for instance. Dogberry's unsuccessful encounters with the King's English belong to a comic convention that extends from the preliterary Greek mime to the typographical "boners" reprinted in contemporary periodicals. The taming of Beatrice, a kind of shrew, had already served Shakespeare as the subject for lighthearted farce, and the conquest of the confirmed bachelor by Cupid is almost a dramatic axiom.

These stereotyped materials have retained their vitality in the long stage history of *Much Ado* for several reasons, but the fundamental one is the context in which they are set. And the context of a drama is the pattern of its action. Shakespeare reworks for his main plot a rather ugly Renaissance story of a calumniated maiden. The innocent Hero is rejected by her betrothed Claudio on the false testimony of Don John. Against this action, Shakespeare sets (1) a comic love affair, in which Beatrice and Benedick are driven into each other's arms by the false testimony of their sportive friends, and (2) a comic deus ex machina, Dogberry, who by his unwitting falsification of legal testimony first prevents and then leads to a solution of the difficulties of the other characters. *Much Ado about Nothing,* incidentally, should not be taken as a title seized upon in desperation or carelessness, but as a precise description of the action of the play—an action that leads to the discovery by the actors of what is known to the audience from the start, that Hero has done nothing, right or wrong, to create ado.

The play is, however, more than a comedy of detection: the ado results in a positive Something. And since the proper subject of romantic comedy is love and marriage, the play properly ends with the union of several pairs of lovers and the prospect of future happiness. Perhaps from the standpoint of psychology, or some other modern theory of determinism, the matings would seem a trifle mechanical or unrealistic. Yet, in the context of the play, they do not appear so. Claudio loves Hero at first sight, and so (somewhat ironically?) Benedick does Beatrice after his eyes have been opened to her reported love for him. A deliberate falsehood awakens love in Benedick, a deliberate falsehood kills love in Claudio. "Reason and love," says a character in *A Midsummer-Night's Dream,* "keep little company together."

At any point the action of Don John, or Beatrice, or Dogberry, might lead to tragedy. But this is the comic view of human relationships. Out of confusion and misunderstanding, both deliberate and unintentional, comes reconciliation. Reconciliation and understanding are, of course, a part of the action of *King Lear;* the materials of tragedy and comedy are similar. The action of a comedy like *Much Ado* differs from the action of a tragedy like *Lear* in intensity and point of view.

The essential difference between the tragic and comic visions of life is strikingly shown in *The Tempest*. Here Shakespeare takes up once again the favorite Elizabethan plot mechanism of revenge (compare the Hamlet story, the Edmund plot in *Lear*). In the main plot, Prospero, the deposed Duke of Milan, contrives to get within his power all his enemies. In the parallel action, Caliban, who has in a sense been deposed by Prospero, seeks vengeance against his master. Yet reading the play, or better still seeing it, one is hardly aware of the ugly political situation, so skillfully has the whole been pervaded by the magic of the enchanted island.

The key word for the action of *The Tempest* is *change*. The warring elements of nature, presented with terrifying detail at the beginning, change at the end to harmony, "calm seas, auspicious gales." Prospero changes from the avenging necromancer to the forgiving Duke; Ferdinand from the gay courtier to the faithful lover. On the magic island all injustices are made equal, all evil natures cleansed, nothing mortal "But doth suffer a sea-change, Into something rich and strange."

Yet the action of *The Tempest,* romantic as it may be, is not wholly fantastic, not without its clear reference to actual life. Prospero was deposed because he was, in a sense, a bad ruler. Loving knowledge, he was content to shut himself up in his study and contemplate his books, a sterile and unprofitable existence. While he was thus withdrawn from life, dissident elements in his court gained the upper hand and exiled him to the magic island where he was forced to put his learning to use in order to survive. The Prospero who returns to Milan at the end of the play is not merely triumphant over his foes but over himself.

To say so much is to hint at a further dimension of the action in Shakespeare's plays—its symbolic value. This is most obvious, of course, in the romances and fantasies, but it emerges clearly at climactic moments in the earlier plays: when Hal stands between the bodies of Falstaff and Hotspur at Shrewsbury, when Lear rages at the storm on the heath. The action of a play, like the words of its poetic dialogue, has several levels of meaning—the literal, related to the total narrative, and the symbolic, related to the central idea, both of which taken together point to the meaning of the whole work. Once this meaning has been discovered, the plays of Shakespeare spring to life in the theater of the mind, ready at will of the reader-producer for repetitions, each of which will reveal added insights into his own nature as he too, in the time of his own choosing, plays many parts in the pulsing action of Shakespeare's theater of life.

ALAN S. DOWNER

Princeton, New Jersey
April, 1951

SOME SUGGESTED READINGS

The best recent study of Shakespeare's life is *Shakespeare of London* by Marcette Chute, New York, 1950. Useful general background material may be found in *A Shakespeare Primer,* by Gerald Sanders, New York, 1950; *The Backgrounds of Shakespeare's Plays,* by Karl J. Helzknecht, New York, 1950. An introduction to the study of the Elizabethan stage and dramatic art may be found in the present editor's *The British Drama: A Handbook and Brief Chronicle,* New York, 1950. The advanced student should consult *The Globe Playhouse,* by John C. Adams, Cambridge (Mass.), 1942; *A Companion to Shakespeare Studies,* edited by Harley Granville-Barker and G. B. Harrison, New York, 1934. Samplings of Shakespeare criticism of three centuries are included in two convenient, small anthologies: D. Nichol Smith, *Shakespeare Criticism* (to Carlyle), Oxford, 1916; Ann Bradby, *Shakespeare Criticism,* 1919–1935, Oxford, 1936.

CONTENTS

William Shakespeare

FIVE PLAYS

The Chronicle History of

KING HENRY
THE FOURTH

Part One

[ACT I • 1] *London. The palace.*

Enter KING HENRY, LORD JOHN OF LANCASTER, *the* EARL OF WESTMORELAND, SIR WALTER BLUNT *with others.*

KING.   So shaken as we are, so wan with care,
Find we a time for frighted Peace to pant
And breathe short-winded accents of new broils
To be commenc'd in strands afar remote.
No more the thirsty entrance of this soil
Shall daub her lips with her own children's blood;
No more shall trenching war channel her fields,
Nor bruise her flowerets with the armed hoofs
Of hostile paces. Those opposed eyes,
Which, like the meteors of a troubled heaven,
All of one nature, of one substance bred,
Did lately meet in the intestine[1] shock
And furious close of civil butchery,
Shall now, in mutual [2] well-beseeming ranks,
March all one way and be no more oppos'd
Against acquaintance, kindred, and allies.
The edge of war, like an ill-sheathed knife,
No more shall cut his master. Therefore, friends,
As far as to the sepulchre of Christ,
Whose soldier now under whose blessed cross
We are impressed[3] and engag'd to fight,
Forthwith a power[4] of English shall we levy;
Whose arms were moulded in their mothers' womb
To chase these pagans in those holy fields
Over whose acres walk'd those blessed feet
Which fourteen hundred years ago were nail'd
For our advantage on the bitter cross.
But this our purpose now is twelve months old,
And bootless[5] 't is to tell you we will go;
Therefore we meet not now. Then let me hear
Of you, my gentle cousin Westmoreland,
What yesternight our council did decree
In forwarding this dear expedience.[6]

---

1. intestine—internal.   2. mutual—united.   3. impressed—enlisted.
4. power—an army.   5. bootless—useless.   6. expedience—enterprise.

WESTMORELAND.   My liege, this haste was hot in question,[7]
And many limits of the charge[8] set down
But yesternight; when all athwart[9] there came
A post[10] from Wales loaden with heavy news;
Whose worst was that the noble Mortimer,
Leading the men of Herefordshire to fight
Against the irregular and wild Glendower,
Was by the rude hands of that Welshman taken,
A thousand of his people butchered;
Upon whose dead corpses there was such misuse,
Such beastly shameless transformation,[11]
By those Welshwomen done as may not be
Without much shame retold or spoken of.

KING.   It seems then that the tidings of this broil
Brake off our business for the Holy Land.

WESTMORELAND.   This match'd with other did, my gracious
    lord;
For more uneven and unwelcome news
Came from the north, and thus it did import:
On Holy-rood day,[12] the gallant Hotspur there,
Young Harry Percy, and brave Archibald,
That ever-valiant and approved[13] Scot,
At Holmedon met,
Where they did spend a sad and bloody hour,
As by discharge of their artillery,
And shape of likelihood,[14] the news was told;
For he that brought them, in the very heat
And pride of their contention did take horse,
Uncertain of the issue any way.

KING.   Here is a dear, a true-industrious friend,
Sir Walter Blunt, new lighted from his horse,
Stain'd with the variation of each soil
Betwixt that Holmedon and this seat of ours;
And he hath brought us smooth and welcome news.
The Earl of Douglas is discomfited.

---

7. question—discussion.   8. charge—expense.
9. all athwart—interrupting.   10. post—courier.
11. transformation—mutilation.   12. Holy-rood day—September 14.
13. approved—well-tested.   14. shape of likelihood—probability.

Ten thousand bold Scots, two and twenty knights,
Balk'd [15] in their own blood did Sir Walter see
On Holmedon's plains. Of prisoners, Hotspur took
Murdoch Earl of Fife and eldest son
To beaten Douglas; and the Earl of Athole,
Of Murray, Angus, and Menteith:
And is not this an honourable spoil?
A gallant prize, ha, cousin, is it not?
   WESTMORELAND.   In faith,
It is a conquest for a prince to boast of.
   KING.   Yea, there thou mak'st me sad, and mak'st me sin
In envy that my Lord Northumberland
Should be the father to so blest a son,
A son who is the theme of Honour's tongue,
Amongst a grove the very straightest plant,
Who is sweet Fortune's minion[16] and her pride;
Whilst I, by looking on the praise of him,
See riot and dishonour stain the brow
Of my young Harry. O that it could be prov'd
That some night-tripping fairy had exchang'd
In cradle-clothes our children where they lay,
And call'd mine Percy, his Plantagenet! [17]
Then would I have his Harry, and he mine.
But let him from my thoughts. What think you, coz,
Of this young Percy's pride? The prisoners,
Which he in this adventure hath supris'd,
To his own use he keeps; and sends me word,
I shall have none but Murdoch Earl of Fife.
   WESTMORELAND. This is his uncle's teaching. This is Wor-
     cester,
Malevolent to you in all aspécts;
Which makes him prune[18] himself, and bristle up
The crest of youth against your dignity.
   KING.   But I have sent for him to answer this;
And for this cause awhile we must neglect
Our holy purpose to Jerusalem.
Cousin, on Wednesday next our council we

---

15. Balk'd—piled in ridges.   16. minion—darling.
17. Plantagenet—surname of the royal family.   18. prune—preen.

Will hold at Windsor; so inform the lords;
But come yourself with speed to us again,
For more is to be said and to be done
Than out of anger can be uttered.
WESTMORELAND.   I will, my liege.   *Exeunt.*

[ACT I · 2] *London. An apartment of the Prince's.*

Enter the PRINCE OF WALES *and* FALSTAFF.

FALSTAFF.   Now, Hal, what time of day is it, lad?
PRINCE.   Thou art so fat-witted, with drinking of old sack[1]
and unbuttoning thee after supper and sleeping up on benches
after noon, that thou hast forgotten to demand that truly which
thou wouldest truly know. What a devil hast thou to do with the
time of the day? Unless hours were cups of sack, and minutes capons, and the clocks the tongues of bawds, and dials the signs of
leaping-houses,[2] and the blessed sun himself a fair hot wench in
flame-coloured taffeta, I see no reason why thou shouldst be so
superfluous to demand the time of the day.
FALSTAFF.   Indeed, you come near me now, Hal; for we that
take purses go by the moon and the seven stars, and not by
Phoebus,[3] he, "that wand'ring knight so fair." And, I prithee,
sweet wag, when thou art king, as, God save thy Grace,—
Majesty I should say, for grace thou wilt have none,—
PRINCE.   What, none?
FALSTAFF.   No, by my troth, not so much as will serve to be
prologue to an egg and butter.
PRINCE.   Well, how then? Come, roundly,[4] roundly.
FALSTAFF.   Marry, then, sweet wag, when thou art king, let
not us that are squires of the night's body be called thieves of the
day's beauty. Let us be Diana's[5] foresters, gentlemen of the
shade, minions of the moon; and let men say we be men of good
government,[6] being governed, as the sea is, by our noble and
chaste mistress the moon, under whose countenance we steal.
PRINCE.   Thou say'st well, and it holds well too; for the
fortune of us that are the moon's men doth ebb and flow like the

---

1. sack—sherry wine.   2. leaping-houses—brothels.
3. Phoebus—Apollo, the sun god.   4. roundly—directly.
5. Diana—goddess of the moon.   6. good government—well-behaved.

sea, being governed, as the sea is, by the moon. As for proof, now: a purse of gold most resolutely snatched on Monday night and most dissolutely spent on Tuesday morning; got with swearing "Lay by" [7] and spent with crying "Bring in";[8] now in as low an ebb as the foot of the ladder, and by and by in as high a flow as the ridge of the gallows.

FALSTAFF. By the Lord, thou say'st true, lad. And is not my hostess of the tavern a most sweet wench?

PRINCE. As the honey of Hybla,[9] my old lad of the castle. And is not a buff jerkin[10] a most sweet robe of durance? [11]

FALSTAFF. How now, how now, mad wag! What, in thy quips and thy quiddities,[12] what a plague have I to do with a buff jerkin?

PRINCE. Why, what a pox have I to do with my hostess of the tavern?

FALSTAFF. Well, thou hast called her to a reckoning many a time and oft.

PRINCE. Did I ever call for thee to pay thy part?

FALSTAFF. No; I'll give thee thy due, thou hast paid all there.

PRINCE. Yea, and elsewhere, so far as my coin would stretch; and where it would not, I have used my credit.

FALSTAFF. Yea, and so used it that, were it not here apparent that thou art heir apparent—But, I prithee, sweet wag, shall there be gallows standing in England when thou art king? and resolution[13] thus fobbed [14] as it is with the rusty curb of old father antic[15] the law? Do not thou, when thou art king, hang a thief.

PRINCE. No; thou shalt.

FALSTAFF. Shall I? O rare! By the Lord, I'll be a brave judge.

PRINCE. Thou judgest false already. I mean, thou shalt have the hanging of the thieves and so become a rare hangman.

---

7. "Lay by"—"Hand over (your money)."
8. "Bring in"—i.e., more wine.   9. Hybla—Sicilian mountain.
10. buff jerkin—sheriff's uniform.
11. durance—durable, with a pun on *imprisonment*.
12. quiddities—playing with words.   13. resolution—courage.
14. fobbed—foiled.   15. antic—clown.

FALSTAFF.   Well, Hal, well; and in some sort it jumps with my humour[16] as well as waiting in the court, I can tell you.

PRINCE.   For obtaining of suits?

FALSTAFF.   Yea, for obtaining of suits, whereof the hangman hath no lean wardrobe.[17] 'Sblood,[18] I am as melancholy as a gib cat[19] or a lugged [20] bear.

PRINCE.   Or an old lion, or a lover's lute.

FALSTAFF.   Yea, or the drone of a Lincolnshire bagpipe.

PRINCE.   What sayest thou to a hare, or the melancholy of Moor Ditch? [21]

FALSTAFF.   Thou hast the most unsavoury similes and art indeed the most comparative,[22] rascalliest, sweet young prince. But, Hal, I prithee, trouble me no more with vanity. I would to God thou and I knew where a commodity[23] of good names were to be bought. An old lord of the council rated [24] me the other day in the street about you, sir, but I marked him not; and yet he talked very wisely, but I regarded him not; and yet he talked wisely, and in the street too.

PRINCE.   Thou didst well; for wisdom[25] cries out in the streets, and no man regards it.

FALSTAFF.   O, thou hast damnable iteration[26] and art indeed able to corrupt a saint. Thou hast done much harm upon me, Hal; God forgive thee for it! Before I knew thee, Hal, I knew nothing; and now am I, if a man should speak truly, little better than one of the wicked. I must give over this life, and I will give it over. By the Lord, an I do not, I am a villain. I'll be damned for never a king's son in Christendom.

PRINCE.   Where shall we take a purse tomorrow, Jack?

FALSTAFF.   'Zounds,[27] where thou wilt, lad; I'll make one.

---

16. jumps with my humour—suits my fancy.
17. wardrobe—the hangman was given the clothes of the persons executed.   18. 'Sblood—By God's blood.
19. gib cat—tomcat.   20. lugged—chained.
21. Moor Ditch—an open sewer outside of London.
22. comparative—apt at making comparisons.
23. commodity—supply.   24. rated—scolded.
25. wisdom—a jesting reference to a familiar biblical quotation; *cf.*, Prov. 1:20–24.
26. iteration—ability to quote.
27. 'Zounds—By the wounds of Christ.

An[28] I do not, call me villain and baffle[29] me.

PRINCE.   I see a good amendment of life in thee; from praying to purse-taking.

FALSTAFF.   Why, Hal, 't is my vocation, Hal: 't is no sin for
a man to labour in his vocation.

Enter POINS.

Poins! Now shall we know if Gadshill have set a match.[30] O, if
men were to be saved by merit, what hole in hell were hot
enough for him? This is the most omnipotent villain that ever
cried "Stand!" [31] to a true man.

PRINCE.   Good morrow, Ned.

POINS.   Good morrow, sweet Hal. What says Monsieur Remorse? What says Sir John Sack and Sugar? Jack! how agrees
the devil and thee about thy soul, that thou soldest him on Good
Friday last for a cup of Madeira and a cold capon's leg?

PRINCE.   Sir John stands to his word, the devil shall have
his bargain; for he was never yet a breaker of proverbs. He will
give the devil his due.

POINS.   Then art thou damned for keeping thy word with the
devil.

PRINCE.   Else he had been damned for cozening[32] the devil.

POINS.   But, my lads, my lads, to-morrow morning, by four
o'clock, early at Gadshill! [33] There are pilgrims going to Canter-
bury with rich offerings, and traders riding to London with fat
purses. I have vizards[34] for you all; you have horses for yourselves: Gadshill lies to-night in Rochester: I have bespoke supper to-morrow night in Eastcheap: we may do it as secure as
sleep. If you will go, I will stuff your purses full of crowns; if you
will not, tarry at home and be hanged.

FALSTAFF.   Hear ye, Yedward;[35] if I tarry at home and go
not, I'll hang you for going.

---

28. An—if.   29. baffle—disgrace.
30. set a match—made arrangements for a holdup.
31. "Stand!"—"Hands up!"
32. cozening—cheating.
33. Gadshill—the place must be distinguished from the name of the
robber.
34. vizards—masks.   35. Yedward—Edward (Poins).

POINS.   You will, chops? [36]

FALSTAFF.   Hal, wilt thou make one?

PRINCE.   Who, I rob? I a thief? Not I, by my faith.

FALSTAFF.   There's neither honesty, manhood, nor good fellowship in thee, nor thou cam'st not of the blood royal,[37] if thou dar'st not stand for ten shillings.

PRINCE.   Well, then, once in my days I'll be a madcap.

FALSTAFF.   Why, that's well said.

PRINCE.   Well, come what will, I'll tarry at home.

FALSTAFF.   By the lord, I'll be a traitor then, when thou art king.

PRINCE.   I care not.

POINS.   Sir John, I prithee, leave the Prince and me alone. I will lay him down such reasons for this adventure that he shall go.

FALSTAFF.   Well, God give thee the spirit of persuasion and him the ears of profiting, that what thou speakest may move and what he hears may be believed, that the true prince may, for recreation sake, prove a false thief; for the poor abuses of the time want countenance.[38] Farewell; you shall find me in East-cheap.

PRINCE.   Farewell, thou latter spring! Farewell, All-hallown summer! [39]   *Exit* FALSTAFF.

POINS.   Now, my good sweet honey lord, ride with us to-morrow; I have a jest to execute that I cannot manage alone. Falstaff, Bardolph, Peto, and Gadshill shall rob those men that we have already waylaid; yourself and I will not be there; and when they have the booty, if you and I do not rob them, cut this head off from my shoulders.

PRINCE.   How shall we part with them in setting forth?

POINS.   Why, we will set forth before or after them, and appoint them a place of meeting, wherein it is at our pleasure to fail, and then will they adventure upon the exploit themselves; which they shall have no sooner achieved, but we'll set upon them.

---

36. chops—fat-face.
37. royal—a pun on *royal*, a coin worth ten shillings.
38. want countenance—lack encouragement.
39. All-hallown summer—Indian summer.

PRINCE. Yea, but 't is like that they will know us by our horses, by our habits,[40] and by every other appointment, to be ourselves.

POINS. Tut! our horses they shall not see; I'll tie them in the wood; our vizards we will change after we leave them; and, sirrah,[41] I have cases of buckram[42] for the nonce,[43] to immask our noted [44] outward garments.

PRINCE. Yea, but I doubt[45] they will be too hard for us.

POINS. Well, for two of them, I know them to be as true-bred cowards as ever turned back; and for the third, if he fight longer than he sees reason, I'll forswear arms. The virtue of this jest will be the incomprehensible[46] lies that this same fat rogue will tell us when we meet at supper; how thirty, at least, he fought with; what wards,[47] what blows, what extremities he endured; and in the reproof [48] of this lies the jest.

PRINCE. Well, I'll go with thee: provide us all things necessary and meet me to-morrow night in Eastcheap; there I'll sup. Farewell.

POINS. Farewell, my lord. *Exit.*

PRINCE. I know you all, and will a while uphold
The unyok'd humour of your idleness;
Yet herein will I imitate the sun,
Who doth permit the base contagious clouds
To smother up his beauty from the world,
That when he please again to be himself,
Being wanted, he may be more wonder'd at
By breaking through the foul and ugly mists
Of vapours that did seem to strangle him.
If all the year were playing holidays,
To sport would be as tedious as to work;
But when they seldom come, they wish'd for come,
And nothing pleaseth but rare accidents.[49]
So, when this loose behaviour I throw off

---

40. habits—clothing.   41. sirrah—my boy.
42. cases of buckram—coveralls of coarse linen.
43. for the nonce—for the occasion.
44. noted—familiar.   45. doubt—fear.
46. incomprehensible—infinite.   47. wards—parries.
48. reproof—disproof.   49. accidents—events.

And pay the debt I never promised,
By how much better than my word I am,
By so much shall I falsify men's hopes;
And like bright metal on a sullen ground,⁵⁰
My reformation, glitt'ring o'er my fault,
Shall show more goodly and attract more eyes
Than that which hath no foil to set it off.
I'll so offend, to make offence a skill,
Redeeming time when men think least I will.   *Exit.*

---

50. sullen ground—dull background.

[ACT I • 3] *London. The palace.*

Enter the KING, NORTHUMBERLAND, WORCESTER, HOTSPUR, SIR
WALTER BLUNT, *with others.*

KING.   My blood hath been too cold and temperate,
Unapt to stir at these indignities,
And you have found me;¹ for accordingly
You tread upon my patience. But be sure
I will from henceforth rather be myself,
Mighty and to be fear'd, than my condition;²
Which hath been smooth as oil, soft as young down,
And therefore lost that title of respect
Which the proud soul ne'er pays but to the proud.
WORCESTER.   Our house, my sovereign liege, little deserves
The scourge of greatness to be us'd on it;
And that same greatness too which our own hands
Have holp to make so portly.
NORTHUMBERLAND.   My lord,—
KING.   Worcester, get thee gone; for I do see
Danger and disobedience in thine eye.
O, sir, your presence is too bold and peremptory,
And majesty might never yet endure
The moody frontier³ of a servant brow.
You have good leave to leave us. When we need

---

1. found me—found me out.   2. condition—natural disposition.
3. moody frontier—frowning forehead.

Your use and counsel, we shall send for you.

Exit WORCESTER.

You were about to speak.

NORTHUMBERLAND.   Yea, my good lord.
Those prisoners in your Highness' name demanded,
Which Harry Percy here at Holmedon took,
Were, as he says, not with such strength denied
As is delivered to your Majesty.
Either envy, therefore, or misprision[4]
Is guilty of this fault, and not my son.

HOTSPUR.   My liege, I did deny no prisoners.
But I remember, when the fight was done,
When I was dry with rage and extreme toil,
Breathless and faint, leaning upon my sword,
Came there a certain lord, neat, and trimly dress'd,
Fresh as a bridegroom; and his chin new reap'd[5]
Show'd like a stubble-land at harvest-home.
He was perfumed like a milliner;
And 'twixt his finger and his thumb he held
A pouncet-box,[6] which ever and anon
He gave his nose and took 't away again;
Who therewith angry, when it next came there,
Took it in snuff; and still he smil'd and talk'd,
And as the soldiers bore dead bodies by,
He call'd them untaught knaves, unmannerly,
To bring a slovenly unhandsome corse[7]
Betwixt the wind and his nobility.
With many holiday and lady terms
He question'd me; amongst the rest, demanded
My prisoners in your Majesty's behalf.
I then, all smarting with my wounds being cold,
To be so pester'd with a popinjay,[8]
Out of my grief,[9] and my impatience
Answer'd neglectingly—I know not what,
He should, or he should not; for he made me mad

---

4. misprision—misunderstanding.
5. chin new reap'd—closely cut beard.
6. pouncet-box—perfume container.   7. corse—corpse.
8. popinjay—fop.   9. grief—pain.

To see him shine so brisk and smell so sweet
And talk so like a waiting-gentlewoman
Of guns and drums and wounds,—God save the mark[10]!—
And telling me the sovereign'st thing on earth
Was parmaceti[11] for an inward bruise;
And that it was great pity, so it was,
This villanous salt-petre should be digg'd
Out of the bowels of the harmless earth,
Which many a good tall[12] fellow had destroy'd
So cowardly; and but for these vile guns,
He would himself have been a soldier.
This bald unjointed chat of his, my lord,
I answered indirectly, as I said;
And I beseech you, let not his report
Come current[13] for an accusation
Betwixt my love and your high Majesty.
    BLUNT.   The circumstance considered, good my lord,
Whate'er Lord Harry Percy then had said
To such a person and in such a place,
At such a time, with all the rest retold,
May reasonably die and never rise
To do him wrong or any way impeach[14]
What then he said, so he unsay it now.
    KING.   Why, yet he doth deny his prisoners
But with proviso[15] and exception
That we at our own charge shall ransom straight
His brother-in-law, the foolish Mortimer;
Who, on my soul, hath wilfully betray'd
The lives of those that he did lead to fight
Against that great magician, damn'd Glendower,
Whose daughter, as we hear, that Earl of March
Hath lately married. Shall our coffers, then,
Be emptied to redeem a traitor home?
Shall we buy treason, and indent[16] with fears,

---

10. God save the mark—God help us.   11. parmaceti—ointment.
12. tall—valiant.   13. come current—be accepted at face value.
14. impeach—subject to blame.
15. But with proviso—unless on the condition.
16. indent—make a contract.

When they have lost and forfeited themselves?
No, on the barren mountains let him starve;
For I shall never hold that man my friend
Whose tongue shall ask me for one penny cost
To ransom home revolted Mortimer.
   HOTSPUR.   Revolted Mortimer!
He never did fall off, my sovereign liege,
But by the chance of war: to prove that true
Needs no more but one tongue for all those wounds,
Those mouthed wounds, which valiantly he took
When on the gentle Severn's sedgy bank,
In single opposition, hand to hand,
He did confound [17] the best part of an hour
In changing hardiment[18] with great Glendower.
Three times they breath'd and three times did they drink,
Upon agreement, of swift Severn's flood;
Who then, affrighted with their bloody looks,
Ran fearfully among the trembling reeds,
And hid his crisp[19] head in the hollow bank
Bloodstained with these valiant combatants.
Never did base and rotten policy[20]
Colour[21] her working with such deadly wounds;
Nor never could the noble Mortimer
Receive so many, and all willingly.
Then let not him be slander'd with revolt.
   KING.   Thou dost belie[22] him, Percy, thou dost belie him;
He never did encounter with Glendower.
I tell thee,
He durst as well have met the devil alone
As Owen Glendower for an enemy.
Art thou not asham'd? But, sirrah, henceforth
Let me not hear you speak of Mortimer.
Send me your prisoners with the speediest means,
Or you shall hear in such a kind [23] from me
As will displease you. My Lord Northumberland,
We license your departure with your son.

---

17. confound—spend.   18. hardiment—blows.
19. crisp—rippled.   20. policy—political trickery.
21. Colour—disguise.   22. belie—lie about.   23. kind—manner.

Send us your prisoners or you'll hear of it.

                      Exeunt KING HENRY, BLUNT, *and train.*

HOTSPUR.   An if the devil come and roar for them,
I will not send them. I will straight
And tell him so; for I will ease my heart,
Albeit[24] I make a hazard of my head.

    NORTHUMBERLAND.   What, drunk with choler? [25] Stay and
        pause a while.
Here comes your uncle.

Re-enter WORCESTER.

    HOTSPUR.   Speak of Mortimer!
'Zounds, I will speak of him; and let my soul
Want mercy, if I do not join with him.
Yea, on his part I'll empty all these veins,
And shed my dear blood drop by drop in the dust,
But I will lift the down-trod Mortimer
As high in the air as this unthankful king,
As this ingrate and canker'd [26] Bolingbroke.[27]

    NORTHUMBERLAND.   Brother, the king hath made your
        nephew mad.

    WORCESTER.   Who struck this heat up after I was gone?

    HOTSPUR.   He will, forsooth, have all my prisoners;
And when I urg'd the ransom once again
Of my wife's brother, then his cheek look'd pale,
And on my face he turn'd an eye of death,
Trembling even at the name of Mortimer.

    WORCESTER.   I cannot blame him. Was not he proclaim'd
By Richard,[28] that dead is, the next of blood?

    NORTHUMBERLAND.   He was; I heard the proclamation.
And then it was when the unhappy king,—
Whose wrongs in us God pardon!—did set forth
Upon his Irish expedition;
From whence he intercepted [29] did return
To be depos'd and shortly murdered.

---

24. Albeit—even if.   25. choler—anger.
26. canker'd—malignant.   27. Bolingbroke—King Henry IV.
28. Richard—King Richard II, forced to abdicate by Bolingbroke.
29. intercepted—interrupted.

WORCESTER.   And for whose death we in the world's wide
     mouth
Live scandaliz'd and foully spoken of.
     HOTSPUR.   But, soft, I pray you; did King Richard then
Proclaim my brother Edmund Mortimer
Heir to the crown?
     NORTHUMBERLAND.   He did; myself did hear it.
     HOTSPUR.   Nay, then I cannot blame his cousin king,
That wish'd him on the barren mountains starve.
But shall it be, that you, that set the crown
Upon the head of this forgetful man
And for his sake wear the detested blot
Of murderous subornation,[30] shall it be,
That you a world of curses undergo,
Being the agents, or base second means,
The cords, the ladder, or the hangman rather?
O, pardon me that I descend so low,
To show the line and the predicament[31]
Wherein you range under this subtle king!
Shall it for shame be spoken in these days,
Or fill up chronicles in time to come,
That men of your nobility and power
Did gage[32] them both in an unjust behalf,
As both of you—God pardon it!—have done,
To put down Richard, that sweet lovely rose,
And plant this thorn, this canker, Bolingbroke?
And shall it in more shame be further spoken,
That you are fool'd, discarded, and shook off
By him for whom these shames ye underwent?
No; yet time serves wherein you may redeem
Your banish'd honours and restore yourselves
Into the good thoughts of the world again,
Revenge the jeering and disdain'd [33] contempt
Of this proud king, who studies day and night
To answer[34] all the debt he owes to you

---

30. murderous subornation—accessory to murder.
31. predicament—category.
32. gage them—pledge themselves.
33. disdain'd—disdainful.   34. answer—pay.

Even with the bloody payment of your deaths.
Therefore, I say,—
WORCESTER.   Peace, cousin, say no more;
And now I will unclasp a secret book,
And to your quick-conceiving[35] discontents
I'll read you matter deep and dangerous,
As full of peril and adventurous spirit
As to o'er-walk a current roaring loud
On the unsteadfast footing of a spear.
HOTSPUR.   If he fall in, good night! or sink or swim.
Send Danger from the east unto the west
So Honour cross it from the north to south,
And let them grapple: O, the blood more stirs
To rouse a lion than to start a hare!
NORTHUMBERLAND.   Imagination of some great exploit
Drives him beyond the bounds of patience.
HOTSPUR.   By heaven, methinks it were an easy leap,
To pluck bright Honour from the pale-fac'd moon,
Or dive into the bottom of the deep,
Where fathom-line could never touch the ground,
And pluck up drowned Honour by the locks;
So he that doth redeem[36] her thence might wear
Without corrival [37] all her dignities.
But out upon this half-fac'd [38] fellowship!
WORCESTER.   He apprehends a world of figures here,
But not the form of what he should attend.
Good cousin, give me audience for a while.
HOTSPUR.   I cry you mercy.
WORCESTER.   Those same noble Scots
That are your prisoners,—
HOTSPUR.   I'll keep them all!
By God, he shall not have a Scot of them;
No, if a Scot would save his soul, he shall not!
I'll keep them, by this hand.
WORCESTER.   You start away
And lend no ear unto my purposes.
Those prisoners you shall keep.

---

35. quick-conceiving—quick-witted.   36. redeem—rescue.
37. corrival—competitor.   38. half-fac'd—half-hearted.

HOTSPUR.   Nay, I will; that's flat.
He said he would not ransom Mortimer;
Forbad my tongue to speak of Mortimer;
But I will find him when he lies asleep,
And in his ear I'll holla "Mortimer!"
Nay,
I'll have a starling shall be taught to speak
Nothing but "Mortimer," and give it him,
To keep his anger still in motion.

    WORCESTER.   Hear you, cousin; a word.

    HOTSPUR.   All studies here I solemnly defy,[39]
Save how to gall [40] and pinch this Bolingbroke;
And that same sword-and-buckler Prince of Wales,
But that I think his father loves him not
And would be glad he met with some mischance,
I would have him poison'd with a pot of ale.

    WORCESTER.   Farewell, kinsman! I'll talk to you
When you are better temper'd to attend.

    NORTHUMBERLAND.   Why, what a wasp-stung and impatient
      fool
Art thou to break into this woman's mood,
Tying thine ear to no tongue but thine own!

    HOTSPUR.   Why, look you, I am whipp'd and scourg'd with
      rods,
Nettled and stung with pismires,[41] when I hear
Of this vile politician, Bolingbroke.
In Richard's time,—what do you call the place?—
A plague upon it, it is in Gloucestershire;
'T was where the madcap duke his uncle kept,[42]
His uncle York; where I first bow'd my knee
Unto this king of smiles, this Bolingbroke,—
'Sblood!—
When you and he came back from Ravenspurgh.

    NORTHUMBERLAND.   At Berkley castle.

    HOTSPUR.   You say true.
Why, what a candy[43] deal of courtesy
This fawning greyhound then did proffer me!

---

39. defy—renounce.   40. gall—make sore.   41. pismires—ants.
42. kept—resided.   43. candy—sickly-sweet.

Look, "when his infant fortune came to age,"
And "gentle Harry Percy," and "kind cousin;"
O, the devil take such cozeners!—God forgive me!
Good uncle, tell your tale; for I have done.

WORCESTER.   Nay, if you have not, to 't again;
We'll stay your leisure.

HOTSPUR.   I have done, i' faith.

WORCESTER.   Then once more to your Scottish prisoners.
Deliver them up without their ransom straight,
And make the Douglas' son your only mean[44]
For powers in Scotland; which, for divers reasons
Which I shall send you written, be assur'd,
Will easily be granted. You, my lord, [*To* NORTHUMBERLAND.]
Your son in Scotland being thus employ'd,
Shall secretly into the bosom creep
Of that same noble prelate, well belov'd,
The Archbishop.

HOTSPUR.   Of York, is it not?

WORCESTER.   True; who bears hard
His brother's death at Bristow, the Lord Scroop.
I speak not this in estimation,[45]
As what I think might be, but what I know
Is ruminated, plotted, and set down,
And only stays but to behold the face
Of that occasion[46] that shall bring it on.

HOTSPUR.   I smell it. Upon my life, it will do well.

NORTHUMBERLAND.   Before the game 's afoot, thou still let'st
slip.

HOTSPUR.   Why, it cannot choose but be a noble plot:
And then the power of Scotland and of York,
To join with Mortimer, ha?

WORCESTER.   And so they shall.

HOTSPUR.   In faith, it is exceedingly well aim'd.

WORCESTER.   And 't is no little reason bids us speed,
To save our heads by raising of a head;[47]
For, bear ourselves as even as we can,
The King will always think him in our debt,

---

44. mean—agent.   45. estimation—conjecture.
46. occasion—opportunity.   47. head—an army.

And think we think ourselves unsatisfied,
Till he hath found a time to pay us home.[48]
And see already how he doth begin
To make us strangers to his looks of love.
   HOTSPUR.   He does, he does. We'll be reveng'd on him.
   WORCESTER.   Cousin, farewell! No further go in this
Than I by letters shall direct your course.
When time is ripe, which will be suddenly,
I'll steal to Glendower and Lord Mortimer;
Where you and Douglas and our powers at once,
As I will fashion it, shall happily meet,
To bear our fortunes in our own strong arms,
Which now we hold at much uncertainty.
   NORTHUMBERLAND.   Farewell, good brother! We shall thrive,
    I trust.
   HOTSPUR.   Uncle, adieu! O, let the hours be short
Till fields and blows and groans applaud our sport!   *Exeunt.*

---

48. home—in full.

[ACT II • 1] *Rochester. An inn yard.*

Enter a CARRIER[1] *with a lantern in his hand.*

   FIRST CARRIER.   Heigh-ho! an it be not four by the day, I'll
be hanged. Charles' wain[2] is over the new chimney, and yet our
horse not packed. What, ostler! [3]
   OSTLER.   [*Within.*] Anon, anon.[4]
   FIRST CARRIER.   I prithee, Tom, beat Cut's saddle, put a few
flocks[5] in the point: the poor jade is wrung in the withers out of
all cess.

Enter another CARRIER.

   SECOND CARRIER.   Peas and beans[6] are as dank here as a
dog, and that is the next way to give poor jades the bots: [7] this
house is turned upside down since Robin Ostler died.

---

1. Carrier—expressman.
2. Charles' wain—the Great Bear, or Big Dipper.
3. ostler—servant in charge of horses.
4. Anon—coming, in a minute.   5. flocks—tufts of wool.
6. Peas and beans—food for horses.   7. bots—worms.

FIRST CARRIER.   Poor fellow, never joyed since the price of oats rose; it was the death of him.

SECOND CARRIER.   I think this be the most villanous house in all London road for fleas: I am stung like a tench.[8]

FIRST CARRIER.   Like a tench! by the mass, there is ne'er a king christen could be better bit than I have been since the first cock.

SECOND CARRIER.   Why, they will allow us ne'er a jordan,[9] and then we leak in your chimney; and your chamber-lye[10] breeds fleas like a loach.[11]

FIRST CARRIER.   What, ostler! come away and be hanged! Come away.

SECOND CARRIER.   I have a gammon of bacon and two razes[12] of ginger, to be delivered as far as Charing Cross.

FIRST CARRIER.   God's body! the turkeys in my pannier[13] are quite starved. What, ostler! A plague on thee! hast thou never an eye in thy head? Canst not hear? An 't were not as good deed as drink, to break the pate on thee, I am a very villain. Come, and be hanged! Hast no faith in thee?

Enter GADSHILL.

GADSHILL.   Good morrow, carriers. What's o'clock?

FIRST CARRIER.   I think it be two o'clock.

GADSHILL.   I prithee, lend me thy lantern, to see my gelding in the stable.

FIRST CARRIER.   Nay, by God, soft;[14] I know a trick worth two of that, i' faith.

GADSHILL.   I pray thee, lend me thine.

SECOND CARRIER.   Ay, when? canst tell? Lend me thy lantern, quoth he? Marry, I'll see thee hanged first.

GADSHILL.   Sirrah carrier, what time do you mean to come to London?

SECOND CARRIER.   Time enough to go to bed with a candle, I warrant thee. Come, neighbour Mugs, we'll call up the gentle-

---

8. tench—a kind of fish.   9. jordan—chamberpot.
10. chamber-lye—urine.   11. loach—a kind of fish.
12. razes—roots.   13. pannier—basket.
14. soft—not so fast.

men: they will along with company, for they have great charge.[15]

Exeunt CARRIERS.

Enter CHAMBERLAIN.

GADSHILL.   What, ho! chamberlain!

CHAMBERLAIN.   At hand, quoth pick-purse.

GADSHILL.   That's even as fair as—at hand, quoth the chamberlain; for thou variest no more from picking of purses than giving direction doth from labouring; thou lay'st the plot how.

CHAMBERLAIN.   Good morrow, Master Gadshill. It holds current that I told you yesternight: there's a franklin[16] in the wild of Kent hath brought three hundred marks with him in gold. I heard him tell it to one of his company last night at supper; a kind of auditor; one that hath abundance of charge too, God knows what. They are up already, and call for eggs and butter: they will away presently.[17]

GADSHILL.   Sirrah, if they meet not with Saint Nicholas' clerks,[18] I'll give thee this neck.

CHAMBERLAIN.   No, I'll none of it. I pray thee, keep that for the hangman; for I know thou worshippest Saint Nicholas as truly as a man of falsehood may.

GADSHILL.   What talkest thou to me of the hangman? If I hang, I'll make a fat pair of gallows; for if I hang, old Sir John hangs with me, and thou knowest he is no starveling. Tut! there are other Troians[19] that thou dream'st not of, the which for sport sake are content to do the profession some grace, that would, if matters should be looked into, for their own credit sake, make all whole. I am joined with no foot land-rakers,[20] no long-staff sixpenny strikers,[21] none of these mad mustachio purple-hued malt-worms;[22] but with nobility and tranquillity, burgomasters and great oneyers;[23] such as can hold in, such as will strike sooner than speak, and speak sooner than drink, and drink sooner than pray; and yet, 'zounds, I lie; for they pray continually to their saint, the commonwealth; or rather, not pray to

---

15. charge—valuables.   16. franklin—rich farmer.
17. presently—at once.   18. St. Nicholas' clerks—highwaymen.
19. Troians—good fellows.   20. foot land-rakers—tramps.
21. sixpenny strikers—petty thieves.
22. purple-hued malt-worms—beer-drinkers.   23. oneyers—great ones.

her, but prey on her, for they ride up and down on her and make her their boots.[24]

CHAMBERLAIN. What, the commonwealth their boots? Will she hold out water in foul way? [25]

GADSHILL. She will, she will; justice hath liquored her. We steal as in a castle, cocksure; we have the receipt of fern-seed, we walk invisible.

CHAMBERLAIN. Nay, by my faith, I think you are more beholding to the night than to fern-seed for your walking invisible.

GADSHILL. Give me thy hand: thou shalt have a share in our purchase,[26] as I am a true man.

CHAMBERLAIN. Nay, rather let me have it as you are a false thief.

GADSHILL. Go to; *homo* is a common name to all men. Bid the ostler bring my gelding out of the stable. Farewell, you muddy knave.   *Exeunt.*

---

24. boots—profit.   25. way—road.   26. purchase—booty.

[ACT II · 2] *The highway near Gadshill.*

Enter PRINCE HENRY *and* POINS.

POINS. Come, shelter, shelter! I have removed Falstaff's horse, and he frets[1] like a gummed velvet.[2]   [*They step back.*]

PRINCE. Stand close.

Enter FALSTAFF.

FALSTAFF. Poins! Poins, and be hanged! Poins!

PRINCE. [*Coming forward.*] Peace, ye fat-kidneyed rascal! what a bawling dost thou keep!

FALSTAFF. Where's Poins, Hal?

PRINCE. He is walked up to the top of the hill; I'll go seek him.   [*Withdraws.*]

FALSTAFF. I am accursed to rob in that thief's company: the rascal hath removed my horse and tied him I know not where. If I travel but four foot by the squire[3] further afoot, I shall break

---

1. frets—complains, but also (of cloth), becomes threadbare.
2. gummed velvet—cheap cloth with stiffening.
3. squire—carpenter's square.

my wind. Well, I doubt not but to die a fair death for all this, if
I scape hanging for killing that rogue. I have forsworn his company hourly any time this two and twenty years, and yet I am
bewitched with the rogue's company. If the rascal have not given
me medicines to make me love him, I'll be hanged. It could not
be else; I have drunk medicines. Poins! Hal! a plague upon you
both! Bardolph! Peto! I'll starve ere I'll rob a foot further. An 't
were not as good a deed as drink, to turn true man and to leave
these rogues, I am the veriest varlet that ever chewed with a
tooth. Eight yards of uneven ground is three score and ten miles
afoot with me; and the stony-hearted villains know it well
enough. A plague upon it when thieves cannot be true one to
another! [*They whistle.*] Whew! [4] A plague upon you all! Give
me my horse, you rogues; give me my horse, and be hanged!

PRINCE. [*Coming forward.*] Peace ye fat-guts! lie down: lay
thine ear close to the ground and list if thou canst hear the tread
of travellers.

FALSTAFF. Have you any levers to lift me up again, being
down? 'Sblood, I'll not bear mine own flesh so far afoot again
for all the coin in thy father's exchequer. What a plague mean ye
to colt[5] me thus?

PRINCE. Thou liest; thou art not colted, thou art uncolted.

FALSTAFF. I prithee, good Prince Hal, help me to my horse,
good king's son.

PRINCE. Out, ye rogue! shall I be your ostler?

FALSTAFF. Hang thyself in thine own heir-apparent garters!
If I be ta'en, I'll peach[6] for this. An I have not ballads made on
you all and sung to filthy tunes, let a cup of sack be my poison.
When a jest is so forward,[7] and afoot too! I hate it.

Enter GADSHILL, BARDOLPH, *and* PETO.

GADSHILL. Stand.

FALSTAFF. So I do, against my will.

POINS. [*Coming forward.*] O, 't is our setter;[8] I know his
voice. Bardolph, what news?

---

4. Whew!—an unsuccessful attempt to whistle in reply.
5. colt—trick.   6. peach—turn informer.
7. forward—goes so far.
8. setter—intelligence officer in thieves' organization.

BARDOLPH.   Case ye, case ye; on with your vizards: there's money of the King's coming down the hill; 't is going to the King's exchequer.

FALSTAFF.   You lie, ye rogue; 't is going to the King's tavern.

GADSHILL.   There's enough to make us all.

FALSTAFF.   To be hanged.

PRINCE.   Sirs, you four shall front them in the narrow lane; Ned Poins and I will walk lower: if they scape from your encounter, then they light on us.

PETO.   How many be there of them?

GADSHILL.   Some eight or ten.

FALSTAFF.   'Zounds, will they not rob us?

PRINCE.   What, a coward, Sir John Paunch?

FALSTAFF.   Indeed, I am not John of Gaunt, your grandfather; but yet no coward, Hal.

PRINCE.   Well, we leave that to the proof.[9]

POINS.   Sirrah Jack, thy horse stands behind the hedge; when thou need'st him, there thou shalt find him. Farewell, and stand fast.

FALSTAFF.   Now cannot I strike him, if I should be hanged.

PRINCE.   [*Aside.*] Ned, where are our disguises?

POINS.   [*Aside.*] Here, hard by: stand close.

Exeunt PRINCE *and* POINS.

FALSTAFF.   Now, my masters, happy man be his dole,[10] say I: every man to his business.

Enter the TRAVELLERS.

FIRST TRAVELLER.   Come, neighbour; the boy shall lead our horses down the hill: we'll walk afoot a while, and ease our legs.

THIEVES.   Stand!

TRAVELLERS.   Jesus bless us!

FALSTAFF.   Strike; down with them! Cut the villains' throats! Ah! whoreson caterpillars! bacon-fed knaves! they hate us youth. Down with them! Fleece them!

TRAVELLERS.   O, we are undone, both we and ours for ever!

FALSTAFF.   Hang ye, gorbellied [11] knaves, are ye undone? No, ye fat chuffs; [12] I would your store were here! On, bacons,[13]

---

9. proof—test.   10. happy man be his dole—good luck to all.
11. gorbellied—fat.   12. chuffs—misers.   13. bacons—clowns.

on! What, ye knaves! young men must live. You are grand-jurors,[14] are ye? We'll jure ye, faith.

[*Here they rob the travellers and bind them.*]
Exeunt.

Re-enter PRINCE HENRY *and* POINS *in buckram suits.*

PRINCE.   The thieves have bound the true men. Now, could thou and I rob the thieves and go merrily to London, it would be argument for a week, laughter for a month, and a good jest for ever.

POINS.   Stand close; I hear them coming.

Enter the THIEVES *again.*

FALSTAFF.   Come, my masters, let us share, and then to horse before day. An the Prince and Poins be not two arrant[15] cowards, there's no equity[16] stirring. There's no more valour in that Poins than in a wild-duck.

PRINCE.   Your money!

POINS.   Villains!

[*As they are sharing, the* PRINCE *and* POINS *set upon them; they all run away; and* FALSTAFF, *after a blow or two, runs away too, leaving the booty behind them.*]

PRINCE.   Got with much ease. Now merrily to horse.
The thieves are all scatter'd and possess'd with fear
So strongly that they dare not meet each other;
Each takes his fellow for an officer.
Away, good Ned. Falstaff sweats to death,
And lards the lean earth as he walks along.
Were 't not for laughing, I should pity him.

POINS.   How the rogue roar'd![17]   *Exeunt.*

---

14. grandjurors—men of property.   15. arrant—complete.
16. equity—justice, sound judgement.   17. roar'd—swaggered.

[ACT II • 3] *Warkworth Castle.*

Enter HOTSPUR, *alone, reading a letter.*

HOTSPUR.   "But, for mine own part, my lord, I could be well contented to be there, in respect of[1] the love I bear your house." [2]

---

1. in respect of—because of.   2. house—family.

He could be contented: why is he not, then? In respect of the love he bears our house: he shows in this, he loves his own barn better than he loves our house. Let me see some more. "The purpose you undertake is dangerous;"—why, that's certain. 'T is dangerous to take a cold, to sleep, to drink; but I tell you, my lord fool, out of this nettle, danger, we pluck this flower, safety. "The purpose you undertake is dangerous; the friends you have named uncertain; the time itself unsorted;[3] and your whole plot too light for the counterpoise of so great an opposition." Say you so, say you so? I say unto you again, you are a shallow, cowardly hind,[4] and you lie. What a lack-brain is this! By the Lord, our plot as a good plot as ever was laid; our friends true and constant: a good plot, good friends, and full of expectation; an excellent plot, very good friends. What a frosty-spirited rogue is this! Why, my Lord of York commends the plot and the general course of the action. 'Zounds, an I were now by this rascal, I could brain him with his lady's fan. Is there not my father, my uncle, and myself? Lord Edmund Mortimer, my Lord of York, and Owen Glendower? Is there not besides the Douglas? Have I not all their letters to meet me in arms by the ninth of the next month? and are they not some of them set forward already? What a pagan rascal is this! an infidel! Ha! you shall see now in very sincerity of fear and cold heart, will he to the King and lay open all our proceedings. O, I could divide myself and go to buffets,[5] for moving such a dish of skim-milk with so honourable an action! Hang him! let him tell the King; we are prepared. I will set forward to-night.

Enter HOTSPUR'S WIFE.

How now, Kate! I must leave you within these two hours.
 LADY PERCY. O, my good lord, why are you thus alone?
For what offence have I this fortnight been
A banish'd woman from my Harry's bed?
Tell me, sweet lord, what is 't that takes from thee
Thy stomach,[6] pleasure, and thy golden sleep?
Why dost thou bend thine eyes upon the earth,
And start so often when thou sit'st alone?

---

3. unsorted—unfit. 4. hind—female deer.
5. buffets—fisticuffs. 6. stomach—appetite.

Why hast thou lost the fresh blood in thy cheeks,
And given my treasures and my rights of thee
To thick-ey'd musing and curst melancholy?
In thy faint slumbers I by thee have watch'd,
And heard thee murmur tales of iron wars;
Speak terms of manage[7] to thy bounding steed;
Cry "Courage! to the field!" And thou hast talk'd
Of sallies and retires, of trenches, tents,
Of palisadoes, frontiers,[8] parapets,
Of basilisks,[9] of cannon, culverin,[10]
Of prisoners' ransom, and of soldiers slain,
And all the currents of a heady fight.
Thy spirit within thee hath been so at war
And thus hath so bestirr'd thee in thy sleep,
That beads of sweat have stood upon thy brow,
Like bubbles in a late-disturbed stream;
And in thy face strange motions have appear'd,
Such as we see when men restrain their breath
On some great sudden hest.[11] O, what portents are these?
Some heavy business hath my lord in hand,
And I must know it, else he loves me not.
    HOTSPUR.   What, ho!

Enter SERVANT.

                      Is Gilliams with the packet gone?
    SERVANT.   He is, my lord, an hour ago.
    HOTSPUR.   Hath Butler brought those horses from the sheriff?
    SERVANT.   One horse, my lord, he brought even now.
    HOTSPUR.   What horse? A roan, a crop-ear, is it not?
    SERVANT.   It is, my lord.
    HOTSPUR.   That roan shall be my throne
Well, I will back him straight. O *Esperance!* [12]
Bid Butler lead him forth into the park.

                              Exit SERVANT.

    LADY PERCY.   But hear you, my lord.
    HOTSPUR.   What say'st thou, my lady?

---

7. manage—horsemanship.   8. frontiers—outworks.
9. basilisks—heavy cannon.   10. culverin—light cannon.
11. hest—command.   12. *Esperance!*—the Percy motto and battle cry.

LADY PERCY.   What is it carries you away?

HOTSPUR.   Why, my horse, my love, my horse.

LADY PERCY.   Out, you mad-headed ape!
A weasel hath not such a deal of spleen[13]
As you are toss'd with. In faith,
I'll know your business, Harry, that I will.
I fear my brother Mortimer doth stir
About his title, and hath sent for you
To line[14] his enterprise; but if you go,—

HOTSPUR.   So far afoot, I shall be weary, love.

LADY PERCY.   Come, come, you paraquito, answer me
Directly unto this question that I ask.
In faith, I'll break thy little finger, Harry,
An if thou wilt not tell me all things true.

HOTSPUR.   Away,
Away, you trifler! Love! I love thee not,
I care not for thee, Kate: this is no world
To play with mammets[15] and to tilt[16] with lips:
We must have bloody noses and crack'd crowns,
And pass them current too. God's me, my horse!
What say'st thou, Kate? What would'st thou have with me?

LADY PERCY.   Do you not love me? Do you not, indeed?
Well, do not then; for since you love me not,
I will not love myself. Do you not love me?
Nay, tell me if you speak in jest or no.

HOTSPUR.   Come, wilt thou see me ride?
And when I am a-horseback, I will swear
I love thee infinitely. But hark you, Kate;
I must not have you henceforth question me
Whither I go, nor reason whereabout.
Whither I must, I must; and, to conclude,
This evening must I leave you, gentle Kate.
I know you wise; but yet no farther wise
Than Harry Percy's wife. Constant you are,
But yet a woman; and for secrecy,
No lady closer; for I well believe
Thou wilt not utter what thou dost not know;

---

13. spleen—excitability.   14. line—support.
15. mammets—dolls.   16. tilt—deliver blows.

And so far will I trust thee, gentle Kate.

LADY PERCY.   How! so far?

HOTSPUR.   Not an inch further. But hark you, Kate:
Whither I go, thither shall you go too;
To-day will I set forth, to-morrow you.
Will this content you, Kate?

LADY PERCY.   It must of force.

Exeunt.

[ACT II • 4] *The Boar's-Head Tavern, Eastcheap.*

Enter the PRINCE *and* POINS.

PRINCE.   Ned, prithee, come out of that fat[1] room, and lend
me thy hand to laugh a little.

POINS.   Where hast been, Hal?

PRINCE.   With three or four loggerheads amongst three or
four score hogsheads. I have sounded the very base-string of
humility. Sirrah, I am sworn brother to a leash of drawers;[2] and
can call them all by their christen names, as Tom, Dick, and
Francis. They take it already upon their salvation, that though
I be but Prince of Wales, yet I am the king of courtesy; and tell
me flatly I am no proud Jack, like Falstaff, but a Corinthian,[3] a
lad of mettle, a good boy (by the Lord, so they call me,) and
when I am King of England, I shall command all the good lads
in Eastcheap. They call drinking deep, dyeing scarlet; and when
you breathe in your watering,[4] they cry "hem!" and bid you
play[5] it off. To conclude, I am so good a proficient in one quarter
of an hour, that I can drink with any tinker in his own language
during my life. I tell thee, Ned, thou hast lost much honour, that
thou wert not with me in this action. But, sweet Ned,—to
sweeten which name of Ned, I give thee this pennyworth of
sugar, clapped even now into my hand by an under-skinker,[6]
one that never spake other English in his life than "Eight shillings and sixpence," and "You are welcome," with this shrill
addition, "Anon, anon, sir! Score a pint of bastard[7] in the Half-

---

1. fat—vat.   2. drawers—waiters.   3. Corinthian—a good sport.
4. breathe in your watering—pause for breath while drinking.
5. play—drink.   6. under-skinker—waiter's assistant.
7. bastard—Spanish wine.

moon," [8] or so. But, Ned, to drive away the time till Falstaff
come, I prithee, do thou stand in some by-room, while I question
my puny drawer to what end he gave me the sugar; and do thou
never leave calling "Francis," that his tale to me may be nothing
but "Anon." Step aside, and I'll show thee a precedent.

POINS.   Francis!

PRINCE.   Thou art perfect.

POINS.   Francis!   *Exit.* POINS.

Enter FRANCIS, *a drawer.*

FRANCIS.   Anon, anon, sir. Look down into the Pomgarnet,[9]
Ralph.

PRINCE.   Come hither, Francis.

FRANCIS.   My lord?

PRINCE.   How long hast thou to serve,[10] Francis?

FRANCIS.   Forsooth, five years, and as much as to—

POINS.   [*Within.*] Francis!

FRANCIS.   Anon, anon, sir.

PRINCE.   Five year! by 'r lady, a long lease for the clinking of
pewter. But, Francis, darest thou be so valiant as to play the
coward with thy indenture[11] and show it a fair pair of heels and
run from it?

FRANCIS.   O Lord, sir, I'll be sworn upon all the books in
England, I could find in my heart—

POINS.   [*Within.*] Francis!

FRANCIS.   Anon, sir.

PRINCE.   How old art thou, Francis?

FRANCIS.   Let me see—about Michaelmas next I shall be—

POINS.   [*Within.*] Francis!

FRANCIS.   Anon, sir. Pray, stay a little, my lord.

PRINCE.   Nay, but hark you, Francis: for the sugar thou
gavest me, 't was a pennyworth, was 't not?

FRANCIS.   O Lord, I would it had been two!

PRINCE.   I will give thee for it a thousand pound. Ask me
when thou wilt, and thou shalt have it.

---

8. Halfmoon—rooms in taverns were given names rather than numbers.
9. Pomgarnet—the Pomegranate Room.
10. serve—i.e., as an apprentice.
11. indenture—apprentice's contract.

POINS.   [*Within.*] Francis!

FRANCIS.   Anon, anon.

PRINCE.   Anon, Francis? No, Francis; but to-morrow, Francis; or Francis, o' Thursday; or indeed, Francis, when thou wilt. But, Francis!

FRANCIS.   My lord?

PRINCE.   Wilt thou rob this leathern jerkin[12] crystal-button, not-pated,[13] agate-ring, puke[14]-stocking, caddis[15]-garter, smooth-tongue, Spanish-pouch,—

FRANCIS.   O Lord, sir, who do you mean?

PRINCE.   Why, then, your brown bastard is your only drink; for look you, Francis, your white canvas doublet[16] will sully. In Barbary, sir, it cannot come to so much.

FRANCIS.   What, sir?

POINS.   [*Within.*] Francis!

PRINCE.   Away, you rogue! dost thou not hear them call?

     [*Here they both call him; the drawer stands amazed, not knowing which way to go.*]

Enter VINTNER.[17]

VINTNER.   What, stand'st thou still, and hear'st such a calling? Look to the guests within. [*Exit* FRANCIS.] My lord, old Sir John with half-a-dozen more are at the door; shall I let them in?

PRINCE.   Let them alone a while, and then open the door. [*Exit* VINTNER.] Poins!

POINS.   [*Within.*] Anon, anon, sir.

Re-enter POINS.

PRINCE.   Sirrah, Falstaff and the rest of the thieves are at the door; shall we be merry?

POINS.   As merry as crickets, my lad. But hark ye; what cunning match[18] have you made with this jest of the drawer? Come, what's the issue?

PRINCE.   I am now of all humours that have showed them-

---

12. jerkin—coat.   13. not-pated—short haircut.
14. puke—dark grey.
15. caddis . . . worsted (these phrases describe Francis' employer).
16. doublet—jacket.   17. Vintner—headwaiter.   18. match—game.

selves humours since the old days of goodman Adam to the pupil age[19] of this present twelve o'clock at midnight.

Re-enter FRANCIS.

What's o'clock, Francis?

FRANCIS.   Anon, anon, sir.   *Exit.*

PRINCE.   That ever this fellow should have fewer words than a parrot, and yet the son of a woman! His industry is upstairs and downstairs; his eloquence the parcel of a reckoning.[20] I am not yet of Percy's mind, the Hotspur of the north; he that kills me some six or seven dozen of Scots at a breakfast, washes his hands, and says to his wife, "Fie upon this quiet life! I want work." "O my sweet Harry," says she, "how many hast thou killed to-day?" "Give my roan horse a drench,[21]" says he; and answers, "Some fourteen," an hour after; "a trifle, a trifle." I prithee, call in Falstaff. I'll play Percy, and that damned brawn shall play Dame Mortimer his wife. "Rivo!" [22] says the drunkard. Call in ribs, call in tallow.

Enter FALSTAFF, GADSHILL, BARDOLPH, *and* PETO; FRANCIS
following with wine.

POINS.   Welcome, Jack! Where hast thou been?

FALSTAFF.   A plague of all cowards, I say, and a vengeance too! marry, and amen! Give me a cup of sack, boy. Ere I lead this life long, I'll sew nether stocks,[23] and mend them and foot them too. A plague of all cowards! Give me a cup of sack, rogue. Is there no virtue extant?   [*He drinks.*]

PRINCE.   Didst thou never see Titan[24] kiss a dish of butter, pitiful-hearted Titan, that melted at the sweet tale of the sun? If thou didst, then behold that compound.[25]

FALSTAFF.   You rogue, here's lime[26] in this sack too: there is nothing but roguery to be found in villanous man; yet a coward is worse than a cup of sack with lime in it. A villanous coward! Go thy ways, old Jack; die when thou wilt, if manhood,

---

19. pupil age—youth.   20. parcel of a reckoning—item of a bill.
21. drench—bran and water.   22. "Rivo!"—"Bottoms up!"
23. nether stocks—stockings.   24. Titan—the sun.
25. compound—melted butter (i.e., Falstaff).
26. lime—used to improve the taste of inferior wine.

good manhood, be not forgot upon the face of the earth, then am
I a shotten[27] herring. There lives not three good men unhanged
in England; and one of them is fat and grows old. God help the
while! [28] a bad world, I say. I would I were a weaver; I could
sing psalms or anything. A plague of all cowards, I say still.

PRINCE.   How now, wool-sack! what mutter you?

FALSTAFF.   A king's son! If I do not beat thee out of thy
kingdom with a dagger of lath, and drive all thy subjects afore
thee like a flock of wild-geese, I'll never wear hair on my face
more. You Prince of Wales!

PRINCE.   Why, you whoreson round man, what's the matter?

FALSTAFF.   Are not you a coward? Answer me to that; and
Poins there?

POINS.   'Zounds, ye fat paunch, an ye call me coward, by the
Lord, I'll stab thee.

FALSTAFF.   I call thee coward! I'll see thee damned ere I call
thee coward; but I would give a thousand pound I could run as
fast as thou canst. You are straight enough in the shoulders; you
care not who sees your back: call you that backing of your
friends? A plague upon such backing! give me them that will
face me. Give me a cup of sack. I am a rogue, if I drunk to-day.

PRINCE.   O villain! thy lips are scarce wiped since thou
drunk'st last.

FALSTAFF.   All's one for that. [*He drinks.*] A plague of all
cowards, still say I.

PRINCE.   What's the matter?

FALSTAFF.   What's the matter? There be four of us here have
ta'en a thousand pound this day morning.

PRINCE.   Where is it, Jack? where is it?

FALSTAFF.   Where is it? Taken from us it is; a hundred upon
poor four of us.

PRINCE.   What, a hundred, man?

FALSTAFF.   I am a rogue, if I were not at half-sword[29] with a
dozen of them two hours together. I have scaped by miracle. I
am eight times thrust through the doublet, four through the
hose; my buckler cut through and through; my sword hack'd

27. shotten—without roe.
28. the while—these days.
29. half-sword—in close combat.

like a hand-saw—*ecce signum!* [30] I never dealt[31] better since I was a man; all would not do. A plague of all cowards! Let them speak; if they speak more or less than truth, they are villains and the sons of darkness.

PRINCE.   Speak, sirs; how was it?

GADSHILL.   We four set upon some dozen—

FALSTAFF.   Sixteen at least, my lord.

GADSHILL.   And bound them.

PETO.   No, no, they were not bound.

FALSTAFF.   You rogue, they were bound, every man of them, or I am a Jew else, an Ebrew Jew.

GADSHILL.   As we were sharing, some six or seven fresh men set upon us—

FALSTAFF.   And unbound the rest, and then come in the other.[32]

PRINCE.   What, fought you with them all?

FALSTAFF.   All! I know not what you call all; but if I fought not with fifty of them, I am a bunch of radish. If there were not two or three and fifty upon poor old Jack, then am I no two-legg'd creature.

PRINCE.   Pray God you have not murdered some of them.

FALSTAFF.   Nay, that's past praying for; I have peppered two of them. Two I am sure I have paid,[33] two rogues in buckram suits. I tell thee what, Hal, if I tell thee a lie, spit in my face, call me horse. Thou knowest my old ward:[34] here I lay, and thus I bore my point. Four rogues in buckram let drive at me—

PRINCE.   What, four? Thou saidst but two even now.

FALSTAFF.   Four, Hal; I told thee four.

POINS.   Ay, ay, he said four.

FALSTAFF.   These four came all a-front, and mainly[35] thrust at me. I made me no more ado but took all their seven points in my target,[36] thus.

PRINCE.   Seven? why, there were but four even now.

FALSTAFF.   In buckram?

POINS.   Ay, four, in buckram suits.

FALSTAFF.   Seven, by these hilts, or I am a villain else.

---

30. *ecce signum*—behold the evidence.   31. dealt—fought.
32. other—the rest.   33. paid—killed.   34. ward—defensive tactics.
35. mainly –with full strength.   36. target—shield.

PRINCE. Prithee, let him alone; we shall have more anon.

FALSTAFF. Dost thou hear me, Hal?

PRINCE. Ay, and mark thee too, Jack.

FALSTAFF. Do so, for it is worth the listening to. These nine in buckram that I told thee of—

PRINCE. So, two more already.

FALSTAFF. Their points[37] being broken,—

POINS. Down fell their hose.

FALSTAFF. Began to give me ground; but I followed me close, came in foot and hand, and with a thought seven of the eleven I paid.

PRINCE. O monstrous! eleven buckram men grown out of two!

FALSTAFF. But, as the devil would have it, three misbegotten knaves in Kendal green came at my back and let drive at me; for it was so dark, Hal, that thou couldst not see thy hand.

PRINCE. These lies are like their father that begets them; gross as a mountain, open, palpable. Why thou clay-brained guts, thou knotty-pated[38] fool, thou whorseon, obscene, greasy tallow-catch,[39]—

FALSTAFF. What, art thou mad? are thou mad? Is not the truth the truth?

PRINCE. Why, how couldst thou know these men in Kendal green, when it was so dark thou couldst not see thy hand? Come, tell us your reason; what say'st thou to this?

POINS. Come, your reason, Jack, your reason.

FALSTAFF. What, upon compulsion? 'Zounds, an I were at the strappado,[40] or all the racks in the world, I would not tell you on compulsion. Give you a reason on compulsion! If reasons[41] were as plenty as blackberries, I would give no man a reason upon compulsion, I.

PRINCE. I'll be no longer guilty of this sin. This sanguine coward, this bed-presser, this horseback-breaker, this huge hill of flesh,—

FALSTAFF. 'Sblood, you starveling, you elf-skin, you dried

---

37. points—sword's points; also, the laces which held the breeches (hose) to the doublet.

38. knotty-pated—blockheaded.   39. tallow-catch—lump of tallow.

40. strappado—a torture.   41. reasons—pronounced like "raisins."

neat's tongue, you bull's pizzle, you stockfish! [42] O for breath to utter what is like thee! you tailor's-yard, you sheath, you bowcase, you vile standing-tuck,[43]—

PRINCE. Well, breathe a while, and then to it again; and when thou hast tired thyself in base comparisons, hear me speak but this:—

POINS. Mark, Jack.

PRINCE. We two saw you four set on four and bound them, and were masters of their wealth. Mark now, how a plain tale shall put you down. Then did we two set on you four; and, with a word, out-faced you from your prize, and have it, yea, and can show it you here in the house; and, Falstaff, you carried your guts away as nimbly, with as quick dexterity, and roared for mercy, and still run and roared, as ever I heard bull-calf. What a slave art thou, to hack thy sword as thou hast done, and then say it was in fight! What trick, what device, what starting-hole,[44] canst thou now find out to hide thee from this open and apparent shame?

POINS. Come, let's hear, Jack; what trick hast thou now?

FALSTAFF. By the Lord, I knew ye as well as he that made ye. Why, hear you, my masters: was it for me to kill the heir-apparent? Should I turn upon the true prince? Why, thou knowest I am as valiant as Hercules; but beware instinct; the lion will not touch the true prince. Instinct is a great matter; I was now a coward on instinct. I shall think the better of myself and thee during my life; I for a valiant lion, and thou for a true prince. But, by the Lord, lads, I am glad you have the money. Hostess, clap, to the doors! Watch to-night, pray to-morrow. Gallants, lads, boys, heart of gold, all the titles of good fellowship come to you! What, shall we be merry? Shall we have a play extempore?

PRINCE. Content; and the argument[45] shall be thy running away.

FALSTAFF. Ah, no more of that, Hal, an thou lovest me!

Enter HOSTESS.

---

42. stockfish—dried cod.
43. standing-tuck—rapier standing on its point.
44. starting-hole—loophole.   45. argument—plot.

HOSTESS.   O Jesu, my lord the Prince!

PRINCE.   How now, my lady the hostess! what say'st thou to me?

HOSTESS.   Marry, my lord, there is a nobleman of the court at door would speak with you. He says he comes from your father.

PRINCE.   Give him as much as will make him a royal [46] man, and send him back again to my mother.

FALSTAFF.   What manner of man is he?

HOSTESS.   An old man.

FALSTAFF.   What doth Gravity out of his bed at midnight? Shall I give him his answer?

PRINCE.   Prithee, do, Jack.

FALSTAFF.   Faith, and I'll send him packing.   *Exit.*

PRINCE.   Now, sirs, by 'r lady, you fought fair; so did you, Peto; so did you, Bardolph. You are lions too, you ran away upon instinct, you will not touch the true prince; no, fie!

BARDOLPH.   Faith, I ran when I saw others run.

PRINCE.   Tell me now in earnest, how came Falstaff's sword so hacked?

PETO.   Why, he hacked it with his dagger, and said he would swear truth out of England but he would make you believe it was done in fight, and persuaded us to do the like.

BARDOLPH.   Yea, and to tickle our noses with spear-grass to make them bleed, and then to beslubber our garments with it and swear it was the blood of true men. I did that I did not this seven year before, I blushed to hear his monstrous devices.

PRINCE.   O villain, thou stolest a cup of sack eighteen years ago, and wert taken with the manner,[47] and ever since thou hast blushed extempore.[48] Thou hadst fire and sword on thy side, and yet thou ran'st away; what instinct hadst thou for it?

BARDOLPH.   My lord, do you see these meteors? Do you behold these exhalations?   [*Pointing to his own face.*]

PRINCE.   I do.

BARDOLPH.   What think you they portend?

---

46. royal—punning on the social rank and the value of the coin; the royal was worth ten shillings, the noble, six shillings, eightpence.

47. with the manner—in the act.

48. blushed extempore—alluding to Bardolph's red face.

PRINCE. Hot livers and cold purses.[49]

BARDOLPH. Choler,[50] my lord, if rightly taken.

Re-enter FALSTAFF.

PRINCE. No, if rightly taken,[51] halter.[52] Here comes lean Jack, here comes bare-bone. How now, my sweet creature of bombast![53] How long is 't ago, Jack, since thou sawest thine own knee?

FALSTAFF. My own knee? When I was about thy years, Hal, I was not an eagle's talon in the waist; I could have crept into any alderman's thumb-ring: a plague of sighing and grief! it blows a man up like a bladder. There's villanous news abroad: here was Sir John Bracy from your father; you must to the court in the morning. That same mad fellow of the north, Percy, and he of Wales that gave Amamon[54] the bastinado[55] and made Lucifer cuckold and swore the devil his true liegeman upon the cross of a Welsh hook—what a plague call you him?

POINS. Owen Glendower.

FALSTAFF. Owen, Owen, the same; and his son-in-law Mortimer, and old Northumberland, and that sprightly Scot of Scots, Douglas, that runs a-horseback up a hill perpendicular,—

PRINCE. He that rides at high speed and with his pistol kills a sparrow flying.

FALSTAFF. You have hit it.

PRINCE. So did he never the sparrow.

FALSTAFF. Well, that rascal hath good mettle in him; he will not run.

PRINCE. Why, what a rascal art thou then, to praise him so for running!

FALSTAFF. A-horseback, ye cuckoo; but afoot he will not budge a foot.

PRINCE. Yes, Jack, upon instinct.

FALSTAFF. I grant ye, upon instinct. Well, he is there too, and one Murdoch, and a thousand blue-caps[56] more: Worcester

---

49. Hot livers and cold purses—disease and poverty (caused by drink).
50. Choler—a quick temper.   51. taken—interpreted; also, arrested.
52. halter—hanging, punning on "choler-collar."
53. bombast—padding.   54. Amamon—a devil.
55. bastinado—thrashing.   56. blue-caps—Scots.

is stolen away to-night: thy father's beard is turn'd white with the news: you may buy land now as cheap as stinking mackerel.

PRINCE.   Why, then, it is like, if there come a hot June and this civil buffeting hold, we shall buy maidenheads as they buy hob-nails, by the hundreds.

FALSTAFF.   By the mass, lad, thou say'st true; it is like we shall have good trading that way. But tell me, Hal, art not thou horrible afeard? Thou being heir-apparent, could the world pick thee out three such enemies again as that fiend Douglas, that spirit Percy, and that devil Glendower? Art thou not horribly afraid? Doth not thy blood thrill at it?

PRINCE.   Not a whit, i' faith; I lack some of thy instinct.

FALSTAFF.   Well, thou wilt be horribly chid to-morrow when thou comest to thy father: if thou love me, practise an answer.

PRINCE.   Do thou stand for my father, and examine me upon the particulars of my life.

FALSTAFF.   Shall I? Content. This chair shall be my state,[57] this dagger my sceptre, and this cushion my crown.

PRINCE.   Thy state is taken for a joined-stool,[58] thy golden sceptre for a leaden dagger, and thy precious rich crown for a pitiful bald crown!

FALSTAFF.   Well, an the fire of grace be not quite out of thee, now shalt thou be moved. Give me a cup of sack to make my eyes look red, that it may be thought I have wept; for I must speak in passion, and I will do it in King Cambyses' [59] vein.

PRINCE.   Well, here is my leg.[60]

FALSTAFF.   And here is my speech. Stand aside, nobility.

HOSTESS.   O Jesu, this is excellent sport, i' faith!

FALSTAFF.   Weep not, sweet queen; for trickling tears are vain.

HOSTESS.   O, the father, how he holds his countenance!

FALSTAFF.   For God's sake, lords, convey[61] my tristful [62] queen;

For tears do stop the flood-gates of her eyes.

---

57. state—throne.
58. joined-stool—wooden stool.
59. Cambyses—hero of a popular tragedy whose ranting speech Falstaff is about to parody.
60. leg—bow.   61. convey—lead away.   62. tristful—sorrowful.

HOSTESS.   O Jesu, he doth it as like one of these harlotry players as ever I see!

FALSTAFF.   Peace, good pint-pot; peace, good tickle-brain.[63] Harry, I do not only marvel where thou spendest thy time, but also how thou art accompanied; for though the camomile, the more it is trodden on the faster it grows, so youth, the more it is wasted the sooner it wears. That thou art my son, I have partly thy mother's word, partly my own opinion, but chiefly a villanous trick of thine eye and a foolish hanging of thy nether lip, that doth warrant me. If then thou be son to me, here lies the point; why, being son to me, art thou so pointed at? Shall the blessed sun of heaven prove a micher[64] and eat blackberries? a question not to be asked. Shall the son of England prove a thief and take purses? a question to be asked. There is a thing, Harry, which thou hast often heard of and it is known to many in our land by the name of pitch. This pitch, as ancient writers do report, doth defile; so doth the company thou keepest: for, Harry, now I do not speak to thee in drink but in tears; not in pleasure but in passion, not in words only, but in woes also; and yet there is a virtuous man whom I have often noted in thy company, but I know not his name.

PRINCE.   What manner of man, an it like your Majesty?

FALSTAFF.   A goodly portly man, i' faith, and a corpulent; of a cheerful look, a pleasing eye, and a most noble carriage; and, as I think, his age some fifty, or, by 'r lady, inclining to threescore; and now I remember me, his name is Falstaff. If that man should be lewdly given, he deceiveth me; for, Harry, I see virtue in his looks. If then the tree may be known by the fruit, as the fruit by the tree, then, peremptorily I speak it, there is virtue in that Falstaff; him keep with, the rest banish. And tell me now, thou naughty varlet, tell me, where hast thou been this month?

PRINCE.   Dost thou speak like a king? Do thou stand for me, and I'll play my father.

FALSTAFF.   Depose me? If thou dost it half so gravely, so majestically, both in word and matter, hang me up by the heels for a rabbit-sucker[65] or a poulter's hare.

---

63. tickle-brain—strong drink.   64. micher—truant.
65. rabbit-sucker—young rabbit.

PRINCE. Well, here I am set.

FALSTAFF. And here I stand: judge, my masters.

PRINCE. Now, Harry, whence come you?

FALSTAFF. My noble lord, from Eastcheap.

PRINCE. The complaints I hear of thee are grievous.

FALSTAFF. 'Sblood, my lord, they are false.—Nay, I'll tickle ye[66] for a young prince, i' faith.

PRINCE. Swearest thou, ungracious boy? Henceforth ne'er look on me. Thou art violently carried away from grace: there is a devil haunts thee in the likeness of an old fat man; a tun of man is thy companion. Why dost thou converse with that trunk of humours, that bolting-hutch of beastliness, that swollen parcel of dropsies, that huge bombard [67] of sack, that stuffed cloak-bag of guts, that roasted Manningtree ox with the pudding in his belly, that reverend vice, that grey iniquity, that father ruffian, that vanity in years? Wherein is he good, but to taste sack and drink it? wherein neat and cleanly, but to carve a capon and eat it? wherein cunning, but in craft? wherein crafty, but in villainy? wherein villanous, but in all things? wherein worthy, but in nothing?

FALSTAFF. I would your Grace would take me with you: whom means your Grace?

PRINCE. That villanous abominable misleader of youth, Falstaff, that old white-bearded Satan.

FALSTAFF. My lord, the man I know.

PRINCE. I know thou dost.

FALSTAFF. But to say I know more harm in him than in myself, were to say more than I know. That he is old, the more the pity, his white hairs do witness it; but that he is, saving your reverence, a whoremaster, that I utterly deny. If sack and sugar be a fault, God help the wicked! If to be old and merry be a sin, than many an old host[68] that I know is damned. If to be fat be to be hated, then Pharaoh's lean kine are to be loved. No, my good lord; banish Peto, banish Bardolph, banish Poins; but for sweet Jack Falstaff, kind Jack Falstaff, true Jack Falstaff, valiant Jack Falstaff, and therefore more valiant, being, as he is, old Jack Falstaff, banish not him thy Harry's company, banish not

---

66. tickle ye—i.e., "show you up."   67. bombard—a wine jug.
68. host—innkeeper.

him thy Harry's company. Banish plump Jack, and banish all the world.

PRINCE.   I do, I will.

[*A knocking heard.*] *Exeunt* HOSTESS, FRANCIS, *and* BARDOLPH.

Re-enter BARDOLPH, *running*.

BARDOLPH.   O, my lord, my lord! the sheriff with a most monstrous watch is at the door.

FALSTAFF.   Out, ye rogue! Play out the play; I have much to say in the behalf of that Falstaff.

Re-enter the HOSTESS.

HOSTESS.   O Jesu, my lord, my lord!

PRINCE.   Heigh, heigh! the devil rides upon a fiddlestick: what's the matter?

HOSTESS.   The sheriff and all the watch are at the door; they are come to search the house. Shall I let them in?

FALSTAFF.   Dost thou hear, Hal? Never call a true piece of gold a counterfeit: thou art essentially mad, without seeming so.

PRINCE.   And thou a natural coward, without instinct.

FALSTAFF.   I deny your major: [69] if you will deny the sheriff, so; if not, let him enter. If I become not a cart[70] as well as another man, a plague on my bringing up! I hope I shall as soon be strangled with a halter as another.

PRINCE.   Go, hide thee behind the arras; [71] the rest walk up above. Now, my masters, for a true face and good conscience.

FALSTAFF.   Both which I have had; but their date is out, and therefore I'll hide me. [*Hides behind the arras.*]

PRINCE.   Call in the sheriff.

Exeunt all except the PRINCE *and* PETO.

Enter SHERIFF *and the* CARRIER.

Now, master sheriff, what is your will with me?

SHERIFF.   First, pardon me, my lord. A hue and cry[72] Hath followed certain men unto this house.

PRINCE.   What men?

---

69. major—major premise.   70. cart—the hangman's cart.
71. arras—tapestry hangings.   72. hue and cry—"posse."

SHERIFF. One of them is well known, my gracious lord,
A gross fat man.

CARRIER. As fat as butter.

PRINCE. The man, I do assure you, is not here,
For I myself at this time have employ'd him.
And, sheriff, I will engage my word to thee
That I will, by to-morrow dinner-time,
Send him to answer thee or any man
For anything he shall be charg'd withal.
And so let me entreat you leave the house.

SHERIFF. I will, my lord. There are two gentlemen
Have in this robbery lost three hundred marks.

PRINCE. It may be so: if he have robb'd these men,
He shall be answerable; and so farewell.

SHERIFF. Good night, my noble lord.

PRINCE. I think it is good morrow, is it not?

SHERIFF. Indeed, my lord, I think it be two o'clock.

Exeunt SHERIFF *and* CARRIER.

PRINCE. This oily rascal is known as well as Paul's.[73] Go, call him forth.

PETO. Falstaff!—Fast asleep behind the arras, and snorting like a horse.

PRINCE. Hark, how hard he fetches breath. Search his pockets. [*He searches his pockets, and finds certain papers.*] What hast thou found?

PETO. Nothing but papers, my lord.

PRINCE. Let's see what they be. Read them.

PETO. [*Reads.*]

Item, A capon.....................................2s. 2d.
Item, Sauce .... 4d.
Item, Sack, two gallons..............................5s. 8d.
Item, Anchovies and sack after supper...............2s. 6d.
Item, Bread .... ob.[74]

PRINCE. O monstrous! but one half-pennyworth of bread to this intolerable deal of sack! What there is else, keep close; we'll read it at more advantage: there let him sleep till day. I'll to the

---

73. Paul's—St. Paul's Church, a famous London landmark.
74. ob.—halfpenny.

court in the morning. We must all to the wars, and thy place shall be honourable. I'll procure this fat rogue a charge of foot; [75] and I know his death will be a march of twelve-score.[76] The money shall be paid back again with advantage.[77] Be with me betimes in the morning; and so, good morrow, Peto.

PETO. Good morrow, good my lord.   *Exeunt.*

---

75. charge of foot—company of infantry.
76. twelve-score—240 yards.   77. advantage—interest.

[ACT III • 1] *Bangor.*[1] *The Archdeacon's house.*

Enter HOTSPUR, WORCESTER, LORD MORTIMER, *and* OWEN GLENDOWER.

MORTIMER.   These promises are fair, the parties sure,
And our induction[2] full of prosperous hope.

HOTSPUR.   Lord Mortimer, and cousin Glendower,
Will you sit down?
And uncle Worcester,—a plague upon it!
I have forgot the map.

GLENDOWER.   No, here it is.
Sit, cousin Percy; sit, good cousin Hotspur,
For by that name as oft as Lancaster[3]
Doth speak of you, his cheek looks pale and with
A rising sigh he wisheth you in heaven.

HOTSPUR.   And you in hell, as oft as he hears Owen Glendower spoke of.

GLENDOWER.   I cannot blame him: at my nativity
The front[4] of heaven was full of fiery shapes,
Of burning cressets;[5] and at my birth
The frame and huge foundation of the earth
Shak'd like a coward.

HOTSPUR.   Why, so it would have done at the same season, if your mother's cat had but kittened, though yourself had never been born.

GLENDOWER.   I say the earth did shake when I was born.

---

1. Bangor—in Wales.   2. induction—beginning.
3. Lancaster—King Henry IV.   4. front—forehead.
5. cressets—torches, i.e., meteors.

HOTSPUR.   And I say the earth was not of my mind,
If you suppose as fearing you it shook.

GLENDOWER.   The heavens were all on fire, the earth did
tremble.

HOTSPUR.   O, then the earth shook to see the heavens on fire,
And not in fear of your nativity.
Diseased nature oftentimes breaks forth
In strange eruptions; oft the teeming earth
Is with a kind of colic pinch'd and vex'd
By the imprisoning of unruly wind
Within her womb; which, for enlargement striving,
Shakes the old beldam[6] earth, and topples down
Steeples and moss-grown towers. At your birth
Our grandam earth, having this distemperature,[7]
In passion shook.

GLENDOWER.   Cousin, of many men
I do not bear these crossings.[8] Give me leave
To tell you once again that at my birth
The front of heaven was full of fiery shapes,
The goats ran from the mountains, and the herds
Were strangely clamorous to the frighted fields.
These signs have mark'd me extraordinary;
And all the courses of my life do show
I am not in the roll of common men.
Where is he living, clipp'd in[9] with the sea
That chides the banks of England, Scotland, Wales,
Which calls me pupil, or hath read to[10] me?
And bring him out that is but woman's son
Can trace[11] me in the tedious ways of art
And hold me pace[12] in deep experiments.

HOTSPUR.   I think there's no man speaks better Welsh. I'll
to dinner.

MORTIMER.   Peace, cousin Percy; you will make him mad.

GLENDOWER.   I can call spirits from the vasty deep.

---

6. beldam—grandmother.   7. distemperature—ailment.
8. crossings—opposition.   9. clipp'd in—enclosed by.
10. read to—instructed.   11. trace—follow.
12. hold me pace—keep up with me.

HOTSPUR.   Why, so can I, or so can any man;
But will they come when you do call for them?
GLENDOWER.   Why, I can teach you, cousin, to command
The devil.
HOTSPUR.   And I can teach thee, coz,[13] to shame the devil
By telling truth. "Tell truth and shame the devil."
If thou have power to raise him, bring him hither,
And I'll be sworn I have power to shame him hence.
O, while you live, tell truth and shame the devil!
MORTIMER.   Come, come, no more of this unprofitable chat.
GLENDOWER.   Three times hath Henry Bolingbroke made
head [14]
Against my power; thrice from the banks of Wye
And sandy-bottom'd Severn have I sent him
Bootless[15] home and weather-beaten back.
HOTSPUR.   Home without books, and in foul weather too!
How scapes he agues, in the devil's name?
GLENDOWER.   Come, here's the map. Shall we divide our
right
According to our threefold order[16] ta'en?
MORTIMER.   The Archdeacon hath divided it
Into three limits very equally.
England, from Trent and Severn hitherto,
By south and east is to my part assign'd;
All westward, Wales beyond the Severn shore,
And all the fertile land within that bound,
To Owen Glendower; and, dear coz, to you
The remnant northward, lying off from Trent.
And our indentures tripartite are drawn;
Which being sealed interchangeably,
A business that this night may execute,
To-morrow, cousin Percy, you and I
And my good Lord of Worcester will set forth
To meet your father and the Scottish power,
As is appointed us, at Shrewsbury.
My father Glendower is not ready yet,

---

13. coz—cousin (loosely used of any relationship).
14. made head—led an army.   15. Bootless—unsuccessful.
16. threefold order—agreement among us three.

Nor shall we need his help these fourteen days.
Within that space you may have drawn together
Your tenants, friends, and neighbouring gentlemen.

GLENDOWER.   A shorter time shall send me to you, lords;
And in my conduct shall your ladies come,
From whom you now must steal and take no leave,
For there will be a world of water shed
Upon the parting of your wives and you.

HOTSPUR.   Methinks my moiety,[17] north from Burton here,
In quantity equals not one of yours.
See how this river comes me cranking in,
And cuts me from the best of all my land
A huge half-moon, a monstrous cantle[18] out.
I'll have the current in this place damm'd up;
And here the smug and silver Trent shall run
In a new channel, fair and evenly.
It shall not wind with such a deep indent,
To rob me of so rich a bottom[19] here.

GLENDOWER.   Not wind? It shall, it must; you see it doth.

MORTIMER.   Yea, but
Mark how he bears his course, and runs me up
With like advantage on the other side;
Gelding[20] the opposed continent as much
As on the other side it takes from you.

WORCESTER.   Yea, but a little charge will trench him here
And on this north side win this cape of land;
And then he runs straight and even.

HOTSPUR.   I'll have it so; a little charge will do it.

GLENDOWER.   I'll not have it alter'd.

HOTSPUR.   Will not you?

GLENDOWER.   No, nor you shall not.

HOTSPUR.   Who shall say me nay?

GLENDOWER.   Why, that will I.

HOTSPUR.   Let me not understand you, then; speak it in
Welsh.

GLENDOWER.   I can speak English, lord, as well as you;
For I was train'd up in the English court;

---

17. moiety—portion.   18. cantle—segment.
19. bottom—fertile land.   20. Gelding—cutting off from.

Where, being but young, I framed [21] to the harp
Many an English ditty lovely well
And gave the tongue a helpful ornament,
A virtue that was never seen in you.
    HOTSPUR.   Marry,
And I am glad of it with all my heart.
I had rather be a kitten and cry mew
Than one of these same metre ballad-mongers;
I had rather hear a brazen canstick[22] turn'd,
Or a dry wheel grate on the axle-tree;
And that would set my teeth nothing on edge,
Nothing so much as mincing poetry.
'T is like the forc'd gait of a shuffling nag.
    GLENDOWER.   Come, you shall have Trent turn'd.
    HOTSPUR.   I do not care. I'll give thrice so much land
To any well-deserving friend;
But in the way of bargain, mark ye me,
I'll cavil [23] on the ninth part of a hair.
Are the indentures drawn? Shall we be gone?
    GLENDOWER.   The moon shines fair; you may away by night.
I'll haste the writer, and withal
Break with[24] your wives of your departure hence.
I am afraid my daughter will run mad,
So much she doteth on her Mortimer.   *Exit.*
    MORTIMER.   Fie, cousin Percy! how you cross my father!
    HOTSPUR.   I cannot choose. Sometime he angers me
With telling me of the moldwarp[25] and the ant,
Of the dreamer Merlin[26] and his prophecies,
And of a dragon and a finless fish,
A clip-wing'd griffin and a moulten[27] raven,
A couching[28] lion and a ramping[29] cat,
And such a deal of skimble-skamble stuff
As puts me from my faith. I tell you what:
He held me last night at least nine hours

---

21. framed—composed.   22. canstick—candlestick.
23. cavil—raise objections.   24. Break with—inform.
25. moldwarp—mole.   26. Merlin—King Arthur's magician.
27. moulten—featherless.   28. couching—lying down.
29. ramping—rearing up.

In reckoning up the several devils' names
That were his lackeys. I cried "hum," and "well, go to,"
But mark'd him not a word. O, he is as tedious
As a tired horse, a railing wife;
Worse than a smoky house. I had rather live
With cheese and garlic in a windmill, far,
Than feed on cates[30] and have him talk to me
In any summer-house in Christendom.

    MORTIMER.   In faith, he is a worthy gentleman,
Exceedingly well read, and profited [31]
In strange concealments,[32] valiant as a lion
And wondrous affable, and as bountiful
As mines of India. Shall I tell you, cousin?
He holds your temper in a high respect
And curbs himself even of his natural scope
When you come 'cross his humour; faith, he does.
I warrant you, that man is not alive
Might so have tempted him as you have done,
Without the taste of danger and reproof:
But do not use it oft, let me entreat you.

    WORCESTER.   In faith, my lord, you are too wilful-blame; [33]
And since your coming hither have done enough
To put him quite besides[34] his patience.
You must needs learn, lord, to amend this fault.
Though sometimes it show greatness, courage, blood,—
And that's the dearest grace[35] it renders you,—
Yet oftentimes it doth present[36] harsh rage,
Defect of manners, want of government,
Pride, haughtiness, opinion,[37] and disdain;
The least of which haunting a nobleman
Loseth men's hearts and leaves behind a stain
Upon the beauty of all parts besides,
Beguiling[38] them of commendation.

---

30. cates—delicacies.   31. profited—expert.
32. concealments—secrets of magic art.
33. wilful-blame—to blame for being wilful.
34. besides—out of.   35. dearest grace—credit.
36. present—indicate.   37. opinion—stubbornness.
38. Beguiling—depriving.

HOTSPUR.   Well, I am school'd: good manners be your
    speed!
Here come our wives, and let us take our leave.

Re-enter GLENDOWER *with the Ladies.*

MORTIMER.   This is the deadly spite that angers me;
My wife can speak no English, I no Welsh.
GLENDOWER.   My daughter weeps; she'll not part with you;
She'll be a soldier too, she'll to the wars.
MORTIMER.   Good father, tell her that she and my aunt
    Percy
Shall follow in your conduct speedily.
                [GLENDOWER *speaks to her in Welsh,*
                   and she answers him in the same.]
GLENDOWER.   She is desperate here; a peevish self-willed
harlotry,[39] one that no persuasion can do good upon. [*The lady
speaks in Welsh.*]
MORTIMER.   I understand thy looks: that pretty Welsh
Which thou pourest down from these swelling heavens
I am too perfect in; and, but for shame,
In such a parley[40] should I answer thee.
              [*The lady speaks again in Welsh.*]
I understand thy kisses and thou mine,
And that's a feeling disputation: [41]
But I will never be a truant, love,
Till I have learn'd thy language; for thy tongue
Makes Welsh as sweet as ditties highly penn'd,
Sung by a fair queen in a summer's bower,
With ravishing division,[42] to her lute.
GLENDOWER.   Nay, if you melt, then will she run mad. [*The
lady speaks again in Welsh.*]
MORTIMER.   O, I am ignorance itself in this!
GLENDOWER.   She bids you on the wanton rushes[43] lay you
    down

---

39. harlotry—wench (a term of affection).
40. parley—language, i.e., tears.
41. feeling disputation—exchange of feelings.
42. division—harmony.
43. wanton rushes—floor covering of thickly spread rushes.

And rest your gentle head upon her lap,
And she will sing the song that pleaseth you
And on your eyelids crown the god of sleep,
Charming your blood with pleasing heaviness,
Making such difference 'twixt wake and sleep
As is the difference betwixt day and night
The hour before the heavenly-harness'd team[44]
Begins his golden progress in the east.

    MORTIMER.   With all my heart I'll sit and hear her sing:
By that time will our book,[45] I think, be drawn.

    GLENDOWER.   Do so;
And those musicians that shall play to you
Hang in the air a thousand leagues from hence,
And straight they shall be here: sit, and attend.

    HOTSPUR.   Come, Kate, thou are perfect in lying down:
come, quick, quick, that I may lay my head in thy lap.

    LADY PERCY.   Go, ye giddy goose.   [*The music plays.*]

    HOTSPUR.   Now I perceive the devil understands Welsh;
And 't is no marvel he is so humorous.
By 'r lady, he is a good musician.

    LADY PERCY.   Then should you be nothing but musical, for
you are altogether governed by humours. Lie still, ye thief, and
hear the lady sing in Welsh.

    HOTSPUR.   I had rather hear Lady, my brach,[46] howl in
Irish.

    LADY PERCY.   Wouldst thou have thy head broken?

    HOTSPUR.   No.

    LADY PERCY.   Then be still.

    HOTSPUR.   Neither; 't is a woman's fault.

    LADY PERCY.   Now God help thee!

    HOTSPUR.   To the Welsh lady's bed.

    LADY PERCY.   What's that?

    HOTSPUR.   Peace! she sings.
                  [*Here the lady sings a Welsh song.*]

    HOTSPUR.   Come, Kate, I'll have your song too.

    LADY PERCY.   Not mine, in good sooth.[47]

---

44. team—horses that draw the chariot of the sun.
45. book—the tripartite pact.
46. brach—bitch.   47. sooth—truth.

HOTSPUR.   Not yours, in good sooth! Heart, you swear like
a comfit-maker's[48] wife. "Not you, in good sooth," and " as true
as I live," and "as God shall mend me," and "as sure as day;"
And givest such sarcenet[49] surety for thy oaths
As if thou never walk'st further than Finsbury.[50]
Swear me, Kate, like a lady as thou art,
A good mouth-filling oath, and leave "in sooth,"
And such protest of pepper-gingerbread,
To velvet-guards[51] and Sunday-citizens.
Come, sing.

LADY PERCY.   I will not sing.

HOTSPUR.   'T is the next way to turn tailor, or be red-breast[52]
teacher. An the indentures be drawn, I'll away within these two
hours; and so, come in when ye will.   *Exit.*

GLENDOWER.   Come, come, Lord Mortimer; you are as slow
As hot Lord Percy is on fire to go.
By this our book is drawn; we'll but seal,
And then to horse immediately.

MORTIMER.   With all my heart. *Exeunt.*

---

48. comfit-maker's—confectioner's.   49. sarcenet—thin silk.
50. Finsbury—recreation grounds for London's middle class.
51. velvet-guards—trimming for the dresses of citizens' wives.
52. red-breast—song bird.

[ACT III • 2] *London. The palace.*

Enter the KING, PRINCE OF WALES, *and others.*

KING.   Lords, give us leave; the Prince of Wales and I
Must have some private conference; but be near at hand,
For we shall presently have need of you.   *Exeunt Lords.*
I know not whether God will have it so,
For some displeasing service I have done,
That, in his secret doom,[1] out of my blood [2]
He'll breed revengement and a scourge for me;
But thou dost in thy passages of life
Make me believe that thou art only mark'd
For the hot vengeance and the rod of heaven

---

1. doom—judgement.   2. blood—child.

To punish my mistreadings. Tell me else,
Could such inordinate and low desires,
Such poor, such bare, such lewd, such mean attempts,
Such barren pleasures, rude society,
As thou art match'd withal and grafted to,
Accompany the greatness of thy blood
And hold their level with[3] thy princely heart?

    PRINCE.   So please your Majesty, I would I could
Quit[4] all offences with as clear excuse
As well as I am doubtless[5] I can purge
Myself of many I am charg'd withal: [6]
Yet such extenuation let me beg,
As, in reproof of many tales devis'd,
Which oft the ear of greatness needs must hear,
By smiling pick-thanks[7] and base newsmongers,
I may, for some things true, wherein my youth
Hath faulty wander'd and irregular,
Find pardon on my true submission.

    KING.   God pardon thee! yet let me wonder, Harry,
At thy affections, which do hold a wing
Quite from the flight of all thy ancestors.
Thy place in council thou hast rudely lost,
Which by thy younger brother is supplied,
And art almost an alien to the hearts
Of all the court and princes of my blood:
The hope and expectation of thy time
Is ruin'd, and the soul of every man
Prophetically do forethink thy fall.
Had I so lavish of my presence been,
So common-hackney'd [8] in the eyes of men,
So stale and cheap to vulgar company,
Opinion, that did help me to the crown,
Had still kept loyal to possession[9]
And left me in reputeless banishment,

---

3. hold their level with—be tolerable to.
4. Quit—prove my innocence of.   5. doubtless—confident.
6. withal—with.   7. pick-thanks—informers.
8. common-hackney'd—commonplace sight.
9. possession—i.e., Richard II.

A fellow of no mark nor likelihood.
By being seldom seen, I could not stir
But like a comet I was wonder'd at;
That men would tell their children, "This is he;"
Others would say, "Where, which is Bolingbroke?"
And then I stole all courtesy from heaven,
And dress'd myself in such humility
That I did pluck allegiance from men's hearts,
Loud shouts and salutations from their mouths,
Even in the presence of the crowned King.
Thus did I keep my person fresh and new,
My presence, like a robe pontifical,
Ne'er seen but wonder'd at; and so my state,[10]
Seldom but sumptuous, show'd like a feast
And won by rareness such solemnity.
The skipping King, he ambled up and down
With shallow jesters and rash bavin[11] wits,
Soon kindled and soon burnt; carded [12] his state,
Mingled his royalty with cap'ring fools,
Had his great name profaned with their scorns,
And gave his countenance, against his name,
To laugh at gibing boys and stand the push
Of every beardless vain comparative; [13]
Grew a companion to the common streets,
Enfeoff'd [14] himself to popularity; [15]
That, being daily swallowed by men's eyes,
They surfeited with honey and began
To loathe the taste of sweetness, whereof a little
More than a little is by much too much.
So when he had occasion to be seen,
He was but as the cuckoo is in June,
Heard, not regarded; seen, but with such eyes
As, sick and blunted with community,[16]
Afford no extraordinary gaze

---

10. state—public appearances.   11. bavin—flashy.
12. carded—debased.   13. comparative—would-be wit.
14. Enfeoff'd—became a subject.
15. to popularity—of the common people.
16. community—familiarity.

Such as is bent on sun-like majesty
When it shines seldom in admiring eyes;
But rather drows'd and hung their eyelids down,
Slept in his face and render'd such aspéct[17]
As cloudy[18] men use to their adversaries,
Being with his presence glutted, gorg'd and full.
And in that very line, Harry, standest thou;
For thou hast lost thy princely privilege
With vile participation.[19] Not an eye
But is a-weary of thy common sight,
Save mine, which hath desir'd to see thee more;
Which now doth that I would not have it do,
Make blind itself with foolish tenderness.

PRINCE.　I shall hereafter, my thrice gracious lord,
Be more myself.

KING.　　　　For all the world
As thou art to this hour was Richard then
When I from France set foot at Ravenspurgh,
And even as I was then is Percy now.
Now, by my sceptre and my soul to boot,
He hath more worthy interest[20] to the state
Than thou, the shadow of succession.
For of no right, nor colour like to right,
He doth fill fields with harness[21] in the realm,
Turns head against the lion's armed jaws,
And, being no more in debt to years than thou,
Leads ancient lords and reverend bishops on
To bloody battles and to bruising arms.
What never-dying honour hath he got
Against renowned Douglas! whose high deeds,
Whose hot incursions and great name in arms
Holds from all soldiers chief majority[22]
And military title capital
Through all the kingdoms that acknowledge Christ.
Thrice hath this Hotspur, Mars in swathling clothes
This infant warrior, in his enterprises

---

17. aspect—look.　　18. cloudy—frowning.
19. participation—companionship.　　20. interest—claim.
21. harness—armor.　　22. majority—claim to supremacy.

Discomfited great Douglas, ta'en him once,
Enlarged [23] him and made a friend of him,
To fill the mouth of deep defiance up
And shake the peace and safety of our throne.
And what say you to this? Percy, Northumberland,
The Archbishop's grace of York, Douglas, Mortimer,
Capitulate[24] against us and are up.[25]
But wherefore do I tell these news to thee?
Why, Harry, do I tell thee of my foes,
Which art my near'st and dearest enemy?
Thou that art like enough, through vassal fear,
Base inclination, and the start of spleen,
To fight against me under Percy's pay,
To dog his heels and curtsy at his frowns,
To show how much thou art degenerate.

    PRINCE.   Do not think so; you shall not find it so:
And God forgive them that so much have sway'd
Your Majesty's good thoughts away from me!
I will redeem all this on Percy's head,
And in the closing of some glorious day
Be bold to tell you that I am your son;
When I will wear a garment all of blood
And stain my favours[26] in a bloody mask,
Which, wash'd away, shall scour my shame with it:
And that shall be the day, whene'er it lights,
That this same child of honour and renown,
This gallant Hotspur, this all-praised knight,
And your unthought-of Harry chance to meet.
For every honour sitting on his helm,
Would they were multitudes, and on my head
My shames redoubled! For the time will come,
That I shall make this northern youth exchange
His glorious deeds for my indignities.[27]
Percy is but my factor,[28] good my lord,
To engross[29] up glorious deeds on my behalf;

---

23. enlarged—freed.   24. Capitulate—combine.
25. up—in rebellion.   26. favours—features.
27. indignities—unworthy actions.   28. factor—purchasing agent.
29. engross—buy on commission for another.

And I will call him to so strict account
That he shall render every glory up,
Yea, even the slightest worship of his time,
Or I will tear the reckoning from his heart.
This, in the name of God, I promise here;
The which if He be pleas'd I shall perform,
I do beseech your Majesty may salve
The long-grown wounds of my intemperance:
If not, the end of life cancels all bands; [30]
And I will die a hundred thousand deaths
Ere break the smallest parcel of this vow.
    KING.   A hundred thousand rebels die in this.
Thou shalt have charge and sovereign trust herein.

Enter BLUNT.

How now, good Blunt? Thy looks are full of speed.
    BLUNT.   So hath the business that I come to speak of.
Lord Mortimer of Scotland hath sent word
That Douglas and the English rebels met
The eleventh of this month at Shrewsbury.
A mighty and a fearful head they are,
If promises be kept on every hand,
As ever offer'd foul play in a state.
    KING.   The Earl of Westmoreland set forth to-day,
With him my son, Lord John of Lancaster,
For this advértisement[31] is five days old.
On Wednesday next, Harry, you shall set forward;
On Thursday we ourselves will march. Our meeting
Is Bridgenorth: and, Harry, you shall march
Through Gloucestershire; by which account,
Our business valued,[32] some twelve days hence
Our general forces at Bridgenorth shall meet.
Our hands are full of business; let's away.
Advantage feeds him fat, while men delay.   *Exeunt.*

---

30. bands—agreements.
31. advértisement—information.
32. Our business valued—considering all that must be done.

[ACT III • 3] *Eastcheap. The Boar's-Head Tavern.*

Enter FALSTAFF *and* BARDOLPH.

FALSTAFF. Bardolph, am I not fallen away vilely since this last action? Do I not bate? [1] Do I not dwindle? Why, my skin hangs about me like an old lady's loose gown; I am withered like an old apple-john.[2] Well, I'll repent, and that suddenly, while I am in some liking:[3] I shall be out of heart[4] shortly, and then I shall have no strength to repent. An I have not forgotten what the inside of a church is made of, I am a peppercorn, a brewer's horse. The inside of a church! Company, villanous company, hath been the spoil of me.

BARDOLPH. Sir John, you are so fretful, you cannot live long.

FALSTAFF. Why, there is it: come sing me a bawdy song; make me merry. I was as virtuously given as a gentleman need to be; virtuous enough, swore little, diced not above seven times a week, went to a bawdy-house not above once in a quarter—of an hour, paid money that I borrowed three or four times, lived well and in good compass;[5] and now I live out of all order, out of all compass.

BARDOLPH. Why, you are so fat, Sir John, that you must needs be out of all compass, out of all reasonable compass, Sir John.

FALSTAFF. Do thou amend thy face, and I'll amend my life: thou art our admiral;[6] thou bearest the lantern in the poop, but 't is in the nose of thee: thou art the Knight of the Burning Lamp.

BARDOLPH. Why, Sir John, my face does you no harm.

FALSTAFF. No, I'll be sworn; I make as good use of it as many a man doth of a Death's-head or a *memento mori;*[7] I never see thy face but I think upon hell-fire and Dives[8] that lived in purple; for there he is in his robes, burning, burning. If thou wert any way given to virtue, I would swear by thy face; my oath

---

1. bate—grown thin.   2. apple-john—shriveled apple.
3. liking—condition.   4. out of heart—depressed.
5. good compass—within bounds.   6. admiral—flagship.
7. *memento mori*—warning of death.
8. Dives—rich man of the parable in Luke 16:19–31.

should be, "By this fire, that's God's angel;" but thou are altogether given over, and wert indeed, but for the light in thy face,
the son of utter darkness. When thou ran'st up Gadshill in the
night to catch my horse, if I did not think thou hadst been an
ignis fatuus[9] or a ball of wildfire, there's no purchase in money.
O, thou art a perpetual triumph,[10] an everlasting bonfire-light!
Thou hast saved me a thousand marks in links[11] and torches,
walking with thee in the night betwixt tavern and tavern; but the
sack that thou hast drunk me would have brought me lights as
good cheap[12] at the dearest chandler's[13] in Europe. I have maintain'd that salamander of yours with fire any time this two and
thirty years; God reward me for it.

BARDOLPH.   'Sblood, I would my face were in your belly!

FALSTAFF.   God-a-mercy! so should I be sure to be heart-
burn'd.

Enter HOSTESS.

How now, Dame Partlet the hen! have you inquired yet who
picked my pocket?

HOSTESS.   Why, Sir John, what do you think, Sir John? Do
you think I keep thieves in my house? I have searched, I have
inquired, so has my husband, man by man, boy by boy, servant
by servant: the tithe[14] of a hair was never lost in my house before.

FALSTAFF.   Ye lie, hostess: Bardolph was shaved and lost
many a hair; and I'll be sworn my pocket was picked. Go to, you
are a woman, go.

HOSTESS.   Who? I? No; I defy thee. God's light, I was never
called so in mine own house before.

FALSTAFF.   Go to, I know you well enough.

HOSTESS.   No, Sir John; you do not know me, Sir John; I
know you, Sir John; you owe me money, Sir John; and now you
pick a quarrel to beguile me of it: I bought you a dozen of shirts
to your back.

---

9. *ignis fatuus*—will-o'-the-wisp.
10. triumph—fireworks, as at a public celebration.
11. links—torches.
12. as good cheap—as cheap.
13. chandler's—candlemaker's.   14. tithe—tenth part.

FALSTAFF. Dowlas,[15] filthy dowlas. I have given them away to bakers' wives; they have made bolters[16] of them.

HOSTESS. Now, as I am a true woman, holland [17] of eight shillings an ell. You owe money here besides, Sir John, for your diet, and by-drinkings,[18] and money lent you, four and twenty pound.

FALSTAFF. He had his part of it; let him pay.

HOSTESS. He? Alas, he is poor; he hath nothing.

FALSTAFF. How! poor? Look upon his face; what call you rich? Let them coin his nose, let them coin his cheeks: I'll not pay a denier.[19] What, will you make a younker[20] of me? Shall I not take mine ease in mine inn but I shall have my pocket picked? I have lost a seal-ring of my grandfather's worth forty mark.

HOSTESS. O Jesu, I have heard the Prince tell him, I know not how oft, that that ring was copper!

FALSTAFF. How! the Prince is a Jack,[21] a sneak-cup: [22] 'sblood, an he were here, I would cudgel him like a dog, if he would say so.

Enter the PRINCE *and* POINS, *marching, and* FALSTAFF *meets them playing on his truncheon[23] like a fife.*

How now, lad! is the wind in that door, i' faith? Must we all march?

BARDOLPH. Yea, two and two, Newgate[24] fashion.

HOSTESS. My lord, I pray you, hear me.

PRINCE. What say'st thou, Mistress Quickly? How doth thy husband? I love him well; he is an honest man.

HOSTESS. Good my lord, hear me.

FALSTAFF. Prithee, let her alone, and list to me.

PRINCE. What say'st thou, Jack?

FALSTAFF. The other night I fell asleep here behind the arras and had my pocket picked. This house is turned bawdy-house; they pick pockets.

---

15. Dowlas—coarse linen. 16. bolters—sieves for flour.
17. holland—fine linen. 18. by-drinkings—drinks between meals.
19. denier—tenth of a penny. 20. younker—greenhorn.
21. Jack—knave. 22. sneak-cup—unsocial drinker.
23. truncheon—short cane, baton. 24. Newgate—a London prison.

PRINCE.   What didst thou lose, Jack?

FALSTAFF.   Wilt thou believe me, Hal? Three or four bonds of forty pound a-piece, and a seal-ring of my grandfather's.

PRINCE.   A trifle, some eight-penny matter.

HOSTESS.   So I told him, my lord, and I said I heard your Grace say so; and, my lord, he speaks most vilely of you, like a foul-mouthed man as he is, and said he would cudgel you.

PRINCE.   What! he did not?

HOSTESS.   There's neither faith, truth, nor womanhood in me else.

FALSTAFF.   There's no more faith in thee than in a stewed prune;[25] nor no more truth in thee than in a drawn[26] fox; and for womanhood, Maid Marian[27] may be the deputy's wife of the ward to thee. Go, you thing, go.

HOSTESS.   Say, what thing? what thing?

FALSTAFF.   What thing? Why, a thing to thank God on.[28]

HOSTESS.   I am no thing to thank God on, I would thou shouldst know it: I am an honest man's wife; and, setting thy knighthood aside, thou art a knave to call me so.

FALSTAFF.   Setting thy womanhood aside, thou art a beast to say otherwise.

HOSTESS.   Say, what beast, thou knave, thou?

FALSTAFF.   What beast? Why, an otter.

PRINCE.   An otter, Sir John! Why an otter?

FALSTAFF.   Why, she's neither fish nor flesh; a man knows not where to have her.

HOSTESS.   Thou art an unjust man in saying so: thou or any man knows where to have me, thou knave, thou!

PRINCE.   Thou say'st true, hostess; and he slanders thee most grossly.

HOSTESS.   So he doth you, my lord; and said this other day you ought[29] him a thousand pound.

PRINCE.   Sirrah, do I owe you a thousand pound?

FALSTAFF.   A thousand pound, Hal! A million. Thy love is worth a million; thou owest me thy love.

---

25. stewed prune—harlot.   26. drawn—cunning.
27. Maid Marian—character in May Games enacted by a man, hence, an awkward, indecorous woman.
28. on—for   29. ought—owed.

HOSTESS.   Nay, my lord, he called you Jack, and said he would cudgel you.

FALSTAFF.   Did I, Bardolph?

BARDOLPH.   Indeed, Sir John, you said so.

FALSTAFF.   Yea, if he said my ring was copper.

PRINCE.   I say 't is copper: dar'st thou be as good as thy word now?

FALSTAFF.   Why, Hal, thou knowest, as thou art but man, I dare; but as thou art Prince, I fear thee as I fear the roaring of the lion's whelp.

PRINCE.   And why not as the lion?

FALSTAFF.   The King himself is to be feared as the lion: dost thou think I'll fear thee as I fear thy father? Nay, an I do, I pray God my girdle break.

PRINCE.   O, if it should, how would thy guts fall about thy knees! But, sirrah, there's no room for faith, truth, nor honesty in this bosom of thine; it is all filled up with guts and midriff. Charge an honest woman with picking thy pocket! Why, thou whoreson, impudent, embossed [30] rascal, if there were anything in thy pocket but tavern-reckonings, memorandums of bawdy-houses, and one poor penny-worth of sugar-candy to make thee long-winded, if thy pocket were enriched with any other injuries[31] but these, I am a villain: and yet you will stand to it; you will not pocket up wrong: art thou not ashamed?

FALSTAFF.   Dost thou hear, Hal? Thou knowest in the state of innocency Adam fell; and what should poor Jack Falstaff do in the days of villainy? Thou seest I have more flesh than another man, and therefore more frailty. You confess then, you picked my pocket?

PRINCE.   It appears so by the story.

FALSTAFF.   Hostess, I forgive thee: go, make ready breakfast; love thy husband, look to thy servants, cherish thy guests: thou shalt find me tractable to any honest reason; thou seest I am pacified. Still? [32] Nay, prithee, be gone.   *Exit* HOSTESS

Now, Hal, to the news at court: for the robbery, lad, how is that answered?

---

30. embossed—swollen.
31. injuries—articles whose loss would injure the owner.
32. Still?—Are you still here?

PRINCE.   O, my sweet beef, I must still be good angel to thee: the money is paid back again.

FALSTAFF.   O, I do not like that paying back; 't is a double labour.

PRINCE.   I am good friends with my father and may do anything.

FALSTAFF.   Rob me the exchequer the first thing thou doest, and do it with unwashed hands[33] too.

BARDOLPH.   Do, my lord.

PRINCE.   I have procured thee, Jack, a charge of foot.

FALSTAFF.   I would it had been of horse. Where shall I find one[34] that can steal well? O for a fine thief, of the age of two and twenty or thereabouts! I am heinously unprovided. Well, God be thanked for these rebels, they offend none but the virtuous. I laud them, I praise them.

PRINCE.   Bardolph!

BARDOLPH.   My lord?

PRINCE.   Go bear this letter to Lord John of Lancaster, to my brother John; this to my Lord of Westmoreland. [*Exit* BAR-DOLPH.] Go, Poins, to horse, to horse; for thou and I have thirty miles to ride yet ere dinner time. [*Exit* POINS.] Jack, meet me to-morrow in the Temple hall at two o'clock in the afternoon. There shalt thou know thy charge, and there receive
Money and order for their furniture.[35]
The land is burning; Percy stands on high;
And either we or they must lower lie.   *Exit.*

FALSTAFF.   Rare words! brave world! Hostess, my breakfast, come!
O, I could wish this tavern were my drum!   *Exit.*

---

33. unwashed hands—without delay.
34. one—as an aide.   35. furniture—equipment.

[ACT IV • 1] *The rebel camp near Shrewsbury.*

Enter HOTSPUR, WORCESTER, *and* DOUGLAS.

HOTSPUR.   Well said, my noble Scot! If speaking truth
In this fine age were not thought flattery,
Such attribution[1] should the Douglas have

---

1. attribution—praise.

As not a soldier of this season's stamp
Should go so general current through the world.
By God, I cannot flatter; I do defy
The tongues of soothers;[2] but a braver place
In my heart's love hath no man than yourself.
Nay, task me to my word; approve[3] me, lord.
    DOUGLAS.   Thou art the king of honour.
No man so potent breathes upon the ground
But I will beard [4] him.

Enter a MESSENGER *with letters.*

    HOTSPUR.   Do so, and 't is well.—
What letters hast thou there?—I can but thank you.
    MESSENGER.   These letters come from your father.
    HOTSPUR.   Letters from him! Why comes he not himself?
    MESSENGER.   He cannot come, my lord; he is grievous sick.
    HOTPUR.   'Zounds! how has he the leisure to be sick
In such a justling time? Who leads his power?
Under whose government come they along?
    MESSENGER.   His letters bear his mind, not I, my lord.
    WORCESTER.   I prithee, tell me, doth he keep his bed?
    MESSENGER.   He did, my lord, four days ere I set forth;
And at the time of my departure thence
He was much fear'd by his physicians.
    WORCESTER.   I would the state of time[5] had first been whole
Ere he by sickness had been visited.
His health was never better worth[6] than now.
    HOTSPUR.   Sick now! droop now! This sickness doth infect
The very life-blood of our enterprise;
'T is catching hither, even to our camp.
He writes me here, that inward sickness—
And that his friends by deputation[7] could not
So soon be drawn, nor did he think it meet
To lay so dangerous and dear a trust
On any soul remov'd but[8] on his own.

---

2. soothers—flatterers.   3. approve—test.
4. beard—face him in battle.   5. time—the times.
6. better worth—of greater consequence.
7. deputation—by deputy of.   8. remov'd but—other than.

Yet doth he give us bold advértisement
That with our small conjunction[9] we should on
To see how fortune is dispos'd to us;
For, as he writes, there is no quailing now,
Because the King is certainly possess'd [10]
Of all purposes. What say you to it?
    WORCESTER. Your father's sickness is a maim to us.
    HOTSPUR. A perilous gash, a very limb lopp'd off.
And yet, in faith, 't is not; his present want[11]
Seems more than we shall find it: were it good
To set the exact wealth[12] of all our states
All at one cast? to set so rich a main[13]
On the nice[14] hazard of one doubtful hour?
It were not good; for therein should we read
The very bottom and the soul of hope,
The very list,[15] the very utmost bound
Of all our fortunes.
    DOUGLAS.   Faith, and so we should;
Where now remains a sweet reversion,[16]
We may boldly spend upon the hope
Of what is to come in.
A comfort of retirement lives in this.
    HOTSPUR. A rendezvous, a home to fly unto,
If that the devil and mischance look big[17]
Upon the maidenhead [18] of our affairs.
    WORCESTER. But yet I would your father had been here.
The quality and hair[19] of our attempt
Brooks no division: it will be thought
By some that know not why he is away,
That wisdom, loyalty, and mere dislike
Of our proceedings kept the earl from hence;
And think how such an apprehension
May turn the tide of fearful faction
And breed a kind of question in our cause;

---

9. conjunction—army.   10. possess'd—informed.
11. want—absence.   12. set the exact wealth—wager all.
13. main—stake.   14. nice—precarious.   15. list—limit.
16. reversion—portion yet to come.   17. look big—frown.
18. maidenhead—onset.   19. hair—nature.

For well you know we of the off'ring[20] side
Must keep aloof from strict arbitrement,[21]
And stop all sight-holes, every loop from whence
The eye of reason may pry in upon us:
This absence of your father's draws a curtain,
That shows the ignorant a kind of fear
Before not dreamt of.

HOTSPUR. You strain too far.
I rather of his absence make this use:
It lends a lustre and more great opinion,[22]
A larger dare to our great enterprise,
Than if the earl were here; for men must think,
If we without his help can make a head
To push against a kingdom, with his help
We shall o'erturn it topsy-turvy down.
Yet all goes well, yet all our joints[23] are whole.

DOUGLAS. As heart can think: there is not such a word
Spoke of in Scotland as this term of fear.

Enter SIR RICHARD VERNON.

HOTSPUR. My cousin Vernon! welcome, by my soul.

VERNON. Pray God my news be worth a welcome, lord.
The Earl of Westmoreland, seven thousand strong,
Is marching hitherwards; with him Prince John.

HOTSPUR. No harm. What more?

VERNON. And further, I have learn'd,
The King himself in person is set forth,
Or hitherwards intended speedily,
With strong and mighty preparation.

HOTSPUR. He shall be welcome to. Where is his son,
The nimble-footed madcap Prince of Wales,
And his comrades, that daff'd [24] the world aside,
And bid it pass?

VERNON. All furnish'd, all in arms;
All plum'd like estridges[25] that with the wind
Bated,[26] like eagles having lately bath'd;

---

20. off'ring—attacking.   21. arbitrement—judgment.
22. opinion—repute.   23. joints—limbs.   24. daff'd—disregarded.
25. estridges—ostriches.   26. bated—beat their wings.

Glittering in golden coats, like images;
As full of spirit as the month of May,
And gorgeous as the sun at midsummer;
Wanton as youthful goats, wild as young bulls.
I saw young Harry, with his beaver[27] on,
His cuisses[28] on his thighs, gallantly arm'd,
Rise from the ground like feathered Mercury,[29]
And vaulted with such ease into his seat,
As if an angel dropp'd down from the clouds
To turn and wind [30] a fiery Pegasus[31]
And witch the world with noble horsemanship.

    HOTSPUR.   No more, no more! Worse than the sun in March,
This praise doth nourish agues. Let them come!
They come like sacrifices in their trim,
And to the fire-ey'd maid [32] of smoky war
All hot and bleeding will we offer them:
The mailed Mars[33] shall on his altar sit
Up to the ears in blood. I am on fire
To hear this rich reprisal is so nigh
And yet not ours. Come, let me taste[34] my horse,
Who is to bear me like a thunderbolt
Against the bosom of the Prince of Wales:
Harry to Harry shall, hot horse to horse,
Meet and ne'er part till one drop down a corse.
O that Glendower were come!

    VERNON.   There is more news.
I learn'd in Worcester, as I rode along,
He cannot draw his power this fourteen days.

    DOUGLAS.   That's the worst tidings that I hear of yet.

    WORCESTER.   Ay, by my faith, that bears a frosty sound.

    HOTSPUR.   What may the King's whole battle[35] reach unto?

    VERNON.   To thirty thousand.

    HOTSPUR.   Forty let it be!

---

27. beaver—helmet.   28. cuisses—thigh armor.
29. feathered Mercury—the gods' messenger, with winged sandals.
30. wind—turn, manage.   31. Pegasus—the winged horse.
32. fire-ey'd maid—Bellona, goddess of war.
33. mailed Mars—god of war in full armor.
34. taste—try.   35. battle—army.

My father and Glendower being both away,
The powers of us may serve so great a day.
Come, let us take a muster speedily.
Doomsday is near; die all, die merrily.
DOUGLAS. Talk not of dying; I am out[36] of fear
Of death or death's hand for this one-half year. *Exeunt.*

---

36. out—free.

[A C T I V • 2] *A public road near Coventry.*

Enter FALSTAFF *and* BARDOLPH.

FALSTAFF. Bardolph, get thee before to Coventry; fill me a
bottle of sack: our soldiers shall march through; we'll to Sutton
Cop-hill to-night.
BARDOLPH. Will you give me money, captain?
FALSTAFF. Lay out, lay out.[1]
BARDOLPH. This bottle makes an angel.[2]
FALSTAFF. An if it do, take it for thy labour; and if it make
twenty, take them all; I'll answer the coinage. Bid my lieutenant
Peto meet me at town's end.
BARDOLPH. I will, captain; farewell. *Exit.*
FALSTAFF. If I be not ashamed of my soldiers, I am a soused
gurnet.[3] I have misused the King's press[4] damnably. I have got,
in exchange of a hundred and fifty soldiers, three hundred and
odd pounds. I press me none but good householders, yeoman's
sons; inquire me out contracted bachelors, such as had been
asked twice on the banns; such a commodity[5] of warm slaves, as
had as lieve hear the devil as a drum; such as fear the report of a
caliver[6] worse than a struck fowl or a hurt wild-duck. I pressed
me none but such toasts-and-butter, with hearts in their bellies
no bigger than pins' heads; and they have bought out their services; and now my whole charge consists of ancients,[7] corporals,
lieutenants, gentlemen of companies, slaves as ragged as Lazarus

---

1. lay out—pay for it yourself.
2. makes an angel—makes ten shillings (you owe me).
3. soused gurnet—a small pickled fish.
4. press—conscription, draft.   5. commodity—supply.
6. caliver—musket.   7. ancients, etc.,—discharged soldiers.

in the painted cloth,[8] where the glutton's dogs licked his sores; and such as, indeed, were never soldiers, but discarded unjust serving-men, younger sons to younger brothers, revolted tapsters and ostlers trade-fallen,[9] the cankers of a calm world and a long peace, ten times more dishonourable ragged than an old feazed ancient: [10] and such have I, to fill up the rooms of them as have bought out their services, that you would think that I had a hundred and fifty tattered prodigals[11] lately come from swine-keeping, from eating draff [12] and husks. A mad fellow met me on the way and told me I had unloaded all the gibbets and pressed the dead bodies. No eye hath seen such scarecrows. I'll not march through Coventry with them, that's flat: nay, and the villains march wide betwixt the legs, as if they had gyves[13] on; for indeed I had the most of them out of prison. There's not a shirt and a half in all my company; and the half shirt is two napkins tacked together and thrown over the shoulders like an herald's coat without sleeves; and the shirt, to say the truth, stolen from my host at Saint Alban's, or the red-nose inn-keeper of Daventry. But that's all one; they'll find linen enough on every hedge.[14]

Enter the PRINCE *and the* LORD OF WESTMORELAND.

PRINCE.   How now, blown[15] Jack! how now, quilt!

FALSTAFF.   What, Hal! how now, mad wag! what a devil dost thou in Warwickshire? My good Lord of Westmoreland, I cry you mercy! I thought your honour had already been at Shrewsbury.

WESTMORELAND.   Faith, Sir John, 't is more than time that I were there, and you too; but my powers are there already. The King, I can tell you, looks for us all: we must away[16] all night.

FALSTAFF.   Tut, never fear me: I am as vigilant as a cat to steal cream.

PRINCE.   I think, to steal cream indeed, for thy theft hath

---

8. painted cloth—a cheap substitute for tapestry.
9. trade-fallen—out of work.   10. feazed ancient—patched flag.
11. prodigals—as in the parable of the Prodigal Son in Luke 15:11*ff*.
12. draff—garbage.   13. gyves—fetters on the legs.
14. on every hedge—where it had been placed to dry.
15. blown—puffed up.   16. away—march on the way.

already made thee butter. But tell me Jack, whose fellows are these that come after?

FALSTAFF.   Mine, Hal, mine.

PRINCE.   I did never see such pitiful rascals.

FALSTAFF.   Tut, tut; good enough to toss;[17] food for powder, food for powder; they'll fill a pit as well as better: tush, man, mortal men, mortal men.

WESTMORELAND.   Ay, but, Sir John, methinks they are exceeding poor and bare, too beggarly.

FALSTAFF.   Faith, for their poverty, I know not where they had that; and for their bareness, I am sure they never learned that of me.

PRINCE.   No, I'll be sworn; unless you call three fingers[18] on the ribs bare. But, sirrah, make haste. Percy is already in the field.

FALSTAFF.   What, is the King encamp'd?

WESTMORELAND.   He is, Sir John: I fear we shall stay[19] too long.

FALSTAFF.   Well,
To the latter end of a fray and the beginning of a feast
Fits a dull fighter and a keen guest.   *Exeunt.*

17. toss—i.e., on pikes or spears.
18. three fingers—a roll of fat.   19. stay—delay.

[ACT IV • 3] *The rebel camp near Shrewsbury.*

Enter HOTSPUR, WORCESTER, DOUGLAS, *and* VERNON.

HOTSPUR.   We'll fight with him to-night.

WORCESTER.   It may not be.

DOUGLAS.   You give him then advantage.

VERNON.   Not a whit.

HOTSPUR.   Why say you so? Looks he not for supply? [1]

VERNON.   So do we.

HOTSPUR.   His is certain, ours is doubtful.

WORCESTER.   Good cousin, be advis'd; stir not to-night.

VERNON.   Do not, my lord.

DOUGLAS.   You do not counsel well.
You speak it out of fear and cold heart.

1. supply—reinforcements.

VERNON.   Do me no slander, Douglas. By my life,
And I dare well maintain it with my life,
If well-respected [2] honour bid me on,
I hold as little counsel with weak fear
As you, my lord, or any Scot that this day lives.
Let it be seen to-morrow in the battle
Which of us fears.

DOUGLAS.   Yea, or to-night.

VERNON.   Content.

HOTSPUR.   To-night, say I.

VERNON.   Come, come, it may not be. I wonder much,
Being men of such great leading[3] as you are,
That you foresee not what impediments
Drag back our expedition: certain horse[4]
Of my cousin Vernon's are not yet come up;
Your uncle Worcester's horse came but to-day;
And now their pride and mettle is asleep,
Their courage with hard labour tame and dull,
That not a horse is half the half of himself.

HOTSPUR.   So are the horses of the enemy
In general, journey-bated [5] and brought low.
The better part of ours are full of rest.

WORCESTER.   The number of the King exceedeth ours.
For God's sake, cousin, stay till all come in.

[*The trumpet sounds a parley.*]

Enter SIR WALTER BLUNT.

BLUNT.   I come with gracious offers from the King,
If you vouchsafe me hearing and respect.

HOTSPUR.   Welcome, Sir Walter Blunt; and would to God
You were of our determination! [6]
Some of us love you well; and even those some
Envy your great deservings and good name,
Because you are not of our quality,[7]
But stand against us like an enemy.

BLUNT.   And God defend but still I should stand so,

2. well-respected—not foolhardy.
3. great leading—experience as leaders.
4. horse—cavalry.   5. journey-bated—travel-weary.
6. determination—party.   7. quality—party.

So long as out of limit and true rule
You stand against anointed majesty.
But to my charge. The King hath sent to know
The nature of your griefs, and whereupon
You conjure from the breast of civil peace
Such bold hostility, teaching his duteous land
Audacious cruelty. If that the King
Have any way your good deserts forgot,
Which he confesseth to be manifold,
He bids you name your griefs; and with all speed
You shall have your desires with interest
And pardon absolute for yourself and these
Herein misled by your suggestion.

   HOTSPUR.   The King is kind; and well we know the King
Knows at what time to promise, when to pay.
My father and my uncle and myself
Did give him that same royalty he wears;
And when he was not six and twenty strong,
Sick in the world's regard, wretched and low,
A poor unminded outlaw sneaking home,
My father gave him welcome to the shore;
And when he heard him swear and vow to God
He came but to be Duke of Lancaster,
To sue his livery[8] and beg his peace,
With tears of innocence and terms of zeal,
My father, in kind heart and pity mov'd,
Swore him assistance and perform'd it too.
Now when the lords and barons of the realm
Perceiv'd Northumberland did lean to him,
The more and less[9] came in with cap and knee;
Met him in boroughs, cities, villages,
Attended him on bridges, stood in lanes,
Laid gifts before him, proffer'd him their oaths,
Gave him their heirs as pages, followed him
Even at the heels in golden multitudes.
He presently, as greatness knows itself,
Steps me a little higher than his vow

8. sue his livery—claim his inheritance.
9. more and less—greater and lesser nobles.

Made to my father, while his blood was poor,
Upon the naked shore at Ravenspurgh;
And now, forsooth, takes on him to reform
Some certain edicts and some strait[10] decrees
That lie too heavy on the commonwealth,
Cries out upon abuses, seems to weep
Over his country's wrongs; and by this face,
This seeming brow of justice, did he win
The hearts of all that he did angle for;
Proceeded further; cut me off the heads
Of all the favourites that the absent king
In deputation left behind him here,
When he was personal [11] in the Irish war.
    BLUNT.   Tut, I came not to hear this.
    HOTSPUR.   Then to the point.
In short time after, he depos'd the King;
Soon after that, depriv'd him of his life;
And in the neck of that, task'd [12] the whole state.
To make that worse, suffer'd his kinsman March,
(Who is, if every owner were well plac'd,[13]
Indeed his king) to be engag'd in Wales,
There without ransom to lie forfeited;
Disgrac'd me in my happy victories,
Sought to entrap me by intelligence;[14]
Rated mine uncle from the council-board;
In rage dismiss'd my father from the court;
Broke oath on oath, committed wrong on wrong,
And in conclusion drove us to seek out
This head of safety; and withal to pry
Into his title, the which we find
Too indirect[15] for long continuance.
    BLUNT.   Shall I return this answer to the King?
    HOTSPUR.   Not so, Sir Walter; we'll withdraw a while.
Go to the King; and let there be impawn'd [16]
Some surety for a safe return again,

---

10. strait—strict.   11. personal—in personal command.
12. task'd—levied taxes on.
13. were well plac'd—had his rightful place.   14. intelligence—spies.
15. indirect—irregular.   16. impawn'd—kept as a hostage.

And in the morning early shall mine uncle
Bring him our purposes: and so farewell.
    BLUNT.   I would you would accept of grace[17] and love.
    HOTSPUR.   And may be so we shall.
    BLUNT.   Pray God you do.
                                          Exeunt.

17. grace—pardon.

[ACT IV • 4] *York. The Archbishop's palace.*

Enter the ARCHBISHOP OF YORK *and* SIR[1] MICHAEL.

    ARCHBISHOP.   Hie, good Sir Michael; bear this sealed brief[2]
With winged haste to the Lord Marshal,
This to my cousin Scroop, and all the rest
To whom they are directed. If you knew
How much they do import, you would make haste.
    SIR MICHAEL.   My good lord,
I guess their tenour.
    ARCHBISHOP.   Like enough you do.
To-morrow, good Sir Michael, is a day
Wherein the fortune of ten thousand men
Must bide the touch; for, sir, at Shrewsbury,
As I am truly given to understand,
The King with mighty and quick-raised power
Meets with Lord Harry; and, I fear, Sir Michael,
What with the sickness of Northumberland,
Whose power was in the first proportion,[3]
And what with Owen Glendower's absence thence,
Who with them was a rated sinew[4] too
And comes not in, over-rul'd by prophecies,
I fear the power of Percy is too weak
To wage an instant trial with the King.
    SIR MICHAEL.   Why, my good lord, you need not fear;
There is Douglas and Lord Mortimer.
    ARCHBISHOP.   No, Mortimer is not there.

1. Sir—i.e., Priest.   2. brief—letter.
3. in the first proportion—larger than the other troops.
4. rated sinew—heavily counted on.

SIR MICHAEL.   But there is Murdoch, Vernon, Lord Harry
     Percy,
And there is my Lord of Worcester, and a head
Of gallant warriors, noble gentlemen.
     ARCHBISHOP.   And so there is; but yet the King hath drawn
The special head of all the land together:
The Prince of Wales, Lord John of Lancaster,
The noble Westmoreland, and warlike Blunt;
And many moe[5] corrivals and dear men
Of estimation and command in arms.
     SIR MICHAEL.   Doubt not, my lord, they shall be well oppos'd.
     ARCHBISHOP.   I hope no less, yet needful 't is to fear;
And, to prevent[6] the worst, Sir Michael, speed;
For if Lord Percy thrive not, ere the King
Dismiss his power he means to visit[7] us,
For he hath heard of our confederacy,
And 't is but wisdom to make strong against him:
Therefore make haste. I must go write again
To other friends; and so farewell, Sir Michael.   *Exeunt.*

---

5. moe—more.   6. prevent—forestall.   7. visit—attack.

[ACT V · 1] *The King's camp near Shrewsbury.*

Enter the KING, PRINCE OF WALES, LORD JOHN OF LANCASTER,
     SIR WALTER BLUNT, *and* FALSTAFF.

     KING.   How bloodily the sun begins to peer
Above yon busky[1] hill! The day looks pale
At his distemperature.
     PRINCE.   The southern wind
Doth play the trumpet to his purposes,
And by his hollow whistling in the leaves
Foretells a tempest and a blust'ring day.
     KING.   Then with the losers let it sympathize,
For nothing can seem foul to those that win.
                         [*The trumpet sounds.*]
Enter WORCESTER *and* VERNON.

How now, my Lord of Worcester! 't is not well

---

1. busky—wooded.

That you and I should meet upon such terms
As now we meet. You have deceiv'd our trust,
And made us doff our easy robes of peace,
To crush our old limbs in ungentle steel:
This is not well, my lord, this is not well.
What say you to it? Will you again unknit
This churlish knot of all-abhorred war?
And move in that obedient orb again
Where you did give a fair and natural light,
And be no more an exhal'd meteor,
A prodigy[2] of fear and a portent
Of broached [3] mischief to the unborn times?
    WORCESTER.   Hear me, my liege.
For mine own part, I could be well content
To entertain the lag-end of my life
With quiet hours; for I do protest,
I have not sought the day of this dislike.[4]
    KING.   You have not sought it! How comes it, then?
    FALSTAFF.   Rebellion lay in his way, and he found it.
    PRINCE.   Peace, chewet,[5] peace!
    WORCESTER.   It pleas'd your Majesty to turn your looks
Of favour from myself and all our house;
And yet I must remember[6] you, my lord,
We were the first and dearest of your friends.
For you my staff of office did I break
In Richard's time; and posted day and night
To meet you on the way, and kiss your hand,
When yet you were in place and in account
Nothing so strong and fortunate as I.
It was myself, my brother, and his son,
That brought you home and boldly did outdare
The dangers of the time. You swore to us,
And you did swear that oath at Doncaster,
That you did nothing purpose 'gainst the state;
Nor claim no further than your new-fall'n[7] right,
The seat of Gaunt, dukedom of Lancaster.

---

2. prodigy—omen.   3. broached—unleashed.
4. dislike—enmity.   5. chewet—jackdaw.
6. remember—remind.   7. new-fall'n—newly inherited.

To this we swore our aid. But in short space
It rain'd down fortune show'ring on your head;
And such a flood of greatness fell on you,
What with our help, what with the absent King,
What with the injuries[8] of a wanton time,[9]
The seeming sufferances[10] that you had borne,
And the contrarious winds that held the King
So long in his unlucky Irish wars
That all in England did repute him dead;
And from this swarm of fair advantages
You took occasion to be quickly woo'd
To gripe the general sway[11] into your hand;
Forgot your oath to us at Doncaster;
And being fed by us you us'd us so
As that ungentle gull, the cuckoo's bird,[12]
Useth the sparrow;.did oppress our nest;
Grew by our feeding to so great a bulk
That even our love durst not come near your sight
For fear of swallowing; [13] but with nimble wing
We were enforc'd, for safety sake, to fly
Out of your sight and raise this present head;
Whereby we stand opposed by such means
As you yourself have forg'd against yourself
By unkind usage, dangerous countenance,
And violation of all faith and troth
Sworn to us in your younger enterprise.
    KING.   These things indeed you have articulate,[14]
Proclaim'd at market-crosses,[15] read in churches,
To face[16] the garment of rebellion
With some fine colour that may please the eye
Of fickle changelings and poor discontents,
Which gape and rub the elbow at the news

---

8. injuries—abuses.   9. wanton time—time of misgovernment.
10. sufferances—injuries.
11. general sway—control of the kingdom.
12. cuckoo's bird—left by the cuckoo to be raised by the sparrow in its nest.
13. swallowing—being swallowed.
14. articulate—drawn up in articles.
15. market crosses—village squares.   16. To face—to cover.

Of hurly-burly innovation.[17]
And never yet did insurrection want
Such water-colours to impaint his cause;
Nor moody beggars, starving for a time
Of pell-mell havoc and confusion.
    PRINCE.   In both your armies there is many a soul
Shall pay full dearly for this encounter,
If once they join in trial. Tell your nephew,
The Prince of Wales doth join with all the world
In praise of Henry Percy: by my hopes,
This present enterprise set off his head,[18]
I do not think a braver gentleman,
More active-valiant or more valiant-young,
More daring or more bold, is now alive
To grace this latter age with noble deeds.
For my part, I may speak it to my shame,
I have a truant been to chivalry;
And so I hear he doth account me too;
Yet this before my father's majesty:
I am content that he shall take the odds[19]
Of his great name and estimation,
And will, to save the blood on either side,
Try fortune with him in a single fight.
    KING.   And, Prince of Wales, so dare we venture thee,
Albeit considerations infinite
Do make against it. No, good Worcester, no,
We love our people well; even those we love
That are misled upon your cousin's part; [20]
And, will they take the offer of our grace,
Both he and they and you, yea, every man
Shall be my friend again and I'll be his:
So tell your cousin, and bring me word
What he will do. But if he will not yield,
Rebuke and dread correction wait on us[21]
And they shall do their office. So, be gone;
We will not now be troubled with reply.

---

17. innovation—rebellion.   18. set off his head—being excepted.
19. the odds—the advantage.   20. part—side.
21. wait on us—are our servants.

We offer fair; take it advisedly.

                       Exeunt WORCESTER *and* VERNON.

PRINCE.   It will not be accepted, on my life.
The Douglas and the Hotspur both together
Are confident against the world in arms.

  KING.   Hence, therefore, every leader to his charge,
For, on their answer, will we set on them;
And God befriend us, as our cause is just!

       Exeunt all but the PRINCE OF WALES *and* FALSTAFF.

FALSTAFF.   Hal, if thou see me down in the battle and be-
stride me, so; 't is a point of friendship.

PRINCE.   Nothing but a Colossus[22] can do thee that friendship. Say thy prayers, and farewell.

FALSTAFF.   I would 't were bed-time, Hal, and all well.

PRINCE.   Why, thou owest God a death.   *Exit.*

FALSTAFF.   'T is not due yet; I would be loath to pay Him
before his day. What need I be so forward with him that calls
not on me? Well, 't is no matter; honour pricks[23] me on. Yea,
but how if honour prick me off [24] when I come on? How then?
Can honour set to a leg? No. Or an arm? No. Or take away the
grief of a wound? No. Honour hath no skill in surgery, then?
No. What is honour? A word. What is that word honour? Air.
A trim reckoning! Who hath it? He that died o' Wednesday.
Doth he feel it? No. Doth he hear it? No. 'T is insensible, then?
Yea, to the dead. But will it not live with the living? No. Why?
Detraction will not suffer it. Therefore I'll none of it. Honour is
a mere scutcheon:[25] and so ends my catechism.   *Exit.*

---

22. Colossus—a statue bestriding the entrance to the harbor of Rhodes.
23. pricks—spurs.   24. prick me off—list me as a casualty.
25. scutcheon—coat of arms set up on a tomb.

[ACT V • 2] *The rebel camp.*

Enter WORCESTER *and* VERNON.

WORCESTER.   O, no, my nephew must not know, Sir Richard,
The liberal and kind offer of the King.

VERNON.   'Twere best he did.

WORCESTER.   Then are we all undone.
It is not possible, it cannot be,

The King should keep his word in loving us.
He will suspect us still, and find a time
To punish this offence in other faults:
Suspicion all our lives shall be stuck full of eyes;
For treason is but trusted like the fox,
Who, ne'er so tame, so cherish'd and lock'd up,
Will have a wild trick[1] of his ancestors.
Look how we can, or sad[2] or merrily,
Interpretation will misquote our looks,   ·
And we shall feed like oxen at a stall,
The better cherish'd, still the nearer death.
My nephew's trespass may be well forgot;
It hath the excuse of youth and heat of blood,
And an adopted name of privilege,[3]
A hare-brain'd Hotspur, govern'd by a spleen.
All his offences live upon my head
And on his father's. We did train[4] him on,
And, his corruption being ta'en[5] from us,
We, as the spring of all, shall pay for all.
Therefore, good cousin, let not Harry know,
In any case, the offer of the King.
  VERNON.   Deliver what you will: I'll say 't is so.
Here comes your cousin.

Enter HOTSPUR *and* DOUGLAS.

  HOTSPUR.   My uncle is return'd;
Deliver up[6] my Lord of Westmoreland.
Uncle, what news?
  WORCESTER.   The King will bid you battle presently.
  DOUGLAS.   Defy him by the Lord of Westmoreland.
  HOTSPUR.   Lord Douglas, go you and tell him so.
  DOUGLAS.   Marry, and shall, and very willingly.   *Exit.*
  WORCESTER.   There is no seeming mercy in the King.
  HOTSPUR.   Did you beg any? God forbid!

---

1. trick—habit.   2. sad—serious.
3. adopted name of privilege—he will be excused for acting in accord
with his nickname, Hotspur.
4. train—lead.   5. ta'en—derived.
6. Deliver up—release (the hostage).

WORCESTER. I told him gently of our grievances,
Of his oath-breaking; which he mended [7] thus,
By now forswearing that he is forsworn.
He calls us rebels, traitors; and will scourge
With haughty arms this hateful name in us.

Re-enter DOUGLAS.

DOUGLAS. Arm, gentlemen; to arms! for I have thrown
A brave defiance in King Henry's teeth,
And Westmoreland, that was engag'd,[8] did bear it;
Which cannot choose but bring him quickly on.
WORCESTER. The Prince of Wales stepp'd forth before the
King,
And, nephew, challeng'd you to single fight.
HOTSPUR. O, would the quarrel lay upon our heads,
And that no man might draw short breath to-day
But I and Harry Monmouth! Tell me, tell me,
How show'd his tasking? Seem'd it in contempt?
VERNON. No, by my soul; I never in my life
Did hear a challenge urg'd more modestly,
Unless a brother should a brother dare
To gentle exercise and proof of arms.
He gave you all the duties of [9] a man,
Trimm'd up your praises with a princely tongue,
Spoke your deservings like a chronicle,
Making you ever better than his praise
By still dispraising praise valued [10] with you;
And, which became him like a prince indeed,
He made a blushing cital [11] of himself,
And chid his truant youth with such a grace
As if he master'd there a double spirit
Of teaching and of learning instantly.
There did he pause; but let me tell the world,
If he outlive the envy[12] of this day,
England did never owe[13] so sweet a hope,
So much misconstrued in his wantonness.

---

7. mended—evaded.   8. engag'd—held as hostage.
9. duties of—respect due to.   10. valued—compared.
11. cital—mention.   12. envy—malice.   13. owe—possess.

HOTSPUR.   Cousin, I think thou art enamoured
On his follies: never did I hear
Of any prince so wild a liberty.
But be he as he will, yet once ere night
I will embrace him with a soldier's arm,
That he shall shrink under my courtesy.
Arm, arm with speed! and, fellows,[14] soldiers, friends,
Better consider what you have to do
Than I, that have not well the gift of tongue,
Can lift your blood up with persuasion.

Enter a MESSENGER.

MESSENGER.   My lord, here are letters for you.
HOTSPUR.   I cannot read them now.
O gentlemen, the time of life is short!
To spend that shortness basely were too long,
If life did ride upon a dial's point,[15]
Still ending at the arrival of an hour.
An if we live, we live to tread on kings;
If die, brave death, when princes die with us!
Now, for our consciences, the arms are fair,
When the intent[16] of bearing them is just.

Enter another MESSENGER.

SECOND MESSENGER.   My lord, prepare; the King comes on
     apace.
HOTSPUR.   I thank him that he cuts me from my tale,
For I profess not talking; only this—
Let each man do his best; and here draw I
A sword, whose temper I intend to stain
With the best blood that I can meet withal
In the adventure of this perilous day.
Now *Esperancé!* Percy! and set on.
Sound all the lofty instruments of war,
And by that music let us all embrace;
For, heaven to earth, some of us never shall
A second time do such a courtesy. [*They embrace and exeunt.*]

---

14. fellows—comrades.
15. dial's point—hour hand (of a clock).   16. intent—cause.

[ACT V • 3] *Plain between the camps.*

The trumpets sound. The KING *enters with his army and passes over the stage. Noises of battle. Then enter* DOUGLAS *and* SIR WALTER BLUNT.

BLUNT.   What is thy name, that in the battle thus
Thou crossest me? What honour dost thou seek
Upon my head?

DOUGLAS.   Know then, my name is Douglas;
And I do haunt thee in the battle thus
Because some tell me that thou art a king.

BLUNT.   They tell thee true.

DOUGLAS.   The Lord of Stafford dear to-day hath bought
Thy likeness, for instead of thee, King Harry,
This sword hath ended him. So shall it thee,
Unless thou yield thee as my prisoner.

BLUNT.   I was not born a yielder, thou proud Scot;
And thou shalt find a king that will revenge
Lord Stafford's death.   [*They fight,* DOUGLAS *kills* BLUNT.]

Enter HOTSPUR.

HOTSPUR.   O Douglas, hadst thou fought at Holmedon thus,
I never had triumph'd upon a Scot.

DOUGLAS.   All's done, all's won; here breathless lies the King.

HOTSPUR.   Where?

DOUGLAS.   Here.

HOTSPUR.   This, Douglas? No. I know this face full well.
A gallant knight he was, his name was Blunt;
Semblably furnish'd [1] like the King himself.

DOUGLAS.   A fool go with thy soul, whither it goes!
A borrowed title hast thou bought too dear:
Why didst thou tell me that thou wert a king?

HOTSPUR.   The King hath many marching in his coats.[2]

DOUGLAS.   Now, by my sword, I will kill all his coats;
I'll murder all his wardrobe, piece by piece,
Until I meet the King.

---

1. Semblably furnish'd—attired.
2. coats—wearing the royal coat of arms.

HOTSPUR.   Up, and away!
Our soldiers stand full fairly for the day.   *Exeunt.*

Alarum. Enter FALSTAFF, *alone.*

FALSTAFF.   Though I could scape shot-free[3] at London, I
fear the shot here; here's no scoring but upon the pate. Soft! who
are you? Sir Walter Blunt: there's honour for you! Here's no
vanity! I am as hot as molten lead, and as heavy too: God keep
lead out of me! I need no more weight than mine own bowels. I
have led my ragamuffins where they are peppered. There's not
three of my hundred and fifty left alive; and they are for the
town's end,[4] to beg during life. But who comes here?

Enter the PRINCE.

PRINCE.   What, stand'st thou idle here? Lend me thy sword.
Many a nobleman lies stark and stiff
Under the hoofs of vaunting enemies,
Whose deaths are yet unreveng'd. I prithee, lend me thy sword.
FALSTAFF.   O Hal, I prithee, give me leave to breathe a
while. Turk Gregory[5] never did such deeds in arms as I have
done this day. I have paid Percy, I have made him sure.
PRINCE.   He is, indeed; and living to kill thee. I prithee, lend
me thy sword.
FALSTAFF.   Nay, before God, Hal, if Percy be alive, thou
gets not my sword; but take my pistol, if thou wilt.
PRINCE.   Give it me. What, is it in the case?
FALSTAFF.   Ay, Hal; 't is hot, 't is hot: there's that will sack a
city.
[*The* PRINCE *draws it out, and finds it to be a bottle of sack.*]
PRINCE.   What, is it a time to jest and dally now?
                          [*He throws the bottle at him. Exit.*]
FALSTAFF.   Well, if Percy be alive, I'll pierce[6] him. If he do
come in my way, so; if he do not, if I come in his willingly, let
him make a carbonado[7] of me. I like not such grinning honour
as Sir Walter hath: give me life, which if I can save, so; if not,
honour comes unlooked for, and there's an end.   *Exit.*

---

3. shot-free—without paying (the bill).
4. town's end—city gates, where beggars congregated.
5. Turk Gregory—Pope Gregory VII, whose name was a byword for
belligerence.   6. pierce—pronounced *perse*.   7. carbonado—steak.

[ACT V • 4] *Another part of the field.*

Alarum. Excursions.[1] *Enter the* KING, *the* PRINCE, LORD JOHN
OF LANCASTER, *and* EARL OF WESTMORELAND.

KING.   I prithee,
Harry, withdraw thyself; thou bleedest too much.
Lord John of Lancaster, go you with him.

   LANCASTER.   Not I, my lord, unless I did bleed too.

   PRINCE.   I beseech your Majesty, make up,[2]
Lest your retirement do amaze[3] your friends.

   KING.   I will do so.
My Lord of Westmoreland, lead him to his tent.

   WESTMORELAND.   Come, my lord, I'll lead you to your tent.

   PRINCE.   Lead me, my lord? I do not need your help:
And God forbid a shallow scratch should drive
The Prince of Wales from such a field as this,
Where stain'd nobility lies trodden on,
And rebels' arms triúmph in massacres!

   LANCASTER.   We breathe[4] too long. Come, cousin Westmore-
     land,
Our duty this way lies; for God's sake, come.

             Exeunt PRINCE JOHN *and* WESTMORELAND.

   PRINCE.   By God, thou hast deceiv'd me, Lancaster;
I did not think thee lord of such a spirit.
Before, I lov'd thee as a brother, John;
But now, I do respect thee as my soul.

   KING.   I saw him hold Lord Percy at the point
With lustier maintenance[5] than I did look for
Of such an ungrown warrior.

   PRINCE.   O, this boy
Lends mettle to us all!   *Exit.*

Enter DOUGLAS.

   DOUGLAS.   Another king! they grow like Hydra's[6] heads.
I am the Douglas, fatal to all those

---

1. Excursions—actors run on and off stage to suggest the confusion of
a battle.   2. make up—attack.   3. amaze—dishearten.
4. breathe—rest.   5. maintenance—vigorous action.
6. Hydra—a fabled monster who grew two heads whenever one was
cut off.

That wear those colours on them. What art thou,
That counterfeit'st the person of a king?
   KING.   The King himself; who, Douglas, grieves at heart
So many of his shadows thou hast met
And not the very King. I have two boys
Seek Percy and thyself about the field;
But, seeing thou fall'st on me so luckily,
I will assay[7] thee; so, defend thyself.
   DOUGLAS.   I fear thou art another counterfeit;
And yet, in faith, thou bear'st thee like a king.
But mine I am sure thou art, whoe'er thou be,
And thus I win thee.

[*They fight; the* KING *being in danger, re-enter* PRINCE OF
WALES.]

   PRINCE.   Hold up thy head, vile Scot, or thou art like
Never to hold it up again! The spirits
Of valiant Shirley, Stafford, Blunt,[8] are in my arms.
It is the Prince of Wales that threatens thee,
Who never promiseth but he means to pay.
                [*They fight:* DOUGLAS *flies.*]
Cheerly, my lord, how fares your Grace?
Sir Nicholas Gawsey hath for succour sent,
And so hath Clifton: I'll to Clifton straight.
   KING.   Stay, and breathe a while.
Thou hast redeem'd thy lost opinion,[9]
And show'd thou mak'st some tender of [10] my life,
In this fair rescue thou hast brought to me.
   PRINCE.   O God! they did me too much injury
That ever said I hearken'd for your death.
If it were so, I might have let alone
The insulting hand of Douglas over you,
Which would have been as speedy in your end
As all the poisonous potions in the world,
And sav'd the treacherous labour of your son.

---

7. assay—make trial of.
8. Shirley, etc.—i.e., King's men killed in the battle.
9. opinion—reputation.
10. mak'st some tender of—have some regard for.

KING.   Make up[11] to Clifton: I'll to Sir Nicholas Gawsey.

Exit.

Enter HOTSPUR.

HOTSPUR.   If I mistake not, thou art Harry Monmouth.
PRINCE.   Thou speak'st as if I would deny my name.
HOTSPUR.   My name is Harry Percy.
PRINCE.   Why, then I see
A very valiant rebel of the name.
I am the Prince of Wales; and think not, Percy,
To share with me in glory any more:
Two stars[12] keep not their motion in one sphere;
Nor can one England brook a double reign
Of Harry Percy and the Prince of Wales.
HOTSPUR.   Nor shall it, Harry; for the hour is come
To end the one of us; and would to God
Thy name in arms were now as great as mine!
PRINCE.   I'll make a greater ere I part from thee;
And all the budding honours on thy crest
I'll crop, to make a garland for my head.
HOTSPUR.   I can no longer brook thy vanities.

[*They fight.*]

Enter FALSTAFF.

FALSTAFF.   Well said, Hal! to it, Hal! Nay, you shall find
no boy's play here, I can tell you.

Re-enter DOUGLAS; *he fights with* FALSTAFF, *who falls down as if
he were dead and exit* DOUGLAS. *The* PRINCE *kills* PERCY.

HOTSPUR.   O, Harry, thou hast robb'd me of my youth!
I better brook the loss of brittle life
Than those proud titles thou hast won of me:
They wound my thoughts worse than thy sword my flesh:
But thought's the slave of life, and life time's fool; [13]
And time, that takes survey of all the world,
Must have a stop. O, I could prophesy,
But that the earthy and cold hand of death

---

11. Make up—go to the aid of.   12. stars—planets.
13. life time's fool—life is subject to time.

Lies on my tongue: no, Percy, thou art dust,
And food for—   [*Dies.*]
   PRINCE. For worms, brave Percy: fare thee well, great
     heart!
Ill-weav'd ambition, how much art thou shrunk!
When that this body did contain a spirit,
A kingdom for it was too small a bound; [14]
But now two paces of the vilest earth
Is room enough: this earth that bears thee dead
Bears not alive so stout a gentleman.
If thou wert sensible [15] of courtesy,
I should not make so dear a show of zeal;
But let my favours [16] hide thy mangled face;
And, even in thy behalf, I'll thank myself
For doing these fair rites of tenderness.
Adieu, and take thy praise with thee to heaven!
Thy ignomy [17] sleep with thee in the grave,
But not remember'd in thy epitaph!
           [*He spies* FALSTAFF *on the ground.*]
What, old acquaintance! could not all this flesh
Keep in a little life? Poor Jack, farewell!
I could have better spar'd a better man:
O, I should have a heavy miss of thee,
If I were much in love with vanity! [18]
Death hath not struck so fat a deer to-day,
Though many dearer, in this bloody fray.
Embowell'd [19] will I see thee by and by;
Till then in blood by noble Percy lie.   *Exit.*
   FALSTAFF. [*Rising up.*] Embowelled! if thou embowel me
to-day, I'll give you leave to powder [20] me and eat me too to-
morrow. 'Sblood, 't was time to counterfeit, or that hot terma-
gant [21] Scot had paid me scot and lot [22] too. Counterfeit? I lie,
I am no counterfeit: to die is to be a counterfeit, for he is but
the counterfeit of a man who hath not the life of a man; but to

---

14. bound—limit.   15. sensible—able to feel.   16. favours—scarf.
17. ignomy—ignominy.   18. vanity—frivolity.
19. Embowell'd—disembowelled (for embalming).
20. powder—pickle.   21. termagant—raging.
22. scot and lot—in full.

counterfeit dying, when a man thereby liveth, is to be no counterfeit, but the true and perfect image of life indeed. The better part[23] of valour is discretion; in the which better part I have saved my life. 'Zounds, I am afraid of this gunpowder Percy, though he be dead: how, if he should counterfeit too and rise? By my faith, I am afraid he would prove the better counterfeit. Therefore I'll make him sure; yea, and I'll swear I killed him. Why may not he rise as well as I? Nothing confutes[24] me but eyes, and nobody sees me. Therefore, sirrah, [*Stabbing him.*] with a new wound in your thigh, come you along with me.

[*Takes up* HOTSPUR *on his back.*]

Re-enter PRINCE *and* JOHN OF LANCASTER.

PRINCE.   Come, brother John; full bravely hast thou flesh'd
Thy maiden sword.[25]
LANCASTER.   But, soft! whom have we here?
Did you not tell me this fat man was dead?
PRINCE.   I did; I saw him dead,
Breathless and bleeding on the ground. Art thou alive?
Or is it fantasy that plays upon our eyesight?
I prithee, speak; we will not trust our eyes
Without our ears: thou art not what thou seem'st.
FALSTAFF.   No, that's certain; I am not a double[26] man; but if I be not Jack Falstaff, then am I a Jack. There is Percy [*Throwing the body down.*] If your father will do me any honour, so; if not, let him kill the next Percy himself. I look to be either earl or duke, I can assure you.
PRINCE.   Why, Percy I killed myself, and saw thee dead.
FALSTAFF.   Didst thou? Lord, Lord, how this world is given to lying! I grant you I was down and out of breath, and so was he; but we rose both at an instant and fought a long hour by Shrewsbury clock. If I may be believed, so; if not, let them that should reward valour bear the sin upon their own heads. I'll take it upon my death, I gave him this wound in the thigh: if the man were alive and would deny it, 'zounds, I would make him eat a piece of my sword.

---

23. part—quality.   24. confutes—could refute.
25. maiden sword—i.e., in your first battle.
26. double—man with two bodies (Falstaff is carrying Hotspur).

LANCASTER.   This is the strangest tale that ever I heard.
PRINCE.   This is the strangest fellow, brother John.
Come, bring your luggage nobly on your back.
For my part, if a lie may do thee grace,
I'll gild it with the happiest terms I have.

> [*A retreat is sounded.*]

The trumpet sounds retreat; [27] the day is ours.
Come, brother, let us to the highest of the field,
To see what friends are living, who are dead.

> *Exeunt* PRINCE *and* LANCASTER.

FALSTAFF.   I'll follow, as they say, for reward. He that
rewards me, God reward him! If I do grow great, I'll grow less;
for I'll purge, and leave sack, and live cleanly as a nobleman
should do.   *Exit.*

---

27. sounds retreat—gives order to cease pursuing the enemy.

[ACT V • 5] *Another part of the field.*

The trumpets sound. Enter the KING, PRINCE OF WALES, LORD
JOHN OF LANCASTER, EARL OF WESTMORELAND, *with* WOR-
CESTER *and* VERNON *prisoners.*

KING.   Thus ever did rebellion find rebuke.
Ill-spirited [1] Worcester! did not we send grace,
Pardon, and terms of love to all of you?
And wouldst thou turn our offers contrary?
Misuse the tenour of thy kinsman's trust?
Three knights upon our party slain to-day,
A noble earl, and many a creature else
Had been alive this hour,
If like a Christian thou hadst truly borne
Betwixt our armies true intelligence.
WORCESTER.   What I have done my safety urg'd me to;
And I embrace this fortune patiently,
Since not to be avoided it falls on me.
KING.   Bear Worcester to the death and Vernon too.
Other offenders we will pause upon.[2]

> *Exeunt* WORCESTER *and* VERNON *guarded.*

How goes the field?

---

1. ill-spirited—evil-minded.   2. pause upon—consider later.

PRINCE.   The noble Scot, Lord Douglas, when he saw
The fortune of the day quite turn'd from him,
The noble Percy slain, and all his men
Upon the foot of fear, fled with the rest;
And falling from a hill, he was so bruis'd
That the pursuers took him. At my tent
The Douglas is; and I beseech your Grace
I may dispose of him.
  KING.   Will all my heart.
  PRINCE.   Then, brother John of Lancaster, to you
This honourable bounty shall belong.
Go to the Douglas, and deliver him
Up to his pleasure, ransomless and free:
His valours shown upon our crests to-day
Have taught us how to cherish such high deeds
Even in the bosom of our adversaries.
  LANCASTER.   I thank your Grace for this high courtesy,
Which I shall give away immediately.
  KING.   Then this remains, that we divide our power.
You, son John, and my cousin Westmoreland
Towards York shall bend you with your dearest speed.
To meet Northumberland and the prelate Scroop,
Who, as we hear, are busily in arms:
Myself and you, son Harry, will towards Wales,
To fight with Glendower and the Earl of March.
Rebellion in this land shall lose his sway,
Meeting the check[3] of such another day;
And since this business so fair is done,
Let us not leave till all our own be won. *Exeunt.*

---

3. meeting the check—if it meets with the hindrance and rebuke.

The Comedy of

MUCH ADO ABOUT NOTHING

CHARACTERS

DON PEDRO, *prince of Arragon.*
DON JOHN, *his bastard brother.*
CLAUDIO, *a young lord of Florence.*
BENEDICK, *a young lord of Padua.*
LEONATO, *governor of Messina.*
ANTONIO, *his brother.*
BALTHASAR, *attendant to* DON PEDRO.

CONRADE, }
BORACHIO, } *followers of* DON JOHN.
FRIAR FRANCIS.
DOGBERRY, *a constable.*
VERGES, *a headborough.*[1]
A SEXTON.
A BOY.
HERO, *daughter to* LEONATO.
BEATRICE, *niece to* LEONATO.
MARGARET, }
URSULA, } gentlewomen attending on HERO

Messengers, Watchmen, Attendants, etc.

SCENE: *Messina.*

[ACT I · 1] *Before Leonato's house.*

Enter LEONATO, HERO, *and* BEATRICE, *with a* MESSENGER.

LEONATO.   I learn in this letter that Don Pedro of Arragon comes this night to Messina.

MESSENGER.   He is very near by this: he was not three leagues off when I left him.

LEONATO.   How many gentlemen have you lost in this action?

MESSENGER.   But few of any sort,[2] and none of name.[3]

---

1. headborough—subordinate officer of the constabulary.
2. sort—rank.   3. name—important family.

• 93

LEONATO. A victory is twice itself when the achiever brings home full numbers. I find here that Don Pedro hath bestowed much honour on a young Florentine called Claudio.

MESSENGER. Much deserved on his part and equally remembered by Don Pedro: he hath borne himself beyond the promise of his age, doing, in the figure of a lamb, the feats of a lion: he hath indeed better bettered expectation than you must expect of me to tell you how.

LEONATO. He hath an uncle here in Messina will be very much glad of it.

MESSENGER. I have already delivered him letters, and there appears much joy in him; even so much that joy could not show itself modest enough without a badge of bitterness.

LEONATO. Did he break out into tears?

MESSENGER. In great measure.

LEONATO. A kind overflow of kindness: there are no faces truer than those that are so washed. How much better is it to weep at joy than to joy at weeping!

BEATRICE. I pray you, is Signior Mountanto[4] returned from the wars or no?

MESSENGER. I know none of that name, lady: there was none such in the army of any sort.

LEONATO. What is he that you ask for, niece?

HERO. My cousin means Signior Benedick of Padua.

MESSENGER. O, he's returned; and as pleasant[5] as ever he was.

BEATRICE. He set up his bills[6] here in Messina and challenged Cupid at the flight; [7] and my uncle's fool, reading the challenge, subscribed for[8] Cupid, and challenged him at the bird-bolt.[9] I pray you, how many hath he killed and eaten in these wars? But how many hath he killed? for indeed I promised to eat all of his killing.

LEONATO. Faith, niece, you tax[10] Signior Benedick too much; but he'll be meet[11] with you, I doubt it not.

---

4. Mountanto—"Upcut" (a fencing term).   5. pleasant—joking.
6. bills—posters.   7. at the flight—as a long-range archer.
8. subscribed for—accepted in place of.
9. bird-bolt—short-range shooting.
10. tax—ridicule.   11. be meet—get even.

MESSENGER.   He hath done good service, lady, in these wars.

BEATRICE.   You had musty victual, and he hath holp[12] to eat it: he is a very valiant trencherman; [13] he hath an excellent stomach.

MESSENGER.   And a good soldier too, lady.

BEATRICE.   And a good soldier to a lady: but what is he to a lord?

MESSENGER.   A lord to a lord, a man to a man; stuffed with all honourable virtues.

BEATRICE.   It is so, indeed; he is no less than a stuffed man: [14] but for the stuffing,—well, we are all mortal.

LEONATO.   You must not, sir, mistake my niece. There is a kind of merry war betwixt Signior Benedick and her: they never meet but there's a skirmish of wit between them.

BEATRICE.   Alas! he gets nothing by that. In our last conflict four of his five wits went halting[15] off, and now is the whole man governed with one; so that if he have wit enough to keep himself warm, let him bear it for a difference between himself and his horse; for it is all the wealth that he hath left, to be known a reasonable creature. Who is his companion now? He hath every month a new sworn brother.

MESSENGER.   Is 't possible?

BEATRICE.   Very easily possible: he wears his faith but as the fashion of his hat; it ever changes with the next block.[16]

MESSENGER.   I see, lady, the gentleman is not in your books.

BEATRICE.   No; an he were, I would burn my study. But, I pray you, who is his companion? Is there no young squarer[17] now that will make a voyage with him to the devil?

MESSENGER.   He is most in the company of the right noble Claudio.

BEATRICE.   O Lord, he will hang upon him like a disease: he is sooner caught than the pestilence, and the taker runs presently[18] mad. God help the noble Claudio! If he have caught the Benedick, it will cost him a thousand pounds ere 'a be cured.

MESSENGER.   I will hold friends with you, lady.

---

12. holp—helped.   13. trencherman—eater.
14. stuffed man—scarecrow.   15. halting—limping.
16. next block—new hat design.   17. squarer—quarreler.
18. presently—at once.

BEATRICE. Do, good friend.

LEONATO. You will never run mad, niece.

BEATRICE. No, not till a hot January.

MESSENGER. Don Pedro is approached.

Enter DON PEDRO, CLAUDIO, BENEDICK, BALTHASAR, *and* DON JOHN.

DON PEDRO. Good Signior Leonato, are you come to meet your trouble? The fashion of the world is to avoid cost, and you encounter it.

LEONATO. Never came trouble to my house in the likeness of your Grace, for trouble being gone, comfort should remain; but when you depart from me, sorrow abides and happiness takes his leave.

DON PEDRO. You embrace your charge[19] too willingly. I think this is your daughter.

LEONATO. Her mother hath many times told me so.

BENEDICK. Were you in doubt, sir, that you asked her?

LEONATO. Signior Benedick, no; for then were you a child.

DON PEDRO. You have it full, Benedick: we may guess by this what you are, being a man.[20] Truly, the lady fathers herself.[21] Be happy lady; for you are like an honourable father.

BENEDICK. If Signior Leonato be her father, she would not have his head on her shoulders for all Messina, as like him as she is.

BEATRICE. I wonder that you will still be talking, Signior Benedick: nobody marks you.

BENEDICK. What, my dear Lady Disdain! are you yet living?

BEATRICE. Is it possible Disdain should die while she hath such meet food to feed it as Signior Benedick? Courtesy itself must convert to disdain, if you come in her presence.

BENEDICK. Then is courtesy a turncoat.[22] But it is certain I am loved of all ladies, only you excepted; and I would I could find in my heart that I had not a hard heart, for truly I love none.

BEATRICE. A dear happiness[23] to women; they would else have been troubled with a pernicious suitor. I thank God and my

---

19. charge—burden.　　20. man—a dangerous man among ladies.
21. fathers herself—is like her father.
22. turncoat—renegade.　　23. dear happiness—great good luck.

cold blood, I am of your humour[24] for that. I had rather hear my dog bark at a crow than a man swear he loves me.

BENEDICK.   God keep your ladyship still in that mind! So some gentleman or other shall scape a predestinate[25] scratched face.

BEATRICE.   Scratching could not make it worse, an 't[26] were such a face as yours were.

BENEDICK.   Well, you are a rare parrot-teacher.

BEATRICE.   A bird of my tongue is better than a beast of yours.

BENEDICK.   I would my horse had the speed of your tongue, and so good a continuer. But keep your way, a[27] God's name; I have done.

BEATRICE.   You always end with a jade's trick; [28] I know you of old.

DON PEDRO.   That is the sum of all, Leonato. Signior Claudio and Signior Benedick, my dear friend Leonato hath invited you all. I tell him we shall stay here at the least a month; and he heartily prays some occasion may detain us longer. I dare swear he is no hypocrite, but prays from his heart.

LEONATO.   If you swear, my lord, you shall not be for-sworn.[29] [*To* DON JOHN.] Let me bid you welcome, my lord: being reconciled to the Prince, your brother, I owe you all duty.

DON JOHN.   I thank you: I am not of many words, but I thank you.

LEONATO.   Please it your Grace lead on?

DON PEDRO.   Your hand, Leonato; we will go together.
                    Exeunt all except BENEDICK *and* CLAUDIO.

CLAUDIO.   Benedick, didst thou note the daughter of Signior Leonato?

BENEDICK.   I noted [30] her not; but I looked on her.

CLAUDIO.   Is she not a modest young lady?

BENEDICK.   Do you question me, as an honest man should do, for my simple true judgement; or would you have me speak after my custom, as being a professed tyrant to their sex?

---

24. humour—mood, turn of mind.   25. predestinate—fated.
26. an't—if it.   27. a—in.   28. jade's trick—evasion.
29. be forsworn—break your oath.   30. noted—took notes on.

CLAUDIO. No; I pray thee speak in sober judgement.

BENEDICK. Why, i' faith, methinks she's too low for a high praise, too brown for a fair praise and too little for a great praise; only this commendation I can afford her, that were she other than she is, she were unhandsome; and being no other but as she is, I do not like her.

CLAUDIO. Thou thinkest I am in sport: I pray thee tell me truly how thou lik'st her.

BENEDICK. Would you buy her, that you inquire after her?

CLAUDIO. Can the world buy such a jewel?

BENEDICK. Yea, and a case to put it into. But speak you this with a sad brow,[31] or do you play the flouting Jack,[32] to tell us Cupid [33] is a good hare-finder and Vulcan[34] a rare carpenter? Come, in what key shall a man take[35] you, to go[36] in the song?

CLAUDIO. In mine eye she is the sweetest lady that ever I looked on.

BENEDICK. I can see yet without spectacles and I see no such matter: there's her cousin, an she were not possessed with a fury, exceeds her as much in beauty as the first of May doth the last of December. But I hope you have no intent to turn husband, have you?

CLAUDIO. I would scare trust myself, though I had sworn the contrary, if Hero would be my wife.

BENEDICK. Is't come to this? In faith, hath not the world one man but he will wear his cap with suspicion? [37] Shall I never see a bachelor of threescore again? Go to, i' faith, an thou wilt needs thrust thy neck into a yoke, wear the print[38] of it, and sigh away Sundays.[39] Look! Don Pedro is returned to seek you.

Re-enter DON PEDRO.

DON PEDRO. What secret hath held you here, that you followed not to Leonato's?

BENEDICK. I would your Grace would constrain me to tell.

---

31. sad brow—seriously.   32. flouting Jack—jesting knave.
33. Cupid—*blind* god of love.   34. Vulcan—the god's blacksmith.
35. take—understand.   36. go—harmonize.
37. suspicion—be suspected of being cuckold.
38. print——impression.
39. sigh away Sundays—spend week-ends at home.

DON PEDRO.   I charge thee on thy allegiance.

BENEDICK.   You hear, Count Claudio: I can be secret as a dumb man; I would have you think so; but, on my allegiance, mark you this, on my allegiance. He is in love. With who? Now that is your Grace's part. Mark how short his answer is:—With Hero, Leonato's short daughter.

CLAUDIO.   If this were so, so were it uttered.

BENEDICK.   Like the old tale, my lord: "It is not so, nor 't was not so, but, indeed, God forbid it should be so."

CLAUDIO.   If my passion change not shortly, God forbid it should be otherwise.

DON PEDRO.   Amen, if you love her; for the lady is very well worthy.

CLAUDIO.   You speak this to fetch me in, my lord.

DON PEDRO.   By my troth, I speak my thought.

CLAUDIO.   And, in faith, my lord, I spoke mine.

BENEDICK.   And, by my two faiths and troths, my lord, I spoke mine.

CLAUDIO.   That I love her, I feel.

DON PEDRO.   That she is worthy, I know.

BENEDICK.   That I neither feel how she should be loved nor know how she should be worthy, is the opinion that fire cannot melt out of me: I will die in at the stake.

DON PEDRO.   Thou wast ever an obstinate heretic in the despite[40] of beauty.

CLAUDIO.   And never could maintain his part but in the force of his will.

BENEDICK.   That a woman conceived me, I thank her; that she brought me up, I likewise give her most humble thanks; but that I will have a recheat[41] winded [42] in my forehead, or hang my bugle in an invisible baldrick,[43] all women shall pardon me. Because I will not do them the wrong to mistrust any, I will do myself the right to trust none; and the fine[44] is, for the which I may go the finer, I will live a bachelor.

DON PEDRO.   I shall see thee, ere I die, look pale with love.

---

40. despite—contempt.
41. recheat—hunter's horn, hence, horn (of the cuckold).
42. winded—sounded.
43. baldrick—belt for carrying the horn.   44. fine—conclusion.

BENEDICK.   With anger, with sickness, or with hunger, my lord, not with love: prove that ever I lose more blood with love than I will get again with drinking, pick out mine eyes with a ballad-maker's pen and hang me up at the door of a brothel-house for the sign of blind Cupid.

DON PEDRO.   Well, if ever thou dost fall from this faith, thou wilt prove a notable argument.

BENEDICK.   If I do, hang me in a bottle[45] like a cat and shoot at me; and he that hits me, let him be clapped on the shoulder and called Adam.[46]

DON PEDRO.   Well, as time shall try.

    "In time the savage bull doth bear the yoke."

BENEDICK.   The savage bull may; but if ever the sensible Benedick bear it, pluck off the bull's horns and set them in my forehead; and let me be vilely painted, and in such great letters as they write "Here is good horse to hire," let them signify under my sign, "Here you may see Benedick the married man."

CLAUDIO.   If this should ever happen, thou wouldst be horn-mad.[47]

DON PEDRO.   Nay, if Cupid have not spent all his quiver in Venice, thou wilt quake for this shortly.

BENEDICK.   I look for an earthquake too, then.

DON PEDRO.   Well, you will temporize with the hours.[48] In the meantime, good Signior Benedick, repair to Leonato's; commend me to him, and tell him I will not fail him at supper; for indeed he hath made great preparation.

BENEDICK.   I have almost matter[49] enough in me for such an embassage; and so I commit you—

CLAUDIO.   To the tuition of God. From my house,—if I had it,—

DON PEDRO.   The sixth of July. Your loving friend, Benedick.

BENEDICK.   Nay, mock not, mock not. The body of your discourse is sometime guarded [50] with fragments, and the guards are but slightly basted on neither. Ere you flout old ends any further, examine your conscience; and so I leave you.   *Exit.*

---

45. bottle—wicker basket.   46. Adam—Adam Bell, champion archer.
47. horn-mad—mad with jealousy.
48. temporize with the hours—surrender in time.
49. matter—sense.   50. guarded—trimmed.

CLAUDIO.   My liege, your Highness now may do me good.

DON PEDRO.   My love is thine to teach; teach it but how,
And thou shalt see how apt it is to learn
Any hard lesson that may do thee good.

CLAUDIO.   Hath Leonato any son, my lord?

DON PEDRO.   No child but Hero; she's his only heir.
Dost thou affect[51] her, Claudio?

CLAUDIO.   O, my lord,
When you went onward on this ended action,
I looked upon her with a soldier's eye,
That lik'd, but had a rougher task in hand
Than to drive liking to the name of love.
But now I am return'd and that war-thoughts
Have left their places vacant, in their rooms
Come thronging soft and delicate desires,
All prompting me how fair young Hero is,
Saying, I lik'd her ere I went to wars.

DON PEDRO.   Thou wilt be like a lover presently
And tire the hearer with a book of words.
If thou dost love fair Hero, cherish it,
And I will break with[52] her and with her father,
And thou shalt have her. Was 't not to this end
That thou began'st to twist so fine a story?

CLAUDIO.   How sweetly you do minister to love,
That know love's grief by his complexion!
But lest my liking might too sudden seem,
I would have salv'd it with a longer treatise.

DON PEDRO.   What need the bridge much broader than the
   flood?
The fairest grant is the necessity.[53]
Look, what will serve is fit: 't is once,[54] thou lovest,
And I will fit thee with the remedy.
I know we shall have revelling to-night.
I will assume thy part in some disguise
And tell fair Hero I am Claudio,
And in her bosom I'll unclasp my heart
And take her hearing prisoner with the force

---

51. affect—love.   52. break with—broach the subject.
53. necessity—one most needed.   54. 'tis once—in a word.

And strong encounter of my amorous tale;
Then after to her father will I break;
And the conclusion is, she shall be thine.
In practice let us put it presently.   *Exeunt.*

[ACT I • 2] *A room in Leonato's house.*

Enter LEONATO *and* ANTONIO, *meeting.*

LEONATO.   How now, brother! Where is my cousin,[1] your
son? Hath he provided this music?

ANTONIO.   He is very busy about it. But, brother, I can tell
you strange news that you yet dreamt not of.

LEONATO.   Are they good?

ANTONIO.   As the event[2] stamps them; but they have a good
cover, they show well outward. The Prince and Count Claudio,
walking in a thick-pleached [3] alley in mine orchard, were thus
much overheard by a man of mine. The Prince discovered to
Claudio that he loved my niece your daughter and meant to acknowledge it this night in a dance; and if he found her accordant,[4] he meant to take the present time by the top[5] and
instantly break with you of it.

LEONATO.   Hath the fellow any wit that told you this?

ANTONIO.   A good sharp fellow: I will send for him; and
question him yourself.

LEONATO.   No, no; we will hold it as a dream till it appear
itself; but I will acquaint my daughter withal,[6] that she may be
the better prepared for an answer, if peradventure this be true.
Go you and tell her of it.
                         Exit ANTONIO. *Enter his son and a musician.*
Cousin, you know what you have to do. O, I cry you mercy,
friend; go you with me, and I will use your skill. Good cousin,
have a care this busy time.   *Exeunt.*

---

1. cousin—any relative, here, nephew.
2. event—outcome.
3. thick-pleached—with intertwining branches overhead.
4. accordant—receptive.
5. top—forelock.
6. withal—with it.

[ACT I • 3] *The same.*

Enter DON JOHN, CONRADE.

CONRADE. What the good-year,[1] my lord! Why are you thus out of measure sad?

DON JOHN. There is no measure in the occasion that breeds; therefore the sadness is without limit.

CONRADE. You should hear reason.

DON JOHN. And when I have heard it, what blessing brings it?

CONRADE. If not a present remedy, at least a patient sufferance.

DON JOHN. I wonder that thou (being as thou say'st thou art, born under Saturn[2]) goest about to apply a moral medicine to a mortifying mischief.[3] I cannot hide what I am. I must be sad when I have cause, and smile at no man's jests; eat when I have stomach, and wait for no man's leisure; sleep when I am drowsy, and tend on no man's business; laugh when I am merry, and claw[4] no man in his humour.

CONRADE. Yea, but you must not make the full show of this till you may do it without controlment. You have of late stood out against your brother, and he hath ta'en you newly into his grace; where it is impossible you should take true root but by the fair weather that you make yourself: it is needful that you frame the season for your own harvest.

DON JOHN. I had rather be a canker[5] in a hedge than a rose in his grace, and it better fits my blood to be disdained of all than to fashion a carriage[6] to rob love from any: in this, though I cannot be said to be a flattering honest man, it must not be denied but I am a plain-dealing villain. I am trusted with a muzzle and enfranchised [7] with a clog; [8] therefore I have decreed not to sing in my cage. If I had my mouth, I would bite; if I had my liberty, I would do my liking: in the meantime let me be that I am and seek not to alter me.

CONRADE. Can you make no use of your discontent?

---

1. good-year—devil.   2. Saturn—i.e., of a morose disposition.
3. mortifying mischief—deadly disease.   4. claw—flatter.
5. canker—wild rose.   6. carriage—behavior.
7. enfranchised—released.   8. clog—ball and chain.

DON JOHN.   I make all use of it, for I use it only. Who comes here?

Enter BORACHIO.

What news, Borachio?

BORACHIO.   I came yonder from a great supper. The Prince your brother is royally entertained by Leonato; and I can give you intelligence[9] of an intended marriage.

DON JOHN.   Will it serve for any model to build mischief on? What is he for a fool that betroths himself to unquietness?

BORACHIO.   Marry, it is your brother's right hand.

DON JOHN.   Who? The most exquisite Claudio?

BORACHIO.   Even he.

DON JOHN.   A proper squire! And who? and who? Which way looks he?

BORACHIO.   Marry, on Hero, the daughter and heir of Leonato.

DON JOHN.   A very forward March-chick! [10] How came you to this?

BORACHIO.   Being entertained for[11] a perfumer, as I was smoking[12] a musty room, comes me the Prince and Claudio, hand in hand, in sad [13] conference: I whipt me behind the arras,[14] and there heard it agreed upon that the Prince should woo Hero for himself, and having obtained her, give her to Count Claudio.

DON JOHN.   Come, come, let us thither; this may prove food to my displeasure. That young start-up hath all the glory of my overthrow: if I can cross[15] him any way, I bless myself every way. You are both sure, and will assist me?

CONRADE.   To the death, my lord.

DON JOHN.   Let us to the great supper; their cheer is the greater that I am subdued. Would the cook were o' my mind! Shall we go prove[16] what's to be done?

BORACHIO.   We'll wait upon your lordship.   *Exeunt.*

---

9. intelligence—information.
10. March-chick—precocious child.
11. entertained for—employed as.   12. smoking—fumigating.
13. sad—serious.   14. arras—tapestry hangings.
15. cross—frustrate.   16. prove—observe.

[ACT II • 1] *A hall in Leonato's house.*

Enter LEONATO, ANTONIO, HERO, BEATRICE, MARGARET *and*
URSULA, *and a kinsman.*

LEONATO.   Was not Count John here at supper?

ANTONIO.   I saw him not.

BEATRICE.   How tartly that gentleman looks! I never can see
him but I am heart-burned an hour after.

HERO.   He is of a very melancholy disposition.

BEATRICE.   He were an excellent man that were made just
in the midway between him and Benedick: the one is too like an
image and says nothing, and the other too like my lady's eldest
son,[1] evermore tattling.

LEONATO.   Then half Signior Benedick's tongue in Count
John's mouth, and half Count John's melancholy in Signior
Benedick's face,—

BEATRICE.   With a good leg and a good foot, uncle, and
money enough in his purse, such a man would win any woman in
the world, if 'a[2] could get her good-will.

LEONATO.   By my troth, niece, thou wilt never get thee a
husband, if thou be so shrewd [3] of thy tongue.

ANTONIO.   In faith, she's too curst.[4]

BEATRICE.   Too curst is more than curst: I shall lessen God's
sending that way; for it is said, "God sends a curst cow short
horns;" but to a cow too curst he sends none.

LEONATO.   So, by being too curst, God will send you no
horns.

BEATRICE.   Just, if he send me no husband; for the which
blessing I am at him upon my knees every morning and evening.
Lord, I could not endure a husband with a beard on his face!
I had rather lie in the woollen.[5]

LEONATO.   You may light on a husband that hath no beard.

BEATRICE.   What should I do with him? Dress him in my
apparel and make him my waiting-gentlewoman? He that hath
a beard is more than a youth, and he that hath no beard is less
than a man; and he that is more than a youth is not for me, and

---

1. my lady's eldest son—any spoiled brat.   2. 'a—he.
3. shrewd—sharp.   4. curst—bad tempered.
5. lie in the woollen—be tickled by blankets.

he that is less than a man, I am not for him; therefore I will even take sixpence in earnest[6] of the bear-ward, and lead his apes into hell.[7]

LEONATO.   Well, then, go you into hell?

BEATRICE.   No, but to the gate; and there will the devil meet me, like an old cuckold, with horns on his head, and say "Get you to heaven, Beatrice, get you to heaven; here's no place for you maids:" so deliver I up my apes, and away to Saint Peter for the heavens: he shows me where the bachelors[8] sit, and there live we as merry as the day is long.

ANTONIO.   [To HERO.] Well, niece, I trust you will be ruled by your father.

BEATRICE.   Yes, faith; it is my cousin's duty to make curtsy and say, "Father, as it please you:" but yet for all that, cousin, let him be a handsome fellow, or else make another curtsy and say, "Father, as it please me."

LEONATO.   Well, niece, I hope to see you one day fitted with a husband.

BEATRICE.   Not till God make men of some other metal than earth. Would it not grieve a woman to be overmastered with a piece of valiant dust? to make an account of her life to a clod of wayward marl?[9] No uncle, I'll none: Adam's sons are my brethren; and truly I hold it a sin to match in my kindred.

LEONATO.   Daughter, remember what I told you: if the Prince do solicit you in that kind, you know your answer.

BEATRICE.   The fault will be in the music, cousin, if you be not wooed in good time: if the Prince be too important,[10] tell him there is measure in everything and so dance out the answer. For, hear me, Hero: wooing, wedding, and repenting, is as a Scotch jig,[11] a measure,[12] and a cinque-pace;[13] the first suit is hot and hasty, like a Scotch jig, and full as fantastical; the wedding mannerly-modest, as a measure, full of state and ancientry;[14] and then comes repentance and, with his bad legs,

6. earnest—advance payment for services to be rendered.
7. lead apes into hell—die an old maid.
8. bachelors—the unmarried of both sexes.   9. marl—clay.
10. important—importunate.   11. Scotch jig—lively, violent dance.
12. measure—stately, formal dance.
13. cinque-pace—quick, intricate dance.
14. ancientry—the old fashion.

falls into the cinque-pace faster and faster, till he sink into his grave.

LEONATO.   Cousin, you apprehend passing[15] shrewdly.

BEATRICE.   I have a good eye, uncle; I can see a church by daylight.

LEONATO.   The revellers are entering, brother; make good room. [ANTONIO *dons a mask.*]

Enter DON PEDRO, CLAUDIO, BENEDICK, BALTHASAR, DON JOHN, BORACHIO, MARGARET, URSULA, *and others, masked, with a drummer.*

DON PEDRO.   Lady, will you walk a bout with your friend?

HERO.   So you walk softly and look sweetly and say nothing, I am yours for the walk; and especially when I walk away.

DON PEDRO.   With me in your company?

HERO.   I may say so when I please.

DON PEDRO.   And when please you to say so?

HERO.   When I like your favour; [16] for God defend the lute should be like the case!

DON PEDRO.   My visor[17] is Philemon's[18] roof; within the house is Jove.

HERO.   Why, then, your visor should be thatched.

DON PEDRO.   Speak low, if you speak love.

[*Drawing her aside.*]

BALTHASAR.   Well, I would you did like me.

MARGARET.   So would not I, for your own sake; for I have many ill qualities.

BALTHASAR.   Which is one?

MARGARET.   I say my prayers aloud.

BALTHASAR.   I love you the better; the hearers may cry, Amen.

MARGARET.   God match me with a good dancer!

BALTHASAR.   Amen.

MARGARET.   And God keep you out of my sight when the dance is done! Answer, clerk.[19]

BALTHASAR.   No more words; the clerk is answered.

---

15. passing—very.   16. favour—face.   17. visor—mask.
18. Philemon—who once entertained Jupiter incognito.
19. clerk—leader of the responsory reading in church service.

URSULA.   I know you well enough; you are Signior Antonio.

ANTONIO.   At a word, I am not.

URSULA.   I know you by the waggling of your head.

ANTONIO.   To tell you true, I counterfeit him.

URSULA.   You could never do him so ill-well,[20] unless you were the very man. Here's his dry hand up and down: you are he, you are he.

ANTONIO.   At a word, I am not.

URSULA.   Come, come, do you think I do not know you by your excellent wit? Can virtue hide itself? Go to, mum, you are he: graces will appear, and there's an end.

BEATRICE.   Will you not tell me who told you so?

BENEDICK.   No, you shall pardon me.

BEATRICE.   Nor will you not tell me who you are?

BENEDICK.   Not now.

BEATRICE.   That I was disdainful, and that I had my good wit out of the "Hundred Merry Tales" [21]:—well, this was Signior Benedick that said so.

BENEDICK.   What's he?

BEATRICE.   I am sure you know him well enough.

BENEDICK.   Not I, believe me.

BEATRICE.   Did he never make you laugh?

BENEDICK.   I pray you, what is he?

BEATRICE.   Why, he is the Prince's jester, a very dull fool; only his gift is in devising impossible slanders: none but libertines delight in him, and the commendation is not in his wit but in his villainy; for he both pleases men and angers them, and then they laugh at him and beat him. I am sure he is in the fleet; [22] I would he had boarded [23] me.

BENEDICK.   When I know the gentleman, I'll tell him what you say.

BEATRICE.   Do, do: he'll but break a comparison or two on me; which, peradventure not marked or not laughed at, strikes him into melancholy; and then there's a partridge wing saved, for the fool will eat no supper that night. [*Music.*] We must follow the leaders.

---

20. do him so ill-well—counterfeit his defects so precisely.
21. "Hundred Merry Tales"—a collection of vulgar stories.
22. in the fleet—among the guests.   23. boarded—accosted.

BENEDICK.   In every good thing.

BEATRICE.   Nay, if they lead to any ill, I will leave them at the next turning.

> *Dance. Then exeunt all except* DON JOHN,
> BORACHIO, *and* CLAUDIO.

DON JOHN.   Sure my brother is amorous on Hero and hath withdrawn her father to break with him about it. The ladies follow her and but one visor remains.

BORACHIO.   And that is Claudio: I know him by his bearing.

DON JOHN.   Are not you Signior Benedick?

CLAUDIO.   You know me well; I am he.

DON JOHN.   Signior, you are very near my brother in his love: he is enamoured on Hero. I pray you, dissuade him from her; she is no equal for his birth. You may do the part of an honest man in it.

CLAUDIO.   How know you he loves her?

DON JOHN.   I heard him swear his affection.

BORACHIO.   So did I too; and he swore he would marry her to-night.

DON JOHN.   Come, let us to the banquet.[24]

> *Exeunt* DON JOHN *and* BORACHIO.

CLAUDIO.   Thus answer I in name of Benedick,
But hear these ill news with the ears of Claudio.
'Tis certain so; the Prince wooes for himself.
Friendship is constant in all other things
Save in the office and affairs of love;
Therefore all hearts in love use their own tongues.
Let every eye negotiate for itself
And trust no agent; for beauty is a witch
Against whose charms faith melteth into blood.[25]
This is an accident of hourly proof,
Which I mistrusted [26] not. Farewell, therefore, Hero!

Re-enter BENEDICK.

BENEDICK.   Count Claudio?

CLAUDIO.   Yea, the same.

BENEDICK.   Come, will you go with me?

---

24. banquet—refreshments.
25. blood—passion.   26. mistrusted—suspected.

CLAUDIO.   Whither?

BENEDICK.   Even to the next willow,[27] about your own business, County. What fashion will you wear the garland of? About your neck, like an usurer's chain, or under your arm, like a lieutenant's scarf? You must wear it one way, for the Prince hath got your Hero.

CLAUDIO.   I wish him joy of her.

BENEDICK.   Why, that's spoken like an honest drover; so they sell bullocks. But did you think the Prince would have served you thus?

CLAUDIO.   I pray you, leave me.

BENEDICK.   Ho! now you strike like the blind man. 'Twas the boy that stole your meat, and you'll beat the post.

CLAUDIO.   If it will not be, I'll leave you.   *Exit.*

BENEDICK.   Alas, poor hurt fowl! now will he creep into sedges.[28] But that my Lady Beatrice should know me, and not know me! The Prince's fool! Ha? It may be I go under that title because I am merry. Yea, but so I am apt to do myself wrong: I am not so reputed: it is the base, though bitter, disposition of Beatrice that puts the world into her person, and so gives me out. Well, I'll be revenged as I may.

Re-enter DON PEDRO, HERO *and* LEONATO.

DON PEDRO.   Now, signior, where's the Count? Did you see him?

BENEDICK.   Troth, my lord, I have played the part of Lady Fame.[29] I found him here as melancholy as a lodge in a warren.[30] I told him, and I think I told him true, that your Grace had got the good will of this young lady; and I offered him my company to a willow-tree, either to make him a garland, as being forsaken, or to bind him up a rod, as being worthy to be whipped.

DON PEDRO.   To be whipped! What's his fault?

BENEDICK.   The flat transgression of a schoolboy, who, being overjoyed with finding a birds' nest, shows it his companion, and he steals it.

---

27. willow—source of garlands for forsaken lovers.
28. sedges—reeds.   29. Lady Fame——Dame Rumor.
30. warren—game preserve.

DON PEDRO. Wilt thou make a trust a transgression? The transgression is in the stealer.

BENEDICK. Yet it had not been amiss the rod had been made, and the garland too; for the garland he might have worn himself, and the rod he might have bestowed on you, who, as I take it, have stolen his birds' nest.

DON PEDRO. I will but teach them to sing, and restore them to the owner.

BENEDICK. If their singing answer your saying, by my faith, you say honestly.

DON PEDRO. The Lady Beatrice hath a quarrel to you: the gentleman that danced with her told her she is much wronged by you.

BENEDICK. O, she misused me past the endurance of a block! An oak but with one green leaf on it would have answered her: my very visor began to assume life and scold with her. She told me, not thinking I had been myself, that I was the Prince's jester, that I was duller than a great thaw; huddling jest upon jest with such impossible conveyance[31] upon me that I stood like a man at a mark, with a whole army shooting at me. She speaks poniards,[32] and every word stabs: if her breath were as terrible as her terminations,[33] there were no living near her; she would infect to the north star. I would not marry her, though she were endowed with all that Adam had left him before he transgressed. She would have made Hercules have turned spit, yea, and have cleft his club to make the fire too. Come, talk not of her; you shall find her the infernal Ate[34] in good apparel. I would to God some scholar would conjure her; for certainly while she is here, a man may live as quiet in hell as in a sanctuary; and people sin upon purpose, because they would go thither; so, indeed, all disquiet, horror, and perturbation follows her.

Enter CLAUDIO *and* BEATRICE.

DON PEDRO. Look, here she comes.

BENEDICK. Will your Grace command me any service to

---

31. impossible conveyance—unbelievable dexterity.
32. poniards—daggers.   33. terminations—words.
34. Ate—goddess of discord.

the world's end? I will go on the slightest errand now to the Antipodes[35] that you can devise to send me on; I will fetch you a toothpicker now from the furthest inch of Asia, bring you the length of Prester John's[36] foot, fetch you a hair off the great Cham's[37] beard, do you any embassage to the Pigmies, rather than hold three words' conference with this harpy. You have no employment for me?

DON PEDRO.   None, but to desire your good company.

BENEDICK.   O God, sir, here's a dish I love not: I cannot endure my Lady Tongue.   *Exit.*

DON PEDRO.   Come, lady, come; you have lost the heart of Signior Benedick.

BEATRICE.   Indeed, my lord, he lent it me awhile; and I gave him use[38] for it, a double heart for his single one: marry, once before he won it of me with false dice, therefore your Grace may well say I have lost it.

DON PEDRO.   You have put him down, lady, you have put him down.

BEATRICE.   So I would not he should do me, my lord, lest I should prove the mother of fools. I have brought Count Claudio, whom you sent me to seek.

DON PEDRO.   Why, how now, Count! wherefore are you sad?

CLAUDIO.   Not sad, my lord.

DON PEDRO.   How, then? Sick?

CLAUDIO.   Neither, my lord.

BEATRICE.   The count is neither sad, nor sick, nor merry, nor well; but civil Count, civil [39] as an orange, and something of that jealous complexion.

DON PEDRO.   I' faith, lady, I think your blazon[40] to be true; though, I'll be sworn, if he be so, his conceit[41] is false. Here, Claudio, I have wooed in thy name, and fair Hero is won: I have broke with her father, and his good will obtained: name the day of marriage, and God give thee joy!

LEONATO.   Count, take of me my daughter, and with her my

---

35. Antipodes—the other side of the world.
36. Prester John—a mythical Asiatic king.
37. great Cham—the Mongol emperor.   38. use—interest.
39. civil—serious, with a pun on *Seville* (oranges).
40. blazon—description.   41. conceit—idea.

fortunes: his Grace hath made the match, and all grace say Amen to it.

BEATRICE.   Speak, Count, 't is your cue.

CLAUDIO.   Silence is the perfectest herald of joy; I were but little happy, if I could say how much. Lady, as you are mine, I am yours: I give away myself for you and dote upon the exchange.

BEATRICE.   Speak, cousin; or, if you cannot, stop his mouth with a kiss, and let not him speak neither.

DON PEDRO.   In faith, lady, you have a merry heart.

BEATRICE.   Yea, my lord; I thank it, poor fool, it keeps on the windy⁴² side of care. My cousin tells him in his ear that he is in her heart.

CLAUDIO.   And so she doth, cousin.

BEATRICE.   Good Lord, for alliance! Thus goes every one to the world but I, and I am sunburnt: ⁴³ I may sit in a corner and cry "Heigh-ho for a husband!"

DON PEDRO.   Lady Beatrice, I will get you one.

BEATRICE.   I would rather have one of your father's getting. Hath your Grace ne'er a brother like you? Your father got excellent husbands, if a maid could come by them.

DON PEDRO.   Will you have me, lady?

BEATRICE.   No, my lord, unless I might have another for working-days: your Grace is too costly to wear every day. But, I beseech your Grace, pardon me; I was born to speak all mirth and no matter.

DON PEDRO.   Your silence most offends me, and to be merry best becomes you; for, out o' question, you were born in a merry hour.

BEATRICE.   No, sure, my lord, my mother cried; but then there was a star danced, and under that was I born. Cousins, God give you joy!

LEONATO.   Niece, will you look to those things I told you of?

BEATRICE.   I cry you mercy, uncle. By your Grace's pardon.

Exit.

DON PEDRO.   By my troth, a pleasant-spirited lady.

LEONATO.   There's little of the melancholy element in her,

42. windy—windward (protected).
43. sunburnt—unfashionably dark-complexioned.

my lord: she is never sad but when she sleeps, and not ever sad then; for I have heard my daughter say, she hath often dreamt of unhappiness and waked herself with laughing.

DON PEDRO.   She cannot endure to hear tell of a husband.

LEONATO.   O, by no means; she mocks all her wooers out of suit.

DON PEDRO.   She were an excellent wife for Benedick.

LEONATO.   O Lord, my lord, if they were but a week married, they would talk themselves mad.

DON PEDRO.   County Claudio, when mean you to go to church?

CLAUDIO.   To-morrow, my lord: time goes on crutches till love have all his rites.

LEONATO.   Not till Monday, my dear son, which is hence a just seven-night; [44] and a time too brief, too, to have all things answer my mind.

DON PEDRO.   Come, you shake the head at so long a breathing; but, I warrant thee, Claudio, the time shall not go dully by us. I will in the interim undertake one of Hercules' [45] labours; which is, to bring Signior Benedick and the Lady Beatrice into a mountain of affection th' one with th' other. I would fain have it a match, and I doubt not but to fashion it, if you three will but minister such assistance as I shall give you direction.

LEONATO.   My lord, I am for you, though it cost me ten nights' watchings.[46]

CLAUDIO.   And I, my lord.

DON PEDRO.   And you too, gentle Hero?

HERO.   I will do any modest office, my lord, to help my cousin to a good husband.

DON PEDRO.   And Benedick is not the unhopefullest husband that I know. Thus far can I praise him: he is of a noble strain, of approved valour, and confirmed honesty. I will teach you how to humour your cousin, that she shall fall in love with Benedick; and I, with your two helps, will so practise on Benedick that, in despite of his quick wit and his queasy stomach,[47] he shall fall

---

44. a just seven-night—a week.
45. Hercules—Greek mythical hero who performed twelve supposedly impossible "labours."
46. watchings—lying awake.   47. queasy stomach—squeamishness.

in love with Beatrice. If we can do this, Cupid is no longer an
archer. His glory shall be ours, for we are the only love-gods.
Go in with me, and I will tell you my drift.   *Exeunt.*

[ACT II • 2] *The same.*

Enter DON JOHN *and* BORACHIO.

DON JOHN.   It is so; the Count Claudio shall marry the
daughter of Leonato.

BORACHIO.   Yea, my lord; but I can cross it.

DON JOHN.   Any bar, any cross, any impediment will be
med'cinable to me: I am sick in displeasure to him, and whatsoever comes athwart his affection ranges evenly[1] with mine. How
canst thou cross this marriage?

BORACHIO.   Not honestly, my lord; but so covertly that no
dishonesty shall appear in me.

DON JOHN.   Show me briefly how.

BORACHIO.   I think I told your lordship a year since how
much I am in the favour of Margaret, the waiting gentlewoman
to Hero.

DON JOHN.   I remember.

BORACHIO.   I can, at any unseasonable instant of the night,
appoint her to look out at her lady's chamber-window.

DON JOHN.   What life is in that, to be the death of this
marriage?

BORACHIO.   The poison of that lies in you to temper.[2] Go you
to the Prince your brother; spare not to tell him that he hath
wronged his honour in marrying the renowned Claudio—whose
estimation do you mightily hold up—to a contaminated stale,[3]
such a one as Hero.

DON JOHN.   What proof shall I make of that?

BORACHIO.   Proof enough to misuse[4] the Prince, to vex
Claudio, to undo Hero, and kill Leonato. Look you for any
other issue?

DON JOHN.   Only to despite them, I will endeavour anything.

BORACHIO.   Go, then; find me a meet[5] hour to draw Don
Pedro and the Count Claudio alone; tell them that you know

1. ranges evenly—runs parallel.   2. temper—mix.
3. stale—harlot.   4. misuse—deceive.   5. meet—proper.

that Hero loves me; intend [6] a kind of zeal both to the Prince and Claudio, as,—in love of your brother's honour, who hath made this match, and his friend's reputation, who is thus like to be cozened [7] with the semblance of a maid,—that you have discovered thus. They will scarcely believe this without trial. Offer them instances; [8] which shall bear no less likelihood than to see me at her chamber-window, hear me call Margaret Hero, hear Margaret term me Claudio; and bring them to see this the very night before the intended wedding,—for in the meantime I will so fashion the matter that Hero shall be absent,—and there shall appear such seeming truth of Hero's disloyalty, that jealousy[9] shall be called assurance[10] and all the preparation overthrown.

DON JOHN.   Grow this to what adverse issue it can, I will put it in practice. Be cunning in the working this, and thy fee is a thousand ducats.

BORACHIO.   Be you constant in the accusation, and my cunning shall not shame me.

DON JOHN.   I will presently go learn their day of marriage.

Exeunt.

---

6. intend—pretend.   7. cozened—cheated.   8. instances—proofs.
9. jealousy—suspicion.   10. assurance—certainty.

[ACT II • 3] *Leonato's orchard.*

Enter BENEDICK *alone.*

BENEDICK.   Boy!

Enter BOY.

BOY.   Signior?
BENEDICK.   In my chamber-window lies a book; bring it hither to me in the orchard.
BOY.   I am here already, sir.
BENEDICK.   I know that; but I would have thee hence, and ere again. [*Exit* BOY.] I do much wonder that one man, seeing how much another man is a fool when he dedicates his behaviours to love, will, after he hath laughed at such shallow follies in others, become the argument[1] of his own scorn by

---

1. argument—subject matter.

falling in love, and such a man is Claudio. I have known when there was no music with him but the drum and the fife; and now had he rather hear the tabor[2] and the pipe. I have known when he would have walked ten miles a-foot to see a good armour; and now will he lie ten nights awake, carving[3] the fashion of a new doublet.[4] He was wont to speak plain and to the purpose, like an honest man and a soldier; and now is he turned orthography;[5] his words are a very fantastical banquet, just so many strange dishes. May I be so converted and see with these eyes? I cannot tell; I think not. I will not be sworn but love may transform me to an oyster; but I'll take my oath on it, till he have made an oyster of me, he shall never make me such a fool. One woman is fair, yet I am well; another is wise, yet I am well; another virtuous, yet I am well; but till all graces be in one woman, one woman shall not come in my grace. Rich she shall be, that's certain; wise, or I'll none; virtuous, or I'll never cheapen[6] her; fair or I'll never look on her; mild, or come not near me; noble, or not I for an angel; of good discourse, an excellent musician, and her hair shall be of what colour it please God. Ha! the Prince and Monsieur Love! I will hide me in the arbour.   [*Withdraws.*]

Enter DON PEDRO, CLAUDIO, *and* LEONATO. *Music within.*

DON PEDRO.   Come, shall we hear this music?
CLAUDIO.   Yea, my good lord. How still the evening is,
As hush'd on purpose to grace harmony!
DON PEDRO.   See you where Benedick hath hid himself?
CLAUDIO.   O, very well, my lord. The music ended,
We'll fit the kid-fox[7] with a pennyworth.[8]

Enter BALTHASAR *with musicians.*

DON PEDRO.   Come, Balthasar, we'll hear that song again.
BALTHASAR.   O, good my lord, tax not so bad a voice
To slander music any more than once.
DON PEDRO.   It is the witness still of excellency

---

2. tabor—small, nonmilitary drum.   3. carving—planning.
4. doublet—jacket.   5. orthography—coiner of fancy phrases.
6. cheapen—bargain for.   7. kid-fox—young fox.
8. pennyworth—bargain (i.e., give him more than he bargains for?).

To put a strange face on his own perfection.
I pray thee, sing, and let me woo no more.
    BALTHASAR.   Because you talk of wooing, I will sing;
Since many a wooer doth commence his suit
To her he thinks not worthy, yet he wooes,
Yet will he swear he loves.
    DON PEDRO.   Now, pray thee, come;
Or, if thou wilt hold longer argument,
Do it in notes.
    BALTHASAR.   Note this before my notes;
There's not a note of mine that's worth the noting.
    DON PEDRO.   Why, these are very crotchets[9] that he speaks;
Note, notes, forsooth, and nothing.[10]   [*Music.*]
    BENEDICK. [*In the arbor.*] Now, divine air! now is his soul
ravished! Is it not strange that sheeps' guts should hale souls
out of men's bodies? Well, a horn for my money, when all's
done.
    BALTHASAR. [*Sings.*]

> Sigh no more, ladies, sigh no more,
>   Men were deceivers ever,
> One foot in sea and one on shore,
>   To one thing constant never.
> Then sigh not so, but let them go,
>   And be you blithe and bonny,
> Converting all your sounds of woe
>   Into Hey nonny nonny.
>
> Sing no more ditties, sing no moe,[11]
>   Of dumps [12] so dull and heavy;
> The fraud of men was ever so,
>   Since summer first was leavy.[13]
>   Then sigh not so, etc.

    DON PEDRO. By my troth, a good song.
    BALTHASAR. And an ill singer, my lord.
    DON PEDRO. Ha, no, no, faith; thou sing'st well enough for a
shift.[14]

---

9. crotchets—whining, also, musical notes.
10. nothing—i.e., with a pun on *noting*.   11. moe—more.
12. dumps—melancholy.   13. leavy—leafy.   14. shift—makeshift.

BENEDICK. An he had been a dog that should have howled thus, they would have hanged him; and I pray God his bad voice bode no mischief. I had as lief have heard the night-raven,[15] come what plague could have come after it.

DON PEDRO. Yea, marry. Dost thou hear, Balthasar? I pray thee, get us some excellent music; for to-morrow night we would have it at the Lady Hero's chamber-window.

BALTHASAR. The best I can, my lord.   *Exit* BALTHASAR.

DON PEDRO. Do so; farewell. Come hither, Leonato. What was it you told me of to-day, that your niece Beatrice was in love with Signior Benedick.

CLAUDIO. [*Aside.*] O, ay, stalk on, stalk on; the fowl sits.— I did never think that lady would have loved any man.

LEONATO. No, nor I neither; but most wonderful that she should so dote on Signior Benedick, whom she hath in all outward behaviours seemed ever to abhor.

BENEDICK. [*In the arbor.*] Is 't possible? Sits the wind in that corner?

LEONATO. By my troth, my lord, I cannot tell what to think of it but that she loves him with an enraged [16] affection: it is past the infinite of thought.

DON PEDRO. May be she doth but counterfeit.

CLAUDIO. Faith, like enough.

LEONATO. O God, counterfeit! There was never counterfeit of passion came so near the life of passion as she discovers[17] it.

DON PEDRO. Why, what effects of passion shows she?

CLAUDIO. [*Aside.*] Bait the hook well; this fish will bite.

LEONATO. What effects, my lord? She will sit you,—you heard my daughter tell you how.

CLAUDIO. She did, indeed.

DON PEDRO. How, how, I pray you? You amaze me; I would have thought her spirit had been invincible against all assaults of affection.

LEONATO. I would have sworn it had, my lord; especially against Benedick.

BENEDICK. I should think this a gull,[18] but that the white-

---

15. night-raven—a bird whose cry foretold ill-fortune.
16. enraged—violent.   17. discovers—reveals.
18. gull—trick.

bearded fellow speaks it. Knavery cannot, sure, hide himself in such reverence.

CLAUDIO.   [*Aside.*] He hath ta'en the infection. Hold [19] it up.

DON PEDRO.   Hath she made her affection known to Benedick?

LEONATO.   No; and swears she never will: that's her torment.

CLAUDIO.   'T is true, indeed; so your daughter says. "Shall I," says she, "that have so oft encountered him with scorn, write to him that I love him?"

LEONATO.   This says she now when she is beginning to write to him; for she'll be up twenty times a night, and there will she sit in her smock[20] till she have writ a sheet of paper. My daughter tells us all.

CLAUDIO.   Now you talk of a sheet of paper, I remember a pretty jest your daughter told us of.

LEONATO.   O, when she had writ it and was reading it over, she found Benedick and Beatrice between the sheet?

CLAUDIO.   That.

LEONATO.   O, she tore the letter into a thousand halfpence; railed at herself, that she should be so immodest to write to one that she knew would flout her. "I measure him," says she, "by my own spirit; for I should flout him, if he writ to me; yea, though I love him, I should."

CLAUDIO.   Then down upon her knees she falls, weeps, sobs, beats her heart, tears her hair, prays, curses: "O sweet Benedick! God give me patience!"

LEONATO.   She doth indeed, my daughter says so; and the ecstasy[21] hath so much overborne her that my daughter is sometime afeard she will do a desperate outrage to herself: it is very true.

DON PEDRO.   It were good that Benedick knew of it by some other, if she will not discover it.

CLAUDIO.   To what end? He would make but a sport of it and torment the poor lady worse.

DON PEDRO.   An he should, it were an alms[22] to hang him. She's an excellent sweet lady and, out of all suspicion, she is virtuous.

---

19. Hold—keep.   20. smock—nightgown.
21. ecstacy—madness.   22. alms—good deed.

CLAUDIO.   And she is exceeding wise.

DON PEDRO.   In every thing but in loving Benedick.

LEONATO.   O, my lord, wisdom and blood combating in so tender a body, we have ten proofs to one that blood hath the victory. I am sorry for her, as I have just cause, being her uncle and her guardian.

DON PEDRO.   I would she had bestowed this dotage on me; I would have daffed [23] all other respects and made her half myself. I pray you, tell Benedick of it, and hear what 'a will say.

LEONATO.   Were it good, think you?

CLAUDIO.   Hero thinks surely she will die; for she says she will die, if he love her not, and she will die, ere she make her ove known, and she will die, if he woo her, rather than she will bate[24] one breath of her accustomed crossness.

DON PEDRO.   She doth well: if she should make tender[25] of her love, 't is very possible he'll scorn it, for the man, as you know all, hath a contemptible[26] spirit.

CLAUDIO.   He is a very proper man.

DON PEDRO.   He hath indeed a good outward happiness.

CLAUDIO.   Before God! and, in my mind, very wise.

DON PEDRO.   He doth indeed show some sparks that are like wit.

CLAUDIO.   And I take him to be valiant.

DON PEDRO.   As Hector,[27] I assure you; and in the managing of quarrels you may say he is wise, for either he avoids them with great discretion, or undertakes them with a most Christian-like fear.

LEONATO.   If he do fear God, 'a must necessarily keep peace: if he break the peace, he ought to enter into a quarrel with fear and trembling.

DON PEDRO.   And so will he do; for the man doth fear God, howsoever it seems not in him by some large[28] jests he will make. Well, I am sorry for your niece. Shall we go seek Benedick and tell him of her love?

CLAUDIO.   Never tell him, my lord: let her wear it out with good counsel.

---

23. daffed—waived.   24. bate—abate.
25. tender—offer.   26. contemptible—contemptuous.
27. Hector—one of the heroes of the Trojan war.   28. large—coarse.

LEONATO. Nay, that's impossible; she may wear her heart out first.

DON PEDRO. Well, we will hear further of it by your daughter: let it cool the while. I love Benedick well; and I could wish he would modestly examine himself, to see how much he is unworthy so good a lady.

LEONATO. My lord, will you walk? Dinner is ready.

CLAUDIO. [*Aside.*] If he do not dote on her upon this, I will never trust my expectation.

DON PEDRO. [*Aside.*] Let there be the same net spread for her; and that must your daughter and her gentlewomen carry. The sport will be, when they hold one an opinion of another's dotage, and no such matter;[29] that's the scene that I would see, which will be merely a dumb-show. Let us send her to call him in to dinner. *Exeunt* DON PEDRO, CLAUDIO, *and* LEONATO.

BENEDICK. [*Coming forward.*] This can be no trick; the conference was sadly borne.[30] They have the truth of this from Hero. They seem to pity the lady; it seems her affections have their full bent. Love me! why, it must be requited. I hear how I am censured: they say I will bear myself proudly if I perceive the love come from her; they say too that she will rather die than give any sign of affection. I did never think to marry. I must not seem proud: happy are they that hear their detractions and can put them to mending. They say the lady is fair; 't is a truth, I can bear them witness; and virtuous; 't is so, I cannot reprove[31] it; and wise, but for loving me; by my troth,[32] it is no addition to her wit, nor no great argument of her folly, for I will be horribly in love with her. I may chance have some odd quirks and remnants of wit broken on me, because I have railed so long against marriage; but doth not the appetite alter? A man loves the meat in his youth that he cannot endure in his age. Shall quips and sentences[33] and these paper[34] bullets of the brain awe a man from the career of his humour? [35] No, the world must be peopled. When I said I would die a bachelor, I did not think I

---

29. no such matter—there be nothing in it.
30. sadly borne—seriously conducted.
31. reprove—disprove.   32. troth—faith.
33. sentences—proverbs.   34. paper—harmless.
35. career of his humour—course of his inclination.

should live till I were married. Here comes Beatrice. By this day! she's a fair lady. I do spy some marks of love in her.

Enter BEATRICE.

BEATRICE.   Against my will I am sent to bid you come in to dinner.

BENEDICK.   Fair Beatrice, I thank you for your pains.

BEATRICE.   I took no more pains for those thanks than you take pains to thank me: if it had been painful, I would not have come.

BENEDICK.   You take pleasure then in the message?

BEATRICE.   Yea, just so much as you may take upon a knife's point and choke a daw[36] withal. You have not stomach, signior: fare you well.   *Exit.*

BENEDICK.   Ha! "Against my will I am sent to bid you come in to dinner"; there's a double meaning in that. "I took no more pains for those thanks than you took pains to thank me"; that's as much as to say, "Any pains that I take for you is as easy as thanks." If I do not take pity of her, I am a villain; if I do not love her, I am a Jew.[37] I will go get her picture.   *Exit.*

---

36. daw—jackdaw.   37. Jew—unbeliever.

[ACT III • 1] *Leonato's orchard.*

Enter HERO, MARGARET, *and* URSULA.

HERO.   Good Margaret, run thee to the parlour;
There shalt thou find my cousin Beatrice
Proposing[1] with the Prince and Claudio.
Whisper her ear and tell her, I and Ursley
Walk in the orchard and our whole discourse
Is all of her; say that thou overheard'st us,
And bid her steal into the pleached bower,
Where honeysuckles, ripened by the sun,
Forbid the sun to enter, like favourites
Made proud by princes, that advance their pride
Against that power that bred it: there will she hide her,

---

1. proposing—conversing

To listen our propose. This is thy office;
Bear thee well in it and leave us alone.

MARGARET.　I'll make her come, I warrant you, presently.[2]

Exit.

HERO.　Now, Ursula, when Beatrice doth come,
As we do trace[3] this alley up and down,
Our talk must only be of Benedick.
When I do name him, let it be thy part
To praise him more than ever man did merit:
My talk to thee must be how Benedick
Is sick in love with Beatrice. Of this matter
Is little Cupid's crafty arrow made,
That only wounds by hearsay. Now begin;

Enter BEATRICE *behind.*

For look where Beatrice, like a lapwing, runs
Close by the ground, to hear our conference.

URSULA.　The pleasant'st angling is to see the fish
Cut with her golden oars[4] the silver stream,
And greedily devour the treacherous bait:
So angle we for Beatrice, who even now
Is couched in the woodbine coverture.
Fear you not my part of the dialogue.

HERO.　Then go we near her, that her ear lose nothing
Of the false sweet bait that we lay for it.

[*Approaching the bower.*]

No, truly, Ursula, she is too disdainful.
I know her spirits are as coy and wild
As haggards[5] of the rock.

URSULA.　　　　　　But are you sure
That Benedick loves Beatrice so entirely?

HERO.　So says the Prince and my new-trothed lord.

URSULA.　And did they bid you tell her of it, madam?

HERO.　They did entreat me to acquaint her of it;
But I persuaded them, if they lov'd Benedick,
To wish him wrestle with affection,
And never to let Beatrice know of it.

---

2. presently—immediately.　3. trace—walk.
4. oars—fins.　5. haggards—wild hawks.

URSULA.   Why did you so? Doth not the gentleman
Deserve as full as fortunate a bed
As ever Beatrice shall couch upon?
    HERO.   O god of love! I know he doth deserve
As much as may be yielded to a man;
But Nature never fram'd a woman's heart
Of prouder stuff than that of Beatrice.
Disdain and scorn ride sparkling in her eyes,
Misprising[6] what they look on, and her wit
Values itself so highly that to her
All matter else seems weak: she cannot love,
Nor take no shape nor project[7] of affection,
She is so self-endeared.
    URSULA.   Sure, I think so;
And therefore certainly it were not good
She knew his love, lest she'll make sport at it.
    HERO.   Why, you speak truth. I never yet saw man,
How wise, how noble, young, how rarely featur'd,
But she would spell him backward.[8] If fairfac'd,
She would swear the gentleman should be her sister;
If black, why, Nature, drawing of an antic,[9]
Made a foul blot: if tall, a lance ill-headed;
If low, an agate[10] very vilely cut;
If speaking, why, a vane blown with all winds;
If silent, why, a block moved with none.
So turns she every man the wrong side out,
And never gives to truth and virtue that
Which simpleness and merit purchaseth.
    URSULA.   Sure, sure, such carping is not commendable.
    HERO.   No; not to be so odd and from all [11] fashions
As Beatrice is, cannot be commendable.
But who dare tell her so? If I should speak,
She would mock me into air; O, she would laugh me
Out of myself, press me to death with wit.
Therefore let Benedick, like cover'd fire,
Consume away in sighs, waste inwardly.

---

6. misprising—undervaluing.   7. project—idea.
8. spell him backwards—say the reverse of it.   9. antic—grotesque.
10. agate—tiny figure cut in a signet ring.   11. from all—contrary to.

It were a better death than die with mocks,
Which is as bad as die with tickling.

URSULA.   Yet tell her of it; hear what she will say.

HERO.   No; rather I will go to Benedick
And counsel him to fight against his passion;
And, truly, I'll devise some honest[12] slanders
To stain my cousin with: one doth not know
How much an ill word may empoison liking.

URSULA.   O, do not do your cousin such a wrong.
She cannot be so much without true judgement—
Having so swift and excellent a wit
As she is priz'd to have—as to refuse
So rare a gentleman as Signior Benedick.

HERO.   He is the only[13] man of Italy,
Always excepted my dear Claudio.

URSULA.   I pray you, be not angry with me, madam,
Speaking my fancy; Signior Benedick,
For shape, for bearing, argument, and valour,
Goes foremost in report through Italy.

HERO.   Indeed, he hath an excellent good name.

URSULA.   His excellence did earn it, ere he had it.
When are you married, madam?

HERO.   Why, every day, to-morrow. Come, go in;
I'll show thee some attires, and have thy counsel
Which is the best to furnish me to-morrow.

URSULA.   [Aside.] She's limed,[14] I warrant you. We have
caught her, madam.

HERO.   [Aside] If it proves so, then loving goes by haps: [15]
Some Cupid kills with arrows, some with traps.

Exeunt HERO and URSULA.

BEATRICE.   [Coming forward.] What fire is in mine ears?
Can this be true?
Stand I condemn'd for pride and scorn so much?
Contempt, farewell! and maiden pride, adieu!
No glory lives behind the back of such.[16]
And, Benedick, love on; I will requite thee,
Taming my wild heart to thy loving hand.

---

12. honest—harmless.   13. only—foremost.   14. limed—caught.
15. haps—chance.   16. such—persons dispraised when absent.

If thou dost love, my kindness shall incite thee
  To bind our loves up in a holy band;
For others say thou dost deserve, and I
Believe it better than reportingly.   *Exit.*

[ACT III • 2] *A room in Leonato's house.*

Enter DON PEDRO, CLAUDIO, BENEDICK, *and* LEONATO.

DON PEDRO.   I do but stay till your marriage be consummate, and then I go toward Arragon.

CLAUDIO.   I'll bring you thither, my lord, if you'll vouchsafe me.

DON PEDRO.   Nay, that would be as great a soil in the new gloss of your marriage as to show a child his new coat and forbid him to wear it. I will only be bold with Benedick for his company; for, from the crown of his head to the sole of his foot, he is all mirth: he hath twice or thrice cut Cupid's bowstring, and the little hangman[1] dare not shoot at him. He hath a heart as sound as a bell and his tongue is the clapper, for what his heart thinks his tongue speaks.

BENEDICK.   Gallants, I am not as I have been.

LEONATO.   So say I; methinks you are sadder.

CLAUDIO.   I hope he be in love.

DON PEDRO.   Hang him, truant! There's no true drop of blood in him, to be truly touched with love. If he be sad, he wants money.

BENEDICK.   I have the toothache.

DON PEDRO.   Draw it.

BENEDICK.   Hang it!

CLAUDIO.   You must hang it first, and draw it afterwards.

DON PEDRO.   What! sigh for the toothache?

LEONATO.   Where is but a humour or a worm.

BENEDICK.   Well, every one can master a grief but he that has it.

CLAUDIO.   Yet say I, he is in love.

DON PEDRO.   There is no appearance of fancy in him, unless it be a fancy that he hath to strange disguises; as, to be a Dutchman to-day, a Frenchman to-morrow, or in the shape of two

---

1. hangman—executioner.

countries at once, as, a German from the waist downward, all slops,[2] and a Spaniard from the hip upward, no doublet. Unless he have a fancy to this foolery, as it appears he hath, he is no fool for fancy, as you would have it appear he is.

CLAUDIO.   If he be not in love with some woman, there is no believing old signs: 'a brushes his hat a mornings; what should that bode?

DON PEDRO.   Hath any man seen him at the barber's?

CLAUDIO.   No, but the barber's man hath been seen with him, and the old ornament of his cheek hath already stuffed tennis-balls.

LEONATO.   Indeed, he looks younger than he did, by the loss of a beard.

DON PEDRO.   Nay, 'a rubs himself with civet:[3] can you smell him out by that?

CLAUDIO.   That's as much as to say, the sweet youth's in love.

DON PEDRO.   The greatest note of it is his melancholy.

CLAUDIO.   And when was he wont to wash his face?

DON PEDRO.   Yea, or to paint himself? For the which, I hear what they say of him.

CLAUDIO.   Nay, but his jesting spirit; which is now crept into a lute-string and now governed by stops.[4]

DON PEDRO.   Indeed, that tells a heavy tale for him: conclude, conclude, he is in love.

CLAUDIO.   Nay, but I know who loves him.

DON PEDRO.   That would I know too: I warrant, one that knows him not.

CLAUDIO.   Yes, and his ill conditions;[5] and, in despite of all, dies for him.

DON PEDRO.   She shall be buried with her face upwards.

BENEDICK.   Yet is this no charm for the toothache. Old signior, walk aside with me; I have studied eight or nine wise words to speak to you, which these hobby-horses[6] must not hear.

Exeunt BENEDICK *and* LEONATO.

DON PEDRO.   For my life, to break with him about Beatrice.

---

2. slops—loose breeches.   3. civet—perfume.
4. stops—frets used as a guide in playing a stringed instrument.
5. conditions—qualities.   6. hobby-horses—buffoons.

CLAUDIO.   'T is even so. Hero and Margaret have by this played their parts with Beatrice; and then the two bears will not bite one another when they meet.

Enter DON JOHN

DON JOHN.   My lord and brother, God save you!

DON PEDRO.   Good-den,[7] brother.

DON JOHN.   If your leisure served, I would speak with you.

DON PEDRO.   In private?

DON JOHN.   If it please you; yet Count Claudio may hear, for what I would speak of concerns him.

CLAUDIO.   What's the matter?

DON JOHN.   [*To Claudio*]. Means your lordship to be married to-morrow?

DON PEDRO.   You know he does.

DON JOHN.   I know not that, when he knows what I know.

CLAUDIO.   If there be any impediment, I pray you discover it.

DON JOHN.   You may think I love you not; let that appear hereafter, and aim better at me by that I now will manifest. For my brother, I think he holds you well, and in dearness of heart hath holp to effect your ensuing marriage;—surely suit ill spent and labour ill bestowed.

DON PEDRO.   Why, what's the matter?

DON JOHN.   I came hither to tell you; and, circumstances shortened, for she has been too long a talking of, the lady is disloyal.

CLAUDIO.   Who? Hero?

DON JOHN.   Even she; Leonato's Hero, your Hero, every man's Hero.

CLAUDIO.   Disloyal?

DON JOHN.   The word is too good to paint out her wickedness; I could say she were worse; think you of a worse title, and I will fit her to it. Wonder not till further warrant: go but with me to-night; you shall see her chamber-window entered, even the night before her wedding-day: if you love her then, to-morrow wed her; but it would better fit your honour to change your mind.

7. Good-den—good afternoon.

CLAUDIO.   May this be so?

DON PEDRO.   I will not think it.

DON JOHN.   If you dare not trust that you see, confess not that you know: if you will follow me, I will show you enough; and when you have seen more and heard more, proceed accordingly.

CLAUDIO.   If I see any thing to-night why I should not marry her to-morrow, in the congregation, where I should wed, there will I shame her.

DON PEDRO.   And, as I wooed for thee to obtain her, I will join with thee to disgrace her.

DON JOHN.   I will disparage her no farther till you are my witnesses: bear it coldly but till midnight, and let the issue show itself.

DON PEDRO.   O day untowardly turned!

CLAUDIO.   O mischief strangely thwarting!

DON JOHN.   O plague right well prevented! So will you say when you have seen the sequel.   *Exeunt.*

[ACT III • 3] *A street.*

Enter DOGBERRY *and his copartner* VERGES *with the* WATCHMEN.

DOGBERRY.   Are you good men and true?

VERGES.   Yea, or else it were pity but they should suffer salvation,[1] body and soul.

DOGBERRY.   Nay, that were a punishment too good for them, if they should have any allegiance in them, being chosen for the Prince's watch.

VERGES.   Well, give them their charge, neighbour Dogberry.

DOGBERRY.   First, who think you the most desartless man to be constable?

FIRST WATCH.   Hugh Oatcake, sir, or George Seacole; for they can write and read.

DOGBERRY.   Come hither, neighbour Seacole. God hath blessed you with a good name. To be a well-favoured man is the gift of fortune, but to write and read comes by nature.

---

1. salvation—by mistake for *damnation.* The following speeches are full of similar blunders, of which only the less obvious have been glossed.

SECOND WATCH.   Both which, master constable,—

DOGBERRY.   You have: I knew it would be your answer. Well, for your favour, sir, why, give God thanks, and make no boast of it; and for your writing and reading, let that appear when there is no need of such vanity. You are thought here to be the most senseless and fit man for the constable of the watch; therefore bear you the lantern. This is your charge: you shall comprehend all vagrom[2] men; you are to bid any man stand, in the Prince's name.

SECOND WATCH.   How if 'a will not stand?

DOGBERRY.   Why, then, take no note of him, but let him go; and presently call the rest of the watch together, and thank God you are rid of a knave.

VERGES.   If he will not stand when he is bidden, he is none of the Prince's subjects.

DOGBERRY.   True, and they are to meddle with none but the Prince's subjects. You shall also make no noise in the streets; for the watch to babble and to talk is most tolerable and not to be endured.

SECOND WATCH.   We will rather sleep than talk; we know what belongs to a watch.

DOGBERRY.   Why, you speak like an ancient and most quiet watchman, for I cannot see how sleeping should offend; only, have a care that your bills[3] be not stolen. Well, you are to call at all the ale-houses, and bid those that are drunk get them to bed.

SECOND WATCH.   How if they will not?

DOGBERRY.   Why, then, let them alone till they are sober: if they make you not then the better answer, you may say they are not the men you took them for.

SECOND WATCH.   Well, sir.

DOGBERRY.   If you meet a thief, you may suspect him, by virtue of your office, to be no true man; and, for such kind of men, the less you meddle or make[4] with them, why, the more is for your honesty.

SECOND WATCH.   If we know him to be a thief, shall we not lay hands on him?

---

2. vagrom—vagrant.   3. bills—the watchmen's weapons.
4. meddle or make—have to do.

DOGBERRY. Truly, by your office, you may; but I think they that touch pitch will be defiled. The most peaceable way for you, if you do take a thief, is to let him show himself what he is and steal out of your company.

VERGES. You have been always called a merciful man, partner.

DOGBERRY. Truly, I would not hang a dog by my will, much more a man who hath any honesty in him.

VERGES. If you hear a child cry in the night, you must call to the nurse and bid her still it.

SECOND WATCH. How if the nurse be asleep and will not hear us?

DOGBERRY. Why, then, depart in peace, and let the child wake her with crying; for the ewe that will not hear her lamb when it baes will never answer a calf when he bleats.

VERGES. 'T is very true.

DOGBERRY. This is the end of the charge: you, constable, are to present[5] the Prince's own person: if you meet the Prince in the night, you may stay him.

VERGES. Nay, by 'r lady, that I think 'a cannot.

DOGBERRY. Five shillings to one on 't, with any man that knows the statues,[6] he may stay him; marry, not without the Prince be willing; for, indeed, the watch ought to offend no man, and it is an offence to stay a man against his will.

VERGES. By 'r lady, I think it be so.

DOGBERRY. Ha, ah ha! Well, masters, good night. And there be any matter of weight chances, call up me: keep your fellows' counsels and your own, and good night. Come, neighbour.

SECOND WATCH. Well, masters, we hear our charge: let us go sit here upon the church bench till two, and then all to bed.

DOGBERRY. One word more, honest neighbours. I pray you, watch about Signior Leonato's door; for the wedding being there to-morrow, there is a great coil [7] to-night. Adieu! Be vigitant, I beseech you.   *Exeunt* DOGBERRY *and* VERGES.

Enter BORACHIO, *drunk, and* CONRADE.

BORACHIO. What, Conrade!

SECOND WATCH. [*Aside.*] Peace! stir not.

---

5. present—represent.   6. statues—statutes.   7. coil—turmoil.

BORACHIO. Conrade, I say!

CONRADE. Here, man; I am at thy elbow.

BORACHIO. Mass, and my elbow itched; I thought there would a scab[8] follow.

CONRADE. I will owe thee an answer for that; and now forward with thy tale.

BORACHIO. Stand thee close, then, under this pent-house,[9] for it drizzles rain; and I will, like a true drunkard, utter all to thee.

SECOND WATCH. [*Aside.*] Such treason, masters: yet stand close.

BORACHIO. Therefore know I have earned of Don John a thousand ducats.

CONRADE. Is it possible that any villainy should be so dear?

BORACHIO. Thou shouldst rather ask if it were possible any villainy should be so rich; for when rich villains have need of poor ones, poor ones may make what price they will.

CONRADE. I wonder at it.

BORACHIO. That shows thou art unconfirmed.[10] Thou knowest that the fashion of a doublet, or a hat, or a cloak, is nothing to a man.

CONRADE. Yes, it is apparel.

BORACHIO. I mean, the fashion.

CONRADE. Yes, the fashion is the fashion.

BORACHIO. Tush! I may as well say the fool's the fool. But seest thou not what a deformed thief this fashion is?

SECOND WATCH. [*Aside.*] I know that Deformed; 'a has been a vile thief this seven year: 'a goes up and down like a gentleman: I remember his name.

BORACHIO. Didst thou not hear somebody?

CONRADE. No; 't was the vane on the house.

BORACHIO. Seest thou not, I say, what a deformed thief this fashion is, how giddily 'a turns about all the hot bloods between fourteen and five-and-thirty, sometimes fashioning them like Pharaoh's soldiers in the reechy[11] painting, sometime like god Bel's priests[12] in the old church-window, sometime like the

---

8. scab—blister; also, low fellow. 9. pent-house—overhanging roof.
10. unconfirmed—inexperienced. 11. reechy—smoky.
12. Bel's priests—defeated by Daniel.

shaven Hercules in the smirched worm-eaten tapestry, where his codpiece seems as massy as his club?

CONRADE.   All this I see; and I see that the fashion wears out more apparel than the man. But are not thou thyself giddy with the fashion too, that thou hast shifted out of thy tale into telling me of the fashion?

BORACHIO.   Not so, neither; but know that I have to-night wooed Margaret, the Lady Hero's gentlewoman, by the name of Hero: she leans me out at her mistress' chamber-window, bids me a thousand times good night,—I tell this tale vilely:—I should first tell thee how the Prince, Claudio, and my master, planted and placed and possessed [13] by my master Don John, saw afar off in the orchard this amiable encounter.

CONRADE.   And thought they Margaret was Hero?

BORACHIO.   Two of them did, the Prince and Claudio; but the devil my master knew she was Margaret; and partly by his oaths, which first possessed them, partly by the dark night, which did deceive them, but chiefly by my villainy, which did confirm any slander that Don John had made, away went Claudio enraged; swore he would meet her, as he was appointed, next morning at the temple, and there, before the whole congregation, shame her with what he saw o'er night, and send her home again without a husband.

SECOND WATCH.   We charge you, in the Prince's name, stand!

FIRST WATCH.   Call up the right master constable. We have here recovered the most dangerous piece of lechery[14] that ever was known in the commonwealth.

SECOND WATCH.   And one Deformed is one of them. I know him; 'a wears a lock.[15]

CONRADE.   Masters, masters,—

SECOND WATCH.   You'll be made bring Deformed forth, I warrant you.

CONRADE.   Masters,—

FIRST WATCH.   Never speak. We charge you let us obey you to go with us.

---

13. possessed—directed.
14. lechery—i.e., treachery.
15. lock—a curl of hair worn over the ear.

BORACHIO.   We are like to prove a goodly commodity,[16] being taken up[17] of these men's bills.[18]

CONRADE.   A commodity in question,[19] I warrant you. Come, we'll obey you.   *Exeunt.*

16. commodity—goods.
17. taken up—arrested; also, bought on credit.
18. bills—weapons; also, bonds.
19. in question—subject to trial by law.

[A C T   I I I • 4] *Hero's apartment.*

Enter HERO, MARGARET, *and* URSULA.

HERO.   Good Ursula, wake my cousin Beatrice, and desire her to rise.

URSULA.   I will, lady.

HERO.   And bid her come hither.

URSULA.   Well.   *Exit.*

MARGARET.   Troth, I think your other rebato[1] were better.

HERO.   No, pray thee, good Meg, I'll wear this.

MARGARET.   By my troth, 's not so good; and I warrant your cousin will say so.

HERO.   My cousin's a fool, and thou art another: I'll wear none but this.

MARGARET.   I like the new tire[2] within[3] excellently, if the hair were a thought browner; and your gown's a most rare fashion, i' faith. I saw the Duchess of Milan's gown that they praise so.

HERO.   O, that exceeds, they say.

MARGARET.   By my troth, 's but a night-gown[4] in respect of yours: cloth o' gold, and cuts,[5] and laced with silver, set with pearls, down sleeves, side sleeves, and skirts, round underborne[6] with a bluish tinsel; but for a fine, quaint, graceful, and excellent fashion, yours is worth ten on 't.

HERO.   God give me joy to wear it! for my heart is exceeding heavy.

MARGARET.   'T will be heavier soon by the weight of a man.

1 rebato—ruff.   2. tire—headdress.
3. within—in the next room.   4. night-gown—dressing gown.
5. cuts—slashes to reveal undermaterial.   6. underborne—lined.

HERO.   Fie upon thee! art not ashamed?

MARGARET.   Of what, lady? Of speaking honourably? Is not marriage honourable in a beggar? Is not your lord honourable without marriage? I think you would have me say, "saving your reverence, a husband:" an bad thinking do not wrest[7] true speaking, I'll offend nobody: is there any harm in "the heavier for a husband"? None, I think, an it be the right husband and the right wife; otherwise 't is light, and not heavy: ask my Lady Beatrice else; here she comes.

Enter BEATRICE.

HERO.   Good morrow, coz.

BEATRICE.   Good morrow, sweet Hero.

HERO.   Why, how now? Do you speak in the sick tune?

BEATRICE.   I am out of all other tune, methinks.

MARGARET.   Clap's into "Light o' love"; that goes without a burden:[8] do you sing it, and I'll dance it.

BEATRICE.   Ye light o' love with your heels! then, if your husband have stables enough, you'll see he shall lack no barns.[9]

MARGARET.   O illegitimate construction! I scorn that with my heels.

BEATRICE.   'T is almost five o'clock, cousin; 't is time you were ready. By my troth, I am exceeding ill: heigh-ho!

MARGARET.   For a hawk, a horse, or a husband?

BEATRICE.   For the letter that begins them all, H.

MARGARET.   Well, an you be not turned Turk,[10] there's no more sailing by the star.

BEATRICE.   What means the fool, trow?

MARGARET.   Nothing I; but God send every one their heart's desire!

HERO.   These gloves the count sent me; they are an excellent perfume.

BEATRICE.   I am stuffed, cousin; I cannot smell.

MARGARET.   A maid, and stuffed! There's goodly catching of cold.

---

7. wrest—violate.   8. burden—bass part.
9. barns—with a pun on *bairns*.
10. turned Turk—completely changed.

BEATRICE.   O God help me! God help me! How long have you professed apprehension? [11]

MARGARET.   Ever since you left it. Doth not my wit become me rarely?

BEATRICE.   It is not seen enough, you should wear it in your cap. By my troth, I am sick.

MARGARET.   Get you some of this distilled Carduus Benedictus,[12] and lay it to your heart: it is the only thing for a qualm.

HERO.   There thou prick'st her with a thistle.

BEATRICE.   Benedictus! why Benedictus? You have some moral in this Benedictus.

MARGARET.   Moral! [13] no, by my troth, I have no moral meaning; I meant, plain holy-thistle. You may think perchance that I think you are in love: nay, by 'r lady, I am not such a fool to think what I list, nor I list not to think what I can, nor indeed I cannot think, if I would think my heart out of thinking, that you are in love or that you will be in love or that you can be in love. Yet Benedick was such another, and now is he become a man: he swore he would never marry, and yet now, in despite of his heart, he eats his meat without grudging; and how you may be converted I know not, but methinks you look with your eyes as other women do.

BEATRICE.   What pace is this that thy tongue keeps?

MARGARET.   Not a false gallop.

Re-enter URSULA.

URSULA.   Madam, withdraw; the Prince, the Count, Signior Benedick, Don John, and all the gallants of the town, are come to fetch you to church.

HERO.   Help to dress me, good coz, good Meg, good Ursula
Exeunt

---

11. apprehension—wit.
12. Carduus Benedictus—the thistle, a medicinal herb (with a complex pun).
13. Moral—hidden meaning.

[ACT III • 5] *The Hall in Leonato's house.*

Enter LEONATO, *with the Constable* DOGBERRY *and the Head-borough* VERGES.

LEONATO.   What would you with me, honest neighbour?

DOGBERRY.   Marry, sir, I would have some confidence with you that decerns you nearly.

LEONATO.   Brief, I pray you; for you see it is a busy time with me.

DOGBERRY.   Marry, this it is, sir.

VERGES.   Yes, in truth it is, sir.

LEONATO.   What is it, my good friends?

DOGBERRY.   Goodman Verges, sir, speaks a little off the matter; an old man, sir, and his wits are not so blunt as, God help, I would desire they were; but, in faith, honest as the skin between his brows.

VERGES.   Yes, I thank God I am as honest as any man living that is an old man and no honester than I.

DOGBERRY.   Comparisons are odorous[1] Palabras,[2] neighbour Verges.

LEONATO.   Neighbours, you are tedious.

DOGBERRY.   It pleases your worship to say so, but we are the poor Duke's officers; but truly, for mine own part, if I were as tedious as a king, I could find in my heart to bestow it all of your worship.

LEONATO.   All thy tediousness on me, ah?

DOGBERRY.   Yea, an 't were a thousand pound more than 't is; for I hear as good exclamation on your worship as of any man in the city; and though I be but a poor man, I am glad to hear it.

VERGES.   And so am I.

LEONATO.   I would fain know what you have to say.

VERGES.   Marry, sir, our watch to-night, excepting your worship's presence, ha' ta'en a couple of as arrant knaves as any in Messina.

DOGBERRY.   A good old man, sir; he will be talking: as they say, When the age[3] is in, the wit is out. God help us! It is a

---

1. odorous—for *odious*.   2. Palabras—be brief.
3. age—the proverb actually goes, "When the *ale* is in . . ."

world to see. Well said, i' faith, neighbour Verges! Well, God's
a good man; an two men ride of a horse, one must ride behind.
An honest soul, i' faith, sir; by my troth he is, as ever broke
bread; but God is to be worshipped; all men are not alike; alas,
good neighbour!

LEONATO.   Indeed, neighbour, he comes too short of you.

DOGBERRY.   Gifts that God gives.

LEONATO.   I must leave you.

DOGBERRY.   One word, sir: our watch, sir, have indeed comprehended two aspicious persons, and we would have them this
morning examined before your worship.

LEONATO.   Take their examination yourself and bring it me:
I am now in great haste, as it may appear unto you.

DOGBERRY.   It shall be suffigance.

LEONATO.   Drink some wine ere you go: fare you well.

Enter a MESSENGER.

MESSENGER.   My lord, they stay for you to give your
daughter to her husband.

LEONATO.   I'll wait upon them; I am ready.

Exeunt LEONATO *and* MESSENGER.

DOGBERRY.   Go, good partner, go, get you to Francis Seacole; bid him bring his pen and inkhorn to the jail: we are now
to examination these men.

VERGES.   And we must do it wisely.

DOGBERRY.   We will spare for no wit, I warrant you: here's
that shall drive some of them to a non-come; [4] only get the
learned writer to set down our excommunication, and meet me at
the jail.   *Exeunt.*

---

4. non-come—confusion.

[ACT IV · 1] *A church.*

Enter DON PEDRO, DON JOHN, LEONATO, FRIAR FRANCIS,
CLAUDIO, BENEDICK, HERO, BEATRICE *and attendants.*

LEONATO.   Come, Friar Francis, be brief; only to the plain
form of marriage, and you shall recount their particular duties
afterwards.

FRIAR.   You come hither, my lord, to marry this lady?

CLAUDIO.   No.

LEONATO.   To be married to her: friar, you come to marry her.

FRIAR.   Lady, you come hither to be married to this count?

HERO.   I do.

FRIAR.   If either of you know any inward impediment why you should not be conjoined, I charge you, on your souls, to utter it.

CLAUDIO.   Know you any, Hero?

HERO.   None, my lord.

FRIAR.   Know you any, Count?

LEON.   I dare make his answer—none.

CLAUDIO.   O, what men dare to do! What men may do! What men daily do, not knowing what they do!

BENEDICK.   How now! interjections? Why, then, some be of laughing, as, ah, ha, he! [1]

CLAUDIO.   Stand thee by, friar. Father, by your leave.
Will you with free and unconstrained soul
Give me this maid, your daughter?

LEONATO.   As freely, son, as God did give her me.

CLAUDIO.   And what have I to give you back, whose worth
May counterpoise this rich and precious gift?

DON PEDRO.   Nothing, unless you render her again.

CLAUDIO.   Sweet Prince, you learn me noble thankfulness.
There, Leonato, take her back again:
Give not this rotten orange to your friend;
She's but the sign and semblance of her honour.
Behold how like a maid she blushes here!
O, what authority and show of truth
Can cunning sin cover itself withal!
Comes not that blood as modest evidence
To witness simple virtue? Would you not swear,
All you that see her, that she were a maid,
By these exterior shows? But she is none:
She knows the heat of a luxurious[2] bed;
Her blush is guiltiness, not modesty.

1. ah, ha, he—examples of interjections from a grammar book.
2. luxurious—lustful.

LEONATO.   What do you mean, my lord?

CLAUDIO.   Not to be married;
Not to knit my soul to an approved³ wanton.

LEONATO.   Dear my lord, if you, in your own proof,
Have vanquish'd the resistance of her youth,
And made defeat of her virginity,—

CLAUDIO.   I know what you would say: if I have known her,
You will say she did embrace me as a husband,
And so extenuate the 'forehand sin.
No, Leonato.
I never tempted her with word too large;
But, as a brother to his sister, show'd
Bashful sincerity and comely love.

HERO.   And seem'd I ever otherwise to you?

CLAUDIO.   Out on the seeming! I will write against it:
You seem to me as Dian⁴ in her orb,
As chaste as is the bud ere it be blown;
But you are more intemperate in your blood
Than Venus, or those pamper'd animals
That rage in savage sensuality.

HERO.   Is my lord well, that he doth speak so wide? ⁵

LEONATO.   Sweet Prince, why speak not you?

DON PEDRO.   What should I speak?
I stand dishonour'd, that have gone about
To link my dear friend to a common stale.

LEONATO.   Are these things spoken, or do I but dream?

DON JOHN.   Sir, they are spoken, and these things are true.

BENEDICK.   This looks not like a nuptial.

HERO.   True! O God!

CLAUDIO.   Leonato, stand I here?
Is this the Prince? Is this the Prince's brother?
Is this face Hero's? Are our eyes our own?

LEONATO.   All this is so; but what of this, my lord?

CLAUDIO.   Let me but move one question to your daughter;
And, by that fatherly and kindly⁶ power
That you have in her, bid her answer truly.

---

3. approved—proved.
4. Dian(a)—goddess of the moon and of chastity.
5. wide—far from the truth.   6. kindly—natural.

LEONATO.   I charge thee do so, as thou art my child.

HERO.   O, God defend me! how am I beset!
What kind of catechising call you this?

CLAUDIO.   To make you answer truly to your name.

HERO.   Is it not Hero? Who can blot that name
With any just reproach?

CLAUDIO.   Marry, that can Hero;
Hero itself can blot out Hero's virtue.
What man was he talk'd with you yester-night
Out at your window betwixt twelve and one?
Now, if you are a maid, answer to this.

HERO.   I talk'd with no man at that hour, my lord.

DON PEDRO.   Why, then are you no maiden. Leonato,
I am sorry you must hear: upon mine honour,
Myself, my brother, and this grieved count
Did see her, hear her, at that hour last night
Talk with a ruffian at her chamber-window;
Who hath indeed, most like a liberal [7] villain,
Confess'd the vile encounters they have had
A thousand times in secret.

DON JOHN.   Fie, fie! they are not to be named, my lord,
Not to be spoke of;
There is not chastity enough in language
Without offence to utter them. Thus, pretty lady,
I am sorry for thy much misgovernment.

CLAUDIO.   O Hero, what a Hero hadst thou been,
If half thy outward graces had been plac'd
About the thoughts and counsels of thy heart!
But fare thee well, most foul, most fair! Farewell,
Thou pure impiety and impious purity!
For thee I'll lock up all the gates of love,
And on my eyelids shall conjecture[8] hang,
To turn all beauty into thoughts of harm,
And never shall it more be gracious.

LEONATO.   Hath no man's dagger here a point for me?

[HERO swoons.]

BEATRICE.   Why, how now, cousin! wherefore sink you down?

---

7. liberal—licentious.   8. conjecture—suspicion.

DON JOHN.   Come, let us go. These things, come thus to
   light,
Smother her spirits up.
                    Exeunt DON PEDRO, DON JOHN, *and* CLAUDIO.
BENEDICK.   How doth the lady?
BEATRICE.   Dead, I think. Help, uncle!
Hero! why, Hero! Uncle!! Signior Benedick! Friar!
LEONATO.   O Fate take not away thy heavy hand.
Death is the fairest cover for her shame
That may be wish'd for.
BEATRICE.   How now, cousin Hero!
FRIAR.   Have comfort, lady.
LEONATO.   Dost thou look up?
FRIAR.   Yea, wherefore should she not?
LEONATO.   Wherefore! Why, doth not every earthly thing
Cry shame upon her? Could she here deny
The story that is printed in her blood?
Do not live, Hero; do not ope thine eyes;
For, did I think thou wouldst not quickly die,
Thought I thy spirits were stronger than thy shames,
Myself would, on the rearward [9] of reproaches,
Strike at thy life. Grieved I, I had but one?
Chid I for that a frugal nature's frame?
O, one too much by thee! Why had I one?
Why ever wast thou lovely in my eyes?
Why had I not with charitable hand
Took up a beggar's issue at my gates,
Who smirched thus and mir'd with infamy,
I might have said "No part of it is mine.
This shame derives itself from unknown loins"?
But mine, and mine I lov'd, and mine I prais'd,
And mine that I was proud on, mine so much
That I myself was to myself not mine,
Valuing of her,—why, she, O, she is fallen
Into a pit of ink, that the wide sea
Hath drops too few to wash her clean again,
And salt too little which may season give
To her foul-tainted flesh!

9. on the rearward of—after.

BENEDICK   Sir, sir, be patient.
For my part, I am so attir'd in wonder,
I know not what to say.
    BEATRICE.   O, on my soul, my cousin is belied! [10]
    BENEDICK.   Lady, were you her bedfellow last night?
    BEATRICE.   No, truly not; although, until last night,
I have this twelvemonth been her bedfellow.
    LEONATO.   Confirm'd, confirm'd! O, that is stronger made
Which was before barr'd up with ribs of iron!
Would the two princes lie, and Claudio lie,
Who lov'd her so, that, speaking of her foulness,
Wash'd it with tears? Hence from her! Let her die.
    FRIAR.   Hear me a little;
For I have only been silent so long
And given way unto this course of fortune,
By noting of the lady. I have mark'd
A thousand blushing apparitions
To start into her face, a thousand innocent shames
In angel whiteness beat away those blushes;
And in her eye there hath appear'd a fire
To burn the errors that these princes hold
Against her maiden truth. Call me a fool;
Trust not my reading nor my observations,
Which with experimental seal [11] doth warrant[12]
The tenour of my book; trust not my age,
My reverence, calling, nor divinity,
If this sweet lady lie not guiltless here
Under some biting error.
    LEONATO.   Friar, it cannot be.
Thou seest that all the grace that she hath left
Is that she will not add to her damnation
A sin of perjury; she not denies it.
Why seek'st thou then to cover with excuse
That which appears in proper nakedness?
    FRIAR.   Lady, what man is he you are accus'd of? [13]
    HERO.   They know that do accuse me; I know none.
If I know more of any man alive

---

10. belied—slandered.   11. experimental seal—the seal of experience.
12. warrant—confirm.   13. of—with.

Than that which maiden modesty doth warrant,
Let all my sins lack mercy! O my father,
Prove you that any man with me convers'd
At hours unmeet, or that I yesternight
Maintain'd the change of words with any creature,
Refuse me, hate me, torture me to death!

    FRIAR.   There is some strange misprision in the princes.

    BENEDICK.   Two of them have the very bent[14] of honour;
And if their wisdoms be misled in this,
The practice[15] of it lives in John the Bastard,
Whose spirits toil in frame of villainies.

    LEONATO.   I know not. If they speak but truth of her,
These hands shall tear her; if they wrong her honour,
The proudest of them shall well hear of it.
Time hath not yet so dried this blood of mine,
Nor age so eat up my invention,
Nor fortune made such havoc of my means,
Nor my bad life reft me so much of friends,
But they shall find, awak'd in such a kind,
Both strength of limb and policy of mind,
Ability in means and choice of friends,
To quit[16] me of them throughly.

    FRIAR.   Pause awhile.
And let my counsel sway you in this case.
Your daughter here the princes left for dead:
Let her awhile be secretly kept in,
And publish it that she is dead indeed:
Maintain a mourning ostentation
And on your family's old monument
Hang mournful epitaphs, and do all rites
That appertain unto a burial.

    LEONATO.   What shall become of this? What will this do?

    FRIAR.   Marry, this well carried shall on her behalf
Change slander to remorse; that is some good:
But not for that dream I on this strange course,
But on this travail look for greater birth.

---

14. very bent—true disposition.
15. practice—plotting.   16. quit—revenge.

She dying, as it must be so maintain'd,
Upon the instant that she was accus'd,
Shall be lamented, pitied, and excus'd
Of every hearer; for it so falls out
That what we have we prize not to the worth
Whiles we enjoy it, but being lack'd and lost,
Why, then we rack[17] the value; then we find
The virtue that possession would not show us
Whiles it was ours. So will it fare with Claudio.
When he shall hear she died upon his words,
Th' idea of her life shall sweetly creep
Into his study of imagination,[18]
And every lovely organ[19] of her life
Shall come apparell'd in more precious habit,
More moving-delicate and full of life,
Into the eye and prospect of his soul,
Than when she liv'd indeed: then shall he mourn,
If ever love had interest in his liver,[20]
And wish he had not so accused her,
No, though he thought his accusation true.
Let this be so, and doubt not but success
Will fashion the event in better shape
Than I can lay it down in likelihood.
But if all aim but this be levell'd false,[21]
The supposition of the lady's death
Will quench the wonder of her infamy.
And if it sort[22] not well, you may conceal her,
As best befits her wounded reputation,
In some reclusive and religious life,
Out of all eyes, tongues, minds, and injuries.
    BENEDICK. Signior Leonato, let the friar advise you;
And though you know my inwardness and love
Is very much unto the Prince and Claudio,
Yet, by mine honour, I will deal in this
As secretly and justly as your soul
Should with your body.

---

17. rack—exaggerate.   18. study of imagination—contemplation.
19. organ—feature.   20. liver—the supposed seat of the passion of love.
21. be levell'd false—miscarry.   22. sort—turn out.

LEONATO.   Being that I flow in grief,
The smallest twine may lead me.

FRIAR.   'T is well consented; presently away,
For to strange sores strangely they strain the cure.
Come, lady, die to live: this wedding-day
Perhaps is but prolong'd; [23] have patience and endure.

Exeunt all but BENEDICK *and* BEATRICE.

BENEDICK.   Lady Beatrice, have you wept all this while?

BEATRICE.   Yea, and I will weep a while longer.

BENEDICK.   I will not desire that.

BEATRICE.   You have no reason; I do it freely.[24]

BENEDICK.   Surely I do believe your fair cousin is wronged.

BEATRICE.   Ah, how much might the man deserve of me that would right her!

BENEDICK.   Is there any way to show such friendship?

BEATRICE.   A very even[25] way, but no such friend.

BENEDICK.   May a man do it?

BEATRICE.   It is a man's office,[26] but not yours.

BENEDICK.   I do love nothing in the world so well as you— is not that strange?

BEATRICE.   As strange as the thing I know not. It were as possible for me to say I loved nothing so well as you: but believe me not; and yet I lie not: I confess nothing, nor I deny nothing. I am sorry for my cousin.

BENEDICK.   By my sword, Beatrice, thou lovest me.

BEATRICE.   Do not swear, and eat it.

BENEDICK.   I will swear by it that you love me; and I will make him eat it that says I love not you.

BEATRICE.   Will you not eat your word?

BENEDICK.   With no sauce that can be devised to it. I protest I love thee.

BEATRICE.   Why, then, God forgive me!

BENEDICK.   What offence, sweet Beatrice?

BEATRICE.   You have stayed [27] me in a happy hour. I was about to protest I loved you.

BENEDICK.   And do it with all thy heart.

---

23. prolong'd—postponed.   24. freely—of my own choice.
25. even—direct.   26. office—business.
27. stayed—stopped.

BEATRICE.   I love you with so much of my heart that none is left to protest.

BENEDICK.   Come, bid me do any thing for thee.

BEATRICE.   Kill Claudio.

BENEDICK.   Ha! not for the wide world.

BEATRICE.   You kill me to deny it. Farewell.

BENEDICK.   Tarry, sweet Beatrice.

BEATRICE.   I am gone, though I am here: there is no love in you: nay, I pray you, let me go.

BENEDICK.   Beatrice,—

BEATRICE.   In faith, I will go.

BENEDICK.   We'll be friends first.

BEATRICE.   You dare easier be friends with me than fight with mine enemy.

BENEDICK.   Is Claudio thine enemy?

BEATRICE.   Is 'a not approved in the height a villain, that hath slandered, scorned, dishonoured my kinswoman? O that I were a man! What, bear her in hand [28] until they come to take hands; and then, with public accusation, uncovered slander, unmitigated rancour,—O God, that I were a man! I would eat his heart in the market-place.

BENEDICK.   Hear me, Beatrice,—

BEATRICE.   Talk with a man out at a window! A proper saying!

BENEDICK.   Nay, but, Beatrice,—

BEATRICE.   Sweet Hero! She is wronged, she is slandered, she is undone.

BENEDICK.   Beat—

BEATRICE.   Princes and Counties! Surely, a princely testimony, a goodly count, Count Comfect; [29] a sweet gallant, surely! O that I were a man for his sake! or that I had any friend would be a man for my sake! But manhood is melted into curtsies, valour into compliment, and men are only turned into tongue, and trim ones too: he is now as valiant as Hercules that only tells a lie and swears it. I cannot be a man with wishing, therefore I will die a woman with grieving.

BENEDICK.   Tarry, good Beatrice. By this hand, I love thee.

---

28. bear her in hand—delude her.   29. Comfect—Sugarcandy.

BEATRICE.   Use it for my love some other way than swearing
by it.

BENEDICK.   Think you in your soul the Count Claudio hath
wronged Hero?

BEATRICE.   Yea, as sure as I have a thought or a soul.

BENEDICK.   Enough! I am engaged; [30] I will challenge him.
I will kiss your hand, and so I leave you. By this hand, Claudio
shall render me a dear account. As you hear of me, so think of
me. Go, comfort your cousin: I must say she is dead; and so,
farewell.   *Exeunt.*

---

30. engaged—pledged.

[ACT IV • 2] *A prison.*

Enter the Constables DOGBERRY, VERGES, *and* SEXTON[1] *in
gowns,*[2] *and the* WATCHMEN, *with* CONRADE *and* BORACHIO.

DOGBERRY.   Is our whole dissembly appeared?

VERGES.   O, a stool and a cushion for the sexton.

SEXTON.   Which be the malefactors?

DOGBERRY.   Marry, that am I and my partner.

VERGES.   Nay, that's certain; we have the exhibition to
examine.

SEXTON.   But which are the offenders that are to be examined? Let them come before master constable.

DOGBERRY.   Yea, marry, let them come before me. What is
your name, friend?

BORACHIO.   Borachio.

DOGBERRY.   Pray, write down Borachio. Yours, sirrah?

CONRADE.   I am a gentleman, sir, and my name is Conrade.

DOGBERRY.   Write down, master gentleman Conrade. Masters, do you serve God?

CONRADE. ⎫
BORACHIO. ⎭ Yea, sir, we hope.

DOGBERRY.   Write down, that they hope they serve God; and
write God first; for God defend but God should go before such
villains! Masters, it is proved already that you are little better

---

1. sexton—village clerk, one able to write.
2. gowns—the judge's robes.

than false knaves; and it will go near to be thought so shortly. How answer you for yourselves?

CONRADE. Marry, sir, we say we are none.

DOGBERRY. A marvellous witty fellow, I assure you; but I will go about with[3] him. Come you hither, sirrah; a word in your ear, sir. I say to you, it is thought you are false knaves.

BORACHIO. Sir, I say to you we are none.

DOGBERRY. Well, stand aside. 'Fore God, they are both in a tale.[4] Have you writ down, that they are none?

SEXTON. Master constable, you go not the way to examine: you must call forth the watch that are their accusers.

DOGBERRY. Yea, marry, that's the eftest[5] way. Let the watch come forth. Masters, I charge you, in the Prince's name, accuse these men.

FIRST WATCH. This man said, sir, that Don John, the Prince's brother, was a villain.

DOGBERRY. Write down Prince John a villain. Why, this is flat perjury, to call a prince's brother villain.

BORACHIO. Master constable,—

DOGBERRY. Pray thee, fellow, peace: I do not like thy look, I promise thee.

SEXTON. What heard you him say else?

SECOND WATCH. Marry, that he had received a thousand ducats of Don John for accusing the Lady Hero wrongfully.

DOGBERRY. Flat burglary as ever was committed.

VERGES. Yea, by mass, that it is.

SEXTON. What else, fellow?

FIRST WATCH. And that Count Claudio did mean, upon his words, to disgrace Hero before the whole assembly, and not marry her.

DOGBERRY. O villain! thou wilt be condemned into everlasting redemption for this.

SEXTON. What else?

WATCHMEN. This is all.

SEXTON. And this is more, masters, than you can deny. Prince John is this morning secretly stolen away: Hero was in

---

3. go about with—get the better of.
4. are both in a tale—have agreed to tell the same story.
5. eftest—quickest (?).

this manner accused, in this very manner refused, and upon the grief of this suddenly died. Master constable, let these men be bound, and brought to Leonato's: I will go before and show him their examination.   *Exit.*

DOGBERRY.   Come, let them be opinioned.[6]

VERGES.   Let them be in the hands—

CONRADE.   Off, coxcomb! [7]

DOGBERRY.   God's my life, where's the sexton? Let him write down the Prince's officer coxcomb. Come, bind them. Thou naughty varlet!

CONRADE.   Away! you are an ass, you are an ass.

DOGBERRY.   Dost thou not suspect[8] my place? Dost thou not suspect my years? O that he were here to write me down an ass! But, masters, remember that I am an ass; though it be not written down, yet forget not that I am an ass. No, thou villain, thou art full of piety, as shall be proved upon thee by good witness. I am a wise fellow, and, which is more, an officer, and, which is more, a householder, and, which is more, as pretty a piece of flesh as any is in Messina, and one that knows the law, go to; [9] and a rich fellow enough, go to; and a fellow that hath had losses, and one that hath two gowns and every thing handsome about him. Bring him away. O that I had been writ down an ass!   *Exeunt.*

---

6. opinioned—i.e., pinioned.   7. coxcomb—fool.
8. suspect—i.e., respect.   9. go to—an exclamation of impatience.

[ACT V • 1] *Before Leonato's house.*

Enter LEONATO *and his brother* ANTONIO.

ANTONIO.   If you go on thus, you will kill yourself;
And 't is not wisdom thus to second [1] grief
Against yourself.

LEONATO.   I pray thee, cease thy counsel,
Which falls into mine ears as profitless
As water in a sieve: give not me counsel;
Nor let no comforter delight mine ear
But such a one whose wrongs do suit[2] with mine.
Bring me a father that so lov'd his child,

---

1. second—aid.   2. suit—match.

Whose joy of her is overwhelm'd like mine,
And bid him speak of patience;
Measure his woe the length and breadth of mine,
And let it answer every strain for strain,
As thus for thus, and such a grief for such,
In every lineament,[3] branch, shape, and form;
If such a one will smile and stroke his beard,
Bid sorrow wag,[4] cry "hem!" when he should groan,
Patch grief with proverbs, make misfortune drunk
With candle-wasters;[5] bring him yet to me,
And I of him will gather patience.
But there is no such man; for, brother, men
Can counsel and speak comfort to that grief
Which they themselves not feel; but, tasting it,
Their counsel turns to passion, which before
Would give preceptial medicine[6] to rage,
Fetter strong madness in a silken thread,
Charm ache with air and agony with words.
No, no; 't is all men's office to speak patience
To those that wring under the load of sorrow,
But no man's virtue nor sufficiency
To be so moral [7] when he shall endure
The like himself. Therefore give me no counsel;
My griefs cry louder than advértisement.[8]
    ANTONIO.   Therein do men from children nothing differ
    LEONATO.   I pray thee, peace: I will be flesh and blood;
For there was never yet philosopher
That could endure the toothache patiently,
However they have writ the style of gods[9]
And made a push at[10] chance and sufferance.
    ANTONIO.   Yet bend not all the harm upon yourself;
Make those that do offend you suffer too.
    LEONATO.   There thou speak'st reason: nay, I will do so.
My soul doth tell me Hero is belied;

---

3. lineament—feature.   4. wag—run off.
5. candle-wasters—revelers.   6. preceptial medicine—good advice.
7. moral—moralistic.   8. advertisement—good advice.
9. style of gods—in a divine manner.
10. made a push at—pretended to brush aside.

And that shall Claudio know; so shall the Prince
And all of them that thus dishonour her.

Enter DON PEDRO *and* CLAUDIO.

ANTONIO.   Here comes the Prince and Claudio hastily.
DON PEDRO.   Good den, good den.
CLAUDIO.   Good day to both of you
LEONATO.   Hear you, my lords,—
DON PEDRO.   We have some haste, Leonato.
LEONATO.   Some haste, my lord! Well, fare you well, my lord.
Are you so hasty now? Well, all is one.
DON PEDRO.   Nay, do not quarrel with us, good old man.
ANTONIO.   If he could right himself with quarrelling,
Some of us would lie low.
CLAUDIO.   Who wrongs him?
LEONATO.   Marry, thou dost wrong me; thou dissembler,
    thou,—
Nay, never lay thy hand upon thy sword;
I fear thee not.
CLAUDIO.   Marry, beshrew[11] my hand,
If it should give your age such cause of fear.
In faith, my hand meant nothing to my sword.
LEONATO.   Tush, tush, man; never fleer[12] and jest at me.
I speak not like a dotard nor a fool,
As under privilege of age to brag
What I have done being young, or what would do
Were I not old. Know, Claudio, to thy head,
Thou hast so wrong'd mine innocent child and me
That I am forc'd to lay my reverence by
And, with grey hairs and bruise of many days,
Do challenge thee to trial of a man.
I say thou hast belied mine innocent child!
Thy slander hath gone through and through her heart,
And she lies buried with her ancestors,
O, in a tomb where never scandal slept,
Save this of hers, fram'd by thy villainy!
CLAUDIO.   My villainy?

---

11. beshrew—curse.   12. fleer—sneer.

LEONATO.   Thine, Claudio; thine, I say.
DON PEDRO.   You say not right, old man.
LEONATO.   My lord, my lord,
I'll prove it on his body, if he dare,
Despite his nice fence[13] and his active practice,
His May of youth and bloom of lustihood.
CLAUDIO.   Away! I will not have to do with you.
LEONATO.   Canst thou so daff me? Thou hast kill'd my child.
If thou kill'st me, boy, thou shalt kill a man.
ANTONIO.   He shall kill two of us, and men indeed.
But that's no matter; let him kill one first.
Win me and wear me; let him answer me.
Come, follow me, boy; come, sir boy, come, follow me:
Sir boy, I'll whip you from your foining[14] fence;
Nay, as I am a gentleman, I will.
LEONATO.   Brother,—
ANTONIO.   Content yourself. God knows I lov'd my niece;
And she is dead, slander'd to death by villains,
That dare as well answer a man indeed
As I dare take a serpent by the tongue.
Boys, apes, braggarts, Jacks,[15] milksops!
LEONATO.   Brother Antony,—
ANTONIO.   Hold you content. What, man! I know them, yea,
And what they weigh, even to the utmost scruple,[16]—
Scambling,[17] out-facing,[18] fashion-monging boys,
That lie and cog[19] and flout, deprave and slander,
Go anticly and show outward hideousness,
And speak off half a dozen dangerous words,
How they might hurt their enemies, if they durst;
And this is all.
LEONATO.   But, brother Antony,—
ANTONIO.   Come, 't is no matter.
Do not you meddle; let me deal in this.
DON PEDRO.   Gentlemen both, we will not wake your patience.
My heart is sorry for your daughter's death;

---

13. nice fence—technical skill in fencing.
14. foining—thrusting.   15. Jacks—knaves.
16. scruple—most minute weight.   17. scambling—quarreling.
18. out-facing—bragging.   19. cog—cheat.

But, on my honour, she was charg'd with nothing
But what was true and very full of proof.

LEONATO.   My lord, my lord,—

DON PEDRO.   I will not hear you.

LEONATO.   No? Come, brother, away! I will be heard.

ANTONIO.   And shall, or some of us will smart for it.

Exeunt LEONATO *and* ANTONIO.

Enter BENEDICK.

DON PEDRO.   See, see; here comes the man we went to seek.

CLAUDIO.   Now, signior, what news?

BENEDICK.   Good day, my lord.

DON PEDRO.   Welcome, signior: you are almost come to part almost a fray.

CLAUDIO.   We had liked to have had our two noses snapped off with[20] two old men without teeth.

DON PEDRO.   Leonato and his brother. What think'st thou? Had we fought, I doubt we should have been too young for them.

BENEDICK.   In a false quarrel there is no true valour. I came to seek you both.

CLAUDIO.   We have been up and down to seek thee; for we are high-proof[21] melancholy and would fain have it beaten away. Wilt thou use thy wit?

BENEDICK.   It is in my scabbard; shall I draw it?

DON PEDRO.   Dost thou wear thy wit by thy side?

CLAUDIO.   Never any did so, though very many have been beside their wit. I will bid thee draw, as we do the minstrels; draw, to pleasure us.

DON PEDRO.   As I am an honest man, he looks pale. Art thou sick, or angry?

CLAUDIO.   What, courage, man! What though care killed a cat, thou hast mettle enough in thee to kill care.

BENEDICK.   Sir, I shall meet your wit in the career,[22] an you charge it against me. I pray you choose another subject.

CLAUDIO.   Nay, then, give him another staff:[23] this last was broke across.

---

20. with—by.   21. high-proof—very.
22. career—onset, charge at a jousting match.
23. staff—lance.

DON PEDRO.   By this light, he changes more and more. I think he be angry indeed.

CLAUDIO.   If he be, he knows how to turn his girdle.[24]

BENEDICK.   Shall I speak a word in your ear?

CLAUDIO.   God bless[25] me from a challenge!

BENEDICK.   [*Aside to* CLAUDIO.] You are a villain! I jest not. I will make it good how you dare, with what you dare, and when you dare. Do me right, or I will protest your cowardice. You have killed a sweet lady, and her death shall fall heavy on you. Let me hear from you.

CLAUDIO.   Well, I will meet you, so I may have good cheer.[26]

DON PEDRO.   What, a feast, a feast?

CLAUDIO.   I' faith, I thank him. He hath bid me to a calf's head and a capon; the which if I do not carve most curiously, say my knife's naught. Shall I not find a woodcock too?

BENEDICK.   Sir, your wit ambles well; it goes easily.

DON PEDRO.   I'll tell thee how Beatrice praised thy wit the other day. I said, thou hadst a fine wit. "True," said she, "a fine little one." "No," said I, "a great wit." "Right," says she, "a great gross one." "Nay," said I, "a good wit." "Just," said she, "it hurts nobody." "Nay," said I, "the gentleman is wise." "Certain," said she, "a wise gentleman." "Nay," said I, "he hath the tongues." [27] "That I believe," said she, "for he swore a thing to me on Monday night, which he forswore on Tuesday morning. There's a double tongue; there's two tongues." Thus did she, an hour together, trans-shape[28] thy particular virtues; yet at last she concluded with a sigh, thou wast the proper'st man in Italy.

CLAUDIO.   For the which she wept heartily and said she cared not.

DON PEDRO.   Yea, that she did; but yet, for all that, an if she did not hate him deadly, she would love him dearly. The old man's daughter told us all.

CLAUDIO.   All, all; and, moreover, God saw him when he was hid in the garden.

---

24. turn his girdle—make a threatening gesture.   25. bless—preserve.
26. cheer—entertainment (with a double meaning).
27. tongues—foreign languages.
28. trans-shape—deform.

DON PEDRO.   But when shall we set the savage bull's horns on the sensible Benedick's head? [29]

CLAUDIO.   Yea, and text underneath, "Here dwells Benedick the married man"?

BENEDICK.   Fare you well, boy; you know my mind. I will leave you now to your gossip-like[30] humour: you break jests as braggarts do their blades, which, God be thanked, hurt not. My lord, for your many courtesies I thank you: I must discontinue your company. Your brother the bastard is fled from Messina: you have among you killed a sweet and innocent lady. For my Lord Lackbeard there, he and I shall meet; and, till then, peace be with him.   *Exit.*

DON PEDRO.   He is in earnest.

CLAUDIO.   In most profound earnest; and, I'll warrant you, for the love of Beatrice.

DON PEDRO.   And hath challenged thee?

CLAUDIO.   Most sincerely.

DON PEDRO.   What a pretty thing man is when he goes in his doublet and hose and leaves off his wit!

CLAUDIO.   He is then a giant to[31] an ape; but then is an ape a doctor[32] to such a man.[33]

DON PEDRO.   But, soft you, let me be: pluck up, my heart, and be sad. Did he not say, my brother was fled?

Enter Constables, DOGBERRY, VERGES, *and the Watchmen, with* CONRADE *and* BORACHIO.

DOGBERRY.   Come you, sir: if justice cannot tame you, she shall ne'er weigh more reasons in her balance: nay, an you be a cursing hypocrite once, you must be looked to.

DON PEDRO.   How now? Two of my brother's men bound! Borachio one!

CLAUDIO.   Hearken after their offence, my lord.

DON PEDRO.   Officers, what offence have these men done?

DOGBERRY.   Marry, sir, they have committed false report; moreover, they have spoken untruths; secondarily, they are slanders; sixth and lastly, they have belied a lady; thirdly, they

---

29. head—see I.1.   30. gossip-like—old womanish.
31. giant to—larger in size than.   32. a doctor—more learned.
33. man—fool.

have verified unjust things; and, to conclude, they are lying
knaves.

DON PEDRO.   First, I ask thee what they have done; thirdly,
I ask thee what's their offence; sixth and lastly, why they are
committed; and, to conclude, what you lay to their charge.

CLAUDIO.   Rightly reasoned, and in his own division; and,
by my troth, there's one meaning well suited.[34]

DON PEDRO.   Who have you offended, masters, that you are
thus bound [35] to your answer? This learned constable is too
cunning to be understood. What's your offence?

BORACHIO.   Sweet Prince, let me go no farther to mine
answer: do you hear me, and let this Count kill me. I have
deceived even your very eyes: what your wisdoms could not
discover, these shallow fools have brought to light, who in the
night overheard me confessing to this man how Don John your
brother incensed [36] me to slander the Lady Hero, how you were
brought into the orchard and saw me court Margaret in Hero's
garments, how you disgraced her, when you should marry her.
My villainy they have upon record; which I had rather seal with
my death than repeat over to my shame. The lady is dead upon
mine and my master's false accusation; and, briefly, I desire
nothing but the reward of a villain.

DON PEDRO.   Runs not this speech like iron through your
    blood?

CLAUDIO.   I have drunk poison whiles he utter'd it.

DON PEDRO.   But did my brother set thee on to this?

BORACHIO.   Yea, and paid me richly for the practice of it.

DON PEDRO.   He is compos'd and fram'd of treachery,
And fled he is upon this villainy.

CLAUDIO.   Sweet Hero! now thy image doth appear
In the rare semblance that I lov'd it first.

DOGBERRY.   Come, bring away the plaintiffs: [37] by this time
our sexton hath reformed Signior Leonato of the matter; and,
masters, do not forget to specify, when time and place shall
serve, that I am an ass.

VERGES.   Here, here comes master Signior Leonato, and the
sexton too.

---

34. well suited—with several costumes.   35. bound—arraigned.
36. incensed—instigated.   37. plaintiffs—i.e., defendants.

Re-enter LEONATO *and* ANTONIO *with the* SEXTON.

LEONATO.   Which is the villain? Let me see his eyes,
That, when I note another man like him,
I may avoid him. Which of these is he?

BORACHIO.   If you would know your wronger, look on me.

LEONATO.   Art thou the slave that with thy breath has kill'd
Mine innocent child?

BORACHIO.   Yea, even I alone.

LEONATO.   No, not so, villain; thou beliest thyself.
Here stand a pair of honourable men,—
A third is fled—that had a hand in it.
I thank you, princes, for my daughter's death.
Record it with your high and worthy deeds.
'T was bravely done, if you bethink you of it.

CLAUDIO.   I know not how to pray your patience;
Yet I must speak. Choose your revenge yourself;
Impose me to what penance your invention
Can lay upon my sin; yet sinn'd I not
But in mistaking.

DON PEDRO.   By my soul, nor I;
And yet, to satisfy this good old man,
I would bend under any heavy weight
That he'll enjoin me to.

LEONATO.   I cannot bid you bid my daughter live,—
That were impossible—but, I pray you both,
Possess[38] the people in Messina here
How innocent she died; and if your love
Can labour ought in sad invention,[39]
Hang her an epitaph upon her tomb
And sing it to her bones, sing it to-night.
To-morrow morning come you to my house,
And since you could not be my son-in-law,
Be yet my nephew: my brother hath a daughter,
Almost the copy of my child that's dead,
And she alone is heir to both of us.
Give her the right you should have given her cousin,
And so dies my revenge.

---

38. Possess—inform.   39. sad invention—funeral ode.

CLAUDIO.   O noble sir,
Your over-kindness doth wring tears from me!
I do embrace your offer; and dispose
For henceforth of poor Claudio.

LEONATO.   To-morrow then I will expect[40] your coming;
To-night I take my leave. This naughty man
Shall face to face be brought to Margaret,
Who I believe was pack'd [41] in all this wrong,
Hir'd to it by your brother.

BORACHIO.   No, by my soul, she was not,
Nor knew not what she did when she spoke to me,
But always hath been just and virtuous
In any thing that I do know by her.

DOGBERRY.   Moreover, sir, which indeed is not under white
and black,[42] this plaintiff here, the offender, did call me ass: I
beseech you, let it be remembered in his punishment. And also,
the watch heard them talk of one Deformed: they say he wears
a key in his ear and a lock hanging by it, and borrows money
in God's name, the which he hath used so long and never paid
that now men grow hard-hearted and will lend nothing for
God's sake: pray you, examine him upon that point.

LEONATO.   I thank thee for thy care and honest pains.

DOGBERRY.   Your worship speaks like a most thankful and
reverend youth, and I praise God for you.

LEONATO.   There's for thy pains.

DOGBERRY.   God save the foundation! [43]

LEONATO.   Go, I discharge thee of thy prisoner, and I thank
thee.

DOGBERRY.   I leave an arrant knave with your worship;
which I beseech your worship to correct yourself, for the example of others. God keep your worship! I wish your worship
well. God restore you to health! I humbly give you leave to
depart; and if a merry meeting may be wished, God prohibit[44]
it! Come neighbour.   *Exeunt* DOGBERRY *and* VERGES.

LEONATO.   Until to-morrow morning, lords, farewell.

ANTONIO.   Farewell, my lords: we look for you to-morrow.

---

40. expect—await.   41. pack'd—involved.
42. white and black—written down.
43. God save the foundation—thank you.   44. prohibit—i.e., grant.

DON PEDRO.   We will not fail.

CLAUDIO.   To-night I'll mourn with Hero.

LEONATO.   [*To the Watchmen.*] Bring you these fellows on.
We'll talk with Margaret,

How her acquaintance grew with this lewd [45] fellow.   *Exeunt.*

45. lewd—evil.

[ACT V · 2] *Leonato's garden.*

Enter BENEDICK *and* MARGARET.

BENEDICK.   Pray thee, sweet Mistress Margaret, deserve well
at my hands by helping me to the speech of Beatrice.

MARGARET.   Will you then write me a sonnet in praise of my
beauty?

BENEDICK.   In so high a style, Margaret, that no man living
shall come over[1] it; for, in most comely truth, thou deservest it.

MARGARET.   To have no man come over me! Why, shall I
always keep below stairs?

BENEDICK.   Thy wit is as quick as the greyhound's mouth; it
catches.

MARGARET.   And yours as blunt as the fencer's foils, which
hit, but hurt not.

BENEDICK.   A most manly wit, Margaret; it will not hurt a
woman: and so, I pray thee, call Beatrice; I give thee the
bucklers.[2]

MARGARET.   Give us the swords; we have bucklers of our
own.

BENEDICK.   If you use them, Margaret, you must put in the
pikes[3] with a vice; [4] and they are dangerous weapons for maids.

MARGARET.   Well, I will call Beatrice to you, who I think
hath legs.   *Exit* MARGARET.

BENEDICK.   And therefore will come.

Sings.   The god of love,
                        That sits above,
                 And knows me, and knows me,
                   How pitiful I deserve,—

1. come over—better.
2. give thee the bucklers—yield the victory to you.
3. pikes—spikes.   4. vice.—screw.

I mean in singing; but in loving, Leander[5] the good swimmer, Troilus the first employer of panders, and a whole bookful of these quondam carpet-mongers,[6] whose names yet run smoothly in the even road of a blank verse, why, they were never so truly turned over and over as my poor self in love. Marry, I cannot show it in rhyme: I have tried: I can find out no rhyme to "lady" but "baby," an innocent rhyme; for "scorn," "horn," a hard rhyme; for "school," "fool," a babbling rhyme, very ominous endings: no, I was not born under a rhyming planet, nor I cannot woo in festival terms.

Enter BEATRICE.

Sweet Beatrice, wouldst thou come when I called thee?

BEATRICE.   Yea, signior, and depart when you bid me.

BENEDICK.   O, stay but till then!

BEATRICE.   "Then" is spoken; fare you well now: and yet, ere I go, let me go with that I came for; which is, with knowing what hath passed between you and Claudio.

BENEDICK.   Only foul words; and thereupon I will kiss thee.

BEATRICE.   Foul words is but foul wind, and foul wind is but foul breath, and foul breath is noisome; therefore I will depart unkissed.

BENEDICK.   Thou hath frighted the word out of his right sense,[7] so forcible is they wit. But I must tell thee plainly, Claudio undergoes my challenge; and either I must shortly hear from him, or I will subscribe[8] him a coward. And, I pray thee now, tell me for which of my bad parts didst thou first fall in love with me?

BEATRICE.   For them all together, which maintained so politic a state of evil that they will not admit any good part to intermingle with them. But for which of my good parts did you first suffer love for me?

BENEDICK.   Suffer love! a good epithet! I do suffer love indeed, for I love thee against my will.

BEATRICE.   In spite of your heart, I think; alas, poor heart! If you spite it for my sake, I will spite it for yours; for I will never love that which my friend hates.

---

5. Leander—i.e., a famous lover, like Troilus.
6. carpet-mongers—who have not fought on the battlefield.
7. sense—meaning.   8. subscribe—proclaim.

BENEDICK.   Thou and I are too wise to woo peaceably.

BEATRICE.   It appears not in this confession: there's not one wise man among twenty that will praise himself.

BENEDICK.   An old, an old instance, Beatrice, that lived in the time of good neighbours.[9] If a man do not erect in this age his own tomb ere he dies, he shall live no longer in monument[10] than the bell rings and the widow weeps.

BEATRICE.   And how long is that, think you?

BENEDICK.   Question! Why, an hour in clamour and a quarter in rheum; [11] therefore is it most expedient for the wise, if Don Worm, his conscience, find no impediment to the contrary, to be the trumpet of his own virtues, as I am to myself. So much for praising myself, who, I myself will bear witness, is praise-worthy. And now tell me, how doth your cousin?

BEATRICE.   Very ill.

BENEDICK.   And how do you?

BEATRICE.   Very ill too.

BENEDICK.   Serve God, love me, and mend. There will I leave you too, for here comes one in haste.

Enter URSULA.

URSULA.   Madam, you must come to your uncle. Yonder's old coil [12] at home: it is proved my Lady Hero hath been falsely accused, the Prince and Claudio mightily abused; and Don John is the author of all, who is fled and gone. Will you come presently? [13]

BEATRICE.   Will you go hear this news, signior?

BENEDICK.   I will live in thy heart, die in thy lap, and be buried in thy eyes; and moreover I will go with thee to thy uncle's.   *Exeunt.*

---

9. in the time of good neighbors—in the past, when neighbors were friendly.   10. monument—memory.
11. rheum—tears.   12. coil—turmoil.   13. presently—at once.

[ACT V • 3] *A church-yard.*

Enter DON PEDRO, CLAUDIO, *and three or four with tapers.*

CLAUDIO.   Is this the monument of Leonato?

A LORD.   It is, my lord.

CLAUDIO.   [*Reading out of a scroll.*]

Epitaph

Done to death by slanderous tongues
 Was the Hero that here lies.
Death, in guerdon[1] of her wrongs,
 Gives her fame which never dies.
So the life that died with shame
Lives in death with glorious fame.

Hang thou there upon the tomb,   [*Hanging up the scroll.*]
Praising her when I am dumb.
Now, music, sound, and sing your solemn hymn.

Song

Pardon, goddess of the night,
Those that slew thy virgin knight;
For the which, with songs of woe,
Round about her tomb they go.
 Midnight, assist our moan;
 Help us to sigh and groan,
  Heavily, heavily.
 Graves, yawn and yield your dead,
 Till death be uttered,[2]
  Heavily, heavily.

CLAUDIO.   Now unto thy bones good night!
    Yearly will I do this rite.
DON PEDRO.   Good morrow, masters; put your torches out.
The wolves have prey'd; and look, the gentle day,
Before the wheels of Phoebus,[3] round about
Dapples the drowsy east with spots of grey.
Thanks to you all, and leave us: fare you well.
CLAUDIO.   Good morrow, masters: each his several way.
DON PEDRO.   Come, let us hence, and put on other weeds;[4]
And then to Leonato's we will go.
CLAUDIO.   And Hymen[5] now with luckier issue speeds
Than this for whom we render'd up this woe.

Exeunt.

---

1. guerdon—reward.   2. uttered—cast out.
3. wheels of Phoebus—wheels of the chariot of the sun god.
4. weeds—clothes.   5. Hymen—god of marriage.

[ACT V · 4] *A room in Leonato's house.*

Enter LEONATO, ANTONIO, BENEDICK, BEATRICE, MARGARET,
URSULA, FRIAR FRANCIS, *and* HERO.

FRIAR. Did I not tell you she was innocent?

LEONATO. So are the Prince and Claudio, who accus'd her.
Upon the error that you heard debated:
But Margaret was in some fault for this,
Although against her will, as it appears
In the true course of all the question.[1]

ANTONIO. Well, I am glad that all things sorts[2] so well.

BENEDICK. And so am I, being else by faith[3] enforc'd
To call young Claudio to a reckoning for it.

LEONATO. Well, daughter, and you gentlewomen all,
Withdraw into a chamber by yourselves,
And when I send for you, come hither mask'd.
The Prince and Claudio promis'd by this hour
To visit me. You know your office, brother:
You must be father to your brother's daughter,
And give her to young Claudio. *Exeunt Ladies.*

ANTONIO. Which I will do with confirm'd countenance.[4]

BENEDICK. Friar, I must entreat your pains, I think.

FRIAR. To do what, signior?

BENEDICK. To bind me, or undo me; one of them.
Signior Leonato, truth it is, good signior,
Your niece regards me with an eye of favour.

LEONATO. That eye my daughter lent her; 't is most true.

BENEDICK. And I do with an eye of love requite her.

LEONATO. The sight whereof I think you had from me,
From Claudio, and the Prince. But what's your will?

BENEDICK. Your answer, sir, is enigmatical;
But, for my will, my will is your good will
May stand with ours, this day to be conjoin'd
In the state of honourable marriage;
In which, good friar, I shall desire your help.

LEONATO. My heart is with your liking.

---

1. question—investigation.   2. sorts—turn out.
3. faith—a vow.   4. confirm'd countenance—straight face.

FRIAR. And my help.
Here comes the Prince and Claudio.

Enter DON PEDRO *and* CLAUDIO, *and two or three others.*

DON PEDRO. Good morrow to this fair assembly.
LEONATO. Good morrow, Prince; good morrow Claudio;
We here attend you. Are you yet determin'd
To-day to marry with my brother's daughter?
CLAUDIO. I'll hold my mind,[5] were she an Ethiope.[6]
LEONATO. Call her forth, brother; here's the friar ready.

Exit ANTONIO.

DON PEDRO. Good morrow, Benedick. Why, what's the matter,
That you have such a February face,
So full of frost, of storm and cloudiness?
CLAUDIO. I think he thinks upon the savage bull.
Tush, fear not, man; we'll tip thy horns with gold
And all Europa shall rejoice at thee,
As once Europa[7] did at lusty Jove,
When he would play the noble beast in love.
BENEDICK. Bull Jove, sir, had an amiable low;
And some such strange bull leap'd your father's cow,
And got a calf in that same noble feat
Much like to you, for you have just his bleat.

Re-enter ANTONIO, *with the Ladies masked.*

CLAUDIO. For this I owe you: [8] here comes other reck'nings.
Which is the lady I must seize upon?
ANTONIO. The same is she, and I do give you her.
CLAUDIO. Why, then she's mine. Sweet, let me see your face.
LEONATO. No, that you shall not, till you take her hand
Before this friar and swear to marry her.
CLAUDIO. Give me your hand: before this holy friar:
I am your husband, if you like of me.
HERO. And when I liv'd, I was your other wife;

[*Unmasking.*]

---

5. mind—purpose.   6. Ethiope—Ethiopian.
7. Europa—a maiden abducted by Jove disguised as a bull.
8. I owe you—I will pay you back.

And when you lov'd, you were my other husband.

CLAUDIO.   Another Hero!

HERO.   Nothing certainer.

One Hero died defil'd, but I do live;

And surely as I live, I am a maid.

DON PEDRO.   The former Hero! Hero that is dead!

LEONATO.   She died, my lord, but whiles[9] her slander liv'd.

FRIAR.   All this amazement can I qualify;

When after that the holy rites are ended,

I'll tell you largely[10] of fair Hero's death.

Meantime let wonder seem familiar,[11]

And to the chapel let us presently.

BENEDICK.   Soft and fair, friar. Which is Beatrice?

BEATRICE.   [*Unmasking.*] I answer to that name. What is
your will?

BENEDICK.   Do not you love me?

BEATRICE.   Why, no; no more than reason.

BENEDICK.   Why, then your uncle and the Prince and Claudio

Have been deceived. They swore you did.

BEATRICE.   Do not you love me?

BENEDICK.   Troth, no; no more than reason.

BEATRICE.   Why, then my cousin, Margaret and Ursula

Are much deceiv'd, for they did swear you did.

BENEDICK.   They swore that you were almost sick for me.

BEATRICE.   They swore that you were well-nigh dead for me.

BENEDICK.   'T is no such matter. Then you do not love me?

BEATRICE.   No truly, but in friendly recompense.

LEONATO.   Come, cousin, I am sure you love the gentleman.

CLAUDIO.   And I'll be sworn upon 't that he loves her;

For here's a paper written in his hand,

A halting[12] sonnet of his own pure brain,

Fashion'd to Beatrice.

HERO.   And here's another

Writ in my cousin's hand, stol'n from her pocket,

Containing her affection unto Benedick.

BENEDICK.   A miracle! here's our own hands against our

---

9. but whiles—only while.   10. largely—in detail.
11. familiar—a normal occurrence.   12. halting—limping,

hearts. Come, I will have thee; but, by this light, I take thee for
pity.

BEATRICE. I would not deny you; but, by this good day, I
yield upon great persuasion; and partly to save your life, for I
was told you were in a consumption.

BENEDICK. Peace! I will stop your mouth. [*Kissing her.*]

DON PEDRO. How dost thou, Benedick, the married man?

BENEDICK. I'll tell thee what, Prince; a college of wit-
crackers cannot flout me out of my humour. Dost thou think I
care for a satire or an epigram? No; if a man will be beaten with
brains,[13] 'a shall wear nothing handsome about him. In brief,
since I do purpose to marry, I will think nothing to any purpose
that the world can say against it; and therefore never flout at me
for what I have said against it, for man is a giddy thing, and this
is my conclusion. For thy part, Claudio, I did think to have
beaten thee; but in that thou art like to be my kinsman, live
unbruised and love my cousin.

CLAUDIO. I had well hoped thou wouldst have denied Beatrice, that I might have cudgelled thee out of thy single life, to
make thee a double-dealer;[14] which, out of question, thou wilt
be, if my cousin do not look exceeding narrowly to thee.

BENEDICK. Come, come, we are friends: let's have a dance
ere we are married, that we may lighten our own hearts and our
wives' heels.

LEONATO. We'll have dancing afterward.

BENEDICK. First, of my word; therefore play, music. Prince,
thou art sad; get thee a wife, get thee a wife: there is no staff
more reverend than one tipped with horn.

Enter a MESSENGER.

MESSENGER. My lord, your brother John is ta'en in flight,
And brought with armed men back to Messina.

BENEDICK. Think not on him till to-morrow: I'll devise thee
brave punishments for him. Strike up, pipers. *Dance. Exeunt.*

---

13. beaten with brains—satirized.
14. double-dealer—married man; also, faithless husband.

The Tragedy of
HAMLET, PRINCE OF DENMARK

CHARACTERS

CLAUDIUS, *King of Denmark.*

HAMLET, *son to the late, and nephew to the present King.*

POLONIUS, *Lord Chamberlain.*

HORATIO, *friend to* HAMLET.

LAERTES, *son to* POLONIUS.

VOLTIMAND,
CORNELIUS, } *councilors.*

ROSENCRANTZ,
GUILDENSTERN,
OSRIC,
A GENTLEMAN, } *courtiers.*

MARCELLUS,
BERNARDO, } *officers.*

FRANCISCO, *a soldier.*

REYNALDO, *servant to* POLONIUS.

A PRIEST.

PLAYERS.

TWO CLOWNS, *grave-diggers.*

FORTINBRAS, *Prince of Norway.*

A CAPTAIN.

ENGLISH AMBASSADORS.

GERTRUDE, *Queen of Denmark, and mother to* HAMLET.

OPHELIA, *daughter to* POLONIUS.

GHOST OF HAMLET'S *Father.*

Lords, Ladies, Officers, Soldiers, Sailors, Messengers, and other Attendants.

SCENE: *Elsinore, Denmark.*

[ACT I · 1] *Elsinore. A platform*[1] *before the castle.*

FRANCISCO *on guard at his post. Enter to him* BERNARDO.

BERNARDO.   Who's there?

FRANCISCO.   Nay, answer me. Stand, and unfold [2] yourself.

1. platform—a paved terrace for mounting cannon.
2. unfold—identify.

BERNARDO.   Long live the king!

FRANCISCO.   Bernardo?

BERNARDO.   He.

FRANCISCO.   You come most carefully upon your hour.

BERNARDO.   'T is now struck twelve: get thee to bed, Francisco.

FRANCISCO.   For this relief much thanks; 't is bitter cold,
And I am sick at heart.

BERNARDO.   Have you had quiet guard?

FRANCISCO.   Not a mouse stirring.

BERNARDO.   Well, good-night.
If you do meet Horatio and Marcellus,
The rivals[3] of my watch, bid them make haste.

Enter HORATIO *and* MARCELLUS.

ꜰRANCISCO.   I think I hear them. Stand, ho! Who is there?

HORATIO.   Friends to this ground.

MARCELLUS.   And liegemen to the Dane.[4]

FRANCISCO.   Give you good-night.

MARCELLUS.   O, farewell, honest soldier:
Who hath reliev'd you?

FRANCISCO.   Bernardo has my place.
Give you good-night.   *Exit.*

MARCELLUS.   Holla! Bernardo!

BERNARDO.   Say,
What, is Horatio there?

HORATIO.   A piece of him.

BERNARDO.   Welcome, Horatio; welcome, good Marcellus.

HORATIO.   What, has this thing appear'd again to-night?

BERNARDO.   I have seen nothing.

MARCELLUS.   Horatio says 't is but our fantasy,[5]
And will not let belief take hold of him
Touching this dreaded sight twice seen of us;
Therefore I have entreated him along
With us to watch the minutes of this night,
That if again this apparition come,

---

3. rivals—partners.   4. the Dane—the Danish king.
5. fantasy—imagination.

He may approve[6] our eyes and speak to it.

HORATIO.   Tush, tush, 't will not appear.

BERNARDO.   Sit down a while,
And let us once again assail your ears,
That are so fortified against our story,
What we have two nights seen.

HORATIO.   Well, sit we down,
And let us hear Bernardo speak of this.

BERNARDO.   Last night of all,
When yond same star that's westward from the pole
Had made his course t' illume that part of heaven
Where now it burns, Marcellus and myself,
The bell then beating one,—

Enter the GHOST.

MARCELLUS.   Peace, break thee off! Look, where it comes
   again!

BERNARDO.   In the same figure, like the King that's dead.

MARCELLUS.   Thou art a scholar; [7] speak to it, Horatio.

BERNARDO.   Looks it not like the King? Mark it, Horatio.

HORATIO.   Most like; it harrows me with fear and wonder.

BERNARDO.   It would be spoke to.

MARCELLUS.   Question it, Horatio.

HORATIO.   What art thou that usurp'st this time of night,
Together with that fair and warlike form
In which the majesty of buried Denmark[8]
Did sometimes march? By heaven I charge thee, speak!

MARCELLUS.   It is offended.

BERNARDO.   See, it stalks away!

HORATIO.   Stay! Speak, speak! I charge thee, speak!

Exit GHOST.

MARCELLUS.   'T is gone, and will not answer.

BERNARDO.   How now, Horatio? you tremble and look pale;
Is not this something more than fantasy?
What think you on 't?

---

6. approve—prove (the trustworthiness of).
7. scholar—i.e., only a learned man would understand the proper way
to address spirits.
8. buried Denmark—the late king, Hamlet's father.

HORATIO.   Before my God, I might not this believe
Without the sensible[9] and true avouch
Of mine own eyes.
    MARCELLUS.   Is it not like the King?
    HORATIO.   As thou art to thyself.
Such was the very armour he had on
When he the ambitious Norway[10] combated;
So frown'd he once, when, in an angry parle,[11]
He smote[12] the sledded Polacks[13] on the ice.
'T is strange.
    MARCELLUS.   Thus twice before, and jump[14] at this dead
      hour,
With martial stalk hath he gone by our watch.
    HORATIO.   In what particular thought to work I know not;
But, in the gross and scope[15] of my opinion,
This bodes some strange eruption to our state.
    MARCELLUS.   Good [16] now, sit down, and tell me, he that
      knows,
Why this same strict and most observant watch
So nightly toils[17] the subject[18] of the land,
And why such daily cast of brazen cannon,
And foreign mart for implements of war;
Why such impress[19] of shipwrights, whose sore task
Does not divide the Sunday from the week;
What might be toward, that this sweaty haste
Doth make the night joint-labourer with the day,
Who is 't that can inform me?
    HORATIO.   That can I;
At least, the whisper goes so. Our last king,
Whose image even but now appear'd to us,
Was, as you know, by Fortinbras of Norway,
Thereto prick'd on by a most emulate[20] pride,

---

9. sensible—perceived by the senses.
10. Norway—the late king of Norway, Fortinbras' father.
11. parle—conference.   12. smote—routed.
13. sledded Polacks—Polanders, riding in sledges.
14. jump—exactly.
15. gross and scope—main conclusion.   16. Good—good friend.
17. toils—causes to work.   18. subject—people.
19. impress—forced labor.   20. emulate—envious.

Dar'd to the combat; in which our valiant Hamlet—
For so this side of our known world esteem'd him—
Did slay this Fortinbras; who, by a seal'd compáct,
Well ratified by law and heraldry,
Did forfeit, with his life, all those his lands
Which he stood seiz'd [21] of, to the conqueror;
Against the which, a moiety competent[22]
Was gaged [23] by our king; which had return'd
To the inheritance of Fortinbras,
Had he been vanquisher; as, by the same comart,[24]
And carriage[25] of the article design'd,
His fell to Hamlet. Now, sir, young Fortinbras,
Of unimproved mettle[26] hot and full,
Hath in the skirts of Norway here and there
Shark'd up a list of lawless resolutes,[27]
For food and diet, to some enterprise
That hath a stomach in 't; which is no other
As it doth well appear unto our state,
But to recover of us, by strong hand
And terms compulsatory, those foresaid lands
So by his father lost; and this, I take it,
Is the main motive of our preparations,
The source of this our watch, and the chief head
Of this post-haste and romage[28] in the land.

   BERNARDO.   I think it be no other but e'en so;
Well may it sort[29] that this portentous figure
Comes armed through our watch, so like the King
That was and is the question of these wars.

   HORATIO.   A mote it is to trouble the mind's eye.
In the most high and palmy state of Rome,
A little ere the mightiest Julius fell,
The graves stood tenantless and the sheeted dead
Did squeak and gibber in the Roman streets.
As[30] stars with trains of fire and dews of blood,

---

21. seiz'd—possessed.   22. moiety competent—adequate portion.
23. gaged—pledged.   24. comart—agreement.
25. carriage—fulfillment.   26. unimproved mettle—untried spirit.
27. resolutes—desperadoes.   28. romage—bustle.
29. sort—fit.   30. As—and so; also, there were.

Disasters in the sun; and the moist star[31]
Upon whose influence Neptune's empire[32] stands
Was sick almost to doomsday with eclipse:
And even the like precurse[33] of fear'd events,
As harbingers[34] preceding still the fates
And prologue to the omen coming on,
Have heaven and earth together demonstrated
Unto our climature[35] and countrymen.

Re-enter GHOST.

But soft, behold! Lo, where it comes again!
I'll cross it, though it blast me. Stay, illusion!
If thou hast any sound, or use of voice,
Speak to me;   [GHOST *spreads his arms.*]
If there be any good thing to be done
That may to thee do ease and grace to me,
Speak to me;
If thou art privy to thy country's fate,
Which, happily, foreknowing may avoid,
O speak!
Or if thou hast uphoarded in thy life
Extorted treasure in the womb of earth,
For which, they say, you spirits oft walk in death,
Speak of it; stay, and speak!   [*The cock crows.*]
                              Stop it, Marcellus.
 MARCELLUS.   Shall I strike at it with my partisan? [36]
 HORATIO.   Do, if it will not stand.
 BERNARDO.   'T is here!
 HORATIO.   'T is here!
                              Exit GHOST.

 MARCELLUS.   'T is gone!
We do it wrong, being so majestical,
To offer it the show of violence;
For it is as the air, invulnerable,
And our vain blows malicious mockery.

---

31. moist star—the moon. 32. Neptune's empire—the ocean.
33. precurse—warning. 34. harbingers—forerunners.
35. climature—country.
36. partisan—spear.

BERNARDO.   It was about to speak, when the cock crew.

HORATIO.   And then it started like a guilty thing
Upon a fearful summons. I have heard,
The cock, that is the trumpet to the morn,
Doth with his lofty and shrill-sounding throat
Awake the god of day; and, at his warning,
Whether in sea or fire, in earth or air,
Th' extravagant and erring[37] spirit hies
To his confine; and of the truth herein
This present object made probation.[38]

MARCELLUS.   It faded on the crowing of the cock.
Some say that ever 'gainst[39] that season comes
Wherein our Saviour's birth is celebrated,
This bird of dawning singeth all night long;
And then, they say, no spirit dare stir abroad;
The nights are wholesome; then no planets strike,[40]
No fairy takes,[41] nor witch hath power to charm,
So hallow'd and so gracious is that time.

HORATIO.   So have I heard and do in part believe it.
But, look, the morn, in russet mantle clad,
Walks o'er the dew of yon high eastward hill:
Break we our watch up; and, by my advice,
Let us impart what we have seen to-night
Unto young Hamlet; for, upon my life,
This spirit, dumb to us, will speak to him.
Do you consent we shall acquaint him with it,
As needful in our loves, fitting our duty?

MARCELLUS.   Let's do 't, I pray; and I this morning know
Where we shall find him most conveniently.   *Exeunt.*

---

37. extravagant and erring—vagrant and wandering.
38. probation—proof.
39. 'gainst—before.
40. planets strike—planets cause disaster.
41. takes—bewitches.

[ACT I • 2] *A room of state in the castle.*

Flourish.[1] *Enter* CLAUDIUS, *King of Denmark*, GERTRUDE, *the Queen*, COUNCILLORS (VOLTIMAND *and* CORNELIUS), POLONIUS, *and his son* LAERTES, HAMLET, ATTENDANT LORDS.

KING.   Though yet of Hamlet our dear brother's death
The memory be green, and that it us befitted
To bear our hearts in grief, and our whole kingdom
To be contracted in one brow of woe,
Yet so far hath discretion fought with nature
That we with wisest sorrow think on him
Together with remembrance of ourselves:
Therefore our sometime sister, now our queen,
Th' imperial jointress[2] to this warlike state,
Have we, as 't were with a defeated joy,—
With an auspicious and a dropping eye,
With mirth[3] in funeral and with dirge in marriage,
In equal scale weighing delight and dole,—
Taken to wife; nor have we herein barr'd
Your better wisdoms, which have freely gone
With this affair along. For all, our thanks.
Now follows that you know: young Fortinbras,
Holding a weak supposal of our worth,
Or thinking by our late dear brother's death
Our state to be disjoint and out of frame,
Colleagued [4] with this dream of his advantage,[5]
He hath not fail'd to pester us with message
Importing the surrender of those lands
Lost by his father, with all bonds of law,
To our most valiant brother. So much for him.
Now for ourself and for this time of meeting,
Thus much the business is: we have here writ
To Norway, uncle of young Fortinbras,—
Who, impotent and bed-rid, scarcely hears
Of this his nephew's purpose,—to suppress
His further gait[6] herein, in that the levies,

---

1. Flourish—trumpet fanfare.   2. jointress—joint ruler.
3. mirth—cheerfulness.   4. colleagued—joined.
5. advantage—opportunity.   6. gait—progress.

The lists and full proportions,[7] are all made
Out of his subject; and we here dispatch
You, good Cornelius, and you, Voltimand,
For bearing of this greeting to old Norway;
Giving to you no further personal power
To business with the king, more than the scope
Of these dilated [8] articles allow.   [*Giving a paper.*]
Farewell, and let your haste commend [9] your duty.

CORNELIUS. ⎱
VOLTIMAND. ⎰ In that and all things will we show our duty.

   KING.   We doubt it nothing; heartily farewell.

                   Exeunt VOLTIMAND *and* CORNELIUS.

And now, Laertes, what's the news with you?
You told us of some suit; what is 't, Laertes?
You cannot speak of reason to the Dane,
And lose[10] your voice: what wouldst thou beg, Laertes,
That shall not be my offer, not thy asking?
The head is not more native[11] to the heart,
The hand more instrumental to the mouth,
Than is the throne of Denmark to thy father.
What wouldst thou have, Laertes?

   LAERTES.   My dread lord,
Your leave and favour to return to France;
From whence though willingly I came to Denmark
To show my duty in your coronation,
Yet now, I must confess, that duty done,
My thoughts and wishes bend again towards France
And bow them to your gracious leave and pardon.

   KING.   Have you your father's leave? What says Polonius?

   POLONIUS.   He hath, my lord, wrung from me my slow leave
By laboursome petition, and at last
Upon his will I seal'd my hard [12] consent:
I do beseech you, give him leave to go.

   KING.   Take thy fair hour, Laertes: time be thine,

---

7. proportions—provisions.   8. dilated—detailed.
9. commend—express.
10. lose—waste.
11. more native—more closely related.
12. seal'd my hard—granted my reluctant.

And thy best graces spend it at thy will!
But now, my cousin[13] Hamlet, and my son,—

HAMLET. [*Aside.*]   A little more than kin, and less than kind.[14]

KING.   How is it that the clouds still hang on you?

HAMLET.   Not so, my lord; I am too much in the sun.

QUEEN.   Good Hamlet, cast thy nighted colour off,
And let thine eye look like a friend on Denmark;
Do not for ever with thy vailed [15] lids
Seek for thy noble father in the dust;
Thou know'st 't is common; [16] all that lives must die,
Passing through nature to eternity.

HAMLET.   Ay, madam, it is common.

QUEEN.   If it be,
Why seems it so particular with thee?

HAMLET.   Seems, madam! Nay, it is; I know not "seems."
'T is not alone my inky cloak, good mother,
Nor customary suits of solemn black,
Nor windy suspiration of forc'd breath,
No, nor the fruitful river in the eye,
Nor the dejected haviour of the visage,
Together with all forms, moods, shapes of grief,
That can denote me truly. These indeed seem,
For they are actions that a man might play; [17]
But I have that within which passeth show,
These but the trappings and the suits of woe.

KING.   'T is sweet and cómmendable in your nature, Hamlet,
To give these mourning duties to your father:
But you must know, your father lost a father,
That father lost, lost his; and the survivor bound
In filial obligation for some term
To do obsequious sorrow; but to perséver
In obstinate condolement[18] is a course
Of impious stubbornness; 't is unmanly grief;
It shows a will most incorrect to heaven,
A heart unfortified, a mind impatient,

---

13. cousin—kinsman, used loosely of any relationship.
14. kind—son; also, natural affection.   15. vailed—downcast.
16. common—universal.   17. play—enact.   18. condolement—grief.

An understanding simple and unschool'd;
For what we know must be, and is as common
As any the most vulgar[19] thing to sense,
Why should we in our peevish opposition
Take it to heart? Fie! 't is a fault to heaven,
A fault against the dead, a fault to nature,
To reason most absurd, whose common theme
Is death of fathers, and who still hath cried,
From the first corse[20] till he that died to-day,
"This must be so." We pray you, throw to earth
This unprevailing[21] woe, and think of us
As of a father; for, let the world take note,
You are the most immediate to our throne,[22]
And with no less nobility of love
Than that which dearest father bears his son,
Do I impart toward you. For your intent
In going back to school in Wittenberg,[23]
It is most retrograde[24] to our desire;
And we beseech you, bend you to remain
Here in the cheer and comfort of our eye,
Our chiefest courtier, cousin, and our son.
      QUEEN.   Let not thy mother lose her prayers, Hamlet:
I prithee, stay with us; go not to Wittenberg.
      HAMLET.   I shall in all my best obey you, madam.
      KING.   Why, 't is a loving and a fair reply:
Be as ourself in Denmark. Madam, come;
This gentle and unforc'd accord of Hamlet
Sits smiling to my heart; in grace whereof,
No jocund health that Denmark drinks to-day,
But the great cannon to the clouds shall tell,
And the King's rouse[25] the heaven shall bruit[26] again,
Re-speaking earthly thunder. Come away.
                        Flourish. Exeunt all but HAMLET.
      HAMLET.   O, that this too too solid flesh would melt,
Thaw, and resolve itself into a dew!

---

19. vulgar—common.   20. corse—corpse.
21. unprevailing—unavailing.   22. to our throne—in succession.
23. Wittenberg—a German university.   24. retrograde—contrary.
25. rouse—drink.   26. bruit—loudly declare.

Or that the Everlasting had not fix'd
His canon[27] 'gainst self-slaughter! O God! God!
How weary, stale, flat, and unprofitable,
Seem to me all the uses[28] of this world!
Fie on 't! ah fie! 'T is an unweeded garden,
That grows to seed; things rank and gross in nature
Possess it merely.[29] That it should come thus!
But two months dead: nay, not so much, not two.
So excellent a king, that was, to this
Hyperion[30] to a satyr; [31] so loving to my mother
That he might not beteem[32] the winds of heaven
Visit her face too roughly—heaven and earth!
Must I remember? Why, she would hang on him,
As if increase of appetite had grown
By what it fed on; and yet, within a month,—
Let me not think on 't!—Frailty, thy name is woman!—
A little month, or e'er those shoes were old
With which she followed my poor father's body,
Like Niobe,[33] all tears,—why she, even she—
O God! a beast, that wants discourse[34] of reason,
Would have mourn'd longer—married with my uncle,
My father's brother, but no more like my father
Than I to Hercules; [35] within a month,
Ere yet the salt of most unrighteous tears
Had left the flushing[36] in her galled eyes,
She married. O, most wicked speed, to post
With such dexterity to incestuous sheets!
It is not, nor it cannot come to good:
But break my heart, for I must hold my tongue.

Enter HORATIO, MARCELLUS, *and* BERNARDO.

HORATIO.   Hail to your lordship!
HAMLET.   I am glad to see you well.
Horatio!—or I do forget myself.

---

27. canon—divine law.   28. uses—customs.   29. merely—entirely.
30. Hyperion—Apollo, most beautiful of the Greek gods.
31. satyr—a monster (half-man, half-goat).   32. beteem—allow.
33. Niobe—whose lamenting caused her to be changed into a rock constantly dripping water.   34. discourse—power.
35. Hercules—strongest of Greek heroes.   36. flushing—redness.

HORATIO. The same, my lord, and your poor servant ever.

HAMLET. Sir, my good friend; I'll change[37] that name with you;

And what make you from[38] Wittenberg, Horatio?

Marcellus.

MARCELLUS. My good lord!

HAMLET. I am very glad to see you. [*To* BERNARDO.] Good even, sir.—

But what, in faith, make you from Wittenberg?

HORATIO. A truant disposition, good my lord.

HAMLET. I would not hear your enemy say so,

Nor shall you do my ear that violence,

To make it truster of your own report

Against yourself: I know you are no truant;

But what is your affair in Elsinore?

We'll teach you for to drink ere you depart.

HORATIO. My lord, I came to see your father's funeral.

HAMLET. I prithee, do not mock me, fellow-student;

I think it was to see my mother's wedding.

HORATIO. Indeed, my lord, it followed hard upon.

HAMLET. Thrift, thrift, Horatio! The funeral bak'd-meats[39]

Did coldly[40] furnish forth the marriage tables.

Would I had met my dearest foe in heaven

Or ever I had seen that day, Horatio!

My father!—methinks I see my father.

HORATIO. Where, my lord?

HAMLET.   In my mind's eye, Horatio.

HORATIO. I saw him once; 'a[41] was a goodly king.

HAMLET. 'A was a man, take him for all in all, I shall not look upon his like again.

HORATIO. My lord, I think I saw him yesternight.

HAMLET. Saw? Who?

HORATIO. My lord, the King your father.

HAMLET.   The King my father!

HORATIO. Season[42] your admiration[43] for a while

With an attent ear, till I may deliver,

---

37. change—exchange.   38. from—away from.
39. bak'd-meats—feast.   40. coldly—when cold.   41. 'a—he.
42. season—control.   43. admiration—amazement.

Upon the witness of these gentlemen,
This marvel to you.

HAMLET.   For God's love, let me hear.

HORATIO. . Two nights together had these gentlemen,
Marcellus and Bernardo, on their watch,
In the dead waste and middle of the night,
Been thus encounter'd. A figure like your father,
Armed at point exactly, cap-a-pie,[44]
Appears before them, and with solemn march
Goes slow and stately by them: thrice he walk'd
By their oppress'd and fear-surprised eyes,
Within his truncheon's[45] length; whilst they, distill'd
Almost to jelly with the act of fear,
Stand dumb and speak not to him. This to me
In dreadful secrecy impart they did,
And I with them the third night kept the watch.
Where, as they had deliver'd, both in time,
Form of the thing, each word made true and good,
The apparition comes. I knew[46] your father;
These hands are not more like.

HAMLET.   But where was this?

MARCELLUS. My lord upon the platform where we watch.

HAMLET. Did you not speak to it?

HORATIO.   My lord, I did;
But answer made it none: yet once methought
It lifted up its head and did address
Itself to motion, like as it would speak;
But even then the morning cock crew loud,
And at the sound it shrunk in haste away,
And vanish'd from our sight.

HAMLET.   'T is very strange.

HORATIO. As I do live, my honour'd lord, 't is true,
And we did think it writ down in our duty
To let you know of it.

HAMLET. Indeed, indeed, sirs. But this troubles me.
Hold you the watch to-night?

MARCELLUS *and* BERNARDO. We do, my lord.

---

44. cap-a-pie—head to foot.   45. truncheon's—baton's.
46. knew—recognized.

HAMLET. Arm'd, say you?

ALL. Arm'd, my lord.

HAMLET. From top to toe?

ALL. My lord, from head to foot.

HAMLET. Then saw you not his face?

HORATIO. O, yes, my lord; he wore his beaver[47] up.

HAMLET. What, look'd he frowningly?

HORATIO. A countenance more in sorrow than in anger.

HAMLET. Pale, or red?

HORATIO. Nay, very pale.

HAMLET. And fix'd his eyes upon you?

HORATIO. Most constantly.

HAMLET. I would I had been there.

HORATIO. It would have much amaz'd you.

HAMLET. Very like, very like. Stay'd it long?

HORATIO. While one with moderate haste might tell [48] a hundred.

MARCELLUS. ⎫
BERNARDO. ⎬ Longer, longer.

HORATIO. Not when I saw 't.

HAMLET. His beard was grizzled,[49] no?

HORATIO. It was, as I have seen it in his life,
A sable silver'd.

HAMLET. I will watch to-night;
Perchance 't will walk again.

HORATIO. I warrant it will.

HAMLET. If it assume[50] my noble father's person,
I'll speak to it, though hell itself should gape
And bid me hold my peace; I pray you all,
If you have hitherto conceal'd this sight,
Let it be tenable[51] in your silence still;
And whatsoever else shall hap to-night,
Give it an understanding, but no tongue;
I will requite your loves. So, fare you well.
Upon the platform 'twixt eleven and twelve,
I'll visit you.

---

47. beaver—the visor of his helmet. 48. tell—count.
49. grizzled—grey. 50. assume—appear in the shape of.
51. tenable—held.

ALL.   Our duty to your honour.

HAMLET.   Your loves, as mine to you; farewell.

Exeunt all but HAMLET.

My father's spirit—in arms? All is not well;
I doubt[52] some foul play; would the night were come!
Till then sit still, my soul: foul deeds will rise,
Though all the earth o'erwhelm them, to men's eyes.   *Exit.*

52. doubt—suspect.

[ACT I • 3] *A room in the house of* POLONIUS.

Enter LAERTES *and* OPHELIA.

LAERTES.   My necessaries[1] are embark'd, farewell;
And, sister, as the winds give benefit
And convoy is assistant, do not sleep,
But let me hear from you.

OPHELIA.   Do you doubt that?

LAERTES.   For Hamlet and the trifling of his favour,
Hold it a fashion and a toy in blood,[2]
A violet in the youth of primy[3] nature,
Forward, not permanent, sweet, not lasting,
The perfume and suppliance[4] of a minute;
No more.

OPHELIA.   No more but so?

LAERTES.   Think it no more:
For nature crescent[5] does not grow alone
In thews and bulk; but, as this temple[6] waxes,
The inward service of the mind and soul
Grows wide withal. Perhaps he loves you now,
And now no soil nor cautel [7] doth besmirch
The virtue of his will; but you must fear,
His greatness weigh'd, his will is not his own;
For he himself is subject to his birth.
He may not, as unvalued [8] persons do,
Carve for himself, for on his choice depends

1. necessaries—baggage.   2. toy in blood—youthful passion.
3. primy—springlike.   4. suppliance—pastime.
5. crescent—growing.   6. temple—i.e., the body.
7. cautel—deceit.   8. unvalued—less important.

The sanity and health of this whole state;
And therefore must his choice be circumscrib'd
Unto the voice and yielding of that body
Whereof he is the head. Then, if he says he loves you,
It fits your wisdom so far to believe it
As he in his particular act and place
May give his saying deed; which is no further
Than the main[9] voice of Denmark goes withal.
Then weigh what loss your honour may sustain
If with too credent ear you list his songs,
Or lose your heart, or your chaste treasure[10] open
To his unmaster'd importunity.
Fear it, Ophelia, fear it, my dear sister,
And keep you in the rear of your affection,
Out of the shot and danger of desire.
The chariest maid is prodigal enough,
If she unmask her beauty to the moon:
Virtue itself scapes not calumnious strokes:
The canker[11] galls the infants[12] of the spring
Too oft before their buttons be disclos'd,
And in the morn and liquid dew of youth
Contagious blastments are most imminent.
Be wary then, best safety lies in fear;
Youth to itself rebels, though none else near.

    OPHELIA.   I shall the effect of this good lesson keep,
As watchman to my heart: but, good my brother,
Do not, as some ungracious[13] pastors do,
Show me the steep and thorny way to heaven,
Whiles, like a puff'd and reckless libertine,
Himself the primrose path of dalliance treads,
And recks[14] not his own rede.[15]

    LAERTES.   O, fear me not;

Enter POLONIUS.

I stay too long: but here my father comes.

---

9. main—mighty.   10. treasure—virginity.
11. canker—worm.   12. infants—buds.
13. ungracious—graceless.   14. recks—heeds.   15. rede—advice.

A double blessing is a double grace,
Occasion smiles upon a second leave.

POLONIUS.   Yet here, Laertes? Aboard, aboard, for shame!
The wind sits in the shoulder of your sail,
And you are stay'd for. There; my blessing with thee!
And these few precepts in thy memory
Look thou chárácter.[16] Give thy thoughts no tongue,
Nor any unproportion'd [17] thought his act;
Be thou familiar, but by no means vulgar;
Those friends thou hast, and their adoption tried,
Grapple them unto thy soul with hoops of steel;
But do not dull thy palm with entertainment
Of each new-hatch'd, unfledg'd comrade. Beware
Of entrance to a quarrel; but being in,
Bear 't that th' opposed may beware of thee.
Give every man thy ear, but few thy voice;
Take each man's censure,[18] but reserve thy judgement.
Costly thy habit as thy purse can buy,
But not express'd in fancy; rich, not gaudy;
For the apparel oft proclaims the man,
And they in France of the best rank and station
Are most select and generous, chief in that.
Neither a borrower nor a lender be;
For loan oft loses both itself and friend,
And borrowing dulleth edge of husbandry; [19]
This above all: to thine own self be true,
And it must follow, as the night the day,
Thou canst not then be false to any man.
Farewell; my blessing season[20] this in thee!

LAERTES.   Most humbly do I take my leave, my lord.

POLONIUS.   The time invites you; go, your servants tend.

LAERTES.   Farewell, Ophelia, and remember well
What I have said to you.

OPHELIA.   'T is in my memory lock'd,
And you yourself shall keep the key of it.

LAERTES.   Farewell.   *Exit* LAERTES.

---

16. character—inscribe.   17. unproportioned—unsuitable.
18. censure—opinion.   19. husbandry—thrift.
20. season—bring to fruition.

POLONIUS.   What is 't, Ophelia, he hath said to you?

OPHELIA.   So please you, something touching the Lord Hamlet.

POLONIUS.   Marry, well bethought.
'T is told me, he hath very oft of late
Given private time to you, and you yourself
Have of your audience been most free and bounteous.
If it be so—as so 't is put on me,
And that in way of caution—I must tell you,
You do not understand yourself so clearly
As it behoves[21] my daughter and your honour.
What is between you? Give me up the truth.

OPHELIA.   He hath, my lord, of late made many tenders[22]
Of his affection to me.

POLONIUS.   Affection! pooh! You speak like a green girl,
Unsifted [23] in such perilous circumstance.
Do you believe his tenders, as you call them?

OPHELIA.   I do not know, my lord, what I should think.

POLONIUS.   Marry, I will teach you: think yourself a baby
That you have ta'en these tenders for true pay,
Which are not sterling. Tender[24] yourself more dearly,
Or—not to crack the wind of the poor phrase,
Running it thus—you'll tender me a fool.

OPHELIA.   My lord, he hath impórtun'd me with love
In honourable fashion.

POLONIUS.   Ay, fashion you may call it: go to,[25] go to!

OPHELIA.   And hath given countenance[26] to his speech, my lord,
With almost all the holy vows of heaven.

POLONIUS.   Ay, springes[27] to catch woodcocks. I do know,
When the blood burns, how prodigal [28] the soul
Lends the tongue vows. These blazes, daughter,
Giving more light than heat, extinct in both
Even in their promise, as it is a-making,

---

21. behoves—is proper for.   22. tenders—offers.
23. Unsifted—inexperienced.   24. Tender—hold.
25. go to—an exclamation of impatience.
26. countenance—confirmation.
27. springes—traps.   28. prodigal—abundantly.

You must not take for fire. From this time
Be somewhat scanter of your maiden presence,
Set your entreatments²⁹ at a higher rate
Than a command to parley: for Lord Hamlet,
Believe so much in him, that he is young,
And with a larger tether³⁰ may he walk
Than may be given you: in few,³¹ Ophelia,
Do not believe his vows, for they are brokers,³²
Not of that dye which their investments³³ show,
But mere implorators of unholy suits,
Breathing like sanctified and pious bawds,
The better to beguile. This is for all:
I would not, in plain terms, from this time forth,
Have you so slander any moment leisure
As to give words or talk with the Lord Hamlet.
Look to 't, I charge you: come your ways.

OPHELIA.   I shall obey, my lord.   *Exeunt.*

29. entreatments—negotiations for surrender.
30. larger tether—greater freedom.   31. in few—to put it briefly.
32. brokers—panders.   33. investments—garments.

[ACT I • 4] *The platform.*

Enter HAMLET, HORATIO, *and* MARCELLUS.

HAMLET.   The air bites shrewdly; ¹ it is very cold.
HORATIO.   It is a nipping and an eager² air.
HAMLET.   What hour now?
HORATIO.   I think it lacks of twelve.
MARCELLUS.   No, it is struck.
HORATIO.   Indeed? I heard it not; it then draws near the
season
Wherein the spirit held his wont to walk.
    [*A flourish of trumpets, and two cannon go off within.*]
What does this mean, my lord?
HAMLET.   The King doth wake³ to-night and takes his rouse,
Keeps wassails, and the swagg'ring up-spring⁴ reels;
And, as he drains his draughts of Rhenish⁵ down,

1. shrewdly—cursedly.   2. eager—sharp.   3. wake—hold revels.
4. up-spring—riotous dance.   5. Rhenish—wine.

The kettle-drum and trumpet thus bray out
The triumph of his pledge.
 HORATIO.   Is it a custom?
 HAMLET. Ay, marry,[6] is 't,
But to my mind, though I am native here
And to the manner born, it is a custom
More honour'd in the breach than the observance.
This heavy-headed revel east and west
Makes us traduc'd [7] and tax'd of other nations:
They clepe[8] us drunkards, and with swinish phrase
Soil our addition; [9] and indeed it takes[10]
From our achievements, though perform'd at height,
The pith and marrow of our attribute.[11]
So oft it chances in particular men,
That for some vicious mole[12] of nature in them,
As, in their birth—wherein they are not guilty,
Since nature cannot choose his origin—
By their o'ergrowth[13] of some complexion
Oft breaking down the pales and forts of reason,
Or by some habit that too much o'er-leavens[14]
The form of plausive[15] manners, that these men,
Carrying, I say, the stamp of one defect,
Being nature's livery[16] or fortune's star,—
Their virtues else—be they as pure as grace,
As infinite as man may undergo—
Shall in the general censure take corruption
From that particular fault: the dram of e'il [17]
Doth all the noble substance[18] often dout[19]
To his own scandal.[20]

Enter GHOST.

 HORATIO.   Look, my lord, it comes!

---

6. marry—a mild oath. 7. traduc'd—disgraced. 8. clepe—call.
9. addition—reputation. 10. takes—detracts.
11. attribute—reputation. 12. mole—defect.
13. o'ergrowth—overdevelopment. 14. o'er-leavens—mixes with.
15. plausive—pleasing. 16. nature's livery—marked by nature.
17. dram of e'il—small amount of evil.
18. noble substance—substantial nobility.
19. dout—nullify. 20. scandal—disgrace.

HAMLET.   Angels and ministers of grace defend us!
Be thou a spirit of health or goblin damn'd,
Bring with thee airs from heaven or blasts from hell,
Be thy intents wicked or charitable,
Thou com'st in such a questionable[21] shape
That I will speak to thee. I'll call thee Hamlet,
King, father, royal Dane. O, answer me!
Let me not burst in ignorance, but tell
Why thy canoniz'd bones, hearsed in death,
Have burst their cerements; [22] why the sepulchre,
Wherein we saw thee quietly interr'd,
Hath op'd his ponderous and marble jaws,
To cast thee up again. What may this mean,
That thou, dead corse, again in cómplete steel [23]
Revisits thus the glimpses of the moon,
Making night hideous, and we fools of nature
So horridly to shake our disposition
With thoughts beyond the reaches of our souls?
Say, why is this? Wherefore? What should we do?

[GHOST *beckons to* HAMLET.]

HORATIO.   It beckons you to go away with it,
As if it some impartment[24] did desire
To you alone.

MARCELLUS.   Look, with what courteous action
It waves you to a more removed ground.
But do not go with it.

HORATIO.   No, by no means.

HAMLET.   It will not speak; then will I follow it.

HORATIO.   Do not, my lord.

HAMLET.   Why, what should be the fear?
I do not set my life at a pin's fee,[25]
And for my soul, what can it do to that,
Being a thing immortal as itself?
It waves me forth again; I'll follow it.

HORATIO.   What if it tempt you toward the flood,[26] my lord,
Or to the dreadful summit of the cliff

---

21. questionable—inviting me to question.
22. cerements—grave clothes.   23. steel—armor.
24. impartment—communication.   25. fee—value.   26. flood—ocean.

That beetles[27] o'er his base into the sea,
And there assume some other, horrible form,
Which might deprive your sovereignty of reason
And draw you into madness? Think of it.
The very place puts toys[28] of desperation,
Without more motive, into every brain
That looks so many fathoms to the sea
And hears it roar beneath.

HAMLET.   It waves me still.
Go on, I'll follow thee.

MARCELLUS.   You shall not go, my lord.

HAMLET.   Hold off your hands.

HORATIO.   Be rul'd; you shall not go.

HAMLET.   My fate cries out,
And makes each petty artery in this body
As hardy as the Némean lion's[29] nerve.
Still am I call'd: unhand me, gentlemen;
By heaven, I'll make a ghost of him that lets[30] me!
I say, away!—Go on, I'll follow thee.

                          Exeunt GHOST *and* HAMLET.

HORATIO.   He waxes desperate with imagination.

MARCELLUS.   Let's follow; 't is not fit thus to obey him.

HORATIO.   Have after—to what issue will this come?

MARCELLUS.   Something is rotten in the state of Denmark.

HORATIO.   Heaven will direct it.

MARCELLUS.   Nay, let's follow him.
                                        Exeunt.

---

27. beetles—juts.   28. toys—impulses.
29. Némean lion—fierce monster slain by Hercules.
30. lets—hinders.

[ACT I • 5] *Another part of the platform.*

Enter GHOST *and* HAMLET.

HAMLET.   Where wilt thou lead me? Speak, I'll go no further.
GHOST.   Mark me.
HAMLET.   I will.
GHOST.   My hour is almost come,

When I to sulph'rous and tormenting flames
Must render up myself.

 HAMLET.   Alas, poor ghost!

 GHOST. Pity me not, but lend thy serious hearing
To what I shall unfold.

 HAMLET.   Speak; I am bound [1] to hear.

 GHOST. So art thou to revenge, when thou shalt hear.

 HAMLET. What?

 GHOST. I am thy father's spirit,
Doom'd for a certain term to walk the night,
And for the day confin'd to fast in fires,[2]
Till the foul crimes done in my days of nature
Are burnt and purg'd away: but that I am forbid
To tell the secrets of my prison-house,
I could a tale unfold whose lightest word
Would harrow up thy soul, freeze thy young blood,
Make thy two eyes, like stars, start from their spheres,
Thy knotty and combined locks to part
And each particular hair to stand an end,
Like quills upon the fretful porpentine.[3]
But this eternal blazon[4] must not be
To ears of flesh and blood. List, list, O, list!
If thou didst ever thy dear father love—

 HAMLET. O God!

 GHOST. Revenge his foul and most unnatural murder.

 HAMLET. Murder!

 GHOST. Murder most foul, as in the best it is,
But this most foul, strange, and unnatural.

 HAMLET. Haste me to know't, that I, with wings as swift
As meditation or the thoughts of love,
May sweep to my revenge.

 GHOST.   I find thee apt;
And duller shouldst thou be than the fat weed
That rots itself in ease on Lethe[5] wharf,
Wouldst thou not stir in this. Now, Hamlet, hear:
'T is given out that, sleeping in my orchard,

---

1. bound—duty-bound. 2. in fires—in Purgatory.
3. porpentine—porcupine. 4. eternal blazon—revelation of eternity
5. Lethe—the river of forgetfulness in Hades.

A serpent stung me; so the whole ear of Denmark
Is by a forged process[6] of my death
Rankly abus'd; but know, thou noble youth,
The serpent that did sting thy father's life
Now wears his crown.
    HAMLET.   O my prophetic soul!
My uncle!
    GHOST.   Ay, that incestuous, that adulterate beast,
With witchcraft of his wit, with traitorous gifts,—
O wicked wit and gifts, that have the power
So to seduce!—won to his shameful lust
The will of my most seeming-virtuous queen;
O Hamlet, what a falling-off was there!
From me, whose love was of that dignity
That it went hand in hand even with the vow
I made to her in marriage, and to decline[7]
Upon a wretch whose natural gifts were poor
To those of mine!
But virtue, as it never will be moved,
Though lewdness court it in a shape of heaven,
So lust, though to a radiant angel link'd,
Will sate[8] itself in a celestial bed
And prey on garbage.
But, soft! methinks I scent the morning air,
Brief let me be. Sleeping within mine orchard,
My custom always of the afternoon,
Upon my secure[9] hour thy uncle stole,
With juice of cursed hebona in a vial,
And in the porches of mine ears did pour
The lep'rous distilment; whose effect
Holds such an enmity with blood of man
That swift as quicksilver it courses through
The natural gates and alleys of the body,
And with a sudden vigour it doth posset[10]
And curd, like eager[11] droppings into milk,
The thin and wholesome blood: so did it mine,

---

6. process—account.   7. decline—fall back.   8. sate—gorge.
9. secure—carefree.   10. posset—curdle.   11. eager—sour.

And a most instant tetter[12] bark'd about,
Most lazar-like,[13] with vile and loathsome crust,
All my smooth body.
Thus was I, sleeping, by a brother's hand
Of life, of crown, of queen, at once dispatch'd;
Cut off even in the blossoms of my sin,
Unhouseled, disappointed, unanel'd,[14]
No reckoning made, but sent to my account
With all my imperfections on my head.
    HAMLET.   O, horrible! O, horrible! most horrible!
    GHOST.   If thou hast nature in thee, bear it not;
Let not the royal bed of Denmark be
A couch for luxury[15] and damned incest.
But, howsomever thou pursuest this act,
Taint not thy mind, nor let thy soul contrive
Against thy mother aught: leave her to heaven
And to those thorns that in her bosom lodge,
To prick and sting her. Fare thee well at once!
The glow-worm shows the matin[16] to be near,
And 'gins to pale his uneffectual fire.
Adieu, adieu, adieu! remember me.   *Exit.*
    HAMLET.   O all you host of heaven! O earth! What else?
And shall I couple hell? O, fie! Hold, hold, my heart,
And you, my sinews, grow not instant old,
But bear me stiffly up. Remember thee?
Ay, thou poor ghost, while memory holds a seat
In this distracted globe.[17] Remember thee?
Yea, from the table[18] of my memory
I'll wipe away all trivial fond [19] recórds,
All saws[20] of books, all forms, all pressures[21] past,
That youth and observation copied there,
And thy commandment all alone shall live
Within the book and volume of my brain,
Unmix'd with baser matter; yes, by heaven!

---

12. tetter—scab.   13. lazar-like—like a leper.
14. Unhouseled, disappointed, unanel'd—without receiving the last rites
of the Church.   15. luxury—lust.   16. matin—morning.
17. globe—head.   18. table—notebook.   19. fond—foolish.
20. saws—wise sayings.   21. pressures—impressions.

O most pernicious woman!
O villain, villain, smiling, damned villain!
My tables!—Meet it is I set it down
That one may smile and smile, and be a villain,
At least I'm sure it may be so in Denmark.
So, uncle, there you are. Now to my word;
It is "Adieu, adieu! remember me."
I have sworn 't.

HORATIO.   [*Within.*] My lord, my lord!
MARCELLUS.   [*Within.*] Lord Hamlet!
HORATIO.   [*Within.*] Heaven secure him!
HAMLET.   So be it!
MARCELLUS.   [*Within.*] Illo, ho, ho,²² my lord!
HAMLET.   Hillo, ho, ho, boy! Come, bird, come.

Enter HORATIO *and* MARCELLUS.

MARCELLUS.   How is 't my noble lord?
HORATIO.   What news, my lord?
HAMLET.   O, wonderful!
HORATIO.   Good my lord, tell it.
HAMLET.   No, you will reveal it.
HORATIO.   Not I, my lord, by heaven.
MARCELLUS.   Nor I, my lord.
HAMLET.   How say you, then, would heart of man once think
   it?—
But you'll be secret?
HORATIO.   ⎫
MARCELLUS. ⎬ Ay, by heaven, my lord.
HAMLET.   There's ne'er a villain dwelling in all Denmark
But he's an arrant knave.
HORATIO.   There needs no ghost, my lord, come from the
   grave
To tell us this.
HAMLET.   Why, right, you are in the right.
And so, without more circumstance²³ at all,
I hold it fit that we shake hands and part;
You, as your business and desire shall point you,

---

22. Illo, ho, ho—a falconer's call.
23. circumstance—ceremony.

For every man has business and desire,
Such as it is; and for mine own poor part,
Look you, I'll go pray.

HORATIO.   These are but wild and whirling words, my lord.

HAMLET.   I'm sorry they offend you, heartily;
Yes, faith, heartily.

HORATIO.   There's no offence, my lord.

HAMLET.   Yes, by Saint Patrick, but there is, Horatio,
And much offence too—touching this vision here,
It is an honest ghost, that let me tell you—
For your desire to know what is between us,
O'ermaster 't as you may. And now, good friends,
As you are friends, scholars, and soldiers,
Give me one poor request.

HORATIO.   What is 't, my lord? We will.

HAMLET.   Never make known what you have seen to-night.

BOTH.   My lord, we will not.

HAMLET.   Nay, but swear 't.

HORATIO.   In faith,
My lord, not I.

MARCELLUS.   Nor I, my lord, in faith.

HAMLET.   Upon my sword.

MARCELLUS.   We have sworn, my lord, already.

HAMLET.   Indeed, upon my sword, indeed.

                    [GHOST *cries under the stage*.]

GHOST.   Swear!

HAMLET.   Ha, ha, boy! say'st thou so? Art thou there, true-
    penny? [24]
Come on; you hear this fellow in the cellarage;
Consent to swear.

HORATIO.   Propose the oath, my lord.

HAMLET.   Never to speak of this that you have seen.
Swear by my sword.

GHOST.   [*Beneath*.] Swear.

HAMLET.   *Hic et ubique?* [25] Then we'll shift our ground.
Come hither, gentlemen,

---

24. truepenny—honest old fellow.
25. *Hic et ubique*—here and everywhere.

And lay your hands again upon my sword:
Never to speak of this that you have heard.
Swear by my sword.

    GHOST.   [*Beneath.*] Swear by his sword.

    HAMLET.   Well said, old mole! Canst work i' th' earth so fast?
A worthy pioner! [26] Once more remove, good friends.

    HORATIO.   O day and night, but this is wondrous strange!

    HAMLET.   And therefore as a stranger give it welcome.
There are more things in heaven and earth, Horatio,
Than are dreamt of in your philosophy.
But come;
Here, as before, never, so help you mercy,
How strange or odd soe'er I bear myself,—
As I perchance hereafter shall think meet
To put an antic disposition[27] on—
That you, at such times seeing me, never shall,
With arms encumber'd [28] thus, or this headshake,
Or by pronouncing of some doubtful phrase
As "Well, well we know," or "We could, an[29] if we would,"
Or "If we list to speak," or "There be, an if they might,"
Or such ambiguous giving out, to note
That you know aught of me,—this not to do,
So grace and mercy at your most need help you.
Swear.

    GHOST.   [*Beneath.*] Swear.

    HAMLET.   Rest, rest, perturbed spirit! [*They swear.*] So,
      gentlemen,
With all my love I do commend me to you;
And what so poor a man as Hamlet is
May do, t' express his love and friending to you,
God willing, shall not lack. Let us go in together;
And still your fingers on your lips, I pray.
The time is out of joint; O cursed spite,
That ever I was born to set it right!
Nay, come, let's go together.   *Exeunt.*

---

26. pioner—miner, trench digger.
27. antic disposition—fantastic behavior.
28. encumber'd—folded.
29. an—if (only).

[ACT II • 1] *A room in the house of* POLONIUS.

Enter POLONIUS *and* REYNALDO.

POLONIUS. Give him this money and these notes, Reynaldo.

REYNALDO. I will, my lord.

POLONIUS. You shall do marvellous wisely, good Reynaldo.
Before you visit him, to make inquire
Of his behaviour.

REYNALDO. My lord, I did intend it.

POLONIUS. Marry, well said, very well said. Look you, sir,
Inquire me first what Danskers[1] are in Paris,
And how, and who, what means,[2] and where they keep,[3]
What company, at what expense; and finding
By this encompassment and drift of question
That they do know my son, come you more nearer
Than your particular demands will touch it:
Take you, as 't were, some distant knowledge of him,
As thus, "I know his father and his friends,
And in part him." Do you mark this, Reynaldo?

REYNALDO. Ay, very well, my lord.

POLONIUS. "And in part him; but," you may say, "not well.
But, if 't be he I mean, he's very wild,
Addicted so and so;" and there put on him
What forgeries[4] you please; marry, none so rank
As may dishonour him,—take heed of that;
But, sir, such wanton, wild, and usual slips
As are companions noted and most known
To youth and liberty.

REYNALDO. As gaming, my lord?

POLONIUS. Ay, or drinking, fencing, swearing, quarrelling,
Drabbing; [5] you may go so far.

REYNALDO. My lord, that would dishonour him.

POLONIUS. Faith, no, as you may season[6] it in the charge.
You must not put another scandal on him,
That he is open to incontinency,[7]

---

1. Danskers—Danes.   2. means—income.
3. keep—lodge.   4. forgeries—imaginary faults.
5. drabbing—licentiousness.   6. season—qualify.
7. incontinency—widely known lewdness.

That's not my meaning; but breathe his faults so quaintly[8]
That they may seem the taints of liberty,
The flash and outbreak of a fiery mind,
A savageness in unreclaimed [9] blood,
Of general assault.[10]

REYNALDO.   But, my good lord,—
POLONIUS.   Wherefore should you do this?
REYNALDO.   Ay, my lord,
I would know that.

POLONIUS.   Marry, sir, here's my drift,
And, I believe, it is a fetch of warrant: [11]
You laying these slight sullies on my son
As 't were a thing a little soil'd i' th' working,
Mark you,
Your party in converse, him you would sound,
Having ever seen in the prenominate[12] crimes
The youth you breathe of guilty, be assur'd
He closes[13] with you in this consequence; [14]
"Good sir," or so, or "friend," or "gentleman,"
According to the phrase or the addition[15]
Of man and country—

REYNALDO.   Very good, my lord.
POLONIUS.   And then, sir, does 'a this—'a does—
What was I about to say? By the mass, I was
About to say something. Where did I leave?
REYNALDO.   At "closes in the consequence," at "friend or
so," and "gentleman."
POLONIUS.   At "closes in the consequence," ay, marry—
He closes thus: "I know the gentleman.
I saw him yesterday, or th' other day,
Or then, or then, with such and such; and, as you say,
There was 'a gaming; there o'ertook[16] in 's rouse;
There falling out[17] at tennis;" or, perchance,

---

8. quaintly—ingeniously.   9. unreclaimed—untamed.
10. of general assault—common to all (young men).
11. fetch of warrant—a trick that cannot fail.
12. prenominate—aforementioned.   13. closes—agrees.
14. consequence—reply.   15. addition—title.
16. o'ertook—intoxicated.   17. falling out—quarrelling.

"I saw him enter such a house of sale,"
Videlicet,[18] a brothel, or so forth.
See you now—
Your bait of falsehood takes this carp of truth;
And thus do we of wisdom and of reach,[19]
With windlasses[20] and with assays of bias,[21]
By indirections find directions out;
So by my former lecture and advice,
Shall you my son. You have[22] me, have you not?

REYNALDO.   My lord, I have.

POLONIUS.   God buy you; fare you well.

REYNALDO.   Good my lord.

POLONIUS.   Observe his inclination in[23] yourself.

REYNALDO.   I shall, my lord

POLONIUS.   And let him ply his music.

REYNALDO.   Well, my lord.

POLONIUS.   Farewell!   *Exit* REYNALDO.

Enter OPHELIA.

How now, Ophelia! what's the matter?

OPHELIA.   O, my lord, my lord, I have been so affrighted!

POLONIUS.   With what: i' th' name of God?

OPHELIA.   My lord, as I was sewing in my closet,[24]
Lord Hamlet, with his doublet[25] all unbrac'd,[26]
No hat upon his head, his stockings fouled,
Ungarter'd, and down-gyved [27] to his ankle,
Pale as his shirt, his knees knocking each other,
And with a look so piteous in purport
As if he had been loosed out of hell
To speak of horrors,—he comes before me.

POLONIUS.   Mad for thy love?

OPHELIA   My lord, I do not know,
But truly, I do fear it.

POLONIUS.   What said he?

---

18. *Videlicet*—that is to say.   19. reach—ability.
20. windlasses—roundabout ways.
21. assays of bias—indirect attempts.   22. have—understand.
23. in—by.   24. closet—boudoir.   25. doublet—jacket.
26. unbrac'd—unlaced.   27. down-gyved—hanging down.

OPHELIA.   He took me by the wrist and held me hard;
Then goes he to the length of all his arm,
And, with his other hand thus o'er his brow,
He falls to such perusal of my face
As 'a would draw it. Long stay'd he so.
At last, a little shaking of mine arm,
And thrice his head thus waving up and down,
He rais'd a sigh so piteous and profound
That it did seem to shatter all his bulk
And end his being; that done, he lets me go;
And, with his head over his shoulder turn'd,
He seem'd to find his way without his eyes,
For out o' doors he went without their help,
And, to the last, bended their light on me.

POLONIUS.   Come, go with me, I will go seek the King.
This is the very ecstasy[28] of love,
Whose violent property[29] fordoes[30] itself
And leads the will to desperate undertakings
As oft as any passion under heaven
That does afflict our natures: I am sorry,—
What, have you given him any hard words of late?

OPHELIA.   No, my good lord, but, as you did command,
I did repel his letters and denied
His access to me.

POLONIUS.   That hath made him mad.
I am sorry that with better heed and judgement
I had not quoted [31] him. I fear'd he did but trifle
And meant to wreck thee; but beshrew my jealousy! [32]
By heaven, it is as proper to[33] our age
To cast beyond [34] ourselves in our opinions
As it is common for the younger sort
To lack discretion. Come, go we to the King.
This must be known, which, being kept close, might move
More grief to hide than hate to utter love.
Come.   *Exeunt.*

---

28. ecstasy—madness.   29. property—quality.
30. fordoes—destroys.   31. quoted—observed.
32. jealousy—suspicious nature.   33. proper to—characteristic of.
34. cast beyond—outsmart.

[ACT II · 2] *A room in the castle.*

Flourish. Enter KING, QUEEN, ROSENCRANTZ, GUILDENSTERN,
with others.

KING.   Welcome, dear Rosencrantz and Guildenstern!
Moreover[1] that we much did long to see you.
The need we have to use you did provoke
Our hasty sending. Something have you heard
Of Hamlet's transformation; so I call it,
Sith[2] nor th' exterior nor the inward man
Resembles that it was. What it should be,
More than his father's death, that thus hath put him
So much from th' understanding of himself,
I cannot dream of: I entreat you both,
That, being of[3] so young days brought up with him
And sith so neighbour'd to[4] his youth and haviour,
That you vouchsafe your rest[5] here in our court
Some little time; so by your companies
To draw him on to pleasures, and to gather
So much as from occasions you may glean,
Whether aught, to us unknown, afflicts him thus,
That, open'd,[6] lies within our remedy.
QUEEN.   Good gentlemen, he hath much talk'd of you;
And sure I am two men there is not living
To whom he more adheres. If it will please you
To show us so much gentry[7] and good will
As to expend your time with us a while
For the supply and profit of our hope,
Your visitation shall receive such thanks
As fits a king's remembrance.
ROSENCRANTZ.   Both your Majesties
Might, by the sovereign power you have of us,
Put your dread pleasures[8] more into command
Than to entreaty.
GUILDENSTERN.   But we both obey,

---

1. Moreover—besides.   2. Sith—since.
3. of—from.   4. neighbor'd to—associated with.
5. vouchsafe your rest—consent to stay.   6. open'd—made known.
7. gentry—courtesy.   8. pleasures—wishes.

And here give up ourselves, in the full bent
To lay our service freely at your feet,
To be commanded.

    KING.   Thanks, Rosencrantz and gentle Guildenstern.

    QUEEN.   Thanks, Guildenstern and gentle Rosencrantz;
And I beseech you instantly to visit
My too much changed son. Go, some of you,
And bring these gentlemen where Hamlet is.

    GUILDENSTERN.   Heavens make our presence and our prac-
        tices
Pleasant and helpful to him!

    QUEEN.   Ay, amen!

                      Exeunt ROSENCRANTZ, GUILDENSTERN,
                              and some Attendants.

Enter POLONIUS.

    POLONIUS.   Th' ambassadors from Norway, my good lord,
Are joyfully return'd.

    KING.   Thou still hast been the father of good news.

    POLONIUS.   Have I, my lord? I assure you, my good liege,
I hold my duty as I hold my soul,
Both to my God and to my gracious king;
And I do think, or else this brain of mine
Hunts not the trail of policy[9] so sure
As it hath us'd to do, that I have found
The very cause of Hamlet's lunacy.

    KING.   O, speak of that; that do I long to hear.

    POLONIUS.   Give first admittance to th' ambassadors.
My news shall be the fruit[10] to that great feast.

    KING.   Thyself do grace[11] to them, and bring them in.

                            [Exit POLONIUS.]
He tells me, my dear Gertrude, he hath found
The head [12] and source of all your son's distemper.[13]

    QUEEN.   I doubt it is no other but the main,[14]
His father's death and our o'erhasty marriage.

---

9. policy—statesmanship.   10. fruit—dessert.
11. grace—honor.   12. head—origin.
13. distemper—strangeness.
14. main—main subject of his thought.

Re-enter POLONIUS, *with* VOLTIMAND *and* CORNELIUS.

KING.   Well, we shall sift him.—Welcome, my good friends!
Say, Voltimand, what from our brother Norway?
VOLTIMAND.   Most fair return of greetings and desires.
Upon our first, he set out to suppress
His nephew's levies, which to him appear'd
To be a preparation 'gainst the Polack,
But, better look'd into, he truly found
It was against your Highness; whereat griev'd,
That so his sickness, age, and impotence
Was falsely borne in hand,[15] sends out arrests
On Fortinbras; which he, in brief, obeys,
Receives rebuke from Norway, and in fine[16]
Makes vow before his uncle never more
To give th' assay of arms against your Majesty:
Whereon old Norway, overcome with joy,
Gives him three thousand crowns in annual fee,
And his commission to employ those soldiers,
So levied as before, against the Polack;
With an entreaty, herein further shown,   [*Giving a paper.*]
That it might please you to give quiet pass
Through your dominions for this enterprise,
On such regards of safety[17] and allowance
As therein are set down.
KING.   It likes[18] us well;
And at our more considered time[19] we'll read,
Answer, and think upon this business:
Meantime we thank you for your well-took labour.
Go to your rest; at night we'll feast together:
Most welcome home!   *Exeunt* AMBASSADORS.
POLONIUS.   This business is well ended.
My liege, and madam, to expostulate[20]
What majesty should be, what duty is,
Why day is day, night night, and time is time,

---

15. borne in hand—taken advantage of.   16. in fine—finally.
17. regards of safety—safeguards.   18. likes—pleases.
19. more considered time—better time for consideration.
20. expostulate—discuss.

Were nothing but to waste night, day, and time;
Therefore, since brevity is the soul of wit[21]
And tediousness the limbs and outward flourishes,
I will be brief. Your noble son is mad.
Mad call I it; for, to define true madness,
What is 't but to be nothing else but mad?
But let that go.

    QUEEN.   More matter, with less art.

    POLONIUS.   Madam, I swear I use no art at all.
That he is mad, 't is true; 't is true 't is pity,
And pity 't is 't is true—a foolish figure! [22]
But farewell it, for I will use no art.
Mad let us grant him then; and now remains
That we find out the cause of this effect,
Or rather say, the cause of this defect,
For this effect defective comes by cause.
Thus it remains, and the remainder thus.
Perpend.[23]
I have a daughter—have while she is mine—
Who, in her duty and obedience, mark,
Hath given me this; now gather, and surmise.

                                    [Reads the letter.]

    To the celestial and my soul's idol, the most beautified [24]
        Ophelia,—

That's an ill phrase, a rule phrase; "beautified" is a vile phrase.
But you shall hear. Thus:

        In her excellent white bosom, these.

    QUEEN.   Came this from Hamlet to her?

    POLONIUS.   Good madam, stay a while; I will be faithful.

                                          [Reads.]

        Doubt thou the stars are fire,
          Doubt that the sun doth move,
          Doubt truth to be a liar,
          But never doubt I love.

---

21. wit—wisdom.   22. figure—i.e., of speech.
23. Perpend—mark my words.   24. beautified—beautiful.

O dear Ophelia, I am ill at these numbers,[25] I have not art to reckon my groans; but that I love thee best, O most best, believe it. Adieu.

Thine evermore, most dear lady,
Whilst this machine[26] is to him,

HAMLET.

This in obedience hath my daughter shown me,
And more above, hath his solicitings,
As they fell out by time, by means, and place,
All given to mine ear.

KING.   But how hath she
Receiv'd his love?

POLONIUS.   What do you think of me?

KING. As of a man faithful and honourable.

POLONIUS. I would fain prove so. But what might you think,
When I had seen this hot love on the wing,—
As I perceiv'd it, I must tell you that,
Before my daughter told me,—what might you
Or my dear Majesty your queen here, think,
If I had play'd the desk or table-book,[27]
Or given[28] my heart a winking,[29] mute and dumb,
Or look'd upon this love with idle sight,
What might you think? No, I went round [30] to work,
And my young mistress thus I did bespeak:
"Lord Hamlet is a prince out of thy star.[31]
This must not be;" and then I prescripts gave her,
That she should lock herself from his resort,
Admit no messengers, receive no tokens.
Which done, she took the fruits[32] of my advice;
And he, repell'd,—a short tale to make—
Fell into a sadness, then into a fast,
Thence to a watch,[33] thence into a weakness,
Thence to a lightness, and, by this declension,
Into the madness wherein now he raves,
And all we mourn for.

---

25. numbers—verse-making. 26. machine—body.
27. table-book—private diary. 28. given—forced.
29. a winking—to shut its eyes. 30. round—directly.
31. star—sphere. 32. took the fruits of—carried out.
33. watch—sleeplessness.

KING.   Do you think 't is this?

QUEEN.   It may be, very like.

POLONIUS.   Hath there been such a time—I would fain know
   that—
That I have positively said, " 'T is so,"
When it prov'd otherwise?

KING.   Not that I know.

POLONIUS.   Take this from this,[34] if this be otherwise:
If circumstances lead me, I will find
Where truth is hid, though it were hid indeed
Within the centre.[35]

KING.   How may we try it further?

POLONIUS.   You know, sometimes he walks four hours together
Here in the lobby.

QUEEN.   So he does, indeed.

POLONIUS.   At such a time I'll loose my daughter to him:
Be you and I behind an arras[36] then;
Mark the encounter, if he love her not
And be not from his reason fall'n thereon,
Let me be no assistant for a state,
But keep a farm and carters.

KING.   We will try it.

Enter HAMLET, *reading a book.*

QUEEN.   But look where sadly the poor wretch comes reading.

POLONIUS.   Away, I do beseech you, both away. I'll board [37]
him presently. O, give me leave.

                         Exeunt KING, QUEEN, *and Attendants.*
How does my good Lord Hamlet?

HAMLET.   Well, God-a-mercy.

POLONIUS.   Do you know me, my lord?

HAMLET.   Excellent well; you are a fishmonger.

POLONIUS.   Not I, my lord.

HAMLET.   Then I would you were so honest a man.

POLONIUS.   Honest, my lord?

---

34. this from this—i.e., head from shoulders.
35. centre—i.e., of the earth.   36. arras—tapestry hanging.
37. board—accost.

HAMLET.   Ay, sir; to be honest, as this world goes, is to be one man picked out of ten thousand.

POLONIUS.   That's very true, my lord.

HAMLET.   For if the sun breed maggots in a dead dog, being a god kissing carrion—Have you a daughter?

POLONIUS.   I have, my lord.

HAMLET.   Let her not walk i' th' sun: conception[38] is a blessing, but as your daughter may conceive—Friend, look to 't.

POLONIUS.   [*Aside*.] How say you by that? Still harping on my daughter: yet he knew me not at first; 'a said I was a fishmonger; 'a is far gone; and truly in my youth I suffered much extremity for love; very near this. I'll speak to him again.—What do you read, my lord?

HAMLET.   Words, words, words.

POLONIUS.   What is the matter, my lord?

HAMLET.   Between who?

POLONIUS.   I mean, the matter that you read, my lord.

HAMLET.   Slanders, sir; for the satirical rogue says here that old men have grey beards, that their faces are wrinkled, their eyes purging thick amber and plum-tree gum, and that they have a plentiful lack of wit, together with most weak hams: [39] all which, sir, though I most powerfully and potently believe, yet I hold it not honesty to have it thus set down; for yourself, sir, shall grow old as I am, if like a crab you could go backward.

POLONIUS.   [*Aside*.] Though this be madness, yet there is method [40] in 't.—Will you walk out of the air, my lord?

HAMLET.   Into my grave?

POLONIUS.   Indeed, that is out of the air. [*Aside*.] How pregnant[41] sometimes his replies are! a happiness[42] that often madness hits on, which reason and sanity could not so prosperously be delivered of. I will leave him, and suddenly contrive the means of meeting between him and my daughter.—My lord, I will take my leave of you.

HAMLET.   You cannot, sir, take from me anything that I will not more willingly part withal,[43]—except my life, except my life, except my life.

---

38. conception—understanding; also, pregnancy.
39. hams—knee joints.   40. method—sense.   **41. pregnant—apt.**
42. happiness—cleverness.   43. withal—with.

POLONIUS.   Fare you well, my lord.

HAMLET.   These tedious old fools!

Enter ROSENCRANTZ *and* GUILDENSTERN.

POLONIUS.   You go to seek the Lord Hamlet? There he is.

ROSENCRANTZ.   [*To* POLONIUS.] God save you, sir!

Exit POLONIUS.

GUILDENSTERN.   My honoured lord!

ROSENCRANTZ.   My most dear lord!

HAMLET.   My excellent good friends! How dost thou, Guildenstern? Ah, Rosencrantz! Good lads, how do you both?

ROSENCRANTZ.   As the indifferent⁴⁴ children of the earth.

GUILDENSTERN.   Happy in that we are not overhappy. On Fortune's cap we are not the very button.

HAMLET.   Nor the soles of her shoe?

ROSENCRANTZ.   Neither, my lord.

HAMLET.   Then you live about her waist, or in the middle of her favours?

GUILDENSTERN.   Faith, her privates we.

HAMLET.   In the secret parts of Fortune? Oh, most true; she is a strumpet. What news?

ROSENCRANTZ.   None, my lord, but that the world's grown honest.

HAMLET.   Then is doomsday near; but your news is not true. Let me question more in particular: what have you, my good friends, deserved at the hands of Fortune, that she sends you to prison hither?

GUILDENSTERN.   Prison, my lord?

HAMLET.   Denmark's a prison.

ROSENCRANTZ.   Then is the world one.

HAMLET.   A goodly one, in which there are many confines, wards, and dungeons, Denmark being one o' th' worst.

ROSENCRANTZ.   We think not so, my lord.

HAMLET.   Why, then, 't is none to you; for there is nothing either good or bad, but thinking makes it so: to me it is a prison.

ROSENCRANTZ.   Why, then, your ambition makes it one: 't is too narrow for your mind.

HAMLET.   O God, I could be bounded in a nutshell and

---

44. indifferent—undistinguished.

count myself a king of infinite space, were it not that I have bad dreams.

GUILDENSTERN. Which dreams indeed are ambition, for the very[45] substance of the ambitious is merely the shadow of a dream.

HAMLET. A dream itself is but a shadow.

ROSENCRANTZ. Truly, and I hold ambition of so airy and light a quality that it is but a shadow's shadow.

HAMLET. Then are our beggars bodies, and our monarchs and outstretched heroes the beggars' shadows. Shall we to th' court? for, by my fay, I cannot reason.[46]

BOTH. We'll wait upon you.

HAMLET. No such matter. I will not sort[47] you with the rest of my servants, for, to speak to you like an honest man, I am most dreadfully attended. But in the beaten way of friendship, what make you at Elsinore?

ROSENCRANTZ. To visit you, my lord; no other occasion.

HAMLET. Beggar that I am, I am even poor in thanks, but I thank you; and sure, dear friends, my thanks are too dear[48] a halfpenny. Were you not sent for? Is it your own inclining? Is it a free visitation? Come, come, deal justly with me: come, come, nay, speak.

GUILDENSTERN. What should we say, my lord?

HAMLET. Why, anything, but to th' purpose. You were sent for; and there is a kind of confession in your looks which your modesties[49] have not craft enough to colour. I know the good king and queen have sent for you.

ROSENCRANTZ. To what end, my lord?

HAMLET. That[50] you must teach me: but let me conjure you, by the rights of our fellowship, by the consonancy[51] of our youth, by the obligation of our ever-preserved love, and by what more dear a better proposer[52] can charge you withal, be even and direct with me, whether you were sent for or no!

ROSENCRANTZ. [Aside to GUILDENSTERN.] What say you?

---

45. very—true.   46. reason—argue.
47. sort—class.   48. too dear—not worth.
49. modesties—sense of shame.   50. that—i.e., that is what.
51. consonancy—harmony.
52. proposer—talker.

HAMLET. [*Aside*.] Nay, then, I have an eye of you.—If you love me, hold not off.

GUILDENSTERN. My lord, we were sent for.

HAMLET. I will tell you why; so shall my anticipation prevent your discovery,[53] and your secrecy to the King and Queen moult no feather. I have of late—but wherefore I know not—lost all my mirth, forgone all custom of [54] exercises; and indeed it goes so heavily with my disposition that this goodly frame, the earth, seems to me a sterile promontory, this most excellent canopy, the air, look you, this brave o'erhanging firmament, this majestical roof fretted [55] with golden fire, why, it appeareth nothing to me but a foul and pestilent congregation of vapours. What a piece of work is a man! How noble in reason! How infinite in faculties! In form and moving how express[56] and admirable! In action how like an angel! In apprehension how like a god! The beauty of the world, the paragon of animals! And yet, to me, what is this quintessence[57] of dust? Man delights not me—no, nor woman neither, though by your smiling you seem to say so.

ROSENCRANTZ. My lord, there was no such stuff in my thoughts.

HAMLET. Why did ye laugh then, when I said, "Man delights not me"?

ROSENCRANTZ. To think, my lord, if you delight not in man, what lenten[58] entertainment the players shall receive from you. We coted [59] them on the way, and hither are they coming to offer you service.

HAMLET. He that plays the king shall be welcome; his majesty shall have tribute on me; the adventurous knight shall use his foil and target; [60] the lover shall not sigh gratis; the humorous[61] man shall end his part in peace; the clown shall make those laugh whose lungs are tickle o' th' sere; [62] and the lady shall say her mind freely, or the blank verse shall halt[63] for 't. What players are they?

---

53. discovery—disclosure.   54. custom of—customary.
55. fretted—ornamented.   56. express—exact.
57. quintessence—finest extract.   58. lenten—poor.
59. coted—passed.   60. foil and target—rapier and shield.
61. humorous—eccentric.   62. tickle o' th' sere—hair-triggered.
63. halt—limp.

ROSENCRANTZ.   Even those you were wont to take such delight in, the tragedians of the city.

HAMLET.   How chances it they travel? Their residence,[64] both in reputation and profit, was better both ways.

ROSENCRANTZ.   I think their inhibition[65] comes by the means of the late innovation.[66]

HAMLET.   Do they hold the same estimation they did when I was in the city? Are they so followed?

ROSENCRANTZ.   No, indeed, they are not.

HAMLET.   How comes it? Do they grow rusty?

ROSENCRANTZ.   Nay, their endeavour keeps in the wonted pace; but there is, sir, an aery of children, little eyases, that cry out on the top of question, and are most tyrannically clapped [67] for 't: these are now the fashion, and so berattle[68] the common stages[69]—so they call them—that many wearing rapiers are afraid of goosequills[70] and dare scarce come thither.

HAMLET.   What, are they children? Who maintains 'em? How are they escoted? [71] Will they pursue the quality[72] no longer than they can sing? [73] Will they not say afterwards, if they should grow themselves to common players,—as it is most like, if their means are no better—their writers do them wrong, to make them exclaim against their own succession?

ROSENCRANTZ.   Faith, there has been much to do on both sides, and the nation holds it no sin to tarre[74] them to controversy. There was for a while no money bid for argument[75] unless the poet and the player went to cuffs in the question.

HAMLET.   Is 't possible?

GUILDENSTERN.   O, there has been much throwing about of brains.

HAMLET.   Do the boys carry it away?

ROSENCRANTZ.   Ay, that they do, my lord; Hercules and his load [76] too.

---

64. residence—acting in the city.   65. inhibition—difficult times.
66. innovation—i.e., a "fad" for companies of child actors ("little eyases").   67. clapped—applauded.   68. berattle—satirize.
69. common stages—the theatres of the adult companies.
70. goosequills—attacks by satirists.   71. escoted—paid.
72. quality—profession.   73. sing—i.e., as "boy sopranos."
74. tarre—provoke.   75. argument—plot of a play.
76. Hercules and his load—the whole world.

HAMLET. It is not very strange; for my uncle is king of Denmark, and those that would make mows[77] at him while my father lived, give twenty, forty, fifty, a hundred ducats apiece for his picture in little.[78] 'Sblood,[79] there is something in this more than natural, if philosophy could find it out.   [*Flourish within.*]

GUILDENSTERN. There are the players.

HAMLET. Gentlemen, you are welcome to Elsinore. Your hands, come, then. Th' appurtenance of welcome is fashion and ceremony: let me comply with you in this garb, lest my extent to the players, which, I tell you, must show fairly outwards, should more appear like entertainment than yours. You are welcome; but my uncle-father and aunt-mother are deceived.

GUILDENSTERN. In what, my dear lord?

HAMLET. I am but mad north-north-west: when the wind is southerly I know a hawk from a handsaw.

Enter POLONIUS.

POLONIUS. Well be with you, gentlemen!

HAMLET. [*Aside to them.*] Hark you, Guildenstern, and you too, at each ear a hearer: that great baby you see there is not yet out of his swaddling-clouts.

ROSENCRANTZ. Happily[80] he is the second time come to them, for they say an old man is twice a child.

HAMLET. I will prophesy he comes to tell me of the players; mark it. [*Aloud.*] You say right, sir; a Monday morning; 't was then indeed.

POLONIUS. My lord, I have news to tell you.

HAMLET. My lord, I have news to tell you. When Roscius was an actor in Rome—

POLONIUS. The actors are come hither, my lord.

HAMLET. Buzz, buzz!

POLONIUS. Upon mine honour,—

HAMLET. "Then came each actor on his ass,"—

POLONIUS. The best actors in the world, either for tragedy, comedy, history, pastoral, pastoral-comical, historical-pastoral,

---

77. mows—grimaces.   78. picture in little—miniature portrait.
79. 'Sblood—by the blood of Christ.
80. Happily—perhaps.

scene individable,[81] or poem unlimited. Seneca[82] cannot be too heavy, nor Plautus[83] too light for the law of writ and the liberty. These are the only men.

HAMLET.   O Jephthah,[84] judge of Israel, what a treasure hadst thou!

POLONIUS.   What a treasure had he, my lord?

HAMLET.   Why.

>"One fair daughter, and no more,
>   The which he loved passing well."

POLONIUS.   [*Aside.*] Still on my daughter.

HAMLET.   Am I not i' th' right, old Jephthah?

POLONIUS.   If you call me Jephthah, my lord, I have a daughter that I love passing well.

HAMLET.   Nay, that follows not.

POLONIUS.   What follows, then, my lord?

HAMLET.   Why,

>   "As by lot, God wot,"

and then, you know,

>   "It came to pass as most like it was,"—

the first row[85] of the pious chanson will show you more, for look where my abridgement[86] comes.

Enter four or five PLAYERS.

You are welcome, masters, welcome all. I am glad to see thee well. Welcome, good friends. O, old friend! Why, thy face is valanced [87] since I saw thee last; com'st thou to beard me in Denmark? What, my young lady[88] and mistress! By 'r Lady, your ladyship is nearer to heaven than when I saw you last, by the altitude of a chopine.[89] Pray God, your voice, like a piece of uncurrent[90] gold, be not cracked within the ring. Masters, you

---

81. scene individable—i.e., play written in classical form, contrasting with "poem unlimited," which disregards the established rules of composition.   82. Seneca—Roman tragic playwright.
83. Plautus—Roman comic playwright.
84. Jephthah—a man who sacrificed his beloved daughter (*cf.,* Judges XI), subject of a popular ballad from which Hamlet pretends to quote.
85. row—stanza.   86. abridgement—those who cut me off.
87. valanced—bearded.
88. young lady—the boy who played women's roles.
89. chopine—thick-soled woman's shoe.   90. uncurrent—invalid.

are all welcome. We'll e'en to 't like French falconers—fly at anything we see; we'll have a speech straight. Come, give us a taste of your quality; come, a passionate speech.

FIRST PLAYER.   What speech, my good lord?

HAMLET.   I heard thee speak me a speech once, but it was never acted; or, if it was, not above once; for the play, I remember, pleased not the million; 't was caviare[91] to the general; [92] but it was—as I received it, and others, whose judgement in such matters cried in the top of[93] mine—an excellent play, well digested in the scenes, set down with as much modesty as cunning. I remember one said there were no sallets[94] in the lines to make the matter savoury, nor no matter in the phrase that might indict the author of affectation; but called it an honest method, as wholesome as sweet, and by very much more handsome than fine.[95] One speech in 't I chiefly loved; 't was Aeneas' [96] tale to Dido,[97] and there about of it especially when he speaks of Priam's[98] slaughter. If it live in your memory, begin at this line: let me see, let me see—

"The rugged Pyrrhus,[99] like th' Hyrcanian beast," [100]

—'T is not so; it begins with Pyrrhus:—

"The rugged Pyrrhus, he whose sable arms,
Black as his purpose, did the night resemble
When he lay couched in th' ominous horse,[101]
Hath now this dread and black complexion smear'd
With heraldry[102] more dismal: head to foot
Now is he total gules,[103] horribly trick'd
With blood of fathers, mothers, daughters, sons,
Bak'd and impasted [104] with the parching streets,
That lend a tyrannous and a damned light
To their lords' murder. Roasted in wrath and fire,

---

91. caviare—too choice.   92. general—common people.
93. in the top of—with a louder voice than.
94. sallets—smutty passages.   95. fine—ornate.
96. Aeneas—Prince of Troy, defeated by the Greeks.
97. Dido—Queen of Carthage.
98. Priam—King of Troy, Aeneas's father.
99. Pyrrhus—a Greek warrior.   100. Hyrcanian beast—tiger.
101. ominous horse—the Wooden Horse by which the Greeks got inside the Trojan walls.   102. heraldry—painting.
103. total gules—all red.   104. impasted—crusted.

And thus o'er-sized [105] with coagulate gore,
With eyes like carbuncles, the hellish Pyrrhus
Old grandsire Priam seeks."
So, proceed you.

POLONIUS. 'Fore God, my lord, well spoken, with good accent and good discretion.

FIRST PLAYER.   "Anon he finds him
Striking too short at Greeks; his antique sword,
Rebellious to his arm, lies where it falls,
Repugnant to command; [106] unequal match'd,
Pyrrhus at Priam drives, in rage strikes wide,
But with the whiff and wind of his fell sword
Th' unnerved father falls. Then senseless Ilium,[107]
Seeming to feel this blow, with flaming top
Stoops to his base, and with a hideous crash
Takes prisoner Pyrrhus' ear; for, lo! his sword,
Which was declining on the milky head
Of reverend Priam, seem'd i' th' air to stick;
So, as a painted tyrant, Pyrrhus stood
And like a neutral to his will and matter,
Did nothing.
But, as we often see, against some storm,
A silence in the heavens, the rack[108] stand still,
The bold winds speechless and the orb[109] below
As hush as death, anon the dreadful thunder
Doth rend the region; so, after Pyrrhus' pause,
Aroused vengeance sets him new a-work;
And never did the Cyclops' [110] hammers fall
On Mars's[111] armour forg'd for proof eterne[112]
With less remorse than Pyrrhus' bleeding sword
Now falls on Priam.
Out, out, thou strumpet Fortune! All you gods,
In general synod take away her power!

---

105. o'er-sized—varnished.
106. Repugnant to command—refusing to obey.
107. Ilium—Trojan citadel.   108. rack—clouds.
109. orb—world.   110. Cyclops—giant armorers of the gods.
111. Mars—god of war.
112. proof eterne—everlasting protection.

Break all the spokes and fellies[113] from her wheel,[114]
And bowl the round nave[115] down the hill of heaven
As low as to the fiends!"

POLONIUS. This is too long.

HAMLET. It shall to the barber's, with your beard. Prithee,
say on; he's for a jig[116] or a tale of bawdry, or he sleeps: say on;
come to Hecuba.[117]

FIRST PLAYER. "But who, Ah, woe! had seen the mobled [118]
   queen"—

HAMLET. "The mobled queen"?

POLONIUS. That's good; "mobled queen" is good.

FIRST PLAYER. "Run barefoot up and down, threat'ning the
   flames
With bisson rheum,[119] a clout[120] about that head
Where late the diadem stood, and for a robe,
About her lank and all o'er-teemed [121] loins,
A blanket, in the alarm of fear caught up;—
Who this had seen, with tongue in venom steep'd,
'Gainst Fortune's state[122] would treason have pronounc'd:
But if the gods themselves did see her then,
When she saw Pyrrhus make malicious sport
In mincing with his sword her husband's limbs,
The instant burst of clamour that she made,
Unless things mortal move them not at all,
Would have made milch[123] the burning eyes of heaven,
And passion in the gods."

POLONIUS. Look, whe'er he has not turn his colour and has
tears in 's eyes. Prithee, no more.

HAMLET. 'T is well; I'll have thee speak out the rest of this
soon. Good my lord, will you see the players well bestowed? Do
you hear? Let them be well used, for they are the abstract and

---

113. fellies—rims.
114. wheel—Fortune was depicted as turning a wheel on which all
men were bound to rise and fall.
115. nave—hub. 116. jig—comic skit.
117. Hecuba—Queen of Troy. 118. mobled—muffled.
119. bisson rheum—blinding tears. 120. clout—cloth.
121. o'er-teemed—worn out by bearing fifty-two children.
122. state—government. 123. milch—tearful.

brief chronicles of the time; after your death you were better
have a bad epitaph than their ill report while you live.

POLONIUS.   My lord, I will use them according to their desert.

HAMLET.   God's bodykins,[124] man, much better! Use every
man after his desert, and who shall scape whipping? Use them
after your own honour and dignity; the less they deserve, the
more merit is in your bounty. Take them in.

POLONIUS.   Come, sirs.   *Exit*.

HAMLET.   Follow him, friends; we'll hear a play to-morrow.
[*Exeunt all the Players but the First.*] Dost thou hear me, old
friend? Can you play "The Murder of Gonzago"?

FIRST PLAYER.   Ay, my lord.

HAMLET.   We'll ha 't to-morrow night. You could, for a need,
study a speech of some dozen lines or sixteen lines, which I
would set down and insert in 't, could you not?

FIRST PLAYER.   Ay, my lord.

HAMLET.   Very well. Follow that lord, and look you mock
him not.   *Exit* FIRST PLAYER.
My good friends, I'll leave you till night: you are welcome to
Elsinore.

ROSENCRANTZ.   Good my lord!
                              Exeunt ROSENCRANTZ *and* GUILDENSTERN.

HAMLET.   Ay, so, God buy to you.—Now I am alone.
O, what a rogue and peasant slave am I!
Is it not monstrous that this player here,
But in a fiction, in a dream of passion,
Could force his soul so to his own conceit[125]
That from her working all his visage wann'd,
Tears in his eyes, distraction in his aspéct,
A broken voice, and his whole function[126] suiting
With forms to his conceit? And all for nothing!
For Hecuba!
What's Hecuba to him, or he to Hecuba,
That he should weep for her? What would he do,
Had he the motive and the cue for passion
That I have? He would drown the stage with tears

---

124. bodikins—little body (the sacramental bread).
125. conceit—conception of his role.
126. whole function—bodily powers.

And cleave the general ear with horrid speech,
Make mad the guilty and appal the free,[127]
Confound the ignorant, and amaze indeed
The very faculties of eyes and ears.
Yet I,
A dull and muddy-mettled [128] rascal, peak[129]
Like John-a-dreams,[130] unpregnant of[131] my cause,
And can say nothing; no, not for a king,
Upon whose property[132] and most dear life
A damn'd defeat was made. Am I a coward?
Who calls me villain, breaks my pate[133] across,
Plucks off my beard and blows it in my face,
Tweaks me by the nose, gives me the lie i' th' throat
As deep as to the lungs, who does me this?
Ha!
'Swounds,[134] I should take it; for it cannot be
But I am pigeon-liver'd and lack gall [135]
To make oppression bitter, or ere this
I should ha' fatted all the region kites[136]
With this slave's offal.[137] Bloody, bawdy villain!
Remorseless, treacherous, lecherous, kindless[138] villain!
O, vengeance!
Why, what an ass am I! This is most brave,
That I, the son of a dear father murdered,
Prompted to my revenge by heaven and hell,
Must, like a whore, unpack my heart with words,
And fall a-cursing, like a very drab,
A scullion! [139]
Fie upon 't! Foh! About,[140] my brain! Hum, I have heard
That guilty creatures sitting at a play
Have by the very cunning of the scene
Been struck so to the soul that presently

---

127. free—innocent.   128. muddy-mettled—poor-spirited.
129. peak—mope.   130. John-a-dreams—a dreamer.
131. unpregnant of—unstirred by.
132. property—his crown and his queen.
133. pate—head.   134. 'Swounds—God's wounds.
135. gall—spirit.   136. kites—scavenging birds.
137. offal—guts.   138. kindless—unnatural.
139. scullion—kitchen maid.   140. About—to work.

They have proclaim'd their malefactions;
For murder, though it have no tongue, will speak
With most miraculous organ: I'll have these players
Play something like the murder of my father
Before mine uncle, I'll observe his looks,
I'll tent[141] him to the quick; if he but blench,[142]
I know my course. The spirit that I have seen
May be a devil; and the devil hath power
T' assume a pleasing shape; yea, and perhaps
Out of my weakness and my melancholy,
As he is very potent with such spirits,[143]
Abuses me to damn me; I'll have grounds
More relative[144] than this—the play's the thing
Wherein I'll catch the conscience of the King.   *Exit*

141. tent—probe.   142. blench—flinch.
143. spirits—moods.   144. relative—conclusive.

[ACT III • 1] *A room in the castle.*

Enter KING, QUEEN, POLONIUS, OPHELIA, ROSENCRANTZ,
GUILDENSTERN, *and Lords.*

KING.   And can you, by no drift of circumstance,[1]
Get from him why he puts on this confusion,
Grating so harshly all his days of quiet
With turbulent and dangerous lunacy?

ROSENCRANTZ.   He does confess he feels himself distracted;
But from what cause 'a will by no means speak.

GUILDENSTERN.   Nor do we find him forward to be sounded,
But, with a crafty madness, keeps aloof
When we would bring him on to some confession
Of his true state.

QUEEN.   Did he receive you well?

ROSENCRANTZ.   Most like a gentleman.

GUILDENSTERN.   But with much forcing of his disposition.[2]

ROSENCRANTZ.   Niggard of question;[3] but, of our demands,
Most free in his reply.

1. circumstance—conversation.
2. forcing of his disposition—effort at cordiality.
3. of question—to make conversation.

QUEEN.   Did you assay him
To any pastime?
ROSENCRANTZ.   Madam, it so fell out, that certain players
We o'er-raught on the way; of these we told him,
And there did seem in him a kind of joy
To hear of it: they are here about the court,
And, as I think, they have already order
This night to play before him.
POLONIUS.   'T is most true.
And he beseech'd me to entreat your Majesties
To hear and see the matter.
KING.   With all my heart; and it doth much content me
To hear him so inclin'd.
Good gentlemen, give him a further edge,[4]
And drive his purpose into these delights.
ROSENCRANTZ.   We shall, my lord.
                    Exeunt ROSENCRANTZ *and* GUILDENSTERN.
KING.   Sweet Gertrude, leave us two,
For we have closely[5] sent for Hamlet hither,
That he, as 't were by accident, may here
Affront[6] Ophelia.
Her father and myself—lawful espials[7]—
We'll so bestow ourselves that, seeing unseen,
We may of their encounter frankly judge,
And gather by him, as he is behav'd,
If 't be th' affliction of his love or no
That thus he suffers for.
QUEEN.   I shall obey you.
And for your part, Ophelia, I do wish
That your good beauties be the happy cause
Of Hamlet's wildness; so shall I hope your virtues
Will bring him to his wonted [8] way again,
To both your honours.
OPHELIA.   Madam, I wish it may.   *Exit* QUEEN.
POLONIUS.   Ophelia, walk you here. Gracious,[9] so please you,

---

4. edge—encouragement.   5. closely—secretly.
6. affront—meet face to face.   7. espials—observers.
8. wonted—normal.
9. Gracious—my gracious lord (Claudius).

We will bestow ourselves. [*To* OPHELIA.] Read on this book,[10]
That show of such an exercise may colour[11]
Your loneliness. We are oft to blame in this,—
'T is too much prov'd—that with devotion's visage
And pious action we do sugar o'er
The devil himself.
  KING. [*Aside.*] O, 't is true!
How smart a lash that speech doth give my conscience!
The harlot's cheek, beautied with plast'ring art,
Is not more ugly to[12] the thing that helps it
Than is my deed to my most painted [13] word:
O heavy burden!
  POLONIUS. I hear him coming; let's withdraw, my lord.
         Exeunt KING *and* POLONIUS.

Enter HAMLET.

  HAMLET. To be, or not to be: that is the question:
Whether 't is nobler in the mind to suffer
The slings and arrows of outrageous[14] fortune,
Or to take arms against a sea of troubles,
And by opposing end them. To die, to sleep—
No more; and by a sleep to say we end
The heart-ache and the thousand natural shocks
That flesh is heir to; 't is a consummation
Devoutly to be wish'd. To die; to sleep;—
To sleep, perchance to dream; ay, there's the rub; [15]
For in that sleep of death what dreams may come,
When we have shuffled off this mortal coil,
Must give us pause; there's the respect[16]
That makes calamity of so long life: [17]
For who would bear the whips and scorns of time,[18]
Th' oppressor's wrong, the proud man's contumely,
The pangs of déspis'd love, the law's delay,
The insolence of office,[19] and the spurns
That patient merit of th' unworthy takes,

---

10. 'book—prayer book. 11. colour—explain.
12. to—compared to. 13. painted—false.
14. outrageous—cruel. 15. rub—difficulty.
16. respect—consideration. 17. of so long life—so lasting.
18. time—the times. 19. office—government officials.

When he himself might his quietus[20] make
With a bare bodkin? [21] Who would these fardels[22] bear,
To grunt and sweat under a weary life,
But that the dread of something after death,
The undiscover'd country from whose bourn[23]
No traveller returns, puzzles the will
And makes us rather bear those ills we have
Than fly to others that we know not of?
Thus conscience[24] does make cowards of us all;
And thus the native hue of resolution
Is sicklied o'er with the pale cast of thought,[25]
And enterprises of great pith[26] and moment
With this regard their currents turn awry,
And lose the name of action.——Soft you now,
The fair Ophelia!——Nymph, in thy orisons[27]
Be all my sins remember'd.
    OPHELIA.   Good my lord,
How does your honour for this many a day?
    HAMLET.   I humbly thank you, well, well, well.
    OPHELIA.   My lord, I have remembrances of yours
That I have longed long to re-deliver.
I pray you, now receive them.
    HAMLET.   No, not I;
I never gave you aught.
    OPHELIA.   My honour'd lord, you know right well you did,
And, with them, words of so sweet breath compos'd
As made the things more rich. Their perfume lost,
Take these again; for to the noble mind
Rich gifts wax poor when givers prove unkind.
There, my lord.
    HAMLET.   Ha, ha! are you honest? [28]
    OPHELIA.   My lord!
    HAMLET.   Are you fair?
    OPHELIA.   What means your lordship?

---

20. quietus—discharge.   21. bodkin—stiletto.
22. fardels—burdens.   23. bourn—boundary.
24. conscience—reflection.   25. thought—despondency.
26. pith—importance.   27. orisons—prayers.
28. honest—chaste.

HAMLET. That if you be honest and fair, your honesty should admit no discourse to your beauty.

OPHELIA. Could beauty, my lord, have better commerce[29] than with honesty?

HAMLET. Ay, truly; for the power of beauty will sooner transform honesty from what it is to a bawd than the force of honesty can translate beauty into his likeness. This was sometime a paradox, but now the time gives it proof. I did love you once.

OPHELIA. Indeed, my lord, you made me believe so.

HAMLET. You should not have believed me, for virtue cannot so inoculate[30] our old stock[31] but we shall relish of it.[32] I loved you not.

OPHELIA. I was the more deceived.

HAMLET. Get thee to a nunnery; why wouldst thou be a breeder of sinners? I am myself indifferent[33] honest, but yet I could accuse me of such things that it were better my mother had not borne me: I am very proud, revengeful, ambitious, with more offences at my beck than I have thoughts to put them in, imagination to give them shape, or time to act them in. What should such fellows as I do crawling between earth and heaven? We are arrant knaves all; believe none of us, go thy ways to a nunnery. Where's your father?

OPHELIA. At home, my lord.

HAMLET. Let the doors be shut upon him, that he may play the fool nowhere but in 's own house. Farewell!

OPHELIA. O, help him, you sweet heavens!

HAMLET. If thou dost marry, I'll give thee this plague for thy dowry: be thou as chaste as ice, as pure as snow, thou shalt not escape calumny. Get thee to a nunnery, farewell! Or, if thou wilt needs marry, marry a fool; for wise men know well enough what monsters[34] you make of them. To a nunnery, go, and quickly too, farewell!

OPHELIA. Heavenly powers, restore him!

HAMLET. I have heard of your paintings, well enough. God hath given you one face, and you make yourselves another. You

---

29. commerce—association.   30. inoculate—change by grafting.
31. old stock—sinful nature.
32. relish of it—have yet a trace of the old stock.
33. indifferent—tolerably.   34. monsters—cuckolds.

jig and amble, and you lisp and nick-name God's creatures and make[35] your wantonness your ignorance. Go to, I'll no more on 't; it hath made me mad. I say, we will have no moe[36] mar-riage: those that are married already, all but one, shall live; the rest shall keep as they are. To a nunnery, go. *Exit.*

OPHELIA.   O, what a noble mind is here o'erthrown!
The courtier's, soldier's, scholar's, eye, tongue, sword;
Th' expectancy and rose of the fair state,
The glass[37] of fashion and the mould of form,
The observ'd of all observers, quite quite down!
And I, of ladies most deject and wretched,
That suck'd the honey of his music vows,
Now see that noble and most sovereign reason,
Like sweet bells jangled out of tune and harsh;
That unmatch'd form and feature of blown[38] youth
Blasted with ecstasy.[39] O, woe is me,
T' have seen what I have seen, see what I see!

Re-enter KING *and* POLONIUS.

KING.   Love! his affections do not that way tend;
Nor what he spake, though it lack'd form a little,
Was not like madness. There's something in his soul
O'er which his melancholy sits on brood,[40]
And I do doubt the hatch and the disclose
Will be some danger; which for to prevent,
I have in quick determination
Thus set it down: he shall with speed to England
For the demand of our neglected tribute.
Haply[41] the seas and countries different
With variable[42] objects shall expel
This something[43]-settled matter in his heart,
Whereon his brains still beating puts him thus
From fashion of himself.[44] What think you on 't?
POLONIUS.   It shall do well; but yet do I believe

---

35. make—call.   36. moe—more.   37. glass—mirror.
38. blown—blooming.   39. ecstasy—madness.
40. on brood—hatching.   41. Haply—perhaps.
42. variable—novel.   43. something—somewhat.
44. fashion of himself—his normal self.

The origin and commencement of his grief
Sprung from neglected love. How now, Ophelia?
You need not tell us what Lord Hamlet said;
We heard it all. My lord, do as you please,
But, if you hold it fit, after the play
Let his queen mother all alone entreat him
To show his grief; let her be round with him,
And I'll be plac'd, so please you, in the ear
Of all their conference. If she find him[45] not,
To England send him, or confine him where
Your wisdom best shall think.
    KING.   It shall be so.
Madness in great ones must not unwatch'd go.   *Exeunt.*

---

45. find him—discover his secret trouble.

[ACT III • 2] *A hall in the castle.*

Enter HAMLET *and three of the* PLAYERS.

HAMLET.   Speak the speech, I pray you, as I pronounced it
to you, trippingly on the tongue; but if you mouth it, as many of
our players do, I had as lief the town-crier spoke my lines. Nor
do not saw the air too much with your hand thus, but use all
gently, for in the very torrent, tempest, and, as I may say, the
whirlwind of your passion, you must acquire and beget a temperance that may give it smoothness. O, it offends me to the
soul to see a robustious periwig-pated [1] fellow tear a passion to
tatters, to very rags, to split the ears of the groundlings,[2] who for
the most part are capable of nothing but inexplicable dumb-
shows and noise: I would have such a fellow whipped for o'er-
doing Termagant; [3] it out-herods Herod: pray you, avoid it.

FIRST PLAYER.   I warrant your honour.

HAMLET.   Be not too tame neither, but let your own discretion be your tutor; suit the action to the word, the word to the
action; with this special observance, that you o'erstep not the

---

1. periwig-pated—bewigged.
2. groundlings—occupants of the least expensive part of the theater.
3. Termagant—Saracen god, presented as a roaring bully in the early
popular drama (as was Herod).

modesty of nature: for anything so o'erdone is from[4] the purpose of playing, whose end, both at the first and now, was and is, to hold, as 't were, the mirror up to nature; to show virtue her own feature, scorn her own image, and the very age and body of the time his form and pressure.[5] Now this overdone, or come tardy off,[6] though it makes the unskilful laugh, cannot but make the judicious grieve; the censure of the which one must, in your allowance, o'erweigh a whole theatre of others. O, there be players that I have seen play, and heard others praise, and that highly, not to speak it profanely, that, neither having th' accent of Christians nor the gait of Christian, pagan, nor man, have so strutted and bellowed that I have thought some of Nature's journeymen[7] had made men and not made them well, they imitated humanity so abominably.

FIRST PLAYER.   I hope we have reformed that indifferently with us.

HAMLET.   O, reform it altogether; and let those that play your clowns speak no more than is set down for them; for there be of them that will themselves laugh to set on some quantity of barren[8] spectators to laugh too, though in the mean time some necessary question of the play be then to be considered. That's villanous, and shows a most pitiful ambition in the fool that uses it. Go, make you ready.   *Exeunt* PLAYERS.

Enter POLONIUS, ROSENCRANTZ, *and* GUILDENSTERN.

How now, my lord! Will the King hear this piece of work?

POLONIUS.   And the Queen too, and that presently.

HAMLET.   Bid the players make haste.   *Exit* POLONIUS.
Will you two help to hasten them?

ROSENCRANTZ.
GUILDENSTERN. } Ay, my lord.

            Exeunt ROSENCRANTZ *and* GUILDENSTERN.
HAMLET.   What ho! Horatio!

Enter HORATIO.

HORATIO.   Here, sweet lord, at your service.

---

4. from—contrary to.   5. pressure—shape.
6. come tardy off—ineffectually acted.
7. journeymen—second-rate workmen.   8. barren—foolish.

HAMLET.   Horatio, thou art e'en as just a man
As e'er my conversation⁹ cop'd ¹⁰ withal.
    HORATIO.   O, my dear lord,—
    HAMLET.   Nay, do not think I flatter,
For what advancement may I hope from thee
That no revénue hast but thy good spirits
To feed and clothe thee? Why should the poor be flatter'd?
No, let the candied ¹¹ tongue lick ábsurd pomp,
And crook the pregnant¹² hinges of the knee
Where thrift¹³ may follow fawning. Dost thou hear?
Since my dear soul was mistress of my choice
And could of men distinguish, her election
Hath seal'd thee for herself, for thou hast been
As one, in suffering all, that suffers nothing,
A man that Fortune's buffets and rewards
Hast ta'en with equal thanks; and blest are those
Whose blood and judgement are so well commingled
That they are not a pipe for Fortune's finger
To sound what stop¹⁴ she please. Give me that man
That is not passion's slave, and I will wear him
In my heart's core, ay, in my heart of heart,
As I do thee.—Something too much of this.—
There is a play to-night before the King;
One scene of it comes near the circumstance
Which I have told thee of my father's death.
I prithee, when thou seest that act a-foot,
Even with the very comment¹⁵ of thy soul
Observe my uncle: if his occulted ¹⁶ guilt
Do not itself unkennel in one speech,
It is a damned ghost that we have seen,
And my imaginations are as foul
As Vulcan's stithy.¹⁷ Give him heedful note;
For I mine eyes will rivet to his face,
And after we will both our judgements join

---

9. conversation—association.   10. cop'd—met.
11. candied—flattering.   12. pregnant—supple.
13. thrift—profit.   14. sound what stop—play upon as.
15. comment—keen observation.   16. occulted—hidden.
17. stithy—forge (of Vulcan, the gods' blacksmith).

In censure[18] of his seeming.

HORATIO.   Well, my lord.
If 'a steal aught the whilst this play is playing,
And scape detecting, I will pay the theft.

Danish march. A flourish. Enter KING, QUEEN, POLONIUS,
OPHELIA, ROSENCRANTZ, GUILDENSTERN, *and other* LORDS *attendant, with the King's guard carrying torches.*

HAMLET.   They are coming to the play. I must be idle; [19]
Get you a place.

KING.   How fares our cousin Hamlet?

HAMLET.   Excellent, i' faith, of the chameleon's dish: I eat
the air, promise-crammed—You cannot feed capons so.

KING.   I have nothing with[20] this answer, Hamlet; these
words are not mine.

HAMLET.   No, nor mine now. [*To* POLONIUS.] My lord, you
played once i' th' university, you say?

POLONIUS.   That did I, my lord, and was accounted a good
actor.

HAMLET.   What did you enact?

POLONIUS.   I did enact Julius Caesar; I was killed i' th'
Capitol; Brutus killed me.

HAMLET.   It was a brute part of him to kill so capital a calf
there. Be the players ready?

ROSENCRANTZ.   Ay, my lord, they stay upon your patience.

QUEEN.   Come hither, my dear Hamlet, sit by me.

HAMLET.   No, good mother, here's metal more attractive.
[*Lying down at* OPHELIA'S *feet.*]

POLONIUS.   [*To the* KING.] O, ho! do you mark that?

HAMLET.   Lady, shall I lie in your lap?

OPHELIA.   No, my lord.

HAMLET.   I mean, my head upon your lap?

OPHELIA.   Ay, my lord.

HAMLET.   Do you think I meant country[21] matters?

OPHELIA.   I think nothing, my lord.

HAMLET.   That's a fair thought to lie between maid's legs.

---

18. censure—judgment.   19. be idle—pretend madness.
20. have nothing with—do not understand.
21. country—indecent.

OPHELIA. What is, my lord?

HAMLET. Nothing.

OPHELIA. You are merry, my lord.

HAMLET. Who, I?

OPHELIA. Ay, my lord.

HAMLET. O God, your only[22] jig-maker. What should a man do but be merry? for, look you, how cheerfully my mother looks, and my father died within 's two hours.

OPHELIA. Nay, 't is twice two months, my lord.

HAMLET. So long? Nay then, let the devil wear black, for I'll have a suit of sables.[23] O heavens! die two months ago, and not forgotten yet? Then there's hope a great man's memory may outlive his life half a year; but, by 'r Lady, 'a must build churches then, or else shall 'a suffer not thinking on, with the hobby-horse,[24] whose epitaph is, "For, O, for, O, the hobby-horse is forgot."

The trumpets sound. The dumb-show[25] enters.

THE DUMB-SHOW

Enter a King and Queen, the Queen embracing him and he her. She kneels and makes show of protestation to him; he takes her up and declines his head upon her neck. He lays him down upon a bank of flowers. She, seeing him asleep, leaves him. Anon[26] comes in another man, takes off his crown, kisses it, pours poison in the sleeper's ears, and leaves him. The Queen returns, finds the King dead, makes passionate action. The poisoner, with some three or four, come in again, seem to condole with her. The dead body is carried away. The poisoner woos the Queen with gifts; she seems harsh a while, but in the end accepts his love.   *Exeunt.*

OPHELIA. What means this, my lord?

HAMLET. Marry, this is miching mallecho;[27] it means mischief.

---

22. only—best.   23. sables—fine fur; also, mourning color.
24. hobby-horse—a character in the May games, in disfavor with the Puritans (hence, "forgot").
25. dumb-show—pantomime.   26. Anon—at once.
27. miching mallecho—sneaking crime.

OPHELIA.   Belike this show imports the argument of the play?

Enter the Speaker of the Prologue.

HAMLET.   We shall know by this fellow. The players cannot keep counsel, they'll tell all.

OPHELIA.   Will 'a tell us what this show meant?

HAMLET.   Ay, or any show that you will show him: be not you ashamed to show, he'll not shame to tell you what it means.

OPHELIA.   You are naught,[28] you are naught; I'll mark the play.

PROLOGUE.

> For us, and for our tragedy,
> Here stooping to your clemency,
> We beg your hearing patiently.

Exit.

HAMLET.   Is this a prologue, or the posy of a ring? [29]

OPHELIA.   'T is brief, my lord.

HAMLET.   As woman's love.

Enter Player King *and* Player Queen.

PLAYER KING.   Full thirty times hath Phoebus' cart[30] gone round
Neptune's salt wash and Tellus' [31] orbed ground,
And thirty dozen moons with borrowed sheen
About the world have times twelve thirties been,
Since love our hearts and Hymen[32] did our hands
Unite commutual in most sacred bands.

PLAYER QUEEN.   So many journeys may the sun and moon
Make us again count o'er ere love be done!
But, woe is me, you are so sick of late,
So far from cheer and from your former state,
That I distrust[33] you. Yet, though I distrust,
Discomfort you, my lord, it nothing must;
For women fear too much, even as they love

---

28. naught—naughty.
29. posy of a ring—motto etched in a finger ring.
30. Phoebus' cart—the sun.   31. Tellus—goddess of the Earth.
32. Hymen—god of marriage.   33. distrust—fear for.

And women's fear and love hold quantity,[34]
In neither aught, or in extremity.[35]
Now, what my love is, proof hath made you know;
And as my love is siz'd, my fear is so:
Where love is great, the littlest doubts are fear;
Where little fears grow great, great love grows there.

 PLAYER KING. Faith, I must leave thee,[36] love, and shortly
  too.

My operant powers their functions leave to do;
And thou shalt live in this fair world behind,
Honour'd, belov'd; and haply one as kind
For husband shalt thou—

 PLAYER QUEEN.   O, confound the rest!

Such love must needs be treason in my breast:
In second husband let me be accurst,
None wed the second but who kill'd the first.

 HAMLET. [*Aside.*] That's wormwood!

 PLAYER QUEEN. The instances[37] that second marriage
  move[38]

Are base respects of thrift,[39] but none of love:
A second time I kill my husband dead,
When second husband kisses me in bed.

 PLAYER KING. I do believe you think what now you speak,

But what we do determine oft we break.
Purpose is but the slave to memory,
Of violent birth, but poor validity; [40]
Which now, the fruit unripe, sticks on the tree,
But fall unshaken when they mellow be.
Most necessary 't is that we forget
To pay ourselves what to ourselves is debt:
What to ourselves in passion we propose,
The passion ending, doth the purpose lose.
The violence of either grief or joy
Their own enactures with themselves destroy:

---

34. quantity—proportion.
35. aught, or in extremity—nothing, or too much.
36. leave thee—die. 37. instances—motives.
38. move—prompt. 39. respects of thrift—considerations of gain.
40. validity—strength.

Where joy most revels, grief doth most lament;
Grief joys, joy grieves, on slender accident.[41]
This world is not for aye,[42] nor 't is not strange
That even our loves should with our fortunes change,
For 't is a question left us yet to prove,
Whether love lead fortune, or else fortune love.
The great man down, you mark his favourite flies;
The poor advanc'd makes friends of enemies:
And hitherto doth love on fortune tend,
For who not needs shall never lack a friend;
And who in want a hollow friend doth try,
Directly seasons[43] him his enemy.
But, orderly to end where I begun,
Our wills and fates do so contrary run
That our devices still are overthrown;
Our thoughts are ours, their ends none of our own:
So think thou wilt no second husband wed;
But die thy thoughts when thy first lord is dead.
    PLAYER QUEEN.   Nor earth to me give food, nor heaven light!
Sport and repose lock from me day and night!
To desperation turn my trust and hope,
An anchor's[44] cheer in prison be my scope!
Each opposite that blanks[45] the face of joy
Meet what I would have well and it destroy!
Both here and hence pursue me lasting strife,
If, once a widow, ever I be wife!
    HAMLET.   If she should break it now!
    PLAYER KING.   'T is deeply sworn. Sweet, leave me here a
      while.
My spirits grow dull, and fain I would beguile
The tedious day with sleep.   *[Sleeps.]*
    PLAYER QUEEN.   Sleep rock thy brain,
And never come mischance between us twain!   *Exit.*
    HAMLET.   Madam, how like you this play?
    QUEEN.   The lady doth protest too much, methinks.
    HAMLET.   O, but she'll keep her word.

---

41. accident—occurrence.   42. aye—ever.   43. seasons—makes.
44. anchor—hermit.   45. blanks—makes pale.

KING. Have you heard the argument? Is there no offence in 't?

HAMLET. No, no, they do but jest, poison in jest; no offence i' th' world.

KING. What do you call the play?

HAMLET. The Mouse-trap. Marry, how? Tropically.[46] This play is the image of a murder done in Vienna; Gonzago is the duke's name; his wife, Baptista. You shall see anon, 't is a knavish piece of work, but what of that? Your Majesty and we that have free[47] souls, it touches us not: let the galled jade[48] wince, our withers[49] are unwrung.

Enter LUCIANUS.

This is one Lucianus, nephew to the king.

OPHELIA. You are as good as a chorus,[50] my lord.

HAMLET. I could interpret between you and your love, if I could see the puppets[51] dallying.

OPHELIA. You are keen, my lord, you are keen.

HAMLET. It would cost you a groaning to take off mine edge.

OPHELIA. Still better, and worse.[52]

HAMLET. So[53] you must take your husbands. Begin, murderer; leave thy damnable faces and begin. Come, "the croaking raven doth bellow for revenge."

LUCIANUS. Thoughts black, hands apt, drugs fit, and time agreeing;
Confederate season,[54] else no[55] creature seeing.
Thou mixture rank, of midnight weeds collected,
With Hecate's[56] ban thrice blasted, thrice infected,
Thy natural magic and dire property[57]
On wholesome life usurps immediately.

                    [*Pours the poison into the sleeper's ears.*]

---

46. Tropically—metaphorically.   47. free—innocent.
48. galled jade—horse covered with sores.
49. withers—shoulders.   50. chorus—commentator.
51. puppets—i.e., toy actors playing the lovers.
52. better and worse—wittier but more obscene.
53. So—i.e., "for better, for worse."
54. Confederate season—the time is ripe.   55. else no—no other.
56. Hecate—goddess of witchcraft.   57. property—nature.

HAMLET. He poisons him i' th' garden for his estate. His name's Gonzago; the story is extant, and writ in very choice Italian; you shall see anon how the murderer gets the love of Gonzago's wife.

OPHELIA. The King rises.

HAMLET. What, frighted with false fire?

QUEEN. How fares my lord?

POLONIUS. Give o'er the play.

KING. Give me some light. Away!

POLONIUS. Lights, lights, lights!

Exeunt all but HAMLET *and* HORATIO.

HAMLET. Why, let the strucken deer go weep,
>The hart ungalled play;
>For some must watch, while some must sleep,—
>Thus runs the world away.

Would not this, sir, and a forest of feathers[58]—if the rest of my fortunes turn Turk[59] with me—with two Provincial roses[60] on my razed [61] shoes, get me a fellowship in a cry[62] of players, sir?

HORATIO. Half a share.

HAMLET. A whole one, I.

For thou dost know, O Damon[63] dear,
>This realm dismantled was
Of Jove himself; and now reigns here
>A very, very—pajock.[64]

HORATIO. You might have rhymed.

HAMLET. O good Horatio, I'll take the ghost's word for a thousand pound. Didst perceive?

HORATIO. Very well, my lord.

HAMLET. Upon the talk of the poisoning?

HORATIO. I did very well note him.

HAMLET. Ah, ha! Come, some music! Come, the recorders! [65]

For if the king like not the comedy,
>Why then, belike, he likes it not, perdy.[66] Come, some music!

---

58. feathers—plumes of the tragedian's headdress.
59. turn Turk—play me false.   60. roses—rosettes.
61. raz'd—slashed.   62. cry—company.
63. Damon—the classic model of friendship.   64. pajock—peacock.
65. recorders—wooden flutes.   66. perdy—by God.

Re-enter ROSENCRANTZ *and* GUILDENSTERN.

GUILDENSTERN.   Good my lord, vouchsafe me a word with you.

HAMLET.   Sir, a whole history.

GUILDENSTERN.   The King, sir,—

HAMLET.   Ay, sir, what of him?

GUILDENSTERN.   Is in his retirement marvellous distempered.[67]

HAMLET.   With drink, sir?

GUILDENSTERN.   No, my lord, with choler.[68]

HAMLET.   Your wisdom should show itself more richer to signify this to the doctor; for, for me to put him to his purgation would perhaps plunge him into more choler.

GUILDENSTERN.   Good my lord, put your discourse into some frame, and start not so wildly from my affair.

HAMLET.   I am tame, sir; pronounce.

GUILDENSTERN.   The Queen, your mother, in most great affliction of spirit, hath sent me to you.

HAMLET.   You are welcome.

GUILDENSTERN.   Nay, good my lord, this courtesy is not of the right breed. If it shall please you to make me a wholesome answer I will do your mother's commandment; if not, your pardon and my return shall be the end of my business.

HAMLET.   Sir, I cannot.

ROSENCRANTZ.   What, my lord?

HAMLET.   Make you a wholesome answer: my wit's diseased. But, sir, such answer as I can make, you shall command, or, rather, as you say, my mother. Therefore no more, but to the matter. My mother, you say,—

ROSENCRANTZ.   Then thus she says: your behavior hath struck her into amazement and admiration.[69]

HAMLET.   O wonderful son, that can so astonish a mother! But is there no sequel at the heels of this mother's admiration? Impart.

ROSENCRANTZ.   She desires to speak with you in her closet ere you go to bed.

---

67. distempered—upset.   68. choler—anger; also, biliousness.
69. admiration—wonder.

HAMLET.   We shall obey, were she ten times our mother. Have you any further trade with us?

ROSENCRANTZ.   My lord, you once did love me.

HAMLET.   And do still, by these pickers and stealers.[70]

ROSENCRANTZ.   Good my lord, what is your cause of distemper? You do surely bar the door upon your own liberty if you deny[71] your griefs to your friend.

HAMLET.   Sir, I lack advancement.

ROSENCRANTZ.   How can that be, when you have the voice of the King himself for your succession in Denmark?

HAMLET.   Ay, but "While the grass grows," [72]—the proverb is something musty.

Re-enter the PLAYERS *with recorders.*

O, the recorders! Let me see one.—To withdraw[73] with you:— why do you go about to recover the wind [74] of me, as if you would drive me into a toil? [75]

GUILDENSTERN.   O, my lord, if my duty be too bold, my love is too unmannerly.

HAMLET.   I do not well understand that. Will you play upon this pipe?

GUILDENSTERN.   My lord, I cannot.

HAMLET.   I pray you.

GUILDENSTERN.   Believe me, I cannot.

HAMLET.   I do beseech you.

GUILDENSTERN.   I know no touch of it, my lord.

HAMLET.   'T is as easy as lying: govern these ventages[76] with your finger and thumb, give it breath with your mouth, and it will discourse most eloquent music. Look you, these are the stops.

GUILDENSTERN.   But these cannot I command to any utt'rance of harmony; I have not the skill.

HAMLET.   Why, look you now, how unworthy a thing you make of me! You would play upon me, you would seem to know

---

70. pickers and stealers—hands.   71. deny—refuse to tell.
72. ". . .grows"—"While the grass grows, the steed starves."
73. withdraw—speak privately.
74. recover the wind—get to the windward.   75. toil—net.
76. ventages—stops (wind holes in the recorder).

my stops, you would pluck out the heart of my mystery, you
would sound me from my lowest note to the top of my compass;
and there is much music, excellent voice, in this little organ, yet
cannot you make it speak. 'Sblood, do you think that I am
easier to be played on than a pipe? Call me what instrument you
will, though you can fret[77] me, yet you cannot play upon me,

Enter POLONIUS.

God bless you, sir.

POLONIUS.   My lord, the Queen would speak with you, and
presently.

HAMLET.   Do you see yonder cloud that's almost in shape
of a camel?

POLONIUS.   By th' mass and 't is like a camel indeed.

HAMLET.   Methinks it is like a weasel.

POLONIUS.   It is backed like a weasel.

HAMLET.   Or like a whale?

POLONIUS.   Very like a whale.

HAMLET.   Then I will come to my mother by and by. [*Aside.*]
They fool [78] me to the top of my bent.[79]—I will come by and by.

POLONIUS.   I will say so.   *Exit.*

HAMLET.   "By and by" is easily said. Leave me, friends.
                                      Exeunt all but HAMLET.

'T is now the very witching time of night
When churchyards yawn and hell itself breathes out
Contagion to this world: now could I drink hot blood,
And do such bitter business as the day
Would quake to look on. Soft! now to my mother.
O heart, lose not thy nature, let not ever
The soul of Nero[80] enter this firm bosom;
Let me be cruel, not unnatural.
I will speak daggers to her, but use none.
My tongue and soul in this be hypocrites;
How in my words somever she be shent,[81]
To give them seals[82] never, my soul, consent!   *Exit.*

---

77. fret—annoy; also, use frets to play an instrument.
78. fool—treat me as a fool.   79. top of my bent—limit.
80. Nero—Roman emperor who murdered his mother.
81. shent—rebuked.   82. give them seals—fulfill them by actions.

[ACT III • 3] *A room in the castle.*

Enter KING, ROSENCRANTZ, *and* GUILDENSTERN.

KING. I like him not, nor stands it safe with us
To let his madness range. Therefore prepare you:
I your commission will forthwith dispatch,
And he to England shall along with you.
The terms of our estate[1] may not endure
Hazard so near us as doth hourly grow
Out of his lunacies.
GUILDENSTERN. We will ourselves provide.
Most holy and religious fear[2] it is
To keep those many many bodies safe
That live and feed upon your Majesty.
ROSENCRANTZ. The single and peculiar life is bound
With all the strength and armour of the mind
To keep itself from noyance,[3] but much more
That spirit upon whose weal [4] depends and rests
The lives of many. The cease[5] of majesty
Dies not alone, but, like a gulf,[6] doth draw
What's near it with it: or it is a massy wheel,
Fix'd on the summit of the highest mount,
To whose huge spokes ten thousand lesser things
Are mortis'd and adjoin'd; which, when it falls,
Each small annexment, petty consequence,
Attends the boisterous ruin. Never alone
Did the King sigh, but with a general groan.
KING. Arm[7] you, I pray you, to this speedy voyage,
For we will fetters put about this fear,
Which now goes too free-footed.
ROSENCRANTZ. We will haste us.
Exeunt ROSENCRANTZ *and* GUILDENSTERN.
Enter POLONIUS.

POLONIUS. My lord, he's going to his mother's closet:
Behind the arras I'll convey myself,

---

1. terms of our estate—condition of royal rank.
2. fear—anxiety. 3. noyance—harm. 4. weal—welfare.
5. cease—death. 6. gulf—whirlpool. 7. Arm—prepare.

To hear the process.[8]—I'll warrant she'll tax[9] him home; [10]
And, as you said, and wisely was it said,
'T is meet that some more audience than a mother,
Since nature makes them partial, should o'erhear
The speech of vantage.[11] Fare you well, my liege.
I'll call upon you ere you go to bed,
And tell you what I know.

KING.   Thanks, dear my lord.

Exit POLONIUS.

O, my offence is rank, it smells to heaven;
It hath the primal eldest curse[12] upon 't,
A brother's murder. Pray can I not,
Though inclination be as sharp as will.
My stronger guilt defeats my strong intent,
And, like a man to double business bound,
I stand in pause where I shall first begin,
And both neglect. What if this cursed hand
Were thicker than itself with brother's blood,
Is there not rain enough in the sweet heavens
To wash it white as snow? Whereto serves mercy
But to confront[13] the visage of offence?
And what's in prayer but this twofold force,
To be forestalled ere we come to fall,
Or pardon'd being down? Then I'll look up;
My fault is past. But, O, what form of prayer
Can serve my turn? "Forgive me my foul murder"?
That cannot be; since I am still possess'd
Of those effects[14] for which I did the murder,
My crown, mine own ambition, and my queen.
May one be pardon'd and retain th' offence? [15]
In the corrupted currents of this world
Offence's gilded hand may shove by justice,
And oft 't is seen the wicked prize itself
Buys out the law: but 't is not so above;

---

8. process—what is said.   9. tax—censure.
10. home—soundly.   11. of vantage—from a place of vantage.
12. curse—i.e., that upon Cain who slew his brother Abel (Genesis
    4: 10–12).
13. confront—look upon.   14. effects—gains.   15. offence—booty.

There is no shuffling, there the action lies
In his true nature; and we ourselves compell'd,
Even to the teeth and forehead of our faults,
To give in evidence. What then? What rests?
Try what repentance can.—What can it not?
Yet what can it when one cannot repent?
O wretched state! O bosom black as death!
O limed [16] soul, that, struggling to be free,
Art more engag'd! [17] Help, angels! Make assay! [18]
Bow, stubborn knees, and, heart with strings of steel,
Be soft as sinews of the new-born babe!
All may be well.   [*He kneels.*]

Enter HAMLET.

   HAMLET.   Now might I do it pat, now 'a is praying,
And now I'll do 't.—And so 'a goes to heaven;
And so am I reveng'd. That would be scann'd: [19]
A villain kills my father, and for that,
I, his sole son, do this same villain send
To heaven.
Oh, this is base and silly, not revenge.
'A took my father grossly, full of bread,
With all his crimes broad blown, as flush as May;
And how his audit[20] stands who knows save Heaven?
But in our circumstance and course of thought
'T is heavy with him: and am I then reveng'd,
To take him in the purging of his soul,
When he is fit and season'd for his passage?
No!
Up, sword, and know thou a more horrid hent,[21]
When he is drunk asleep, or in his rage,
Or in th' incestuous pleasure of his bed,
At game a-swearing, or about some act
That has no relish of salvation in 't,
Then trip him, that his heels may kick at heaven,

---

16. limed—trapped.   17. engag'd—ensnared.
18. assay—attempt.   19. scann'd—scrutinized.
20. audit—account (in the Book of Judgement).
21. hent—opportunity.

And that his soul may be as damn'd and black
As hell, whereto it goes. My mother stays.
This physic but prolongs thy sickly days.   *Exit.*
   KING.   [*Rising.*] My words fly up, my thoughts remain below:
Words without thoughts never to heaven go.   *Exit.*

[ACT III • 4] *The* QUEEN'S *closet.*

Enter QUEEN *and* POLONIUS.

   POLONIUS.   'A will come straight, look you lay home to him:
Tell him his pranks have been too broad to bear with,
And that your Grace hath screen'd and stood between
Much heat and him. I'll silence me e'en here.
Pray you, be round with him.
   HAMLET.   [*Within.*] Mother, mother, mother!
   QUEEN.   I'll warrant you, fear me not.
Withdraw, I hear him coming.
                 [POLONIUS *hides behind the arras.*]
Enter HAMLET.

   HAMLET.   Now, mother, what's the matter?
   QUEEN.   Hamlet, thou hast thy father much offended.
   HAMLET.   Mother, you have my father much offended.
   QUEEN.   Come, come, you answer with an idle tongue.
   HAMLET.   Go, go, you question with a wicked tongue.
   QUEEN.   Why, how now, Hamlet!
   HAMLET.   What's the matter now?
   QUEEN.   Have you forgot me?
   HAMLET.   No, by the rood,[1] not so.
You are the Queen, your husband's brother's wife;
And, would it were not so, you are my mother.
   QUEEN.   Nay, then, I'll set those to you that can speak.
   HAMLET.   Come, come, and sit you down; you shall not
      budge;
You go not till I set you up a glass
Where you may see the inmost part of you.
   QUEEN.   What wilt thou do? Thou wilt not murder me?
Help, ho!

---

1. rood—cross.

POLONIUS.   [*Behind.*] What, ho! help!

HAMLET.   [*Drawing.*] How now! A rat? Dead, for a ducat,
   dead!   [*Stabs* POLONIUS *through the arras.*]

POLONIUS.   [*Behind.*] O, I am slain!

QUEEN.   O me, what hast thou done?

HAMLET.   Nay, I know not.
Is it the King?

QUEEN.   O, what a rash and bloody deed is this!

HAMLET.   A bloody deed. Almost as bad, good mother,
As kill a king, and marry with his brother.

QUEEN.   As kill a king!

HAMLET.   Ay, lady it was my word.
              [*Lifts up the arras and discovers* POLONIUS.]
Thou wretched, rash, intruding fool, farewell!
I took thee for thy better; take thy fortune;
Thou find'st to be too busy is some danger.
—Leave wringing of your hands; peace, sit you down,
And let me wring your heart; for so I shall,
If it be made of penetrable stuff,
If damned custom have not braz'd [2] it so
That it be proof and bulwark against sense.[3]

QUEEN.   What have I done, that thou dar'st wag thy tongue
In noise so rude against me?

HAMLET.   Such an act
That blurs the grace and blush of modesty,
Calls virtue hypocrite, takes off the rose
From the fair forehead of an innocent love
And sets a blister[4] there, makes marriage-vows
As false as dicers' oaths; O, such a deed
As from the body of contraction[5] plucks
The very soul, and sweet religion makes
A rhapsody of words.[6] Heaven's face doth glow,[7]
And this solidity and compound mass,[8]
With heated visage, as against the doom,
Is thought-sick at the act.

---

2. braz'd—hardened.   3. sense—feeling.
4. blister—harlot's brand.   5. contraction—the marriage contract.
6. rhapsody of words—meaningless words.   7. glow—blush.
8. solidity and compound mass—the solid earth.

QUEEN.   Ay me, what act,
That roars so loud and thunders in the index?
HAMLET.   Look here, upon this picture, and on this,
The counterfeit presentment of two brothers.
See, what a grace was seated on this brow:
Hyperion's curls, the front of Jove[9] himself,
An eye like Mars, to threaten and command,
A station[10] like the herald Mercury
New-lighted on a heaven-kissing hill,
A combination and a form indeed,
Where every god did seem to set his seal,
To give the world assurance of a man:
This was your husband.—Look you now what follows:
Here is your husband, like a mildew'd ear,
Blasting his wholesome brother. Have you eyes?
Could you on this fair mountain leave to feed,
And batten[11] on this moor? Ha! have you eyes?
You cannot call it love, for at your age
The hey-day[12] in the blood is tame, it's humble,
And waits upon[13] the judgement; and what judgement
Would step from this to this? Sense sure you have,
Else could you not have motion; but sure, that sense
Is apoplex'd; [14] for madness would not err,
Nor sense to ecstasy was ne'er so thrall'd
But it reserv'd some quantity of choice,[15]
To serve in such a difference. What devil was 't
That thus hath cozen'd [16] you at hoodman-blind? [17]
Eyes without feeling, feeling without sight,
Ears without hands or eyes, smelling sans[18] all,
Or but a sickly part of one true sense
Could not so mope.
O shame! where is thy blush? Rebellious hell,
If thou canst mutine[19] in a matron's bones,

---

9. front of Jove—forehead of the king of the gods.
10. station—posture.   11. batten—gorge.
12. hey-day—youthful passion.   13. waits upon—defers to.
14. apoplex'd—paralyzed.   15. choice—discrimination.
16. cozen'd—cheated.   17. hoodman-blind—blindman's-buff.
18. sans—without.   19. mutine—mutiny.

To flaming youth let virtue be as wax,
And melt in her own fire. Proclaim no shame
When the compulsive ardour[20] gives the charge,
Since frost itself as actively doth burn
And reason panders[21] will.
    QUEEN.   O Hamlet, speak no more!
Thou turn'st mine eyes into my very soul,
And there I see such black and grained [22] spots
As will leave there their tinct.
    HAMLET.   Nay, but to live
In the rank sweat of an enseamed [23] bed,
Stew'd in corruption, honeying and making love
Over the nasty sty—
    QUEEN.   O, speak to me no more!
These words like daggers enter in mine ears.
No more, sweet Hamlet!
    HAMLET.   A murderer and a villain,
A slave that is not twentieth part the tithe[24]
Of your precedent lord! A vice[25] of kings,
A cutpurse of the empire and the rule,
That from a shelf the precious diadem stole,
And put it in his pocket!
    QUEEN.   No more!

Enter GHOST *in his night-gown.*[26]

    HAMLET.   A king of shreds and patches—
Save me, and hover o'er me with your wings,
You heavenly guards! What would your gracious figure?
    QUEEN.   Alas, he's mad!
    HAMLET.   Do you not come your tardy son to chide,
That, laps'd in[27] time and passion, lets go by
Th' important acting of your dread command?
O, say!
    GHOST.   Do not forget! This visitation
Is but to whet thy almost blunted purpose.

---

20. ardor—lust.   21. panders—becomes subject to.
22. grained—fast-dyed.   23. enseamed—greasy.
24. tithe—tenth part.   25. vice—rascally buffoon.
26. night-gown—dressing gown.   27. laps'd-in—allowed to slip by.

But, look, amazement on thy mother sits;
O, step between her and her fighting soul.
Conceit[28] in weakest bodies strongest works.
Speak to her, Hamlet.

HAMLET.   How is it with you, lady?

QUEEN. Alas, how is 't with you,
That you do bend your eye on vacancy
And with th' incorporal [29] air do hold discourse?
Forth at your eyes your spirits wildly peep,
And, as the sleeping soldiers in th' alarm,[30]
Your bedded [31] hair, like life in excrements,[32]
Start up and stand on end. O gentle son,
Upon the heat and flame of thy distemper
Sprinkle cool patience. Whereon do you look?

HAMLET. On him, on him! Look you, how pale he glares!
His form and cause[33] conjoin'd, preaching to stones,
Would make them capable.[34] Do not look upon me,
Lest with this piteous action you convert
My stern effects; then what I have to do
Will want true colour, tears perchance for blood.

QUEEN. To whom do you speak this?

HAMLET.   Do you see nothing there?

QUEEN. Nothing at all, yet all that is I see.

HAMLET. Nor did you nothing hear?

QUEEN.   No, nothing but ourselves.

HAMLET. Why, look you there! Look, how it steals away!
My father, in his habit[35] as[36] he lived!
Look, where he goes, even now, out at the portal! *Exit* GHOST.

QUEEN. This is the very coinage of your brain:
This bodiless creation ecstasy
Is very cunning[37] in.

HAMLET.   Ecstasy!
My pulse, as yours, doth temperately keep time,

---

28. conceit—imagination. 29. incorporeal—bodiless.
30. —in th' alarm—at the call to arms. 31. bedded—lying flat.
32. life in excrements—hairs with life.
33. cause—the reason for his appearance.
34. capable—i.e., of being moved. 35. habit—garments.
36. as—when. 37. cunning—skillful.

And makes as healthful music: it is not madness
That I have utter'd: bring me to the test,
And I the matter will re-word, which madness
Would gambol [38] from. Mother, for love of grace,
Lay not that flattering unction[39] to your soul,
That not your trespass, but my madness speaks;
It will but skin and film the ulcerous place,
Whilst rank corruption, mining[40] all within,
Infects unseen. Confess yourself to Heaven;
Repent what's past, avoid what is to come,
And do not spread the compost[41] on the weeds,
To make them ranker.[42] Forgive me this my virtue,
For in the fatness of these pursy[43] times
Virtue itself of vice must pardon beg,
Yea, curb[44] and woo for leave to do him good.
    QUEEN.   O Hamlet, thou hast cleft my heart in twain.
    HAMLET.   O, throw away the worser part of it,
And live the purer with the other half.
Good-night; but go not to my uncle's bed.
Assume a virtue, if you have it not.
That monster, custom, who all sense doth eat
Of habits evil, is angel yet in this,
That to the use of actions fair and good
He likewise gives a frock or livery,
That aptly is put on. Refrain to-night,
And that shall lend a kind of easiness
To the next abstinence; the next more easy;
For use[45] almost can change the stamp of nature,
And either curb the devil or throw him out,
With wondrous potency. Once more, good-night;
And when you are desirous to be blest,
I'll blessing beg of you. For this same lord,
                              [Pointing to POLONIUS.]
I do repent; but Heaven hath pleas'd it so,
To punish me with this and this with me,

---

38. gambol—wander fantastically.   39. unction—salve.
40. mining—undermining.   41. compost—manure.
42. ranker—more luxuriant.   43. pursy—short-winded.
44. curb—bow.   45. use—practice.

That I must be their scourge and minister.[46]
I will bestow him, and will answer well
The death I gave him. So, again, good-night.
I must be cruel, only to be kind.
Thus bad begins and worse remains behind.
One word more, good lady.

QUEEN.   What shall I do?

HAMLET.   Not this, by no means, that I bid you do:
Let the bloat[47] king tempt you again to bed,
Pinch wanton on your cheek, call you his mouse,
And let him, for a pair of reechy[48] kisses,
Or paddling in your neck with his damn'd fingers,
Make you to ravel [49] all this matter out,
That I essentially[50] am not in madness,
But mad in craft. 'T were good you let him know;
For who, that's but a queen, fair, sober, wise,
Would from a paddock,[51] from a bat, a gib,[52]
Such dear concernings hide? Who would do so?
No, in despite of sense and secrecy,
Unpeg[53] the basket on the house's top,
Let the birds fly, and like the famous ape,[54]
To try conclusions,[55] in the basket creep,
And break your own neck down.

QUEEN.   Be thou assur'd, if words be made of breath,
And breath of life, I have no life to breathe
What thou hast said to me.

HAMLET.   I must to England; you know that?

QUEEN.   Alack,
I had forgot. 'T is so concluded on.

HAMLET.   There's letters seal'd, and my two school-fellows,
Whom I will trust as I will adders fang'd,
They bear the mandate; [56] they must sweep my way,
And marshal me to knavery. Let it work;

---

46. minister—agent.   47. bloat—bloated with drinking.
48. reechy—nauseous.   49. ravel . . . out—explain.
50. essentially—in fact.   51. paddock—toad.
52. gib—tomcat.   53. Unpeg—open.
54. ape—who attempted to fly and broke his neck.
55. conclusions—an experiment.   56. mandate—command.

For 't is the sport to have the énginer[57]
Hoist with his own petar;[58] and 't shall go hard
But I will delve[59] one yard below their mines,
And blow them at the moon. O, 't is most sweet,
When in one line two crafts[60] directly meet.
This man shall set me packing.
I'll lug the guts into the neighbour room.
Mother, good-night indeed. This counsellor
Is now most still, most secret, and most grave,
Who was in life a foolish prating knave.
Come, sir, to draw toward an end with you.
Good-night, mother.

        Exeunt severally,[61] HAMLET *tugging in* POLONIUS.

---

57. énginer—army engineer.   58. petar—bomb.   59. delve—dig.
60. crafts—plots.   61. severally—by opposite doors.

[ACT IV • 1] *A room in the castle.*

Enter KING, QUEEN, ROSENCRANTZ, *and* GUILDENSTERN.

    KING.   There's matter[1] in these sighs, these profound heaves;
You must translate, 't is fit we understand them.
Where is your son?
    QUEEN.   Bestow this place on us a little while.

        Exeunt ROSENCRANTZ *and* GUILDENSTERN.
Ah, mine own lord, what have I seen to-night!
    KING.   What, Gertrude? How does Hamlet?
    QUEEN.   Mad as the sea and wind, when both contend
Which is the mightier—in his lawless fit,
Behind the arras hearing something stir,
Whips out his rapier, cries, "A rat, a rat!"
And in this brainish apprehension[2] kills
The unseen good old man.
    KING.   O heavy deed!
It had been so with us, had we been there.
His liberty is full of threats to all,
To you yourself, to us, to every one.
Alas, how shall this bloody deed be answer'd?

---

1. matter—meaning.   2. brainish apprehension—insane notion.

It will be laid to us, whose providence[3]
Should have kept short, restrain'd, and out of haunt,[4]
This mad young man; but so much was our love,
We would not understand what was most fit,
But, like the owner of a foul disease,
To keep it from divulging,[5] let it feed
Even on the pith of life. Where is he gone?
   QUEEN.   To draw apart the body he hath kill'd,
O'er whom his very madness, like some ore
Among a mineral of metals base,
Shows itself pure; 'a weeps for what is done.
   KING.   O Gertrude, come away!
The sun no sooner shall the mountains touch,
But we will ship him hence, and this vile deed
We must, with all our majesty and skill,
Both countenance[6] and excuse. Ho, Guildenstern!

Re-enter ROSENCRANTZ *and* GUILDENSTERN.

Friends both, go join you with some further aid;
Hamlet in madness hath Polonius slain,
And from his mother's closet hath he dragg'd him.
Go seek him out, speak fair, and bring the body
Into the chapel. I pray you, haste in this.
         Exeunt ROSENCRANTZ *and* GUILDENSTERN.
Come, Gertrude, we'll call up our wisest friends
To let them know both what we mean to do
And what's untimely done; so, haply, slander
Whose whisper o'er the world's diameter,
As level [7] as the cannon to his blank,[8]
Transports his poison'd shot, may miss our name,
And hit the woundless[9] air. O, come away!
My soul is full of discord and dismay.   *Exeunt.*

---

3. providence—foresight.
4. haunt—society.
5. divulging—coming to light.
6. countenance—defend.
7. level—sure an aim.
8. blank—target.
9. woundless—invulnerable.

[ACT IV • 2] *Another room in the castle.*

Enter HAMLET.

HAMLET.   Safely stowed.
GENTLEMEN.   [*Within.*] Hamlet! Lord Hamlet!
HAMLET.   But soft, what noise? Who calls on Hamlet?
O, here they come.

Enter ROSENCRANTZ *and* GUILDENSTERN.

ROSENCRANTZ.   What have you done, my lord, with the dead
   body?
HAMLET.   Compounded it with dust, whereto 't is kin.
ROSENCRANTZ.   Tell us where 't is, that we may take it thence
And bear it to the chapel.
HAMLET.   Do not believe it.
ROSENCRANTZ.   Believe what?
HAMLET.   That I can keep your counsel and not mine own.
Besides, to be demanded of [1] a sponge, what replication[2] should
be made by the son of a king?
ROSENCRANTZ.   Take you me for a sponge, my lord?
HAMLET.   Ay, sir, that soaks up the King's countenance, his
rewards, his authorities. But such officers do the King best serv-
ice in the end: he keeps them, like an ape an apple, in the corner
of his jaw; first mouthed, to be last swallowed: when he needs
what you have gleaned, it is but squeezing you, and, sponge, you
shall be dry again.
ROSENCRANTZ.   I understand you not, my lord.
HAMLET.   I am glad of it: a knavish speech sleeps in a foolish
ear.
ROSENCRANTZ.   My lord, you must tell us where the body is,
and go with us to the King.
HAMLET.   The body is with the King, but the King is not with
the body. The King is a thing—
GUILDENSTERN.   A thing, my lord!
HAMLET.   Of nothing; bring me to him. Hide fox, and all
after.[3]   *Exeunt.*

---

1. to be demanded of—being questioned by.
2. replication—answer.   3. Hide fox, and all after—hide and seek.

[ACT IV • 3] *Another room in the castle.*

Enter KING *and Attendants.*

KING. I have sent to seek him, and to find the body.
How dangerous is it that this man goes loose!
Yet must not we put the strong law on him;
He's lov'd of the distracted [1] multitude,
Who like not in their judgement, but their eyes,
And where 't is so, the offender's scourge[2] is weigh'd,
But never the offence. To bear[3] all smooth and even,
This sudden sending him away must seem
Deliberate pause.[4] Diseases desperate grown
By desperate appliance are reliev'd,
Or not at all.

Enter ROSENCRANTZ *and others.*

How now! What hath befall'n?
ROSENCRANTZ. Where the dead body is bestow'd, my lord,
We cannot get from him.
KING.   But where is he?
ROSENCRANTZ. Without, my lord, guarded, to know your
    pleasure.
KING. Bring him before us.
ROSENCRANTZ. Ho! bring in the lord.

Enter HAMLET *guarded and* GUILDENSTERN.

KING. Now, Hamlet, where's Polonius?
HAMLET. At supper.
KING. At supper! Where?
HAMLET. Not where he eats, but where 'a is eaten: a certain
convocation of politic[5] worms are e'en at him. Your worm is your
only emperor for diet: we fat[6] all creatures else to fat us, and we
fat ourselves for maggots. Your fat king and your lean beggar
is but variable service,[7] two dishes, but to one table; that's the
end.

---

1. distracted—turbulent.   2. scourge—punish.
3. bear—manage.   4. pause—planning.
5. politic—statesmanlike.   6. fat—fatten.
7. variable service—two ways of serving the same food.

KING.   Alas, alas!

HAMLET.   A man may fish with the worm that hath eat of a king, and eat of the fish that hath fed of that worm.

KING.   What dost thou mean by this?

HAMLET.   Nothing but to show you how a king may go a progress[8] through the guts of a beggar.

KING.   Where is Polonius?

HAMLET.   In heaven; send thither to see: if your messenger find him not there, seek him i' th' other place yourself. But if indeed, you find him not within this month, you shall nose him as you go up the stairs into the lobby.

KING.   Go seek him there.   [*To some Attendants.*]

HAMLET.   'A will stay till you come.

Exeunt Attendants.

KING.   Hamlet, this deed, for thine especial safety,—
Which we do tender,[9] as we dearly grieve
For that which thou hast done,—must send thee hence
With fiery quickness; therefore prepare thyself.
The bark is ready, and the wind at help,[10]
Th' associates tend, and everything is bent
For England.

HAMLET.   For England?

KING.   Ay, Hamlet.

HAMLET.   **Good.**

KING.   So is it, if thou knew'st our purposes.

HAMLET.   I see a cherub that sees them. But, come, for England! Farewell, dear mother.

KING.   Thy loving father, Hamlet.

HAMLET.   My mother: father and mother is man and wife, man and wife is one flesh, and so, my mother. Come, for England!   *Exit.*

KING.   Follow him at foot,[11] tempt him with speed aboard,
Delay it not; I'll have him hence to-night.
Away! for everything is seal'd and done
That else leans on[12] th' affair, pray you, make haste.

Exeunt ROSENCRANTZ *and* GUILDENSTERN.

---

8. progress—journey of state.   9. tender—regard highly.
10. at help—favorable.   11. at foot—at his heels.
12. leans on—pertains to.

And, England,[13] if my love thou hold'st at aught,—
As my great power thereof may give thee sense,
Since yet thy cicatrice[14] looks raw and red
After the Danish sword, and thy free awe[15]
Pays homage to us—thou mayst not coldly set[16]
Our sovereign process,[17] which imports at full,
By letters congruing[18] to that effect,
The present[19] death of Hamlet. Do it, England;
For like the hectic[20] in my blood he rages,
And thou must cure me: till I know 't is done,
Howe'er my haps, my joys were ne'er begun.   *Exit.*

---

13. England—the king of England.   14. cicatrice—scar.
15. free awe—voluntary submission.   16. coldly set—ignore.
17. process—command.   18. congruing—agreeing.
19. present—instant.   20. hectic—fever.

[ACT IV • 4] *A plain in Denmark.*

Enter FORTINBRAS, *and a* CAPTAIN, *marching with his army over the stage.*

FORTINBRAS.   Go, captain, from me greet the Danish king.
Tell him that, by his license, Fortinbras
Craves the conveyance[1] of a promis'd march
Over his kingdom. You know the rendezvous.
If that his Majesty would aught with us,
We shall express our duty in his eye; [2]
And let him know so.
          CAPTAIN.   I will do 't, my lord.
          FORTINBRAS.   Go softly on.
               Exeunt FORTINBRAS *and army.* CAPTAIN *remains.*

Enter HAMLET, ROSENCRANTZ, GUILDENSTERN *and others.*

          HAMLET.   Good sir, whose powers[3] are these?
          CAPTAIN.   They are of Norway, sir.
          HAMLET.   How purpos'd, sir, I pray you?
          CAPTAIN.   Against some part of Poland.
          HAMLET.   Who commands them, sir?

---

1. conveyance—escort.   2. eye—presence.
3. powers—soldiers.

CAPTAIN. The nephew to old Norway, Fortinbras.

HAMLET. Goes it against the main[4] of Poland, sir,
Or for some frontier?

CAPTAIN. Truly to speak, and with no addition,
We go to gain a little patch of ground
That hath in it no profit but the name.
To pay five ducats, five, I would not farm it;
Nor will it yield to Norway or the Pole
A ranker[5] rate, should it be sold in fee.[6]

HAMLET. Why, then the Polack never will defend it.

CAPTAIN. Yes, it is already garrison'd.

HAMLET. Two thousand souls and twenty thousand ducats
Will not debate the question of this straw.
This is th' imposthume[7] of much wealth and peace,
That inward breaks, and shows no cause without
Why the man dies. I humbly thank you, sir.

CAPTAIN. God buy you, sir.   *Exit.*

ROSENCRANTZ. Will 't please you go, my lord?

HAMLET. I'll be with you straight; go a little before.

                                    Exeunt all except HAMLET.

How all occasions do inform against[8] me,
And spur my dull revenge! What is a man,
If his chief good and market[9] of his time
Be but to sleep and feed? A beast, no more.
Sure He that made us with such large discourse,[10]
Looking before and after, gave us not
That capability and god-like reason
To fust[11] in us unus'd. Now, whether it be
Bestial oblivion,[12] or some craven scruple
Of thinking too precisely on th' event,[13]—
A thought which, quarter'd, hath but one part wisdom
And ever three parts coward,—I do not know
Why yet I live to say, "This thing's to do,"
Sith I have cause and will and strength and means

---

4. main—whole country.   5. ranker—higher.   6. in fee—outright.
7. imposthume—abscess.   8. inform against—denounce.
9. market—profit.   10. discourse—faculty of reasoning.
11. fust—grow musty.   12. oblivion—forgetfulness.
13. event—outcome.

To do 't: examples gross[14] as earth exhort me;
Witness this army of such mass and charge
Led by a delicate and tender prince,
Whose spirit with divine ambition puff'd
Makes mouths at the invisible event,
Exposing what is mortal and unsure
To all that fortune, death, and danger dare,
Even for an egg-shell.[15] Rightly to be great
Is not to stir without great argument,[16]
But[17] greatly to find quarrel in a straw
When honour's at the stake. How stand I then,
That have a father kill'd, a mother stain'd,
Excitements of my reason and my blood,
And let all sleep, while to my shame I see
The imminent death of twenty thousand men,
That for a fantasy and trick of fame[18]
Go to their graves like beds, fight for a plot
Whereon the numbers cannot try the cause,
Which is not tomb enough and continent[19]
To hide the slain? O, from this time forth,
My thoughts be bloody, or be nothing worth!   *Exit.*

---

14. gross—obvious.   15. eggshell—trifle.
16. argument—cause.   17. But—i.e., but rather.
18. trick of fame—trifle of reputation.   19. continent—receptacle

[ACT IV • 5] *Elsinore. A room in the castle.*

Enter QUEEN, HORATIO, *and a* GENTLEMAN.

QUEEN.   I will not speak with her.
GENTLEMAN.   She is importunate, indeed distract;
Her mood will needs be pitied.
QUEEN.   What would she have?
GENTLEMAN.   She speaks much of her father; says she hears
There's tricks i' th' world, and hems, and beats her heart,
Spurns enviously[1] at straws, speaks things in doubt[2]
That carry but half sense. Her speech is nothing,

---

1. Spurns enviously—kicks spitefully.   2. in doubt—ambiguously.

Yet the unshaped [3] use of it doth move
The hearers to collection.[4] They aim[5] at it
And botch[6] the words up fit to their own thoughts;
Which, as her winks, and nods, and gestures yield them,
Indeed would make one think there would be thought,
Though nothing sure, yet much unhappily.

HORATIO.   'T were good she were spoken with, for she may strew
Dangerous conjectures in ill-breeding minds.
Let her come in.   *Exit* GENTLEMAN.

QUEEN.   [*Aside.*] To my sick soul, as sin's true nature is,
Each toy[7] seems prologue to some great amiss; [8]
So full of artless jealousy[9] is guilt,
It spills[10] itself in fearing to be spilt.

Enter OPHELIA, *playing on a lute, with her hair down, singing.*

OPHELIA.   Where is the beauteous majesty of Denmark?
QUEEN.   How now, Ophelia!
OPHELIA.   [*Sings.*]

> How should I your true love know
>   From another one?
> By his cockle[11] hat and staff,
>   And his sandal shoon.

QUEEN.   Alas, sweet lady, what imports this song?
OPHELIA.   Say you? Nay, pray you, mark.
[*Sings.*]

> He is dead and gone, lady,
>   He is dead and gone;
> At his head a grass-green turf
>   At his heels a stone.

Enter KING.

QUEEN.   Nay, but, Ophelia,—
OPHELIA.   Pray you, mark.
[*Sings.*]

> White his shroud as the mountain snow,—

---

3. unshaped—disconnected.   4. collection—conjecture.
5. aim—guess.   6. botch—patch.
7. toy—trifle.   8. amiss—misfortune.
9. artless jealousy—unreasonable suspicion.   10. spills—destroys.
11. cockle—pilgrim's (i.e., adorned with a shell).

QUEEN. Alas, look here, my lord.

OPHELIA. [*Sings.*]

> Larded [12] all with sweet flowers;
> Which bewept to the ground did not go
> With true-love showers.[13]

KING. How do you, pretty lady?

OPHELIA. Well, God 'ild [14] you! They say the owl was a baker's daughter.[15] Lord, we know what we are, but know not what we may be. God be at your table!

KING. Conceit[16] upon her father.

OPHELIA. Pray let's have no words of this, but when they ask you what it means, say you this:
[*Sings.*]

> To-morrow is Saint Valentine's day,
>   All in the morning betime,[17]
> And I a maid at your window,
>   To be your Valentine.
>
> Then up he rose and donn'd his clothes,
>   And dupp'd [18] the chamber door;
> Let in the maid, that out a maid
>   Never departed more.

KING. Pretty Ophelia!

OPHELIA. Indeed, without an oath I'll make an end on 't.

> By Gis,[19] and by Saint Charity,
>   Alack, and fie for shame!
> Young men will do 't, if they come to 't;
>   By Cock,[20] they are to blame.
>
> Quoth she, "Before you tumbled me,
>   You promis'd me to wed."
> He answers:
> "So would I ha' done, by yonder sun,
>   An thou hadst not come to my bed."

KING. How long hath she been thus?

OPHELIA. I hope all will be well. We must be patient; but I

---

12. Larded—bedecked.   13. showers—tears.   14. 'ild—repay.
15. daughter—transformed into an owl for uncharitableness.
16. Conceit—brooding.   17. betime—early.
18. dupp'd—opened.   19. Gis—Jesus.   20. Cock—God.

cannot choose but weep, to think they should lay him i' th' cold
ground. My brother shall know of it; and so I thank you for your
good counsel. Come, my coach! Good-night, ladies; good-night,
sweet ladies; good-night, good-night.   *Exit.*

    KING.   Follow her close; give her good watch, I pray you.
                           Exeunt HORATIO *and* GENTLEMAN.
O, this is the poison of deep grief; it springs
All from her father's death—and now behold!
O Gertrude, Gertrude,
When sorrows come, they come not single spies,
But in battalions. First, her father slain;
Next, your son gone; and he most violent author
Of his own just remove; the people muddied,[21]
Thick and unwholesome in their thoughts and whispers,
For good Polonius' death; and we have done but greenly[22]
In hugger-mugger[23] to inter him; poor Ophelia
Divided from herself and her fair judgement,
Without the which we are pictures, or mere beasts;
Last, and as much containing as all these,
Her brother is in secret come from France,
Feeds on his wonder, keeps himself in clouds,
And wants not buzzers[24] to infect his ear
With pestilent speeches of his father's death,
Wherein necessity, of matter beggar'd,[25]
Will nothing stick our persons to arraign
In ear and ear. O my dear Gertrude, this,
Like to a murd'ring-piece,[26] in many places
Gives me superfluous death.   [*A noise within.*]

    QUEEN.   Alack, what noise is this?
    KING.   Attend!   *Enter a* MESSENGER.
Where are my Switzers? [27] Let them guard the door.
What is the matter?
    MESSENGER.   Save yourself, my lord!

---

21. muddied—confused.   22. greenly—foolishly.
23. In hugger-mugger—secretly and hastily.
24. wants not buzzers—does not lack whisperers.
25. of matter beggar'd—without knowing the true facts.
26. murd'ring piece—cannon which scatters its shot.
27. Switzers—Swiss Guard.

The ocean, overpeering[28] of his list,[29]
Eats not the flats with more impetuous haste
Than young Laertes, in a riotous head,[30]
O'erbears your officers: the rabble call him lord;
And, as the world were now but to begin,
Antiquity forgot, custom not known,
The ratifiers and props of every word,
They cry, "Choose we! Laertes shall be king!"
Caps, hands, and tongues applaud it to the clouds,
"Laertes shall be king, Laertes king!"

    QUEEN.   How cheerfully on the false trail they cry!
O, this is counter,[31] you false Danish dogs!

Noise within. Enter LAERTES, *armed, with other* DANES.

    KING.   The doors are broke.
    LAERTES.   Where is this king? Sirs, stand you all without.
    DANES.   No, let's come in.
    LAERTES.   I pray you, give me leave.
    DANES.   We will, we will.   [*They retire without the door.*]
    LAERTES.   I thank you; keep the door. O thou vile king,
Give me my father!
    QUEEN.   Calmly, good Laertes.
    LAERTES.   That drop of blood that's calm proclaims me
      bastard,
Cries cuckold to my father, brands the harlot[32]
Even here, between the chaste unsmirched brow
Of my true mother.
    KING.   What is the cause, Laertes,
That thy rebellion looks so giant-like?
Let him go, Gertrude; do not fear our person:
There's such divinity doth hedge a king,
That treason can but peep to[33] what it would,
Acts little of his[34] will. Tell me, Laertes,
Why thou art thus incens'd. Let him go, Gertrude.
Speak, man.

---

28. overpeering—flooding.   29. list—banks.
30. riotous head—rebellious armed force.   31. counter—off the scent.
32. harlot—i.e., with a "blister" (*cf*. III.4.44).
33. peep to—see from a distance.   34. his—its.

LAERTES. Where is my father?

KING. Dead.

QUEEN. But not by him.

KING. Let him demand his fill.

LAERTES. How came he dead? I'll not be juggled with.
To hell allegiance! Vows to the blackest devil!
Conscience and grace to the profoundest pit!
I dare damnation. To this point I stand,
That both the worlds I give to negligence,
Let come what comes; only I'll be reveng'd
Most throughly for my father.

KING. Who shall stay[35] you?

LAERTES. My will, not all the world's:
And for my means, I'll husband[36] them so well,
They shall go far with little.

KING. Good Laertes,
If you desire to know the certainty
Of your dear father, is 't writ in your revenge
That, swoopstake,[37] you will draw[38] both friend and foe,
Winner and loser?

LAERTES. None but his enemies.

KING. Will you know them then?

LAERTES. To his good friends thus wide I'll ope my arms,
And like the kind life-rend'ring pelican,
Repast[39] them with my blood. -

KING Why, now you speak
Like a good child and a true gentleman.
That I am guiltless of your father's death,
And am most sensibly in grief for it,
It shall as level to your judgement pierce
As day does to your eye.

[*A noise within.* "Let her come in!"]

LAERTES. How now! what noise is that?

Re-enter OPHELIA.

O heat, dry up my brains! Tears seven times salt

---

35. stay—support.   36. husband—use them thriftily.
37. swoopstake—you will clear the gaming-table of all money.
38. draw—include.   39. Repast—feed.

Burn out the sense and virtue of mine eye!
By heaven, thy madness shall be paid with weight
Till our scale turn the beam. O rose of May!
Dear maid, kind sister, sweet Ophelia!
O heavens! is 't possible, a young maid's wits
Should be as mortal as an old man's life?
Nature[40] is fine in love, and where 't is fine,
It sends some precious instance[41] of itself
After the thing it loves.

> OPHELIA. [*Sings.*]
>
> > They bore him barefac'd on the bier;
> >   Hey non nonny, nonny, hey nonny; [42]
> > And in his grave rain'd many a tear,—

Fare you well, my dove!

LAERTES.   Hadst thou thy wits and didst persuade revenge,
It could not move thus.[43]

OPHELIA.   You must sing, "A-down a-down, and you call him
a-down-a." O, how the wheel [44] becomes it! [45] It is[46] the false
steward, that stole his master's daughter.

LAERTES.   This nothing's more than matter.

OPHELIA.   There's rosemary, that's for remembrance; pray
you, love, remember; and there is pansies, that's for thoughts.

LAERTES.   A document[47] in madness, thoughts and remembrance fitted.

OPHELIA.   There's fennel for you, and columbines; there's
rue for you, and here's some for me; we may call it herb of grace
o' Sundays; O, you must wear your rue with a difference. There's
a daisy. I would give you some violets, but they withered all
when my father died; they say 'a made a good end,—
[*Sings.*]

> For bonny sweet Robin is all my joy.

---

40. Nature—human nature.
41. instance—sample; also, proof.
42. hey nonny—a meaningless refrain (like "A-down-a").
43. thus—as this does.
44. wheel—spinning wheel.
45. it—i.e., the song sung to the rhythm of the spinning wheel.
46. It is—i.e., the song tells the story of.
47. document—lesson taught.

LAERTES.   Thought and affliction, passion, hell itself,
She turns to favour and to prettiness.
OPHELIA.   [*Sings.*]

> And will 'a not come again?
> And will 'a not come again?
>   No, no, he is dead;
>   Go to thy death-bed;
> He never will come again.
>
> His beard was as white as snow,
> All flaxen was his poll.[48]
>   He is gone, he is gone,
>   And we cast away moan.
> God ha' mercy on his soul!

And of all Christian souls, I pray God. God buy ye.   *Exit.*
LAERTES.   Do you see this, O God?
KING.   Laertes, I must cómmune with your grief,
Or you deny me right. Go but apart,
Make choice of whom your wisest friends you will,
And they shall hear and judge 'twixt you and me.
If by direct or by collateral hand
They find us touch'd,[49] we will our kingdom give,
Our crown, our life, and all that we call ours,
To you in satisfaction; but if not,
Be you content to lend your patience to us,
And we shall jointly labour with your soul
To give it due content.
LAERTES.   Let this be so.
His means of death, his óbscure burial,
No trophy, sword, nor hatchment[50] o'er his bones,
No noble rite nor formal ostentation,
Cry to be heard, as 't were from heaven to earth,
That I must call 't in question.
KING.   So you shall;
And where th' offence is let the great axe fall.
I pray you, go with me.   *Exeunt.*

---

48. poll—head.
49. touch'd—implicated.
50. hatchment—memorial tablet.

[ACT IV • 6] *Another room in the castle.*

Enter HORATIO *with an Attendant.*

HORATIO. What are they that would speak with me?
ATTENDANT. Sea-faring men, sir; they say they have letters
  for you.
HORATIO. Let them come in. *Exit Attendant.*
I do not know from what part of the world
I should be greeted, if not from Lord Hamlet.

Enter SAILORS.

FIRST SAILOR. God bless you, sir.
HORATIO. Let Him bless thee too.
FIRST SAILOR. 'A shall, sir, an[1] 't please Him. There's a letter
for you, sir— it came from th' ambassador that was bound for
England—if your name be Horatio, as I am let to know it is.
HORATIO. [*Reads.*]

Horatio, when thou shalt have overlooked this, give these fellows
some means[2] to the King; they have letters for him. Ere we were
two days old at sea, a pirate of very warlike appointment gave us
chase. Finding ourselves too slow of sail, we put on a compelled
valour and in the grapple I boarded them. On the instant they got
clear of our ship, so I alone became their prisoner. They have dealt
with me like thieves of mercy,[3] but they knew what they did: I am
to do a good turn for them. Let the King have the letters I have
sent, and repair thou to me with as much haste as thou wouldest
fly death. I have words to speak in thine ear will make thee dumb,
yet are they much too light for the bore[4] of the matter. These good
fellows will bring thee where I am. Rosencrantz and Guildenstern
hold their course for England; of them I have much to tell thee.
Farewell.

> He that thou knowest thine,
> HAMLET.

Come, I will give you way for these your letters;
And do 't the speedier, that you may direct me
To him from whom you brought them. *Exeunt.*

---

1. an—if.   2. means—access.
3. thieves of mercy—merciful thieves.
4. bore—size.

[ACT IV • 7] *Another room in the castle.*

Enter KING *and* LAERTES.

KING. Now must your conscience my acquittance seal;
And you must put me in your heart for friend,
Sith you have heard, and with a knowing ear,
That he which hath your noble father slain
Pursued my life.

LAERTES. It well appears: but tell me
Why you proceeded not against these feats,[1]
So criminal and so capital in nature,
As by your safety, wisdom, all things else,
You mainly were stirr'd up.

KING. O, for two special reasons,
Which may to you, perhaps, seem much unsinew'd,[2]
And yet to me they are strong. The Queen his mother
Lives almost by his looks; and for myself—
My virtue or my plague, be it either which—
She is so conjunctive[3] to my life and soul,
That, as the star moves not but in his sphere,
I could not but by her. The other motive
Why to a public count[4] I might not go,
Is the great love the general gender[5] bear him;
Who, dipping[6] all his faults in their affection,
Would, like the spring that turneth wood to stone,
Convert his gyves[7] to graces; so that my arrows,
Too slightly timber'd for so loud a wind,
Would have reverted to my bow again,
And not where I have aim'd them.

LAERTES. And so have I a noble father lost,
A sister driven into desp'rate terms,
Whose worth, if praises may go back again,
Stood challenger on mount of all the age[8]
For[9] her perfections. But my revenge will come.

KING. Break not your sleeps for that; you must not think

---

1. feats—deeds.   2. unsinew'd—weak.
3. conjunctive—inseparably joined.   4. count—reckoning.
5. general gender—common people.   6. dipping—gilding.
7. gyves—fetters.   8. age—world.   9. For—to match.

That we are made of stuff so flat and dull
That we can let our beard be shook with danger
And think it pastime. You shortly shall hear more.
I lov'd your father, and we love ourself,
And that, I hope, will teach you to imagine—

Enter a MESSENGER *with letters.*

How now! What news?
    MESSENGER.   Letters, my lord, from Hamlet.
These to your Majesty; this to the Queen.
    KING.   From Hamlet! Who brought them?
    MESSENGER.   Sailors, my lord, they say; I saw them not.
They were given me by Claudio. He received them
Of him that brought them.
    KING.   Laertes, you shall hear them.
Leave us.   *Exit* MESSENGER.
[*Reads.*]

    High and mighty, You shall know I am set naked [10] on your
kingdom. To-morrow shall I beg leave to see your kingly eyes, when
I shall, first asking you pardon, thereunto recount the occasion of
my sudden and more strange return.
                                    HAMLET.

What should this mean? Are all the rest come back?
Or is it some abuse,[11] and no such thing?
    LAERTES.   Know you the hand?
    KING.   'T is Hamlet's character.[12] "Naked!"
And in a postscript here, he says, "alone."
Can you advise me?
    LAERTES.   I'm lost in it, my lord; but let him come:
It warms the very sickness in my heart
That I shall live and tell him to his teeth,
"Thus didest thou."
    KING.   If it be so, Laertes,—
And how should it be so? How otherwise?—
Will you be rul'd by me?

---

10. naked—destitute.   11. abuse—delusion.
12. character—handwriting.

LAERTES.   Ay, my lord,
So you will not o'errule[13] me to a peace.
　　KING.   To thine own peace. If he be now return'd,
As checking[14] at his voyage, and that he means
No more to undertake it, I will work him
To an exploit, now ripe in my device,
Under the which he shall not choose but fall;
And for his death no wind of blame shall breathe,
But even his mother shall uncharge the practice[15]
And call it accident.
　　LAERTES.   My lord, I will be rul'd;
That rather, if you could devise it so
That I might be the organ.[16]
　　KING.   It falls right.
You have been talk'd of since your travel much,
And that in Hamlet's hearing, for a quality
Wherein, they say, you shine. Your sum of parts
Did not together pluck such envy from him
As did that one, and that, in my regard,
Of the unworthiest siege.[17]
　　LAERTES.   What part is that, my lord?
　　KING.   A very riband [18] in the cap of youth,
Yet needful too; for youth no less becomes
The light and careless livery that it wears
Than settled age his sables and his weeds,
Importing health and graveness. Two months since,
Here was a gentleman of Normandy;—
I have seen myself, and serv'd against, the French,
And they can well [19] on horseback; but this gallant
Had witchcraft in 't; he grew unto his seat,
And to such wondrous doing brought his horse,
As had he been incorps'd [20] and demi-natur'd
With the brave beast. So far he topp'd my thought,

---

13. o'errule—order.
14. checking—swerving aside from.
15. uncharge the practice—fail to see the plot.
16. organ—agent.   17. siege—rank.
18. very riband—mere ornament.   19. can well—are skillful.
20. incorps'd—made into one body with.

That I, in forgery of shapes and tricks,[21]
Come short of what he did.

LAERTES.   A Norman, was 't?

KING.   A Norman.

LAERTES.   Upon my life, Lamound.

KING.   The very same.

LAERTES.   I know him well: he is the brooch[22] indeed
And gem of all their nation.

KING.   He made confession of you,
And gave you such a masterly report
For art and exercise in your defence,[23]
And for your rapier most especial,
That he cried out, 't would be a sight indeed
If one could match you. The scrimers[24] of their nation,
He swore, had neither motion, guard, nor eye,
If you oppos'd them. Sir, this report of his
Did Hamlet so envenom with his envy
That he could nothing do but wish and beg
Your sudden coming o'er to play with you.
Now, out of this—

LAERTES.   What out of this, my lord?

KING.   Laertes, was your father dear to you?
Or are you like the painting of a sorrow,
A face without a heart?

LAERTES.   Why ask you this?

KING.   Not that I think you did not love your father,
But that I know love is begun by time,
And that I see, in passages of proof,[25]
Time qualifies[26] the spark and fire of it.
There lives within the very flame of love
A kind of wick or snuff that will abate it,
And nothing is at a like goodness still;
For goodness, growing to a plurisy,[27]
Dies in his own too-much. That[28] we would do,

---

21. forgery of shapes and tricks—imagining feats of horsemanship.
22. brooch—ornament.   23. defence—fencing.
24. scrimers—fencers.
25. passages of proof—experiences which prove.
26. qualifies—weakens.   27. plurisy—excess.   28. That—what.

We should do when we would; for this "would" changes,
And hath abatements and delays as many
As there are tongues, are hands, are accidents;
And then this "should" is like a spendthrift[29] sigh,
That hurts by easing. But, to the quick[30] of th' ulcer—
Hamlet comes back. What would you undertake,
To show yourself in deed your father's son
More than in words?
    LAERTES.   To cut his throat i' th' church.
    KING.   No place, indeed, should murder sanctuarize; [31]
Revenge should have no bounds. But, good Laertes,
Will you do this, keep close within your chamber?
Hamlet return'd shall know you are come home:
We'll put on those[32] shall praise your excellence
And set a double varnish on the fame
The Frenchman gave you, bring you in fine[33] together
And wager on your heads; he, being remiss,[34]
Most generous and free from all contriving,
Will not peruse the foils, so that, with ease,
Or with a little shuffling, you may choose
A sword unbated,[35] and in a pass of practice[36]
Requite him for your father.
    LAERTES.   I will do 't;
And, for that purpose, I'll anoint my sword.
I bought an unction of a mountebank,[37]
So mortal that, but dip a knife in it,
Where it draws blood no cataplasm[38] so rare,
Collected from all simples[39] that have virtue
Under the moon, can save the thing from death
That is but scratch'd withal. I'll touch my point

---

29. spendthrift—wasteful (a sigh was thought to draw blood from the heart).
30. quick—sensitive part.
31. murder sanctuarize—give asylum to a murderer.
32. put on those—instigate persons who.
33. fine—short.   34. remiss—unsuspicious.
35. unbated—without the blunt point commonly used in fencing matches.
36. pass of practice—treacherous thrust.
37. mountebank—quack doctor.
38. cataplasm—poultice.   39. simples—medicinal herbs.

With this contagion, that, if I gall him slightly,
It may be death.

KING.　　　　Let's further think of this,
Weigh what convenience both of time and means
May fit us to our shape. If this should fail,
And that our drift[40] look through our bad [41] performance,
'T were better not assay'd; therefore this project
Should have a back or second, that might hold
If this did blast in proof. Soft! let me see:
We'll make a solemn wager on your cunnings—
I ha 't!
When in your motion you are hot and dry—
As make your bouts more violent to that end—
And that he calls for drink, I'll have prepar'd him
A chalice for the nonce,[42] whereon but sipping,
If he by chance escape your venom'd stuck,
Our purpose may hold there. But stay, what noise?

Enter QUEEN.

QUEEN.　One woe doth tread upon another's heel,
So fast they follow: your sister's drown'd, Laertes.

LAERTES.　Drown'd! O, where?

QUEEN.　There is a willow grows aslant the brook,
That shows his hoar leaves in the glassy stream,
Therewith fantastic garlands did she make
Of crow-flowers, nettles, daisies, and long purples
That liberal [43] shepherds give a grosser name,
But our cold [44] maids do dead men's fingers call them;
There, on the pendent boughs her coronet weeds
Clamb'ring to hang, an envious sliver broke,
When down her weedy trophies and herself
Fell in the weeping brook. Her clothes spread wide,
And, mermaid-like, awhile they bore her up;
Which time she chanted snatches of old tunes,
As one incapable[45] of her own distress,
Or like a creature native and indued [46]

---

40. drift—purpose.　　41. bad—bungling.　　42. nonce—purpose.
43. liberal—vulgar-tongued.　　44. cold—chaste.
45. incapable—insensitive.　　46. indued—adapted.

Unto that element. But long it could not be
Till that her garments, heavy with their drink,
Pull'd the poor wretch from her melodious lay
To muddy death.

LAERTES.　　　　Alas, then, she is drown'd.

QUEEN.　Drown'd, drown'd.

LAERTES.　Too much of water hast thou, poor Ophelia,
And therefore I forbid my tears; but yet
It is our trick:[47] nature her custom holds,
Let shame say what it will; when these are gone,
The woman[48] will be out. Adieu, my lord;
I have a speech o' fire that fain would blaze,
But that this folly drowns it.　　　　*Exit.*

KING.　　　　　Let's follow, Gertrude.
How much I had to do to calm his rage!
Now fear I this will give it start again,
Therefore let's follow.　　　　*Exeunt.*

---

47. trick—human trait.　　48. woman—effeminate qualities.

[ACT V • I] *A churchyard.*

Enter two CLOWNS, GRAVEDIGGERS, *with spades and pickaxes.*

FIRST CLOWN.[1]　Is she to be buried in Christian burial when she wilfully seeks her own salvation?[2]

SECOND CLOWN.　I tell thee she is, therefore make her grave straight. The crowner[3] hath sat on her, and finds it Christian burial.

FIRST CLOWN.　How can that be, unless she drowned herself in her own defence?

SECOND CLOWN.　Why, 't is found so.

FIRST CLOWN.　It must be *"se offendendo,"* [4] it cannot be else. For here lies the point: if I drown myself wittingly, it argues an act, and an act hath three branches; it is, to act, to do, and to perform; argal,[5] she drowned herself wittingly.

---

1. First Clown—i.e., countryman.
2. salvation—i.e., by suicide.　　3. crowner—coroner.
4. *se offendendo*—self-offence, blunder for self-defence.
5. argal—therefore (*ergo*).

SECOND CLOWN. Nay, but hear you, goodman delver,[6]—

FIRST CLOWN. Give me leave. Here lies the water; good. Here stands the man; good. If the man go to this water and drown himself, it is, will he, nill he, he goes,—mark you that? But if the water come to him and drown him, he drowns not himself; argal, he that is not guilty of his own death shortens not his own life.

SECOND CLOWN. But is this law?

FIRST CLOWN. Ay, marry, is 't; crowner's quest[7] law.

SECOND CLOWN. Will you ha' the truth on 't? If this had not been a gentlewoman, she should have been buried out o' Christian burial.

FIRST CLOWN. Why, there thou say'st; and the more pity that great folk should have countenance[8] in this world to drown or hang themselves, more than their even-Christian.[9] Come, my spade! There is no ancient gentlemen but gardeners, ditchers, and grave-makers; they hold up Adam's profession.

SECOND CLOWN. Was he a gentleman?

FIRST CLOWN. 'A was the first that ever bore arms.

SECOND CLOWN. Why, he had none.

FIRST CLOWN. What, art a heathen? How dost thou understand the Scripture? The Scripture says Adam digged; could he dig without arms? I'll put another question to thee. If thou answerest me not to the purpose, confess thyself—

SECOND CLOWN. Go to.

FIRST CLOWN. What is he that builds stronger than either the mason, the shipwright, or the carpenter?

SECOND CLOWN. The gallows-maker; for that frame outlives a thousand tenants.

FIRST CLOWN. I like thy wit well, in good faith. The gallows does well; but how does it well? It does well to those that do ill. Now, thou dost ill to say the gallows is built stronger than the church, argal, the gallows may do well to thee. To 't again, come.

SECOND CLOWN. "Who builds stronger than a mason, a shipwright, or a carpenter?"

FIRST CLOWN. Ay, tell me that, and unyoke.[10]

---

6. delver—digger.   7. quest—inquest.
8. countenance—authorization.   9. even-Christian—fellow Christians.
10. unyoke—call it a day.

SECOND CLOWN. Marry, now I can tell.

FIRST CLOWN. To 't.

SECOND CLOWN. Mass, I cannot tell.

FIRST CLOWN. Cudgel thy brains no more about it, for your dull ass will not mend his pace[11] with beating; and, when you are asked this question next, say "a grave-maker"; the houses that he makes last till doomsday. Go, get thee in; and fetch me a stoup[12] of liquor. *Exit* SECOND CLOWN.

[FIRST CLOWN *digs, and sings.*]

In youth, when I did love, did love,
    Methought it was very sweet,
To contract,[13] O, the time for-a-my behove,[14]
    O, methought, there-a-was nothing-a meet.

Enter HAMLET *and* HORATIO.

HAMLET. Has this fellow no feeling of his business? 'A sings at grave-making.

HORATIO. Custom hath made it in him a property of easiness.[15]

HAMLET. 'T is e'en so: the hand of little[16] employment hath the daintier sense.

FIRST CLOWN. [*Sings.*]

But age, with his stealing steps,
    Hath clawed me in his clutch,
And hath shipped me into the land,
    As if I had never been such.

[*Throws up a skull.*]

HAMLET. That skull had a tongue in it, and could sing once. How the knave jowls[17] it to the ground, as if it were Cain's jaw-bone, that did the first murder! This might be the pate of a politician, which this ass now o'erreaches;[18] one that would circumvent God, might it not?

HORATIO. It might, my lord.

---

11. mend his pace—go faster.   12. stoup—pot.
13. contract—cut short.   14. behove—advantage.
15. property of easiness—action to which he gives no second thought.
16. of little—unaccustomed to.   17. jowls—dashes.
18. o'erreaches—gets the better of.

HAMLET. Or of a courtier, which could say, "Good morrow, sweet lord! How dost thou, sweet lord?" This might be my lord such-a-one that praised my lord such-a-one's horse, when 'a meant to beg it; might it not?

HORATIO. Ay, my lord.

HAMLET. Why, e'en so; and now my Lady Worm's; chapless,[19] and knocked about the mazzard [20] with a sexton's spade: here's fine revolution, an we had the trick to see 't. Did these bones cost no more the breeding, but to play at loggats[21] with 'em? Mine ache to think on 't.

FIRST CLOWN.   [*Sings.*]

> A pick-axe, and a spade, a spade
> For and [22] a shrouding sheet;
> O, a pit of clay for to be made
> For such a guest is meet.

[*Throws up another skull.*]

HAMLET. There's another. Why may not that be the skull of a lawyer? Where be his quiddities now, his quillets,[23] his cases, his tenures, and his tricks? Why does he suffer this mad knave now to knock him about the sconce with a dirty shovel, and will not tell him of his action of battery? Hum! This fellow might be in 's time a great buyer of land, with his statutes, his recognizances, his fines, his double vouchers, his recoveries. Is this the fine of his fines, and the recovery of his recoveries, to have his fine pate full of fine dirt? Will his vouchers vouch him no more of his purchases, and double ones too, than the length and breadth of a pair of indentures? The very conveyances of his lands will hardly lie in this box,[24] and must th' inheritor himself have no more, ha?

HORATIO. Not a jot more, my lord.

HAMLET. Is not parchment made of sheepskins?

HORATIO. Ay, my lord, and of calf-skins too.

HAMLET. They are sheep and calves which seek out assurance in that. I will speak to this fellow. Whose grave's this, sirrah?

---

19. chapless—jawless.   20. mazzard—head.
21. loggats—a game like bowling.   22. For and—and also.
23. quillets—quibbles.   24. box—coffin.

FIRST CLOWN. Mine, sir.

[*Sings.*]

O, a pit of clay for to be made
For such a guest is meet.

HAMLET. I think it be thine indeed, for thou liest in 't.

FIRST CLOWN. You lie out on 't, sir, and therefore it is not yours: for my part, I do not lie in 't, yet it is mine.

HAMLET. Thou dost lie in 't, to be in 't and say it is thine. 'T is for the dead, not for the quick, therefore thou liest.

FIRST CLOWN. 'T is a quick lie, sir; 't will away again, from me to you.

HAMLET. What man dost thou dig it for?

FIRST CLOWN. For no man, sir.

HAMLET. What woman, then?

FIRST CLOWN. For none, neither.

HAMLET. Who is to be buried in 't?

FIRST CLOWN. One that was a woman, sir; but, rest her soul, she's dead.

HAMLET. How absolute[25] the knave is! We must speak by the card,[26] or equivocation[27] will undo us. By the Lord, Horatio, this three years I have took note of it; the age is grown so picked [28] that the toe of the peasant comes so near the heel of the courtier, he galls his kibe.[29] How long hast thou been a grave-maker?

FIRST CLOWN. Of all the days i' th' year, I came to 't that day that our last king Hamlet overcame Fortinbras.

HAMLET. How long is that since?

FIRST CLOWN. Cannot you tell that? Every fool can tell that. It was that very day that young Hamlet was born; he that is mad, and sent into England.

HAMLET. Ay, marry, why was he sent into England?

FIRST CLOWN. Why, because 'a was mad: 'a shall recover his wits there; or, if he do not, 't is no great matter there.

HAMLET. Why?

FIRST CLOWN. 'T will not be seen in him there; there the men are as mad as he.

---

25. absolute—precise.   26. by the card—punctiliously.
27. equivocation—ambiguity, "double talk."
28. picked—refined.   29. kibe—chilblains.

HAMLET. How came he mad?

FIRST CLOWN. Very strangely, they say.

HAMLET. How "strangely"?

FIRST CLOWN. Faith, e'en with losing his wits.

HAMLET. Upon what ground?

FIRST CLOWN. Why, here in Denmark: I have been sexton here, man and boy, thirty years.

HAMLET. How long will a man lie i' th' earth ere he rot?

FIRST CLOWN. Faith, if 'a be not rotten before 'a die—as we have many pocky[30] corses now-a-days, that will scarce hold the laying in—'a will last you some eight year or nine year. A tanner will last you nine year.

HAMLET. Why he more than another?

FIRST CLOWN. Why, sir, his hide is so tanned with his trade that 'a will keep out water a great while, and your water is a sore decayer of your whoreson[31] dead body. Here's a skull now; this skull hath lain i' th' earth three and twenty years.

HAMLET. Whose was it?

FIRST CLOWN. A whoreson mad fellow's it was. Whose do you think it was?

HAMLET. Nay, I know not.

FIRST CLOWN. A pestilence on him for a mad rogue! 'A poured a flagon of Rhenish on my head once. This same skull, sir, was, sir, Yorick's skull, the King's jester.

HAMLET. This?

FIRST CLOWN. E'en that.

HAMLET. Let me see that. [*Takes the skull.*] Alas, poor Yorick! I knew him, Horatio; a fellow of infinite jest, of most excellent fancy. He hath borne me on his back a thousand times. And now how abhorred in my imagination it is! My gorge rises at it. Here hung those lips that I have kissed I know not how oft. Where be your gibes now, your gambols, your songs, your flashes of merriment, that were wont to set the table on a roar? Not one now, to mock your own grinning? Quite chop-fallen?[32] Now get you to my lady's chamber, and tell her, let her paint an inch thick, to this favour[33] she must come. Make her laugh at that. Prithee, Horatio, tell me one thing.

---

30. pocky—with venereal disease.   31. whoreson—bastard.
32. chop-fallen—downcast.   33. favour—appearance.

HORATIO.   What's that, my lord?

HAMLET.   Dost thou think Alexander looked o' this fashion i' th' earth?

HORATIO.   E'en so.

HAMLET.   And smelt so? Pah!   *[Puts down the skull.]*

HORATIO.   E'en so, my lord.

HAMLET.   To what base uses we may return, Horatio! Why may not imagination trace the noble dust of Alexander, till 'a find it stopping a bung-hole?

HORATIO.   'T were to consider too curiously,[34] to consider so.

HAMLET.   No, faith, not a jot; but to follow him thither with modesty[35] enough and likelihood to lead it; as thus: Alexander died, Alexander was buried, Alexander returneth to dust, the dust is earth, of earth we make loam, and why of that loam whereto he was converted might they not stop a beer-barrel?

> Imperious Caesar, dead and turn'd to clay,
> Might stop a hole to keep the wind away.
> O, that that earth, which kept the world in awe,
> Should patch a wall t' expel the winter's flaw!

But soft, but soft, awhile! Here comes the King.

Enter KING, QUEEN, LAERTES, *and a Coffin, with a* PRIEST *and Attendant Lords.*

The Queen, the courtiers. Who is this they follow?
And with such maimed [36] rites? This doth betoken
The corse they follow did with desp'rate hand
Fordo[37] its own life: 't was of some estate.
Couch we a while, and mark.   *Retiring with* HORATIO.

LAERTES.   What ceremony else?

HAMLET.   That is Laertes, a very noble youth. Mark.

LAERTES.   What ceremony else?

PRIEST.   Her obsequies have been as far enlarg'd
As we have warranty. Her death was doubtful;
And, but[38] that great command o'ersways the order,[39]
She should in ground unsanctified have lodg'd
Till the last trumpet; for[40] charitable prayers,

---

34. curiously—minutely.   35. modesty—reasonableness.
36. maimed—abridged.   37. Fordo—take.   38. but—only.
39. order—usual rule of the church.   40. for—instead of.

Shards, flints, and pebbles should be thrown on her:
Yet here she is allowed her virgin crants,[41]
Her maiden strewments, and the bringing home
Of bell and burial.

    LAERTES.   Must there no more be done?

    PRIEST.   No more be done.
We should profane the service of the dead
To sing a requiem and such rest to her
As to peace-parted souls.

    LAERTES.   Lay her i' th' earth,
And from her fair and unpolluted flesh
May violets spring! I tell thee, churlish priest,
A minist'ring angel shall my sister be,
When thou liest howling.

    HAMLET.   What, the fair Ophelia!

    QUEEN.   Sweets to the sweet; farewell!

                         [Scattering flowers.]
I hop'd thou shouldst have been my Hamlet's wife;
I thought thy bride-bed to have deck'd, sweet maid,
And not have strew'd thy grave.

    LAERTES.   O, treble woe
Fall ten times treble on that cursed head
Whose wicked deed thy most ingenious sense[42]
Depriv'd thee of! Hold off the earth a while,
Till I have caught her once more in mine arms.

                      [Leaps in the grave.]
Now pile your dust upon the quick and dead,
Till of this flat a mountain you have made
T' o'ertop old Pelion,[43] or the skyish head
Of blue Olympus.

    HAMLET.   *[Advancing.]* What is he whose grief
Bears such an emphasis, whose phrase of sorrow
Conjures the wand'ring stars and makes them stand
Like wonder-wounded hearers? This is I,
Hamlet, the Dane!

---

41. crants—garland.
42. ingenious sense—lively intelligence.
43. Pelion—like Olympus and Ossa, a mountain in Greece.

LAERTES.   The devil take thy soul!   [*Grappling with him.*]
HAMLET.   Thou pray'st not well.
I prithee, take thy fingers from my throat,
For, though I am not splenitive[44] and rash,
Yet have I something in me dangerous,
Which let thy wiseness fear. Hold off thy hand!
KING.   Pluck them asunder.
QUEEN.   Hamlet, Hamlet!
ALL.   Gentlemen,—
HORATIO.   Good my lord, be quiet.
                              [*The Attendants part them.*]
HAMLET.   Why, I will fight with him upon this theme
Until my eyelids will no longer wag.[45]
QUEEN.   O my son, what theme?
HAMLET.   I lov'd Ophelia: forty thousand brothers
Could not, with all their quantity of love,
Make up my sum. What wilt thou do for her?
KING.   O, he is mad, Laertes.
QUEEN.   For love of God, forbear[46] him.
HAMLET.   'Swounds,[47] show me what thou 't do.
Woo 't weep? Woo 't fight? Woo 't fast? Woo 't tear thyself?
Woo 't drink up eisel? [48] Eat a crocodile?
I'll do 't. Dost come here to whine?
To outface me with leaping in her grave?
Be buried quick with her, and so will I;
And, if thou prate of mountains, let them throw
Millions of acres on us, till our ground,
Singeing his pate against the burning zone,[49]
Make Ossa like a wart! Nay, an thou 'lt mouth,
I'll rant as well as thou.
QUEEN.   This is mere madness,
And thus a while the fit will work on him;
Anon, as patient as the female dove,
When that her golden couplets[50] are disclos'd
His silence will sit drooping.

---

44. splenitive—quick-tempered.   45. wag—open and shut.
46. forbear—leave him alone.   47. 'Swounds—by God's wounds.
48. eisel—vinegar.   49. burning zone—sun's sphere.
50. couplets—twins.

HAMLET. Hear you, sir,
What is the reason that you use me thus?
I lov'd you ever. But it is no matter.
Let Hercules himself do what he may,
The cat will mew and dog will have his day. *Exit.*
KING. I pray thee, good Horatio, wait upon him.
Exit HORATIO.
[*To* LAERTES.] Strengthen your patience[51] in our last night's
speech;
We'll put the matter to the present push.[52]
Good Gertrude, set some watch over your son.
This grave shall have a living[53] monument.
An hour of quiet shortly shall we see;
Till then, in patience our proceeding be. *Exeunt.*

---

51. patience—endurance.
52. to the present push—into immediate operation.
53. living—lifelike; but also, the killing of Hamlet.

[ACT V • 2] *A hall in the castle.*

Enter HAMLET *and* HORATIO.

HAMLET. So much for this, sir; now you shall see the other—
You do remember all the circumstance?
HORATIO. Remember it, my lord!
HAMLET. Sir, in my heart there was a kind of fighting,
That would not let me sleep; methought I lay
Worse than the mutines in the bilboes.[1] Rashly,—
And prais'd be rashness for it: let us know
Our indiscretion sometime serves us well
When our deep plots do pall;[2] and that should learn us
There's a divinity that shapes our ends,
Rough-hew them how we will—
HORATIO. That is most certain.
HAMLET. Up from my cabin,
My sea-gown scarf'd about me, in the dark
Grop'd I to find out them, had my desire,
Finger'd[3] their packet; and in fine withdrew

---

1. bilboes—shackles. 2. pall—fail. 3. Finger'd—laid hold on.

To mine own room again, making so bold,
My fears forgetting manners, to unseal
Their grand commission; where I found, Horatio,—
Ah, royal knavery!—an exact command,
Larded with many several sorts of reasons
Importing Denmark's health and England's too,
With, ho! such bugs[4] and goblins in my life,
That, on the supervise,[5] no leisure bated,[6]
No, not to stay the grinding of the axe,
My head should be struck off.

HORATIO.   Is 't possible?

HAMLET.   Here's the commission; read it at more leisure.
But wilt thou hear now how I did proceed?

HORATIO.   I beseech you.

HAMLET.   Being thus be-netted round with villainies,—
Ere I could make a prologue to my brains,
They had begun the play,—I sat me down,
Devis'd a new commission, wrote it fair;
I once did hold it, as our statists[7] do,
A baseness to write fair, and labour'd much
How to forget that learning; but, sir, now
It did me yeoman's[8] service. Wilt thou know
Th' effect of what I wrote?

HORATIO.   Ay, good my lord.

HAMLET.   An earnest conjuration from the King,
As England was his faithful tributary,
As love between them like the palm might flourish,
As peace should still her wheaten garland wear
And stand a comma[9] 'tween their amities,
And many such-like "As"-es of great charge,[10]
That, on the view and knowing of these contents,
Without debatement further, more or less,
He should those bearers put to sudden death,
Not shriving time allow'd.

HORATIO.   How was this seal'd?

---

4. bugs—bugbears.   5. on the supervise—after the first meeting.
6. bated—allowed.   7. statists—statesmen.
8. yeomen's—substantial.   9. comma—connecting link.
10. charge—burden.

HAMLET. Why, even in that was Heaven ordinant.[11]
I had my father's signet in my purse,
Which was the model [12] of that Danish seal;
Folded the writ up in the form of th' other,
Subscrib'd it, gave 't th' impression, plac'd it safely,
The changeling never known. Now, the next day
Was our sea-fight; and what to this was sequent
Thou knowest already.

HORATIO. So Guildenstern and Rosencrantz go to 't.

HAMLET. Why man, they did make love to this employment;
They are not near[13] my conscience; their defeat[14]
Does by their own insinuation[15] grow:
'Tis dangerous when the baser nature comes
Between the pass[16] and fell [17] incensed points
Of mighty opposites.

HORATIO.   Why, what a king is this!

HAMLET. Does it not, think thee, stand me now upon—[18]
He that hath kill'd my king and whor'd my mother,
Popp'd in between th' election and my hopes,
Thrown out his angle for my proper[19] life,
And with such cozenage— is 't not perfect conscience,
To quit him[20] with this arm? And is 't not to be damn'd,
To let this canker of our nature come
In further evil?

HORATIO. It must be shortly known to him from England
What is the issue[21] of the business there.

HAMLET. It will be short; the interim is mine,
And a man's life's no more than to say "One."
But I am very sorry, good Horatio,
That to Laertes I forgot myself;
For, by the image of my cause, I see
The portraiture of his. I'll court his favours:
But, sure, the bravery[22] of his grief did put me
Into a tow'ring passion.

---

11. ordinant—in control.   12. model—copy.   13. near—on.
14. defeat—destruction.   15. insinuation—meddling.   16. pass—thrust.
17. fell—fierce.   18. stand me now upon—become my duty.
19. proper—own.   20. quit him—pay him off.
21. issue—outcome.   22. bravery—ostentation.

HORATIO.   Peace! who comes here?

Enter young OSRIC.

OSRIC.   Your lordship is right welcome back to Denmark.

HAMLET.   I humbly thank you, sir. [*To* HORATIO.] —Dost know this water-fly?

HORATIO.   No, my good lord.

HAMLET.   Thy state is the more gracious, for 't is a vice to know him. He hath much land, and fertile; let a beast be lord of beasts, and his crib shall stand at the King's mess. 'T is a chough,[23] but, as I say, spacious in the possession of dirt.

OSRIC.   Sweet lord, if your lordship were at leisure, I should impart a thing to you from his Majesty.

HAMLET.   I will receive it, sir, with all diligence of spirit. Put your bonnet to his right use; 't is for the head.

OSRIC.   I thank your lordship, it is very hot.

HAMLET.   No, believe me, 't is very cold; the wind is northerly.

OSRIC.   It is indifferent cold, my lord, indeed.

HAMLET.   Methinks it is very sultry and hot for my complexion.

OSRIC.   Exceedingly, my lord; it is very sultry,—as 't were —I cannot tell how. But, my lord, his Majesty bade me signify to you that 'a has laid a great wager on your head. Sir, this is the matter,—

HAMLET.   I beeseech you, remember—

                    [HAMLET *directs him to put on his hat.*]

OSRIC.   Nay, good my lord; for my ease, in good faith. Sir, here is newly come to court Laertes, believe me, an absolute[24] gentleman, full of most excellent differences,[25] of very soft society and great showing; indeed, to speak feelingly of him, he is the card or calendar of gentry, for you shall find in him the continent[26] of what parts a gentleman would see.

HAMLET.   Sir, his definement suffers no perdition in you; though, I know, to divide him inventorially would dizzy th' arithmetic of memory, and yet but yaw[27] neither, in respect of

---

23. chough—jackdaw, chattering bird.
24. absolute—perfect.   25. differences—distinctions.
26. continent—sum total.   27. yaw—falter.

his quick sail. But, in the verity of extolment, I take him to be a soul of great article, and his infusion of such dearth and rareness, as, to make true diction of him, his semblable is his mirror; and who else would trace him, his umbrage,[28] nothing more.

OSRIC.   Your lordship speaks most infallibly of him.

HAMLET.   The concernancy, sir? Why do we wrap the gentleman in our more rawer breath? [29]

OSRIC.   Sir?

HORATIO.   Is 't not possible to understand in another tongue? You will do 't, sir, really.

HAMLET.   What imports the nomination of this gentleman?

OSRIC.   Of Laertes?

HORATIO.   His purse is empty already; all 's golden words are spent.

HAMLET.   Of him, sir.

OSRIC.   I know you are not ignorant—

HAMLET.   I would you did, sir; yet, in faith, if you did, it would not much approve me. Well, sir?

OSRIC.   You are not ignorant of what excellence Laertes is—

HAMLET.   I dare not confess that, lest I should compare with him in excellence; but to know a man well were to know himself.

OSRIC.   I mean, sir, for his weapon; but in the imputation laid on him by them, in his meed [30] he's unfellowed.

HAMLET.   What's his weapon?

OSRIC.   Rapier and dagger.

HAMLET.   That's two of his weapons; but well.

OSRIC.   The King, sir, hath wagered with him six Barbary horses, against the which he has impawned, as I take it, six French rapiers and poniards, with their assigns,[31] as girdle, hangers, and so. Three of the carriages, in faith, are very dear to fancy, very responsive to the hilts, most delicate carriages, and of very liberal conceit.

HAMLET.   What call you the carriages?

HORATIO.   I knew you must be edified by the margent[32] ere you had done.

OSRIC.   The carriages, sir, are the hangers.

---

28. umbrage—shadow.   29. rawer breath—crude speech.
30. meed—deserts.   31. assigns—accessories.
32. by the margent—an explanatory footnote.

HAMLET.   The phrase would be more germane to the matter, if we could carry cannon by our sides; I would it might be hangers till then. But, on: six Barbary horses against six French swords, their assigns, and three liberal-conceited carriages; that's the French bet against the Danish. Why is all this "impawned," as you call it?

OSRIC.   The King, sir, hath laid, sir, that in a dozen passes between yourself and him, he shall not exceed you three hits; he hath laid on twelve for nine; and it would come to immediate trial, if your lordship would vouchsafe the answer.

HAMLET.   How if I answer no?

OSRIC.   I mean, my lord, the opposition of your person in trial.

HAMLET.   Sir, I will walk here in the hall; if it please his Majesty, it is the breathing time[33] of day with me. Let the foils be brought, the gentleman willing, and the King hold his purpose, I will win for him an I can; if not, I will gain nothing but my shame and the odd hits.

OSRIC.   Shall I deliver you so?

HAMLET.   To this effect, sir; after what flourish your nature will.

OSRIC.   I commend my duty to your lordship.

HAMLET.   Yours, yours. [*Exit* OSRIC.] He does well to commend it himself; there are no tongues else for 's turn.

HORATIO.   This lapwing runs away with the shell on his head.[34]

HAMLET.   'A did, sir, comply[35] with his dug[36] before 'a suck'd it. Thus has he—and many more of the same bevy that I know the drossy[37] age dotes on—only got the tune of the time and, out of an habit of encounter, a kind of yeasty[38] collection, which carries them through and through[39] the most fanned and

---

33. breathing time—exercise period.
34. shell on his head—i.e., before he is completely hatched.
35. comply—spoke ceremonious compliments.
36. dug—his mother's breast.
37. drossy—this degenerate.
38. yeasty—frothy.
39. carries them through and through—makes them completely acceptable to those of.

winnowed opinions; and do but blow them to their trial,[40] the bubbles are out.

Enter a Lord.

LORD. My lord, his Majesty commended him to you by young Osric, who brings back to him, that you attend him in the hall. He sends to know if your pleasure hold to play with Laertes, or that you will take longer time.

HAMLET. I am constant to my purposes; they follow the King's pleasure. If his fitness speaks, mine is ready, now or whensoever, provided I be so able as now.

LORD. The King and Queen and all are coming down.

HAMLET. In happy time.

LORD. The Queen desires you to use some gentle entertainment to Laertes before you fall to play.

HAMLET. She well instructs me. *Exit Lord.*

HORATIO. You will lose, my lord.

HAMLET. I do not think so; since he went into France, I have been in continual practice. I shall win at the odds. But thou wouldst not think how ill all's here about my heart; but it is no matter.

HORATIO. Nay, good my lord,—

HAMLET. It is but foolery; but it is such a kind of gain-giving,[41] as would perhaps trouble a woman.

HORATIO. If your mind dislike anything, obey it. I will forestall their repair hither, and say you are not fit.

HAMLET. Not a whit; we defy augury; there is special providence in the fall of a sparrow. If it be now, 't is not to come; if it be not to come, it will be now; if it be not now, yet it will come; the readiness is all. Since no man of aught he leaves knows, what is 't to leave betimes? Let be.

Enter KING, QUEEN, LAERTES, OSRIC, *and all the Officers of State and other Attendants, with foils and daggers; a table and flagons of wine on it. Trumpets, drums, and Officers with cushions.*

KING. Come, Hamlet, come, and take this hand from me.

[*The* KING *puts* LAERTES' *hand into* HAMLET'S.]

---

40. trial—speak sense.   41. gain-giving—misgiving.

HAMLET.   Give me your pardon, sir. I have done you wrong,
But pardon 't, as you are a gentleman.
This presence[42] knows, and you must needs have heard,
How I am punish'd with a sore distraction.
What I have done
That might your nature, honour, and exception[43]
Roughly awake, I here proclaim was madness.
Was 't Hamlet wrong'd Laertes? Never Hamlet!
If Hamlet from himself be ta'en away,
And when he's not himself does wrong Laertes,
Then Hamlet does it not, Hamlet denies it.
Who does it, then? His maddness. If 't be so,
Hamlet is of the faction that is wrong'd;
His madness is poor Hamlet's enemy.
Sir, in this audience,
Let my disclaiming from a purpos'd evil
Free me so far in your most generous thoughts,
That I have shot my arrow o'er the house
And hurt my brother.

LAERTES.   I am satisfied in nature,
Whose motive, in this case, should stir me most
To my revenge; but in my terms of honour
I stand aloof, and will no reconcilement,
Till by some elder masters of known honour
I have a voice and precedent[44] of peace,
To keep my name ungor'd.[45] But till that time,
I do receive your offer'd love like love,
And will not wrong it.

HAMLET.   I embrace it freely,
And will this brother's wager frankly play.
Give us the foils.

LAERTES.   Come, one for me.

HAMLET.   I'll be your foil,[46] Laertes; in mine ignorance
Your skill shall, like a star i' th' darkest night,
Stick fiery off indeed.

LAERTES   You mock me, sir.

---

42. presence—the assembled court.   43. exception—resentment.
44. voice and precedent—decision serving as a precedent.
45. ungor'd—free from disgrace.   46. foil—rapier; also, antithesis.

HAMLET.   No, by this hand.

KING.   Give them the foils, young Osric. Cousin Hamlet,
You know the wager?

HAMLET.   Very well, my lord.
Your Grace hath laid the odds o' th' weaker side.

KING.   I do not fear it, I have seen you both;
But since he is better'd, we have therefore odds.

LAERTES.   This is too heavy; let me see another.

HAMLET.   This likes me well. These foils have all a⁴⁷ length?
                               [*They prepare to fence.*]

OSRIC.   Ay, my good lord.

KING.   Set me the stoups of wine upon that table.
If Hamlet give the first or second hit,
Or quit⁴⁸ in answer of the third exchange,
Let all the battlements their ordnance fire.
The King shall drink to Hamlet's better breath,
And in the cup an union⁴⁹ shall he throw,
Richer than that which four successive kings
In Denmark's crown have worn. Give me the cups,
And let the kettle⁵⁰ to the trumpet speak,
The trumpet to the cannoneer without,
The cannons to the heavens, the heaven to earth,
"Now the King drinks to Hamlet." Come, begin;
And you, the judges, bear a wary eye.   [*Trumpets sound.*]

HAMLET.   Come on, sir.

LAERTES.   Come, my lord.   [*They fence.*]

HAMLET.   One.

LAERTES   No.

HAMLET.   Judgement.

OSRIC.   A hit, a very palpable hit.

LAERTES.   Well; again.

KING.   Stay, give me drink. Hamlet, this pearl is thine;
Here's to thy health! Give him the cup.
                 [*Trumpets sound, and shot goes off within.*]

HAMLET.   I'll play this bout first; set it by a while.
Come. [*They play.*] Another hit; what say you?

LAERTES.   A touch, a touch, I do confess 't.

---

47. a—equal.   48. quit—strike back.
49. union—pearl.   50. kettle—drum.

KING.   Our son shall win.

QUEEN.   He's fat, and scant of breath.
Here, Hamlet, take my napkin, rub thy brows.
The Queen carouses[51] to thy fortune, Hamlet.

HAMLET.   Good madam!

KING.   Gertrude, do not drink.

QUEEN.   I will, my lord; I pray you, pardon me.

KING.   [*Aside.*] It is the poison'd cup; it is too late.

HAMLET.   I dare not drink yet, madam; by and by.

QUEEN.   Come, let me wipe thy face.

LAERTES.   My lord, I'll hit him now.

KING.   I do not think 't.

LAERTES.   [*Aside.*] And yet it is almost against my conscience.

HAMLET.   Come, for the third, Laertes; you but dally.
I pray you, pass with your best violence.
I am afeard you make a wanton of me.[52]

LAERTES.   Say you so? Come on.   [*They fence.*]

OSRIC.   Nothing, neither way.

LAERTES.   Have at you now!

                        [LAERTES *wounds* HAMLET; *then, in
                        scuffling, they change rapiers.*]

KING.   Part them; they are incens'd.

HAMLET.   Nay, come, again.

                        [HAMLET *wounds* LAERTES. *The Queen falls.*]

OSRIC.   Look to the Queen there! Ho!

HORATIO.   They bleed on both sides. How is 't, my lord!

OSRIC.   How is 't, Laertes?

LAERTES.   Why, as a woodcock to mine own springe, Osric;
I am justly kill'd with mine own treachery.

HAMLET.   How does the Queen?

KING.   She swounds to see them bleed.

QUEEN.   No, no, the drink, the drink,—O my dear Hamlet,—
The drink, the drink! I am poison'd.   [*Dies.*]

HAMLET.   O villainy! Ho! let the door be lock'd:
Treachery! Seek it out.

LAERTES.   It is here, Hamlet. Hamlet, thou art slain.

---

51. carouses—drinks a full draught.
52. make a wanton of me—indulge me as if I were a child.

No med'cine in the world can do thee good;
In thee there is not half an hour of life;
The treacherous instrument is in thy hand,
Unbated and envenom'd: the foul practice
Hath turn'd itself on me; lo, here I lie,
Never to rise again. Thy mother's poison'd.
I can no more:—the King, the King's to blame.
    HAMLET.   The point envenom'd too!
Then, venom, to thy work.   [*Wounds the* KING.]
    ALL.   Treason! treason!
    KING.   O, yet defend me, friends; I am but hurt.
    HAMLET.   Here, thou incestuous, murd'rous, damned Dane,
Drink off this potion! Is thy union here?
Follow my mother!   [KING *dies.*]
    LAERTES.   He is justly serv'd;
It is a poison temper'd [53] by himself.
Exchange forgiveness with me, noble Hamlet;
Mine and my father's death come not upon thee,[54]
Nor thine on me!   [*Dies.*]
    HAMLET.   Heaven make thee free of it! I follow thee.
I am dead, Horatio. Wretched queen, adieu!
You that look pale and tremble at this chance,
That are but mutes[55] or audience to this act,
Had I but time—as this fell sergeant, Death,
Is strict in his arrest—O, I could tell you—
But let it be. Horatio, I am dead;
Thou livest; report me and my cause aright
To the unsatisfied.[56]
    HORATIO.   Never believe it:
I am more an antique Roman[57] than a Dane;
Here's yet some liquor left.
    HAMLET.   As thou 'rt a man,
Give me the cup; let go, by heaven, I'll have 't!
O God, Horatio, what a wounded name,

---

53. temper'd—compounded.
54. come not upon thee—are not on thy head.
55. mutes—actors without speaking parts.
56. unsatisfied—uninformed.
57. antique Roman—for whom suicide was an honorable act.

Things standing thus unknown, shall live behind me!
If thou didst ever hold me in thy heart,
Absent thee from felicity[58] a while
And in this harsh world draw thy breath in pain
To tell my story.   [*March afar off, and shot within.*]
                    What warlike noise is this?
   OSRIC.   Young Fortinbras, with conquest come from **Poland,**
To th' ambassadors of England gives
This warlike volley.
   HAMLET.   O, I die, Horatio;
The potent poison quite o'er-crows[59] my spirit:
I cannot live to hear the news from England,
But I do prophesy th' election lights
On Fortinbras; he has my dying voice.
So tell him, with th' occurrents, more and less,
Which have solicited [60]—the rest is silence.   [*Dies.*]
   HORATIO.   Now cracks a noble heart. Good-night, sweet
        prince,
And flights of angels sing thee to thy rest!
Why does the drum come hither?

Enter FORTINBRAS *and the English* AMBASSADORS, *with drum-*
        mers, colour-bearers, and Attendants.

   FORTINBRAS.   Where is this sight?
   HORATIO.   What is it you would see?
If aught of woe or wonder, cease your search.
   FORTINBRAS.   This quarry[61] cries on havoc.[62] O proud **Death,**
What feast is toward in thine eternal cell,
That thou so many princes at a shot
So bloodily hast struck?
   FIRST AMBASSADOR.   The sight is dismal,
And our affairs from England come too late:
The ears are senseless that should give us hearing,
To tell him his commandment is fulfill'd,
That Rosencrantz and Guildenstern are dead.
Where should we have our thanks?

---

58. felicity—death.   59. o'ercrows—overcomes.
60. solicited—caused my actions.   61. quarry—dead bodies.
62. havoc—massacre.

HORATIO. Not from his mouth,
Had it th' ability of life to thank you.
He never gave commandment for their death:
But since, so jump[63] upon this bloody question,
You from the Polack wars, and you from England,
Are here arrived, give order that these bodies
High on a stage[64] be placed to the view;
And let me speak to th' yet unknowing world
How these things came about: so shall you hear
Of carnal, bloody, and unnatural acts,
Of accidental judgements,[65] casual slaughters,
Of deaths put on by cunning and forc'd cause,
And, in this upshot, purposes mistook
Fall'n on th' inventors' heads: all this can I
Truly deliver.
    FORTINBRAS.   Let us haste to hear it,
And call the noblest to the audience.
For me, with sorrow I embrace my fortune:
I have some rights of memory[66] in this kingdom,
Which now to claim, my vantage doth invite me.
    HORATIO.   Of that I shall have also cause to speak,
And from his mouth whose voice will draw on more:
But let this same be presently perform'd
Even while men's minds are wild, lest more mischance,
On plots and errors, happen.
    FORTINBRAS.   Let four captains
Bear Hamlet, like a soldier, to the stage,
For he was likely, had he been put on,
To have prov'd most royal; and, for his passage,
The soldiers' music and the rites of war
Speak loudly for him.
Take up the bodies: such a sight as this
Becomes the field, but here shows much amiss.
Go, bid the soldiers shoot.

> *Exeunt marching, after the which a*
> *peal of ordnance is shot off.*

---

63. jump—opportunely.   64. stage—platform.
65. accidental judgements—judgments executed by accidental means.
66. of memory—still remembered.

The Tragedy of
KING LEAR

CHARACTERS

LEAR, *King of Britain.*	DOCTOR.
KING OF FRANCE.	FOOL.
DUKE OF BURGUNDY.	OSWALD, *steward to* GONERIL.
DUKE OF CORNWALL.	A CAPTAIN *employed by*
DUKE OF ALBANY.	EDMUND.
EARL OF KENT.	GENTLEMAN *attendant on*
EARL OF GLOUCESTER.	CORDELIA.
EDGAR, *son to* GLOUCESTER.	A HERALD.
EDMUND, *bastard son to*	SERVANTS *to* CORNWALL.
GLOUCESTER.	
CURAN, a courtier.	GONERIL,
OLD MAN, *tenant to*	REGAN, }*daughters to* LEAR
GLOUCESTER.	CORDELIA,

Knights of Lear's Train, Captains, Messengers, Soldiers,
and Attendants.

SCENE: *Britain.*

[ACT I • 1] *King Lear's palace.*

Enter KENT, GLOUCESTER, *and* EDMUND.

KENT. I thought the King had more affected [1] the Duke of
Albany than Cornwall.

GLOUCESTER. It did always seem so to us; but now, in the
division of the kingdom, it appears not which of the Dukes he
values most; for equalities[2] are so weigh'd,[3] that curiosity[4] in
neither can make choice of [5] either's moiety.[6]

---

1. affected—favored.　2. equalities—shares.　3. weigh'd—balanced.
4. curiosity—close examination.　5. of—between.　6. moiety—share.

KENT.   Is not this your son, my lord?

GLOUCESTER.   His breeding, sir, hath been at my charge. I have so often blushed to acknowledge him, that now I am brazed [7] to 't.

KENT.   I cannot conceive[8] you.

GLOUCESTER.   Sir, this young fellow's mother could; whereupon she grew round-wombed, and had, indeed, sir, a son for her cradle ere she had a husband for her bed. Do you smell a fault?

KENT.   I cannot wish the fault undone, the issue of it being so proper.

GLOUCESTER.   But I have a son, sir, by order of law, some year elder than this, who yet is no dearer in my account. Though this knave came something saucily into the world before he was sent for, yet was his mother fair; there was good sport at his making, and the whoreson[9] must be acknowledged. Do you know this noble gentleman, Edmund?

EDMUND.   No, my lord.

GLOUCESTER.   My Lord of Kent. Remember him hereafter as my honourable friend.

EDMUND.   My services to your lordship.

KENT.   I must love you, and sue to know you better.

EDMUND.   Sir, I shall study deserving.

GLOUCESTER.   He hath been out nine years, and away he shall again. The King is coming.

Sennet.[10] *Enter one bearing a coronet, then* KING LEAR, *then the* DUKES OF ALBANY *and* CORNWALL, *next* GONERIL, REGAN, CORDELIA, *with followers.*

LEAR.   Attend the lords of France and Burgundy, Gloucester.

GLOUCESTER.   I shall, my liege.

>   *Exeunt* GLOUCESTER *and* EDMUND.

LEAR.   Meantime we shall express our darker[11] purpose.
Give me the map there. Know that we have divided
In three our kingdom; and 't is our fast intent
To shake all cares and business from our age,

---

7. brazed—hardened.   8. conceive—understand.
9. whoreson—bastard.   10. Sennet—trumpet fanfare.
11. darker—hitherto secret.

Conferring them on younger strengths, while we
Unburden'd crawl toward death. Our son of Cornwall,
And you, our no less loving son of Albany,
We have this hour a constant will to publish
Our daughters' several [12] dowers, that future strife
May be prevented now. The Princes, France and Burgundy,
Great rivals in our youngest daughter's love,
Long in our court have made their amorous sojourn,
And here are to be answer'd. Tell me, my daughters,—
Since now we will divest us both of rule,
Interest[13] of territory, cares of state,—
Which of you shall we say doth love us most,
That we our largest bounty may extend
Where nature[14] doth with merit[15] challenge? [16] Goneril,
Our eldest-born, speak first.

    GONERIL.   Sir, I do love you more than words can wield [17]
    the matter;
Dearer than eye-sight, space, and liberty:
Beyond what can be valued, rich or rare;
No less than life, with grace, health, beauty, honour;
As much as child e'er lov'd, or father found;
A love that makes breath poor, and speech unable:
Beyond all manner of so much[18] I love you.

    CORDELIA.   [Aside.] What shall Cordelia speak? Love and be
    silent.

    LEAR.   Of all these bounds, even from this line to this,
With shadowy forest and with champains[19] rich'd,
With plenteous rivers and wide-skirted meads,
We make thee lady. To thine and Albany's issues
Be this perpetual. What says our second daughter,
Our dearest Regan, wife of Cornwall? Speak.

    REGAN.   I am made of that self [20] metal as my sister,
And prize me at her worth.[21] In my true heart

---

12. several—separate.   13. Interest—possession.
14. nature—natural affection.   15. with merit—plus individual merit.
16. challenge—make a claim.   17. wield—express.
18. of so much—of these things.
19. champains—fields.   20. self—same.
21. prize me at her worth—appraise myself her equal.

I find she names my very deed of love;
Only she comes too short, that I profess
Myself an enemy to all other joys
Which the most precious square[22] of sense possesses;
And find I am alone felicitate[23]
In your dear Highness' love.

CORDELIA.   [*Aside*.] Then poor Cordelia!
And yet not so; since, I am sure, my love's
More ponderous[24] than my tongue.

LEAR.   To thee and thine hereditary ever
Remain this ample third of our fair kingdom;
No less in space, validity,[25] and pleasure,
Than that conferr'd on Goneril. Now, our joy,
Although our last and least, to whose young love
The vines of France and milk of Burgundy
Strive to be interess'd,[26] what can you say to draw
A third more opulent than your sisters? Speak.

CORDELIA.   Nothing, my lord.

LEAR.   Nothing!

CORDELIA.   Nothing.

LEAR.   Nothing will come of nothing. Speak again.

CORDELIA.   Unhappy that I am, I cannot heave
My heart into my mouth. I love your Majesty
According to my bond; [27] nor more nor less.

LEAR.   How, how, Cordelia! Mend your speech a little,
Lest you may mar your fortune.

CORDELIA.   Good my lord,
You have begot me, bred me, lov'd me: I
Return those duties back as are right fit;
Obey you, love you, and most honour you.
Why have my sisters husbands, if they say
They love you all? Haply,[28] when I shall wed,
That lord whose hand must take my plight[29] shall carry
Half my love with him, half my care and duty.

---

22. square—criterion.   23. felicitate—made happy.
24. more ponderous—weightier.   25. validity—value.
26. be interess'd—enter a claim.   27. bond—bounden duty.
28. Haply—It may happen.   29. plight—troth.

Sure, I shall never marry like my sisters
To love my father all.

 LEAR. But goes thy heart with this?

 CORDELIA.   Ay, my good lord.

 LEAR. So young, and so untender?

 CORDELIA. So young, my lord, and true.

 LEAR. Let it be so; thy truth, then, be thy dower!
For, by the sacred radiance of the sun,
The mysteries of Hecate,[30] and the night;
By all the operation of the orbs[31]
From whom we do exist, and cease to be;
Here I disclaim all my paternal care,
Propinquity[32] and property of blood,
And as a stranger to my heart and me
Hold thee, from this, for ever. The barbarous Scythian,[33]
Or he that makes his generation messes[34]
To gorge his appetite, shall to my bosom
Be as well neighbour'd, piti'd, and reliev'd,
As thou my sometime daughter.

 KENT.   Good my liege,—

 LEAR. Peace, Kent!
Come not between the dragon[35] and his wrath.
I lov'd her most, and thought to set my rest[36]
On her kind nursery. [*To* CORDELIA.] Hence, and avoid [37] my
 sight!—
So be my grave my peace, as here I give
Her father's heart from her! Call France.—Who stirs?
Call Burgundy. Cornwall and Albany,
With my two daughters' dowers digest[38] this third;
Let pride, which she calls plainness, marry her.
I do invest you jointly in my power,

---

30. Hecate—goddess of witchcraft.
31. orbs—stars.   32. Propinquity—relationship.
33. Scythian—South Russian, regarded as extremely savage.
34. makes his generation messes—makes food of his children.
35. dragon—traditional symbol of British kings.
36. set my rest—rely completely.
37. avoid—leave.
38. digest—incorporate.

Pre-eminence,[39] and all the large effects[40]
That troop with majesty. Ourself, by monthly course,
With reservation of an hundred knights,
By you to be sustain'd, shall our abode
Make with you by due turn. Only we still retain
The name, and all th' additions[41] to a king;
The sway, revénue, execution of the rest,
Beloved sons, be yours; which to confirm,
This coronet part betwixt you.

    KENT.   Royal Lear,
Whom I have ever honour'd as my king,
Lov'd as my father, as my master follow'd,
As my great patron thought on in my prayers,—

    LEAR.   The bow is bent and drawn; make from the shaft.[42]

    KENT.   Let it fall rather, though the fork[43] invade
The region of my heart: be Kent unmannerly
When Lear is mad. What wouldst thou do, old man?
Think'st thou that duty shall have dread to speak
When power to flattery bows? To plainness honour's bound,
When majesty falls to folly. Reserve thy state;
And, in thy best consideration, check
This hideous rashness. Answer my life my judgement,
Thy youngest daughter does not love thee least;
Nor are those empty-hearted whose low sounds
Reverb[44] no hollowness.

    LEAR.   Kent, on thy life, no more.

    KENT.   My life I never held but as a pawn[45]
To wage[46] against thine enemies, nor fear to lose it,
Thy safety being the motive.

    LEAR.   Out of my sight!

    KENT.   See better, Lear; and let me still remain
The true blank[47] of thine eye.

    LEAR.   Now, by Apollo,—

---

39. Pre-eminence—authority.   40. large effects—show of power.
41. additions—titles.   42. shaft—arrow.   43. fork—barb.
44. Reverb—echo.   45. pawn—pledge.
46. wage—stake.   47. blank—target.

KENT.   Now, by Apollo, king,
Thou swear'st thy gods in vain.
    LEAR.   O, vassal! miscreant!
                        [*Laying his hand on his sword.*]

ALBANY. ⎫
CORNWALL. ⎬ Dear sir, forbear.
    KENT.   Kill thy physician, and thy fee bestow
Upon the foul disease. Revoke thy doom;
Or, whilst I can vent clamour from my throat,
I'll tell thee thou dost evil.
    LEAR.   Hear me, recreant!
On thine allegiance, hear me!
That thou hast sought to make us break our vows,
Which we durst never yet, and with strain'd pride
To come betwixt our sentence and our power,
Which nor our nature nor our place can bear,
Our potency made good,[48] take thy reward.
Five days we do allot thee, for provision
To shield thee from diseases of the world;
And on the sixth to turn thy hated back
Upon our kingdom. If, on the tenth day following,
Thy banish'd trunk be found in our dominions,
The moment is thy death. Away! By Jupiter,[49]
This shall not be revok'd.
    KENT.   Fare thee well, king! Sith[50] thus thou wilt appear,
Freedom lives hence, and banishment is here.
[*To* CORDELIA.] The gods to their dear shelter take thee, maid,
That justly think'st, and hast most rightly said!
[*To* REGAN *and* GONERIL.] And your large speeches may your
         deeds approve,[51]
That good effects[52] may spring from words of love.
Thus Kent, O princes, bids you all adieu;
He'll shape his old course[53] in a country new.   *Exit.*

---

48. our potency made good—my royal will having been asserted.
49. Jupiter—chief of the Roman gods. The classic pantheon is used
in this play to fit a pagan, not necessarily Roman, society.
50. Sith—since.   51. approve—confirm.   52. effects—actions.
53. old course—i.e., as a faithful, plain-spoken subject.

Flourish.[54] *Enter* GLOUCESTER, *with* FRANCE *and* BURGUNDY, *Attendants.*

GLOUCESTER.   Here's France[55] and Burgundy,[56] my noble lord.

LEAR.   My Lord of Burgundy,
We first address toward you, who with this king
Hath rivall'd for our daughter. What, in the least,
Will you require[57] in present[58] dower with her,
Or cease your quest of love?

BURGUNDY.   Most royal Majesty.
I crave no more than hath your Highness offer'd,
Nor will you tender[59] less.

LEAR.   Right noble Burgundy,
When she was dear to us, we did hold her so;
But now her price is fal'n. Sir, there she stands:
If aught within that little-seeming substance,
Or all of it, with our displeasure piec'd,[60]
And nothing more, may fitly like your Grace,
She's there, and she is yours.

BURGUNDY.   I know no answer.

LEAR.   Will you, with those infirmities she owes,[61]
Unfriended, new-adopted to our hate,
Dower'd with our curse, and stranger'd with our oath,
Take her, or leave her?

BURGUNDY.   Pardon me, royal sir;
Election[62] makes not up in such conditions.

LEAR.   Then leave her, sir; for, by the power that made me,
I tell you all her wealth. [*To* FRANCE.] For you, great king,
I would not from your love make such a stray,
To match you where I hate; therefore beseech you
T' avert your liking a more worthier way
Than on a wretch whom Nature is asham'd
Almost t' acknowledge hers.

FRANCE.   This is most strange,

---

54. Flourish—trumpet fanfare.   55. France—the king of France.
56. Burgundy—the duke of Burgundy.
57. require—request.   58. present—immediate.
59. tender—offer.   60. piec'd—added.
61. owes—possesses.   62. Election—choice.

That she, that even but now was your best object,[63]
The argument of your praise, balm of your age,
Most best, most dearest, should in this trice[64] of time
Commit a thing so monstrous, to dismantle
So many folds of favour. Sure, her offence
Must be of such unnatural degree,
That monsters[65] it, or your fore-vouch'd [66] affection
Fall'n into taint;[67] which to believe of her,
Must be a faith that reason without miracle
Should never plant in me.

    CORDELIA.   I yet beseech your Majesty,—
If for I want that glib and oily art,
To speak and purpose not; since what I well intend,
I'll do 't before I speak,—that you make known
It is no vicious blot,[68] murder, or foulness,
No unchaste action, or dishonoured step,
That hath depriv'd me of your grace and favour;
But even for want[69] of that for which I am richer,
A still-soliciting[70] eye, and such a tongue
That I am glad I have not, though not to have it
Hath lost me in your liking.

    LEAR.   Better thou
Hadst not been born than not to have pleas'd me better.

    FRANCE.   It is but this,—a tardiness[71] in nature
Which often leaves the history unspoke
That it intends to do? My Lord of Burgundy,
What say you to the lady? Love is not love
When it is mingled with regards[72] that stands
Aloof from th' entire point.[73] Will you have her?
She is herself a dowry.

    BURGUNDY.   Royal Lear,
Give but that portion which yourself propos'd,

---

63. best object—favorite.   64. trice—moment.
65. monsters—makes monstrous.
66. fore-vouch'd—previously declared.
67. into taint—decay.   68. vicious blot—immoral act.
69. want—lack.   70. still-soliciting—always asking favors.
71. tardiness—reticence.   72. regards—considerations.
73. entire point—love.

And here I take Cordelia by the hand,
Duchess of Burgundy.

LEAR.   Nothing. I have sworn; I am firm.

BURGUNDY.   I am sorry, then, you have so lost a father
That you must lose a husband.

CORDELIA.   Peace be with Burgundy!
Since that respects of fortune[74] are his love,
I shall not be his wife.

FRANCE.   Fairest Cordelia, that art most rich being poor,
Most choice forsaken, and most lov'd despis'd!
Thee and thy virtues here I seize upon,
Be it lawful I take up what's cast away.
Gods, gods! 't is strange that from their cold'st neglect
My love should kindle to inflam'd [75] respect.
Thy dowerless daughter, king, thrown to my chance,
Is queen of us, of ours, and our fair France.
Not all the dukes of waterish Burgundy
Shall buy this unpriz'd precious maid of me.
Bid them farewell, Cordelia, though unkind;
Thou losest here, a better where[76] to find.

LEAR.   Thou hast her, France. Let her be thine; for we
Have no such daughter, nor shall ever see
That face of hers again.—[*To* CORDELIA.] Therefore be gone
Without our grace, our love, our benison.[77]—
Come, noble Burgundy.

                         Flourish. Exeunt LEAR *and* BURGUNDY.

FRANCE.   Bid farewell to your sisters.

CORDELIA.   The jewels of our father, with wash'd eyes
Cordelia leaves you. I know you what you are;
And like a sister am most loath to call
Your faults as they are named. Use well our father,
To your professed [78] bosoms I commit him;
But yet, alas, stood I within his grace,
I would prefer him to a better place.
So, farewell to you both.

REGAN.   Prescribe not us our duties.

---

74. respects of fortune—considerations of my dowry.
75. inflam'd—passionate.   76. where—place.
77. benison—blessing.   78. professed—professing (love).

GONERIL.   Let your study
Be to content your lord, who hath receiv'd you
At fortune's alms.[79] You have obedience scanted,[80]
And well are worth[81] the want[82] that you have wanted.[83]

CORDELIA.   Time shall unfold what plighted [84] cunning hides;
Who covers faults, at last shame them derides.
Well may you prosper!

FRANCE.   Come, my fair Cordelia.

                                 Exeunt FRANCE *and* CORDELIA.

GONERIL.   Sister, it is not little I have to say of what most
nearly appertains to us both. I think our father will hence to-
night.

REGAN.   That's most certain, and with you; next month with
us.

GONERIL.   You see how full of changes his age is; the observation we have made of it hath not been little. He always
loved our sister most; and with what poor judgement he hath
now cast her off appears too gross.[85]

REGAN.   'T is the infirmity of his age; yet he hath ever but
slenderly known himself.

GONERIL.   The best and soundest of his time[86] hath been but
rash; then must we look to receive from his age not alone the
imperfections of long-engrafted condition,[87] but therewithal the
unruly waywardness that infirm and choleric years bring with
them.

REGAN.   Such unconstant starts[88] are we like to have from
him as this of Kent's banishment.

GONERIL.   There is further compliment of leave-taking between France and him. Pray you, let's hit[89] together; if our father
carry authority with such disposition as he bears, this last surrender of his will but offend [90] us.

---

79. at fortune's alms—as charity from fortune.
80. scanted—fallen short in.   81. worth—deserve.
82. want—lack of love (from your husband).
83. wanted—as you have shown lack of love for your father.
84. plighted—folded.   85. gross—obvious.
86. of his time—periods of his life.
87. long-engrafted condition—natural temperament.
88. starts—whims.   89. hit—agree.
90. offend—give trouble.

REGAN.   We shall further think on 't.
GONERIL.   We must do something, and i' th' heat.[91]

Exeunt.

91. i' th' heat—while the iron is hot.

[ACT I • 2] *The Earl of Gloucester's castle.*

Enter EDMUND *with a letter.*

EDMUND.   Thou, Nature, art my goddess; to thy law
My services are bound. Wherefore should I
Stand in the plague[1] of custom, and permit
The curiosity[2] of nations to deprive me,
For that I am some twelve or fourteen moonshines
Lag[3] of a brother? Why bastard? Wherefore base?
When my dimensions are as well compact,
My mind as generous, and my shape as true,
As honest madam's issue? Why brand they us
With base? with baseness? bastardy? base, base?
Who, in the lusty stealth of nature, take
More composition[4] and fierce quality[5]
Than doth, within a dull, stale, tired bed,
Go to th' creating a whole tribe of fops,
Got[6] 'tween asleep and wake? Well then,
Legitimate Edgar, I must have your land.
Our father's love is to the bastard Edmund
As to th' legitimate. Fine word, "legitimate"!
Well, my legitimate, if this letter speed [7]
And my invention thrive, Edmund the base
Shall top th' legitimate. I grow; I prosper.
Now, gods, stand up for bastards!

Enter GLOUCESTER.

GLOUCESTER.   Kent banish'd thus! and France in choler[8]
   parted!
And the King gone to-night! subscrib'd [9] his power!

1. plague—vexation.   2. curiosity—absurd law.   3. Lag—behind.
4. composition—strength.   5. fierce quality—energy.
6. Got—conceived.   7. speed—prosper.
8. choler—anger.   9. subscrib'd—signed away.

Confin'd to exhibition! [10] All this done
Upon the gad! [11] Edmund, how now! what news?

EDMUND.   So please your lordship, none.

[Putting up the letter.]

GLOUCESTER.   Why so earnestly seek you to put up that letter?

EDMUND.   I know no news, my lord.

GLOUCESTER.   What paper were you reading?

EDMUND.   Nothing, my lord.

GLOUCESTER.   No? What needed, then, that terrible dispatch of it into your pocket? The quality of nothing hath not such need to hide itself. Let's see. Come, if it be nothing, I shall not need spectacles.

EDMUND.   I beseech you, sir, pardon me. It is a letter from my brother, that I have not all o'erread; and for so much as I have perused, I find it not fit for your o'erlooking.

GLOUCESTER.   Give me the letter, sir.

EDMUND.   I shall offend, either to detain or give it. The contents, as in part I understand them, are to blame.[12]

GLOUCESTER.   Let's see, let's see.

EDMUND.   I hope, for my brother's justification, he wrote this but as an essay[13] or taste of my virtue.

GLOUCESTER.   *[Reads.]*

This policy[14] and reverence of age makes the world bitter to the best of our times; [15] keeps our fortunes from us till our oldness cannot relish them. I begin to find an idle and fond [16] bondage in the oppression of aged tyranny; who sways, not as it hath power, but as it is suffered.[17] Come to me, that of this I may speak more. If our father would sleep till I waked him, you should enjoy half his revénue for ever, and live the beloved of your brother,

EDGAR.

Hum—conspiracy!—"Sleep till I wake him, you should enjoy half his revénue!"—My son Edgar! Had he a hand to write this?

---

10. exhibition—a pension.   11. gad—spur of the moment.
12. to blame—blameworthy.   13. essay—test.
14. policy and reverence—strategy of requiring reverence for.
15. our times—our youth.
16. fond—foolish.
17. suffered—submitted to.

a heart and brain to breed it in?—When came this to you? Who brought it?

EDMUND.   It was not brought me, my lord; there's the cunning of it. I found it thrown in at the casement of my closet.[18]

GLOUCESTER.   You know the character[19] to be your brother's?

EDMUND.   If the matter were good, my lord, I durst swear it were his; but, in respect of that, I would fain think it were not.

GLOUCESTER.   It is his.

EDMUND.   It is his hand, my lord; but I hope his heart is not in the contents.

GLOUCESTER.   Hath he never heretofore sounded you in this business?

EDMUND.   Never, my lord; but I have heard him oft maintain it to be fit that, sons at perfect age, and fathers declined, the father should be as ward to the son, and the son manage his revénue.

GLOUCESTER.   O villain, villain! His very opinion in the letter! Abhorred villain! Unnatural, detested, brutish villain! worse than brutish! Go, sirrah, seek him; I'll apprehend him. Abominable villain! Where is he?

EDMUND.   I do not well know, my lord. If it shall please you to suspend your indignation against my brother till you can derive from him better testimony of his intent, you should run a certain course;[20] where, if you violently proceed against him, mistaking his purpose, it would make a great gap in your own honour, and shake in pieces the heart of his obedience. I dare pawn down my life for him, that he hath wrote this to feel my affection to your honour, and to no further pretence of danger.

GLOUCESTER.   Think you so?

EDMUND.   If your honour judge it meet, I will place you where you shall hear us confer of this, and by an auricular assurance[21] have your satisfaction; and that without any further delay than this very evening.

GLOUCESTER.   He cannot be such a monster—

---

18. closet—private room.   19. character—handwriting.
20. certain course—proceed more surely.
21. auricular assurance—hearing the evidence.

EDMUND.   Nor is not, sure.

GLOUCESTER.   To his father, that so tenderly and entirely loves him. Heaven and earth! Edmund, seek him out; wind me into him,[22] I pray you. Frame the business after your own wisdom. I would unstate[23] myself, to be in a due resolution.[24]

EDMUND.   I will seek him, sir, presently; [25] convey[26] the business as I shall find means, and acquaint you withal.[27]

GLOUCESTER.   These late eclipses in the sun and moon portend no good to us. Though the wisdom of nature can reason[28] it thus and thus, yet nature finds itself scourged by the sequent[29] effects. Love cools, friendship falls off, brothers divide: in cities, mutinies; in countries, discord; in palaces, treason; and the bond cracked 'twixt son and father. This villain of mine comes under the prediction; there's son against father: the King falls from bias of nature; there's father against child. We have seen the best of our time; machinations, hollowness, treachery, and all ruinous disorders, follow us disquietly to our graves. Find out this villain, Edmund; it shall lose thee nothing; do it carefully. And the noble and true-hearted Kent banished! his offence, honesty! 'T is strange.   *Exit.*

EDMUND.   This is the excellent foppery[30] of the world, that, when we are sick in fortune,—often the surfeit[31] of our own behaviour,—we make guilty of our disasters the sun, the moon, and the stars, as if we were villains on necessity, fools by heavenly compulsion, knaves, thieves, and treachers by spherical predominance,[32] drunkards, liars, and adulterers by an enforced obedience of planetary influence, and all that we are evil in, by a divine thrusting on. An admirable evasion of whoremaster man, to lay his goatish[33] disposition on the charge of a star! My father compounded with my mother under the dragon's tail; and my

---

22. wind me into him—gain his confidence.
23. unstate—give up my earldom.
24. in a due resolution—freed of doubts.
25. presently—immediately.   26. convey—conduct.
27. withal—with the results.   28. reason—explain.
29. sequent—consequent.   30. foppery—folly.
31. surfeit—overeating, i.e., because of our own overindulgence.
32. spherical predominance—influence of the planets.
33. goatish—lustful.

nativity was under *Ursa major;* [34] so that it follows, I am rough and lecherous. Fut, I should have been that I am, had the maidenliest star in the firmament twinkled on my bastardizing. Edgar—

Enter EDGAR.

and pat he comes like the catastrophe[35] of the old comedy. My cue is villanous melancholy, with a sigh like Tom o' Bedlam.[36]— O, these eclipses do portend these divisions! *fa, sol, la, mi.*

EDGAR. How now, brother Edmund! what serious contemplation are you in?

EDMUND. I am thinking, brother, of a prediction I read this other day, what should follow these eclipses.

EDGAR. Do you busy yourself with that?

EDMUND. I promise you, the effects he writ of succeed [37] unhappily; as of unnaturalness between the child and the parent; death, dearth,[38] dissolutions of ancient amities; divisions in state, menaces and maledictions against king and nobles; needless diffidences, banishment of friends, dissipation of cohorts, nuptial breaches, and I know not what.

EDGAR. How long have you been a sectary astronomical? [39]

EDMUND. Come, come; when saw you my father last?

EDGAR. Why, the night gone by.

EDMUND. Spake you with him?

EDGAR. Ay, two hours together.

EDMUND. Parted you in good terms? Found you no displeasure in him by word nor countenance?

EDGAR. None at all.

EDMUND. Bethink yourself wherein you may have offended him; and at my entreaty forbear his presence until some little time hath qualified [40] the heat of his displeasure, which at this instant so rageth in him, that with the mischief of [41] your person it would scarce allay.

EDGAR. Some villain hath done me wrong.

---

34. *Ursa major*—the constellation of the Great Bear.
35. catastrophe—final event.   36. Tom o' Bedlam—lunatic beggar.
37. succeed—follow.   38. dearth—famine.
39. sectary astronomical—believer in astrology.
40. qualified—modified.   41. mischief of—injury to.

EDMUND.   That's my fear. I pray you, have a continent forbearance[42] till the speed of his rage goes slower; and, as I say,
retire with me to my lodging, from whence I will fitly bring you
to hear my lord speak. Pray ye, go; there's my key. If you do
stir abroad, go armed.

EDGAR.   Armed, brother!

EDMUND.   Brother, I advise you to the best; I am no honest
man if there be any good meaning towards you. I have told you
what I have seen and heard; but faintly, nothing like the image
and horror of it. Pray you, away.

EDGAR.   Shall I hear from you anon? [43]

EDMUND.   I do serve you in this business.   *Exit* EDGAR.
A credulous father, and a brother noble,
Whose nature is so far from doing harms
That he suspects none; on whose foolish honesty
My practices[44] ride easy. I see the business.
Let me, if not by birth, have lands by wit:
All with me's meet[45] that I can fashion fit.   *Exit.*

---

42. continent forbearance—self-control.   43. anon—soon.
44. practices—plots.   45. meet—proper.

[ACT I • 3] *The Duke of Albany's palace.*

Enter GONERIL, *and* OSWALD, *her Steward.*

GONERIL.   Did my father strike my gentleman for chiding of
   his Fool?

OSWALD.   Ay, madam.

GONERIL.   By day and night he wrongs me; every hour
He flashes into one gross crime or other
That sets us all at odds. I'll not endure it.
His knights grow riotous, and himself upbraids us
On every trifle. When he returns from hunting,
I will not speak with him; say I am sick.
If you come slack of former services,
You shall do well; the fault of it I'll answer.

OSWALD.   He's coming, madam; I hear him.

                                           [*Horns within.*]

GONERIL.   Put on what weary negligence you please,
You and your fellows; I'd have it come to question,[1]
If he distaste[2] it, let him to our sister,
Whose mind and mine, I know, in that are one,
Not to be over-rul'd. Idle old man,
That still would manage those authorities
That he hath given away! Now, by my life,
Old fools are babes again, and must be us'd
With checks[3] as[4] flatteries, when they are seen abus'd.[5]
Remember what I have said.
OSWALD.   Well, madam.
GONERIL.   And let his knights have colder looks among you;
What grows of it, no matter. Advise your fellow so.
I would breed from hence occasions,[6] and I shall,
That I may speak. I'll write straight to my sister,
To hold my very course. Prepare for dinner.   *Exeunt.*

---

1. question—open discussion.   2. distaste—dislike.
3. checks—rebukes.   4. as—as well as.
5. abus'd—misled.   6. occasions—opportunities.

[ACT I • 4]   *A hall in the same.*

Enter KENT *disguised.*

KENT.   If but as well I other accents borrow,
That can my speech defuse,[1] my good intent
May carry through itself to that full issue
For which I raz'd [2] my likeness. Now, banish'd Kent,
If thou canst serve where thou dost stand condemn'd,
So may it come, thy master, whom thou lov'st,
Shall find thee full of labours.

Horns within. Enter LEAR, KNIGHTS, *and Attendants.*

LEAR.   Let me not stay a jot for dinner; go get it ready.
[*Exit an Attendant.*] How now! what art thou?
KENT.   A man, sir.
LEAR.   What dost thou profess? What wouldst thou with us?
KENT.   I do profess to be no less than I seem; to serve him

---

1. defuse—disguise.   2. raz'd—shaved off (my beard).

truly that will put me in trust; to love him that is honest; to converse with him that is wise and says little; to fear judgement; to fight when I cannot choose; and to eat no fish.[3]

LEAR. What art thou?

KENT. A very honest-hearted fellow, and as poor as the King.

LEAR. If thou be as poor for a subject as he is for a king, thou art poor enough. What wouldst thou?

KENT. Service.

LEAR. Who wouldst thou serve?

KENT. You.

LEAR. Dost thou know me, fellow?

KENT. No, sir; but you have that in your countenance which I would fain call master.

LEAR. What's that?

KENT. Authority.

LEAR. What services canst thou do?

KENT. I can keep honest counsel, ride, run, mar a curious tale in telling it, and deliver a plain message bluntly. That which ordinary men are fit for, I am qualified in; and the best of me is diligence.

LEAR. How old art thou?

KENT. Not so young, sir, to love a woman for singing, nor so old to dote on her for anything. I have years on my back forty-eight.

LEAR. Follow me; thou shalt serve me. If I like thee no worse after dinner, I will not part from thee yet. Dinner, ho, dinner! Where's my knave? my Fool? Go you, and call my Fool hither. *Exit an Attendant.*

Enter the Steward, OSWALD.

You, you, sirrah, where's my daughter?

OSWALD. So please you,— *Exit.*

LEAR. What says the fellow there? Call the clotpoll [4] back. [*Exit a* KNIGHT.] Where's my Fool, ho? I think the world's asleep.

Enter KNIGHT.

How now! where's that mongrel?

---

3. eat no fish—be a Protestant.   4. clotpoll—blockhead.

KNIGHT.   He says, my lord, your daughter is not well.

LEAR.   Why came not the slave back to me when I called him?

KNIGHT.   Sir, he answered me in the roundest[5] manner, he would not.

LEAR.   'A[6] would not!

KNIGHT.   My lord, I know not what the matter is; but, to my judgement, your Highness is not entertain'd with that ceremonious affection as you were wont. There's a great abatement of kindness appears as well in the general dependants as in the Duke himself also and your daughter.

LEAR.   Ha! say'st thou so?

KNIGHT.   I beseech you, pardon me, my lord, if I be mistaken; for my duty cannot be silent when I think your Highness wronged.

LEAR.   Thou but rememb'rest me of mine own conception.[7] I have perceived a most faint neglect of late, which I have rather blamed as mine own jealous curiosity[8] than as a very pretence and purpose of unkindness. I will look further into 't. But where's my Fool? I have not seen him this two days.

KNIGHT.   Since my young lady's going into France, sir, the Fool hath much pined away.

LEAR.   No more of that; I have noted it well. Go you, and tell my daughter I would speak with her. [*Exit an Attendant.*] Go you, call hither my Fool.   *Exit an Attendant.*

Enter OSWALD.

O, you sir, you sir, come you hither. Who am I, sir?

OSWALD.   My lady's father.

LEAR.   "My lady's father"! My lord's knave! You whoreson dog! you slave! you cur!

OSWALD.   I am none of these, my lord; I beseech your pardon.

LEAR.   Do you bandy[9] looks with me, you rascal?

[*Striking him.*]

OSWALD.   I'll not be strucken, my lord.

---

5. roundest—most direct.   6. 'A—he.
7. conception—idea, thought.   8. curiosity—watchfulness.
9. bandy—exchange.

KENT.   Nor tripped neither, you base football player.
[Tripping up his heels.]

LEAR.   I thank thee, fellow. Thou serv'st me, and I'll love thee.

KENT.   Come, sir, arise, away! I'll teach you differences.[10] Away, away! If you will measure your lubber's length again, tarry; but away! go to.[11] Have you wisdom? So.
[Pushes OSWALD out.]

LEAR.   Now, my friendly knave, I thank thee. There's earnest[12] of thy service.   [Giving KENT money.]

Enter FOOL.

FOOL.   Let me hire him too; here's my coxcomb.[13]
[Offering KENT his cap.]

LEAR.   How now, my pretty knave! how dost thou?

FOOL.   Sirrah, you were best take my coxcomb.

KENT.   Why, Fool?

FOOL.   Why? For taking one's part that's out of favour. Nay, an thou canst not smile as the wind sits,[14] thou 'lt catch cold shortly. There, take my coxcomb. Why, this fellow hath banished two on[15] 's daughters, and did the third a blessing against his will; if thou follow him, thou must needs wear my coxcomb. —How now, nuncle! [16] Would I had two coxcombs and two daughters!

LEAR.   Why, my boy?

FOOL.   If I gave them all my living, I'd keep my coxcombs myself. There's mine; beg another of thy daughters.

LEAR.   Take heed, sirrah; the whip.

FOOL.   Truth's a dog must to kennel; he must be whipped out, when Lady the brach[17] may stand by the fire and stink.

LEAR.   A pestilent gall [18] to me!

FOOL.   Sirrah, I'll teach thee a speech.

---

10. differences—distinctions (of rank).
11. go to—an exclamation of impatience.
12. earnest—advance money.
13. coxcomb—fool's cap, the badge of the fool's profession.
14. smile as the wind sits—agree with those in power.
15. on—of.   16. nuncle—uncle.   17. brach—favorite bitch
18. pestilent gall—always rubbing a sore spot.

LEAR.   Do.

FOOL.   Mark it, nuncle:

> Have more than thou showest,
> Speak less than thou knowest,
> Lend less than thou owest,[19]
> Ride more than thou goest,
> Learn more than thou trowest,[20]
> Set[21] less than thou throwest;
> Leave thy drink and thy whore,
> And keep in-a-door,
> And thou shalt have more
> Than two tens to a score.

KENT.   This is nothing, Fool.

FOOL.   Then 'tis like the breath of an unfee'd lawyer; you gave me nothing for 't. Can you make no use of nothing, nuncle?

LEAR.   Why, no, boy; nothing can be made out of nothing.

FOOL.   [*To* KENT.] Prithee, tell him so much the rent[22] of his land comes to. He will not believe a Fool.

LEAR.   A bitter fool!

FOOL.   Dost thou know the difference, my boy, between a bitter fool and a sweet fool?

LEAR.   No, lad; teach me.

FOOL.

> That lord that counsell'd thee
>   To give away thy land,
> Come place him here by me,
>   Do thou for him stand:
> The sweet and bitter fool
>   Will presently appear;
> The one in motley[23] here,
>   The other found out there.

LEAR.   Dost thou call me fool, boy?

FOOL.   All thy other titles thou hast given away; that thou wast born with.

KENT.   This is not altogether fool, my lord.

FOOL.   No, faith, lords and great men will not let me; if I

---

19. owest—own.   20. trowest—believe.
21. Set—wager.   22. rent—income.
23. motley—the professional fool's parti-colored costume.

had a monopoly[24] out, they would have part[25] on 't. And ladies, too, they will not let me have all the fool to myself; they'll be snatching. Nuncle, give me an egg, and I'll give thee two crowns.

LEAR.   What two crowns shall they be?

FOOL.   Why, after I have cut the egg i' th' middle, and eat up the meat, the two crowns of the egg. When thou clovest thy crown i' th' middle, and gav'st away both parts, thou bor'st thine ass[26] on thy back o'er the dirt. Thou hadst little wit in thy bald crown, when thou gav'st thy golden one away. If I speak like myself[27] in this, let him be whipped that first finds it so.

> Fools had ne'er less grace[28] in a year;
>   For wise men are grown foppish,
> And know not how their wits to wear,
>   Their manners are so apish.[29]

LEAR.   When were you wont to be so full of songs, sirrah?

FOOL.   I have used it, nuncle, ever since thou mad'st thy daughters thy mother, for when thou gav'st them the rod, and puttest down thine own breeches,

> Then they for sudden joy did weep,
>   And I for sorrow sung,
> That such a king should play bo-peep[30]
>   And go the fools among.

Prithee, nuncle, keep a schoolmaster that can teach thy Fool to lie. I would fain learn to lie.

LEAR.   An[31] you lie, sirrah, we'll have you whipped.

FOOL.   I marvel what kin thou and thy daughters are. They'll have me whipped for speaking true, thou 'lt have me whipped for lying; and sometimes I am whipp'd for holding my peace. I had rather be any kind o' thing than a Fool; and yet I would not be thee, nuncle; thou hast pared thy wit o' both sides, and left nothing i' the middle. Here comes one o' the parings.

---

24. monopoly—the right to be sole dealer (in folly).
25. part—their share.
26. thine ass—like the countryman who carried his **donkey when the** roads were bad.   27. like myself—foolishly.
28. grace—favor.   29. apish—i.e., imitating fools.
30. bo-peep—hide and seek.   31. An—if.

Enter GONERIL.

LEAR.　How now, daughter! what makes that frontlet[32] on?
Methinks you are too much of late i' th' frown.

FOOL.　Thou wast a pretty fellow when thou hadst no need
to care for her frowning; now thou art an O[33] without a figure.
I am better than thou art now; I am a Fool, thou art nothing.
[*To* GONERIL.] Yes, forsooth, I will hold my tongue; so your face
bids me, though you say nothing.

> Mum, mum,
> He that keeps nor crust nor crumb,
> Weary of all, shall want some.

[*Pointing to* LEAR.] That's a sheal'd peascod. [34]

GONERIL.　Not only, sir, this your all-licens'd [35] Fool,
But other of your insolent retinue
Do hourly carp and quarrel, breaking forth
In rank and not-to-be-endured riots. Sir,
I had thought, by making this well known unto you,
To have found a safe redress; but now grow fearful,
By what yourself, too, late have spoke and done,
That you protect this course, and put it on[36]
By your allowance; [37] which if you should, the fault
Would not scape censure, nor the redresses sleep,
Which, in the tender[38] of a wholesome weal,[39]
Might in their working do you that offence,
Which else were shame, that then necessity
Will call discreet proceeding.

FOOL.　For, you know, nuncle,
"The hedge-sparrow fed the cuckoo[40] so long,
That it had it head bit off by it young." [41]
So, out went the candle, and we were left darkling.[42]

LEAR.　Are you our daughter?

---

32. frontlet—frown.　　　33. O—zero.
34. sheal'd peascod—shelled peapod (nothing).
35. all-licens'd—privileged to say and do as he pleases.
36. put it on—encourage it.　　　37. allowance—approval.
38. tender—care for.　　　39. weal—commonwealth.
40. cuckoo—i.e., the cuckoo's young.
41. young—ungrateful nestling.　　　42. darkling—in the dark.

GONERIL. Come, sir,
I would you would make use of that good wisdom,
Whereof I know you are fraught,[43] and put away
These dispositions,[44] which of late transport you
From what you rightly are.

FOOL. May not an ass know when the cart draws the horse?
"Whoop,[45] Jug! I love thee."

LEAR. Doth any here know me? This is not Lear.
Doth Lear walk thus? speak thus? Where are his eyes?
Either his notion[46] weakens, or his discernings
Are lethargied—Ha! waking? [47] 'T is not so.
Who is it that can tell me who I am?

FOOL. Lear's shadow.

LEAR. I would learn that; for, by the marks of sovereignty,
knowledge, and reason, I should be false persuaded I had
daughters.

FOOL. Which they will make an obedient father.

LEAR. Your name, fair gentlewoman?

GONERIL. This admiration,[48] sir, is much o' th' savour
Of other your new pranks. I do beseech you
To understand my purposes aright.
As you are old and reverend, you should be wise.
Here do you keep a hundred knights and squires;
Men so disorder'd, so debosh'd [49] and bold,
That this our court, infected with their manners,
Shows like a riotous inn. Epicurism[50] and lust
Makes it more like a tavern or a brothel
Than a grac'd palace. The shame itself doth speak
For instant remedy. Be then desir'd
By her, that else will take the thing she begs,
A little to disquantity[51] your train;
And the remainders, that shall still depend,
To be such men as may besort[52] your age,
Which know themselves and you.

---

43. fraught—furnished with.   44. dispositions—moods.
45. "Whoop, etc."—nonsense.   46. notion—understanding.
47. waking—am I awake?   48. admiration—pretended surprise.
49. debosh'd—debauched.   50. Epicurism—gluttony.
51. disquantity—reduce.   52. besort—befit.

LEAR.   Darkness and devils!
Saddle my horses; call my train together!
Degenerate bastard! I'll not trouble thee;
Yet have I left a daughter.

GONERIL.   You strike my people; and your disorder'd rabble
Make servants of their betters.

Enter ALBANY.

LEAR.   Woe, that too late repents!—O, sir, are you come?
Is it your will? Speak, sir.—Prepare my horses.—
Ingratitude, thou marble-hearted fiend,
More hideous when thou show'st thee in a child
Than the sea-monster!

ALBANY.   Pray, sir, be patient.[53]

LEAR.   [*To* GONERIL.] Detested kite! [54] thou liest.
My train are men of choice and rarest parts,
That all particulars of duty know,
And in the most exàct regard [55] support
The worships[56] of their name. O most small fault,
How ugly didst thou in Cordelia show!
Which, like an engine,[57] wrench'd my frame of nature
From the fix'd place; drew from my heart all love,
And added to the gall.[58] O Lear, Lear, Lear!
Beat at this gate, that let thy folly in,   [*Striking his head.*]
And thy dear judgement out! Go, go, my people.

ALBANY.   My lord, I am guiltless as I am ignorant
Of what hath moved you.

LEAR.   It may be so, my lord.
Hear, Nature! hear, dear goddess, hear!
Suspend thy purpose, if thou didst intend
To make this creature fruitful!
Into her womb convey sterility!
Dry up in her the organs of increase,[59]
And from her derogate[60] body never spring
A babe to honour her! If she must teem,[61]

---

53. patient—calm.   54. Detested kite—detestable scavenger.
55. regard—detail.   56. worships—honor.   57. engine—machine.
58. gall—bitterness.   59. increase—fertility.
60. derogate—blighted.   61. teem—conceive.

Create her child of spleen,[62] that it may live
And be a thwart[63] disnatur'd [64] torment to her!
Let it stamp wrinkles in her brow of youth,
With cadent[65] tears fret[66] channels in her cheeks,
Turn all her mother's pains and benefits
To laughter and contempt, that she may feel
How sharper than a serpent's tooth it is
To have a thankless child!—Away, away!   *Exit.*
 ALBANY. Now, gods that we adore, whereof comes this?
 GONERIL. Never afflict yourself to know the cause;
But let his disposition[67] have that scope
That dotage gives it.

Re-enter LEAR.

 LEAR. What, fifty of my followers at a clap!
Within a fortnight!
 ALBANY.   What's the matter, sir?
 LEAR. I'll tell thee. [*To* GONERIL.] Life and death! I am
  asham'd
That thou hast power to shake my manhood thus;
That these hot tears, which break from me perforce,
Should make thee worth them. Blasts[68] and fogs upon thee!
The untented [69] woundings of a father's curse
Pierce every sense about thee! Old fond eyes,
Beweep this cause again, I'll pluck ye out,
And cast you, with the waters that you loose,
To temper clay. Ha! is 't come to this?
Let it be so: I have another daughter,
Who, I am sure, is kind and comfortable.
When she shall hear this of thee, with her nails
She'll flay thy wolvish visage. Thou shalt find
That I'll resume the shape which thou dost think
I have cast off for ever. Thou shalt, I warrant thee.
     Exeunt LEAR, KENT, *and Attendants.*
 GONERIL. Do you mark that, my lord?

---

62. spleen—malice. 63. thwart—perverse.
64. disnatur'd—unnatural. 65. cadent—falling.
66. fret—wear away. 67. disposition—mood.
68. Blasts—pestilence. 69. untented—to deep to be probed.

ALBANY.   I cannot be so partial,[70] Goneril,
To the great love I bear you,—
    GONERIL.   Pray you, content.—What, Oswald, ho!
[*To the* FOOL.] You, sir, more knave than fool, after your master.
    FOOL.   Nuncle Lear, nuncle Lear! tarry and take the Fool
with thee.

> A fox, when one has caught her,
> And such a daughter,
> Should sure to the slaughter,
> If my cap would buy a halter.
> So the Fool follows after.

Exit.

    GONERIL.   This man hath had good counsel,—a hundred
        knights!
'T is politic and safe to let him keep
At point[71] a hundred knights; yes, that, on every dream,
Each buzz, each fancy, each complaint, dislike,
He may enguard his dotage with their powers,
And hold our lives in mercy.[72] Oswald, I say!
    ALBANY.   Well, you may fear too far.
    GONERIL.   Safer than trust too far.
Let me still take away the harms I fear,
Not fear still to be taken.[73] I know his heart.
What he hath utter'd I have writ my sister.
If she sustain him and his hundred knights,
When I have show'd the unfitness,—

Enter OSWALD.

                                How now, Oswald!
What, have you writ that letter to my sister?
    OSWALD.   Ay, madam.
    GONERIL.   Take you some company, and away to horse:
Inform her full of my particular[74] fear;
And thereto add such reasons of your own
As may compact it more. Get you gone;
And hasten your return. [*Exit* OSWALD.] No, no, my lord,

---

70. partial . . . To—influenced by.   71. at point—fully armed.
72. in mercy—at his mercy.   73. taken—i.e., by some harm.
74. particular—own.

This milky gentleness and course of yours
Though I condemn not, yet, under pardon,
You are much more at task[75] for want of wisdom
Than prais'd for harmful mildness.

ALBANY.   How far your eyes may pierce I cannot tell.
Striving to better, oft we mar what's well.

GONERIL.   Nay, then—

ALBANY.   Well, well; the event.   *Exeunt.*

75. at task—to be criticized.

[ACT I • 5] *Court before the same.*

Enter LEAR, KENT, *and* FOOL.

LEAR.   Go you before to Gloucester with these letters. Acquaint my daughter no further with anything you know than comes from her demand out of the letter. If your diligence be not speedy, I shall be there afore you.

KENT.   I will not sleep, my lord, till I have delivered your letter.   *Exit.*

FOOL.   If a man's brains were in 's heels, were 't not in danger of kibes?[1]

LEAR.   Ay, boy.

FOOL.   Then, I prithee, be merry; thy wit shall ne'er go slip-shod.[2]

LEAR.   Ha, ha, ha!

FOOL.   Shalt see thy other daughter will use thee kindly;[3] for though she's as like this as a crab[4] 's like an apple, yet I can tell what I can tell.

LEAR.   What canst tell, boy?

FOOL.   She will taste as like this as a crab does to a crab. Thou canst tell why one's nose stands i' th' middle on 's face?

LEAR.   No.

FOOL.   Why, to keep one's eyes of[5] either side 's nose, that what a man cannot smell out, he may spy into.

LEAR.   I did her wrong—

1. kibes—chilblains.
2. slip-shod—in slippers (to protect you from chilblains).
3. kindly—charitably; also, according to her nature.
4. crab—crab apple.   5. of—on.

FOOL. Canst tell how an oyster makes his shell?

LEAR. No.

FOOL. Nor I neither; but I can tell why a snail has a house.

LEAR. Why?

FOOL. Why, to put 's head in; not to give it away to his daughters, and leave his horns without a case.

LEAR. I will forget my nature. So kind a father! Be my horses ready?

FOOL. Thy asses are gone about 'em. The reason why the seven stars are no moe[6] than seven is a pretty reason.

LEAR. Because they are not eight?

FOOL. Yes, indeed: Thou wouldst make a good Fool.

LEAR. To take 't again perforce! Monster ingratitude!

FOOL. If thou wert my Fool, nuncle, I'd have thee beaten for being old before thy time.

LEAR. How's that?

FOOL. Thou shouldst not have been old till thou hadst been wise.

LEAR. O, let me not be mad, not mad, sweet heaven! Keep me in temper; [7] I would not be mad!

Enter GENTLEMAN.

How now! are the horses ready?

GENTLEMAN. Ready, my lord.

LEAR. Come, boy.

FOOL. She that's a maid now, and laughs at my departure, Shall not be a maid long, unless things be cut shorter. *Exeunt.*

---

6. moe—more.   7. temper—sanity.

[ACT II • 1] *The Earl of Gloucester's castle.*

Enter EDMUND *and* CURAN, *meeting.*

EDMUND. Save thee, Curan.

CURAN. And you, sir. I have been with your father, and given him notice that the Duke of Cornwall and Regan his duchess will be here with him this night.

EDMUND. How comes that?

CURAN. Nay, I know not. You have heard of the news

abroad; I mean the whispered ones, for they are yet but ear-kissing[1] arguments?

    EDMUND.   Not I. Pray you, what are they?

    CURAN.   Have you heard of no likely wars toward[2] 'twixt the Dukes of Cornwall and Albany?

    EDMUND.   Not a word.

    CURAN.   You may, then, in time. Fare you well, sir. *Exit.*

    EDMUND.   The Duke be here to-night? The better! best!
This weaves itself perforce into my business.
My father hath set guard to take my brother;
And I have one thing, of a queasy question,[3]
Which I must act. Briefness and fortune, work!
Brother, a word; descend. Brother, I say!

Enter EDGAR.

My father watches; O sir, fly this place;
Intelligence[4] is given where you are hid;
You have now the good advantage of the night.
Have you not spoken 'gainst the Duke of Cornwall?
He's coming hither, now, i' th' night, i' th' haste,
And Regan with him. Have you nothing said
Upon his party 'gainst the Duke of Albany?
Advise yourself.[5]

    EDGAR.   I am sure on 't, not a word.

    EDMUND.   I hear my father coming: pardon me;
In cunning[6] I must draw my sword upon you.
Draw; seem to defend yourself; now quit[7] you well.
Yield! Come before my father. Light, ho, here!
Fly, brother. Torches, torches! So, farewell.   *Exit* EDGAR.
Some blood drawn on me would beget opinion
                      [Wounds his arm.]
Of my more fierce endeavour. I have seen drunkards
Do more than this in sport. Father! father!
Stop, stop! No help?

---

1. ear-kissing—whispered.   2. toward—imminent.
3. of a queasy question—requiring delicate handling.
4. Intelligence—information.
5. Advise yourself—consider.
6. cunning—pretense.   7. quit—acquit.

Enter GLOUCESTER, *and Servants with torches.*

GLOUCESTER.   Now, Edmund, where's the villain?
EDMUND.   Here stood he in the dark, his sharp sword out,
Mumbling of wicked charms, conjuring the moon
To stand 's auspicious mistress,[8]—
     GLOUCESTER.   But where is he?
     EDMUND.   Look, sir, I bleed.
     GLOUCESTER.   Where is the villain, Edmund?
     EDMUND.   Fled this way, sir. When by no means he could—
     GLOUCESTER.   Pursue him, ho! Go after. [*Exeunt some Serv-*
     ants.] "By no means" what?
     EDMUND.   Persuade me to the murder of your lordship;
But that I told him, the revenging gods
'Gainst parricides did all their thunders bend;
Spoke, with how manifold and strong a bond
The child was bound to the father; sir, in fine,[9]
Seeing how loathly opposite I stood
To his unnatural purpose, in fell [10] motion,
With his prepared sword he charges home
My unprovided body, lanc'd mine arm;
But when he saw my best alarum'd spirits,
Bold in the quarrel's right, rous'd to the encounter,
Or whether gasted [11] by the noise I made,
Full suddenly he fled.
     GLOUCESTER.   Let him fly far.
Not in this land shall he remain uncaught;
And found,—dispatch.[12] The noble Duke my master,
My worthy arch[13] and patron, comes to-night.
By his authority I will proclaim it,
That he which finds him shall deserve our thanks,
Bringing the murderous coward to the stake;
He that conceals him, death.
     EDMUND.   When I dissuaded him from his intent,
And found him pight[14] to do it, with curst[15] speech

---

8. 's auspicious mistress—be favorable to him.   9. in fine—briefly.
10. fell—fierce.   11. gasted—panic-stricken.
12. dispatch—kill him.   13. arch—chief.
14. pight—determined.   15. curst—angry.

I threaten'd to discover[16] him; he replied,
"Thou unpossessing bastard! dost thou think,
If I would stand against thee, would the reposal
Of any trust, virtue, or worth in thee
Make thy words faith'd? [17] No! what I should deny,—
As this I would; ay, though thou didst produce
My very character,—I'd turn it all
To thy suggestion, plot, and damned practice;
And thou must make a dullard of the world
If they not thought the profits of my death
Were very pregnant[18] and potential [19] spurs
To make thee seek it."

GLOUCESTER.   O strong and fasten'd [20] villain!
Would he deny his letter? I never got him.   [*Tucket*[21] *within.*]
Hark, the Duke's trumpets! I know not why he comes.
All ports[22] I'll bar, the villain shall not scape;
The Duke must grant me that. Besides, his picture
I will send far and near, that all the kingdom
May have due note of him; and of my land,
Loyal and natural boy, I'll work the means
To make thee capable.[23]

Enter CORNWALL, REGAN, *and Attendants.*

CORNWALL.   How now, my noble friend! since I came hither,
Which I can call but now, I have heard strange news.

REGAN.   If it be true, all vengeance comes too short
Which can pursue the offender. How dost, my lord?

GLOUCESTER.   O, madam, my old heart is crack'd, is crack'd!

REGAN.   What, did my father's godson seek your life?
He whom my father nam'd? your Edgar?

GLOUCESTER.   O, lady, lady, shame would have it hid!

REGAN.   Was he not companion with the riotous knights
That tends upon my father?

GLOUCESTER.   I know not, madam. 'T is too bad, too bad.

EDMUND.   Yes, madam, he was of that consórt.[24]

---

16. discover—reveal.   17. faith'd—believed.   18. pregnant—ready.
19. potential—powerful.   20. fasten'd—hardened.
21. Tucket—trumpet signal.   22. ports—seaports.
23. capable—i.e., legitimate.   24. consórt—gang.

REGAN.   No marvel, then, though he were ill affected: [25]
'T is they have put him on[26] the old man's death,
To have th' expense[27] and waste of his revénues.
I have this present evening from my sister
Been well inform'd of them; and with such cautions,
That if they come to sojourn at my house,
I'll not be there.

    CORNWALL.   Nor I, assure thee, Regan.
Edmund, I hear that you have shown your father
A child-like[28] office.

    EDMUND.   'T was my duty, sir.

    GLOUCESTER.   He did bewray[29] his practice; and receiv'd
This hurt you see, striving to apprehend him.

    CORNWALL. Is he pursued?

    GLOUCESTER.   Ay, my good lord.

    CORNWALL. If he be taken, he shall never more
Be fear'd of doing harm. Make your own purpose,
How in my strength[30] you please. For you, Edmund,
Whose virtue and obedience doth this instant
So much command itself, you shall be ours.
Natures of such deep trust we shall much need;
You we first seize on.

    EDMUND.   I shall serve you, sir,
Truly, however else.

    GLOUCESTER.   For him I thank your Grace.

    CORNWALL. You know not why we came to visit you,—

    REGAN.   Thus out of season, threading[31] dark-ey'd night?
Occasions, noble Gloucester, of some poise,[32]
Wherein we must have use of your advice.
Our father he hath writ, so hath our sister,
Of differences, which I best thought it fit
To answer from[33] our home; the several messengers
From hence attend [34] dispatch. Our good old friend,
Lay comforts to your bosom; and bestow

---

25. ill affected—disloyal.   26. put him on—incited him to.
27. expense—spending.   28. child-like—dutiful.
29. bewray—reveal.   30. strength—authority.
31. threading—traveling through.   32. poise—importance.
33. from—away from.   34. attend—await.

Your needful counsel to our business,
Which craves the instant use.

GLOUCESTER.   I serve you, madam.
Your Graces are right welcome.   *Exeunt. Flourish.*

[ACT II • 2] *Before Gloucester's castle.*

Enter KENT *and the Steward* OSWALD, *meeting.*

OSWALD.   Good dawning to thee, friend. Art of this house?
KENT.   Ay.
OSWALD.   Where may we set our horses?
KENT.   I' th' mire.
OSWALD.   Prithee, if you lov'st me, tell me.
KENT.   I love thee not.
OSWALD.   Why, then, I care not for thee.
KENT.   If I had thee in Lipsbury pinfold,[1] I would make thee
care for me.
OSWALD.   Why dost thou use me thus? I know thee not.
KENT.   Fellow, I know thee.
OSWALD.   What dost thou know me for?
KENT.   A knave; a rascal; an eater of broken meats;[2] a base,
proud, shallow, beggarly, three-suited, hundred-pound, filthy,
worsted-stocking knave; a lily-livered, action-taking[3] knave; a
whoreson, glass-gazing, super-serviceable, finical rogue; onc-
trunk-inheriting[4] slave; one that wouldst be a bawd, in way of
good service, and art nothing but the composition[5] of a knave,
beggar, coward, pandar, and the son and heir of a mongrel
bitch; one whom I will beat into clamorous whining, if thou
deni'st the least syllable of thy addition.
OSWALD.   Why, what a monstrous fellow art thou, thus to
rail on one that is neither known of thee nor knows thee!
KENT.   What a brazen-faced varlet art thou, to deny thou
knowest me! Is it two days since I tripped up thy heels, and
beat thee before the King? Draw, you rogue; for, though it be

---

1. Lipsbury pinfold—between my jaws (?).
2. broken meats—left-overs, food for the lower servants.
3. action-taking—going to law instead of fighting for his rights.
4. one-trunk-inheriting—one trunk will hold all his possessions.
5. composition—combination.

night, yet the moon shines. I'll make a sop o' th' moonshine[6] of you, you whoreson cullionly[7] barber-monger! [8] Draw! [*Drawing his sword.*]

OSWALD.   Away! I have nothing to do with thee.

KENT.   Draw, you rascal! You come with letters against the King; and take Vanity the puppet's part against the royalty of her father. Draw, you rogue, or I'll so carbonado[9] your shanks, —draw, you rascal! Come your ways.

OSWALD.   Help, ho! murder! help!

KENT.   Strike, you slave! Stand, rogue, stand! You neat slave, strike.   [*Beating him.*]

OSWALD.   Help, ho! murder! murder!

Enter EDMUND *with his rapier drawn,* CORNWALL, REGAN, GLOUCESTER, *and Servants.*

EDMUND.   How now! What's the matter?

KENT.   With you, goodman boy, an you please: come, I'll flesh[10] ye; come on, young master.

GLOUCESTER.   Weapons! arms! What's the matter here?

CORNWALL.   Keep peace, upon your lives! He dies that strikes again. What is the matter?

REGAN.   The messengers from our sister and the King.

CORNWALL.   What is your difference? Speak.

OSWALD.   I am scarce in breath, my lord.

KENT.   No marvel, you have so bestirred your valour. You cowardly rascal. Nature disclaims in thee. A tailor made thee.

CORNWALL.   Thou art a strange fellow: a tailor make a man?

KENT.   A tailor, sir. A stone-cutter[11] or a painter could not have made him so ill, though they had been but two hours at the trade.

CORNWALL.   Speak yet, how grew your quarrel?

OSWALD.   This ancient ruffian, sir, whose life I have spared at suit of his grey beard,—

KENT.   Thou whoreson zed! [12] thou unnecessary letter! My lord, if you will give me leave, I will tread this unbolted [13]

---

6. sop o' the moonshine—mess(?).   7. cullionly—vile.
8. barber-monger—fop.   9. carbonado—slice (into steaks).
10. flesh—initiate you to fighting.   11. stone-cutter—sculptor.
12. zed—the letter Z.   13. unbolted—coarse.

villain into mortar, and daub the wall of a jakes[14] with him.
Spare my grey beard, you wagtail?

    CORNWALL.   Peace, sirrah!
You beastly knave, know you no reverence?

    KENT.   Yes, sir; but anger hath a privilege.

    CORNWALL.   Why art thou angry?

    KENT.   That such a slave as this should wear a sword,
Who wears no honesty. Such smiling rogues as these,
Like rats, oft bite the holy cords[15] a-twain
Which are too intrinse t' unloose; smooth[16] every passion
That in the natures of their lords rebel;
Bring oil to fire, snow to their colder moods;
Renege, affirm, and turn their halcyon[17] beaks
With every gale and vary of their masters,
Knowing nought, like dogs, but following.
A plague upon your epileptic visage!
Smile you my speeches, as I were a fool?
Goose, an I had you upon Sarum[18] Plain,
I'd drive ye cackling home to Camelot.[19]

    CORNWALL.   What, art thou mad, old fellow?

    GLOUCESTER.   How fell you out? Say that.

    KENT.   No contraries hold more antipathy
Than I and such a knave.

    CORNWALL.   Why dost thou call him knave? What is his
      fault?

    KENT.   His countenance likes[20] me not.

    CORNWALL.   No more, perchance, does mine, nor his, nor
      hers.

    KENT.   Sir, 't is my occupation to be plain;
I have seen better faces in my time
Than stands on any shoulder that I see
Before me at this instant.

    CORNWALL.   This is some fellow
Who, having been prais'd for bluntness, doth affect

---

14. jakes—privy.   15. holy cords—bonds of natural affection.
16. smooth—encourage.
17. halcyon—the kingfisher, supposed to be a natural weathervane.
18. Sarum—Salisbury.   19. Camelot—site of King Arthur's court.
20. likes—pleases.

A saucy roughness, and constrains[21] the garb
Quite from his nature. He cannot flatter, he;
An honest mind and plain, he must speak truth!
An they will take it, so; if not, he's plain.
These kind of knaves I know, which in this plainness
Harbour more craft and more corrupter ends
Than twenty silly ducking óbservants[22]
That stretch their duties nicely.[23]

KENT.   Sir, in good sooth, in sincere verity,
Under th' allowance of your great aspéct,
Whose influence, like the wreath of radiant fire
On flickering Phoebus' front,[24]—

CORNWALL.   What mean'st by this?

KENT.   To go out of my dialect, which you discommend so
much. I know, sir, I am no flatterer. He that beguiled you in a
plain accent was a plain knave; which for my part I will not be,
though I should win your displeasure to entreat me to 't.

CORNWALL.   What was th' offence you gave him?

OSWALD.   I never gave him any.
It pleas'd the King his master very late
To strike at me, upon his misconstruction; [25]
When he, conjunct, and flattering his displeasure,
Tripp'd me behind; being down, insulted, rail'd,
And put upon him such a deal of man
That worthied him,[26] got praises of the King
For him attempting who was self-subdued; [27]
And, in the fleshment[28] of this dread exploit,
Drew on me here again.

KENT.   None of these rogues and cowards
But Ajax[29] is their fool.[30]

CORNWALL.   Fetch forth the stocks!

---

21. constrains—puts on.   22. observants—obsequious parasites.
23. nicely—punctiliously.
24. Phoebus' front—sun's forehead.
25. upon his misconstruction—because of a misunderstanding.
26. worthied him—won him favor.
27. was self-subdued—made no resistance.
28. fleshment—excitement.
29. Ajax—the famous Greek braggart warrior.
30. their fool—inferior to them.

You stubborn ancient knave, you reverend braggart,
We'll teach you—
    KENT.   Sir, I am too old to learn.
Call not your stocks for me; I serve the King,
On whose employment I was sent to you.
You shall do small respects, show too bold malice
Against the grace and person of my master,
Stocking his messenger.
    CORNWALL.   Fetch forth the stocks! As I have life and
      honour,
There shall he sit till noon.
    REGAN.   Till noon! Till night, my lord; and all night too.
    KENT.   Why, madam, if I were your father's dog,
You should not use me so.
    REGAN.   Sir, being his knave, I will.
                                    [*Stocks brought out.*]
    CORNWALL.   This is a fellow of the self-same colour
Our sister speaks of. Come, bring away the stocks!
    GLOUCESTER.   Let me beseech your Grace not to do so.
His fault is much, and the good King his master
Will check[31] him for 't. Your purpos'd low correction
Is such as basest and contemned'st wretches
For pilferings and most common trespasses
Are punish'd with. The King must take it ill
That he, so slightly valued in his messenger,
Should have him thus restrained.
    CORNWALL.   I'll answer that.
    REGAN.   My sister may receive it much more worse
To have her gentleman abus'd, assaulted,
For following her affairs. Put in his legs.
                     [KENT *is put in the stocks.*]
Come, my good lord, away.
                  Exeunt all but GLOUCESTER *and* KENT.
    GLOUCESTER.   I am sorry for thee, friend; 't is the Duke's
      pleasure,
Whose disposition, all the world well knows,
Will not be rubb'd nor stopp'd. I'll entreat for thee.

---

31. check—rebuke.

KENT. Pray, do not, sir. I have watch'd [32] and travell'd hard;
Some time I shall sleep out, the rest I'll whistle.
A good man's fortune may grow out at heels.
Give you good morrow!
GLOUCESTER. The Duke's to blame in this; 't will be ill took.
Exit.

KENT. Good King, that must approve the common saw,[33]
Thou out of heaven's benediction com'st
To the warm sun!
Approach, thou beacon[34] to this under globe,
That by thy comfortable beams I may
Peruse this letter! Nothing almost sees miracles
But misery. I know 't is from Cordelia,
Who hath most fortunately been inform'd
Of my obscured [35] course; [*Reads.*] "—and shall find time
From this enormous state[36]—seeking to give
Losses their remedies."—All weary and o'erwatch'd,
Take vantage,[37] heavy eyes, not to behold
This shameful lodging.
Fortune, good-night! Smile once more; turn thy wheel! [38]
[*Sleeps.*]

---

32. watch'd—gone without sleep. 33. saw—saying.
34. beacon—rising sun. 35. obscured—in disguise.
36. this enormous state—these evil times.
37. vantage—advantage of drowsiness.
38. wheel—i.e., the wheel, turned by the goddess Fortune, on which all men were bound to rise and fall.

[ACT II • 3] *Near Gloucester's Castle.*

Enter EDGAR.

EDGAR. I heard myself proclaim'd;
And by the happy hollow of a tree
Escap'd the hunt. No port is free; no place
That guard and most unusual vigilance
Does not attend my taking.[1] Whiles I may scape

---

1. attend my taking—await my capture.

I will preserve myself, and am bethought
To take the basest and most poorest shape
That ever penury,[2] in contempt[3] of man,
Brought near to beast. My face I'll grime with filth,
Blanket my loins, elf [4] all my hairs in knots,
And with presented [5] nakedness out-face
The winds and persecutions of the sky.
The country gives me proof and precedent[6]
Of Bedlam[7] beggars, who, with roaring voices,
Strike in their numb'd and mortified bare arms
Pins, wooden pricks, nails, sprigs of rosemary;
And with this horrible object, from low farms,
Poor pelting[8] villages, sheep-cotes, and mills,
Sometimes with lunatic bans,[9] sometimes with prayers,
Enforce their charity. "Poor Turlygod! [10] poor Tom!"
There's something yet. Edgar I nothing[11] am.   *Exit.*

---

2. penury—poverty.   3. in contempt—to show the worthlessness.
4. elf—mat.   5. presented—exposed.
6. proof and precedent—examples.
7. Bedlam—from Bethlehem Hospital for lunatics.
8. pelting—insignificant.   9. bans—curses.
10. "Poor Turlygod!"—the bedlam's cry.
11. nothing—as good as dead.

[ACT II • 4] *Gloucester's Castle. Kent in the stocks.*

Enter LEAR, FOOL, *and* GENTLEMAN.

LEAR.   'T is strange that they should so depart from home,
And not send back my messenger.
     GENTLEMAN.   As I learn'd,
The night before there was no purpose in them
Of this remove.
     KENT.   Hail to thee, noble master!
     LEAR.   Ha!
Mak'st thou this shame thy pastime?
     KENT.   No, my lord.
     FOOL.   Ha, ha! he wears cruel garters. Horses are tied by the
heads, dogs and bears by the neck, monkeys by the loins, and

men by the legs. When a man's over-lusty at legs,[1] then he
wears wooden nether-stocks.[2]

LEAR.   What's he that hath so much thy place[3] mistook
To set thee here?

KENT.   It is both he and she;
Your son and daughter.

LEAR.   No.

KENT.   Yes.

LEAR.   No, I say.

KENT.   I say, yea.

LEAR.   No, no, they would not.

KENT.   Yes, they have.

LEAR.   By Jupiter, I swear, no.

KENT.   By Juno,[4] I swear, ay.

LEAR.   They durst not do 't;
They could not, would not do 't. 'T is worse than murder,
To do upon respect[5] such violent outrage.
Resolve[6] me, with all modest[7] haste, which way
Thou mightst deserve, or they impose, this usage,
Coming from us.

KENT.   My lord, when at their home
I did commend [8] your Highness' letters to them,
Ere I was risen from the place that show'd
My duty kneeling, came there a reeking post,
Stew'd in his haste, half breathless, panting forth
From Goneril his mistress salutations;
Deliver'd letters, spite of intermission,[9]
Which presently, they read. On whose contents,
They summon'd up their meiny,[10] straight took horse;
Commanded me to follow, and attend
The leisure of their answer; gave me cold looks:
And meeting here the other messenger,

---

1. over-lusty at legs—a vagabond.   2. nether-stocks—stockings.
3. place—position.   4. Juno—queen of the gods.
5. upon respect—against the respect due a king.
6. Resolve—inform.   7. modest—moderate.
8. commend—deliver.
9. spite of intermission—in spite of interrupting me.
10. meiny—attendants.

Whose welcome, I perceiv'd, had poison'd mine,—
Being the very fellow which of late
Display'd [11] so saucily against your Highness,—
Having more man than wit about me, drew:
He rais'd the house with loud and coward cries.
Your son and daughter found this trespass worth[12]
The shame which here it suffers.

    FOOL.   Winter's[13] not gone yet, if the wild geese fly that way.

> Fathers that wear rags
>   Do make their children blind;
> But fathers that bear bags[14]
>   Shall see their children kind.
> Fortune, that arrant whore,
> Ne'er turns the key[15] to the poor.

But, for all this, thou shalt have as many dolours[16] for thy daughters as thou canst tell [17] in a year.

    LEAR.   O, how this mother[18] swells up toward my heart!
Hysterica passio, down, thou climbing sorrow,
Thy element[19] 's below!—Where is this daughter?

    KENT.   With the Earl, sir; here within.

    LEAR.   Follow me not; stay here.
                                                  Exit.

    GENTLEMAN.   Made you no more offence but what you speak of?

    KENT.   None.
How chance the King comes with so small a number?

    FOOL.   An thou hadst been set i' th' stocks for that question, thou hadst well deserv'd it.

    KENT.   Why, Fool?

    FOOL.   We'll set thee to school to an ant, to teach thee there's no labouring i' th' winter. All that follow their noses are led by their eyes but blind men; and there's not a nose among twenty but can smell him that's stinking. Let go thy hold when a great

---

11. Display'd—acted.   12. worth—deserving of.
13. Winter's—trouble's.   14. bags—moneybags.
15. turns the key—admits.
16. dolours—griefs, with a pun on "dollars."
17. tell—count.   18. mother—hysteria (*hysterica passio*).
19. element—proper place.

wheel runs down a hill, lest it break thy neck with following;
but the great one that goes upward, let him draw thee after.
When a wise man gives thee better counsel, give me mine again;
I would have none but knaves follow it, since a fool gives it.

> That sir which serves and seeks for gain,
>   And follows but for form,
> Will pack[20] when it begins to rain,
>   And leave thee in the storm.
> But I will tarry; the Fool will stay,
>   And let the wise man fly.
> The knave turns fool that runs away;
>   The Fool no knave, perdy.[21]

Enter LEAR *and* GLOUCESTER.

    KENT.   Where learn'd you this, Fool?

    FOOL.   Not i' th' stocks, fool.

    LEAR.   Deny to speak with me! They are sick? They are
    weary?
They have travell'd all the night? Mere fetches,[22]
The images[23] of revolt and flying off.
Fetch me a better answer.

    GLOUCESTER.   My dear lord,
You know the fiery quality of the Duke;
How unremovable and fix'd he is
In his own course.

    LEAR.   Vengeance! plague! death! confusion!
Fiery! What quality? Why, Gloucester, Gloucester,
I'd speak with the Duke of Cornwall and his wife.

    GLOUCESTER.   Well, my good lord, I have inform'd them so.

    LEAR.   Inform'd them! Dost thou understand me, man?

    GLOUCESTER.   Ay, my good lord.

    LEAR.   The King would speak with Cornwall; the dear father
Would with his daughter speak, commands her service.
Are they inform'd of this? My breath and blood!
Fiery? The fiery duke? Tell the hot duke that—
No, but not yet; may be he is not well.
Infirmity doth still neglect all office[24]

---

20. pack—desert.   21. perdy—by God.
22. fetches—pretexts.   23. images—signs.   24. office—duty.

Whereto our health is bound; we are not ourselves
When nature, being oppress'd, commands the mind
To suffer with the body. I'll forbear;
And am fallen out[25] with my more headier will,[26]
To take the indispos'd and sickly fit
For the sound man.—Death on my state! wherefore
                                    [*Looking on* KENT.]
Should he sit here? This act persuades me
That this remotion[27] of the Duke and her
Is practice only. Give me my servant forth.[28]
Go tell the Duke and 's wife I'd speak with them,
Now, presently. Bid them come forth and hear me,
Or at their chamber-door I'll beat the drum
Till it cry sleep to death.[29]

   GLOUCESTER.   I would have all well betwixt you.   *Exit.*
   LEAR.   O me, my heart, my rising heart! But, down!
   FOOL.   Cry to it, nuncle, as the cockney did to the eels when
she put 'em i' th' paste[30] alive; she knapped 'em o' th' coxcombs[31] with a stick, and cried, "Down, wantons, down!" 'T was
her brother that, in pure kindness to his horse, buttered his hay.

Enter CORNWALL, REGAN, GLOUCESTER, *and Servants.*

   LEAR.   Good morrow to you both.
   CORNWALL.   Hail to your Grace!
                             [KENT *here set at liberty.*]
   REGAN.   I am glad to see your Highness.
   LEAR.   Regan, I think you are; I know what reason
I have to think so. If thou shouldst not be glad,
I would divorce me from thy mother's tomb,
Sepúlchring an adultress. [*To* KENT.] O, are you free?
Some other time for that. Beloved Regan,
Thy sister's naught.[32] O Regan, she hath tied

---

25. fallen out—angry.   26. more headier will—hastiness.
27. remotion—keeping away from me.
28. Give me my servant forth—release my servant.
29. cry sleep to death—make sleep impossible.
30. paste—pastry crust.
31. knapped 'em o' th' coxcombs—rapped them on the heads.
32. naught—wicked.

Sharp-tooth'd unkindness, like a vulture, here.

[Points to his heart.]

I can scarce speak to thee; thou 'lt not believe
With how deprav'd a quality—O Regan!

REGAN.   I pray you, sir, take patience. I have hope
You less know how to value her desert
Than she to scant[33] her duty.

     LEAR.   Say, how is that?

     REGAN.   I cannot think my sister in the least
Would fail her obligation. If, sir, perchance
She have restrain'd the riots of your followers,
'T is on such ground, and to such wholesome end,
As clears her from all blame.

     LEAR.   My curses on her!

     REGAN.   O, sir, you are old;
Nature in you stands on the very verge
Of her confine.[34] You should be rul'd and led
By some discretion that discerns your state[35]
Better than you yourself. Therefore, I pray you,
That to our sister you do make return;
Say you have wrong'd her, sir.

     LEAR.   Ask her forgiveness?
Do you but mark how this becomes the house: [36]
"Dear daughter, I confess that I am old;   *[Kneeling.]*
Age is unnecessary.[37] On my knees I beg,
That you'll vouchsafe me raiment, bed, and food."

     REGAN.   Good sir, no more; these are unsightly tricks.
Return you to my sister.

     LEAR.   *[Rising.]* Never, Regan:
She hath abated me of half my train;
Look'd black upon me; struck me with her tongue,
Most serpent-like, upon the very heart.
All the stor'd vengeances of heaven fall
On her ingrateful top! [38] Strike her young bones,
You taking[39] airs, with lameness!

---

33. scant—fall short in.   34. confine—boundary.
35. state—condition of mind.   36. the house—royal family.
37. Age is unnecessary—the old are useless.
38. top—head.   39. taking—infectious.

CORNWALL.   Fie, sir, fie!
LEAR.   You nimble lightnings, dart your blinding flames
Into her scornful eyes! Infect her beauty,
You fen-suck'd fogs, drawn by the powerful sun,
To fall [40] and blast her pride!
REGAN.   O the blest gods! so will you wish on me,
When the rash mood is on.
LEAR.   No, Regan, thou shalt never have my curse.
Thy tender-hefted [41] nature shall not give
Thee o'er to harshness. Her eyes are fierce; but thine
Do comfort and not burn. 'T is not in thee
To grudge my pleasures, to cut off my train,
To bandy hasty words, to scant my sizes,[42]
And in conclusion to oppose the bolt[43]
Against my coming in. Thou better know'st
The offices[44] of nature, bond of childhood,
Effects of courtesy, dues of gratitude.
Thy half o' th' kingdom hast thou not forgot,
Wherein I thee endow'd.
REGAN.   Good sir, to the purpose.
                                              [Tucket within.]

LEAR.   Who put my man i' th' stocks?

Enter OSWALD.

CORNWALL.   What trumpet's that?
REGAN.   I know 't; my sister's. This approves her letter,
That she would soon be here. [*To* OSWALD.] Is your lady come?
LEAR.   This is a slave whose easy-borrowed pride[45]
Dwells in the fickle grace of her he follows.
Out, varlet,[46] from my sight!
CORNWALL.   What means your Grace?

Enter GONERIL.

LEAR.   Who stock'd my servant? Regan, I have good hope
Thou didst not know on 't. Who comes here? O heavens,

---

40. fall—humble.   41. tender-hefted—moved by tenderness.
42. sizes—allowances.   43. oppose the bolt—bar the door.
44. offices—duties.   45. easy-borrowed pride—vanity.
46. varlet—low fellow.

If you do love old men, if your sweet sway
Allow[47] obedience, if you yourselves are old,
Make it your cause; send down, and take my part!
[*To* GONERIL.] Art not asham'd to look upon this beard?
O Regan, wilt thou take her by the hand?

    GONERIL.   Why not by the hand, sir? How have I offended?
All's not offence that indiscretion finds
And dotage terms so.

    LEAR.   O sides, you are too tough;
Will you yet hold? How came my man i' th' stocks?

    CORNWALL.   I set him there, sir; but his own disorders
Deserv'd much less advancement

    LEAR.   You! did you?

    REGAN.   I pray you, father, being weak, seem so.
If, till the expiration of your month,
You will return and sojourn with my sister,
Dismissing half your train, come then to me.
I am now from home, and out of [48] that provision
Which shall be needful for your entertainment.

    LEAR.   Return to her, and fifty men dismiss'd!
No, rather I abjure all roofs, and choose
To wage against the enmity o' th' air;
To be a comrade with the wolf and owl,—
Necessity's sharp pinch. Return with her?
Why, the hot-blooded France, that dowerless took
Our youngest born, I could as well be brought
To knee his throne, and, squire-like, pension beg
To keep base life afoot. Return with her?
Persuade me rather to be slave and sumpter[49]
To this detested groom.   [*Pointing at* OSWALD.]

    GONERIL.   At your choice, sir.

    LEAR.   I prithee, daughter, do not make me mad;
I will not trouble thee, my child; farewell!
We'll no more meet, no more see one another
But yet thou art my flesh, my blood, my daughter;
Or rather a disease that's in my flesh,
Which I must needs call mine; thou art a boil,

---

47. Allow—approve.   48. out of—lack.
49. sumpter—pack horse.

A plague-sore, an embossed [50] carbuncle,
In my corrupted blood. But I'll not chide thee;
Let shame come when it will, I do not call it.
I do not bid the thunder-bearer [51] shoot,
Nor tell tales of thee to high-judging[52] Jove.
Mend when thou canst; be better at thy leisure.
I can be patient; I can stay with Regan,
I and my hundred knights.

REGAN.   Not altogether so;
I look'd not for you yet, nor am provided
For your fit welcome. Give ear, sir, to my sister;
For those that mingle reason with your passion[53]
Must be content to think you old, and so—
But she knows what she does.

LEAR.   Is this well spoken?

REGAN.   I dare avouch it, sir. What, fifty followers!
Is it not well? [54] What should you need of more?
Yea, or so many, sith that both charge[55] and danger
Speak 'gainst so great a number? How, in one house,
Should many people, under two commands,
Hold amity? 'T is hard; almost impossible.

GONERIL.   Why might not you, my lord, receive attendance
From those that she calls servants or from mine?

REGAN.   Why not, my lord? If then they chanc'd to slack[56] ye,
We could control them. If you will come to me,—
For now I spy a danger—I entreat you
To bring but five and twenty; to no more
Will I give place or notice.

LEAR.   I gave you all.

REGAN.   And in good time you gave it.

LEAR.   Made you my guardians, my depositaries;
But kept a reservation [57] to be followed

---

50. embossed—swollen.
51. thunder-bearer—Jupiter.   52. high-judging—almighty.
53. mingle reason with your passion—consider your anger from a
reasonable point of view.
54. well—enough.   55. charge—expense.
56. lack—neglect.
57. reservation—condition.

With such a number. What, must I come to you
With five and twenty, Regan? Said you so?

    REGAN.   And speak 't again, my lord; no more with me.

    LEAR.   Those wicked creatures yet do look well-favour'd [58]
When others are more wicked; not being the worst
Stands in some rank of praise. [*To* GONERIL.] I'll go with thee.
Thy fifty yet doth double five and twenty,
And thou art twice her love.

    GONERIL.   Hear me, my lord:
What need you five and twenty, ten, or five,
To follow[59] in a house where twice so many
Have a command to tend you?

    REGAN.   What need one?

    LEAR.   O, reason not the need! Our basest beggars
Are in the poorest thing superfluous.[60]
Allow not nature more than nature needs,
Man's life is cheap as beast's. Thou art a lady;
If only to go warm were gorgeous,
Why, nature needs not what thou gorgeous wear'st,
Which scarcely keeps thee warm. But, for true need,—
You heavens, give me that patience, patience I need!
You see me here, you gods, a poor old man,
As full of grief as age; wretched in both!
If it be you that stirs these daughters' hearts
Against their father, fool [61] me not so much
To bear it tamely; touch me with noble anger,
And let not women's weapons, water-drops,
Stain my man's cheeks! No, you unnatural hags,
I will have such revenges on you both
That all the world shall—I will do such things,—
What they are, yet I know not; but they shall be
The terrors of the earth. You think I'll weep:
No, I'll not weep.
I have full cause of weeping; but this heart

                            [*Storm and tempest.*]

Shall break into a hundred thousand flaws,[62]

---

58. well-favor'd—handsome.   59. follow—attend you.
60. are . . . superfluous—have more than is absolutely necessary.
61. fool—degrade.   62. flaws—bits.

Or ere[63] I'll weep. O, Fool! I shall go mad!

Exeunt LEAR, GLOUCESTER, KENT *and* FOOL.

CORNWALL.   Let us withdraw, 't will be a storm.

REGAN.   This house is little: the old man and 's people
Cannot be well bestow'd.

GONERIL.   'T is his own blame; hath put himself from rest,
And must needs taste his folly.

REGAN.   For his particular,[64] I'll receive him gladly,
But not one follower.

GONERIL.   So am I purpos'd.
Where is my Lord of Gloucester?

Enter GLOUCESTER.

CORNWALL.   Followed the old man forth. He is return'd.

GLOUCESTER.   The King is in high rage.

CORNWALL.   Whither is he going?

GLOUCESTER.   He calls to horse; but will I know not whither.

CORNWALL.   'T is best to give him way; he leads himself.

GONERIL.   My lord, entreat him by no means to stay.

GLOUCESTER.   Alack, the night comes on, and the bleak
    winds
Do sorely ruffle;[65] for many miles about
There's scarce a bush.

REGAN.   O, sir, to wilful men,
The injuries that they themselves procure
Must be their schoolmasters. Shut up your doors.
He is attended with a desperate train;
And what they may incense[66] him to, being apt
To have his ear abus'd,[67] wisdom bids fear.

CORNWALL.   Shut up your doors, my lord; 't is a wild night:
My Regan counsels well: come out o' th' storm.   *Exeunt.*

---

63. Or ere—before.   64. particular—himself alone.
65. ruffle—rage.   66. incense—instigate.   67. abus'd—deceived.

[ACT III • 1] *A Heath.*

Storm still. Enter KENT *and a* GENTLEMAN, *meeting.*

KENT.   Who's there, besides foul weather?

GENTLEMAN.   One minded like the weather, most unquietly.

KENT. I know you. Where's the King?

GENTLEMAN.   Contending with the fretful elements;
Bids the wind blow the earth into the sea,
Or swell the curled waters 'bove the main,[1]
That things might change or cease; tears his white hair,
Which the impetuous blasts, with eyeless[2] rage,
Catch in their fury, and make nothing of;
Strives in his little world of man to out-scorn
The to-and-fro-conflicting wind and rain.
This night, wherein the cub-drawn[3] bear would couch,[4]
The lion and the belly-pinched wolf
Keep their fur dry, unbonneted he runs,
And bids what will take all.

KENT.   But who is with him?

GENTLEMAN.   None but the Fool; who labours to outjest
His heart-struck injuries.

KENT.   Sir, I do know you;
And dare, upon the warrant of my note,
Commend a dear[5] thing to you. There is division,
Although as yet the face of it be cover'd
With mutual cunning, 'twixt Albany and Cornwall;
Who have—as who have not, that their great stars
Thron'd and set high?—servants, who seem no less,
Which are to France the spies and speculations[6]
Intelligent[7] of our state; what hath been seen,
Either in snuffs[8] and packings[9] of the Dukes,
Or the hard rein which both of them have borne
Against the old kind king, or something deeper,
Whereof perchance these are but furnishings[10]
But, true it is, from France there comes a power[11]
Into this scattered [12] kingdom; who already,
Wise in our negligence, have secret feet
In some of our best ports, and are at point[13]

---

1. main—land.   2. eyeless—blind.   3. cub-drawn—sucked dry.
4. couch—take shelter.   5. dear—important.
6. speculations—informers.   7. Intelligent—giving information.
8. snuffs—resentment.   9. packings—plottings.
10. furnishings—excuses.   11. power—army.
12. scattered—divided.   13. at point—ready.

To show their open banner. Now to you:
If on my credit you dare build so far
To make your speed to Dover, you shall find
Some that will thank you, making just[14] report
Of how unnatural and bemadding sorrow
The King hath cause to plain.
I am a gentleman of blood and breeding;
And, from some knowledge and assurance, offer
This office to you.

    GENTLEMAN.   I will talk further with you.
    KENT.   No, do not.
For confirmation that I am much more
Than my out-wall,[15] open this purse, and take
What it contains. If you shall see Cordelia,—
As fear not but you shall,—show her this ring;
And she will tell you who your fellow is
That yet you do not know. Fie on this storm!
I will go seek the King.

    GENTLEMAN.   Give me your hand. Have you no more to say?
    KENT.   Few words, but, to effect,[16] more than all yet;
That, when we have found the King,—in which your pain[17]
That way, I'll this,—he that first lights on him
Holla the other.   *Exeunt severally.*

---

14. just—accurate.
15. out-wall—appearance., i.e., in servant's livery.
16. to effect—in importance.   17. pain—best efforts.

[ACT III · 2] *Another part of the Heath. Storm still.*

Enter LEAR *and* FOOL.

    LEAR.   Blow, winds, and crack your cheeks! Rage! Blow!
You cataracts and hurricanoes, spout
Till you have drench'd our steeples, drown'd the cocks! [1]
You sulph'rous and thought-executing[2] fires,
Vaunt-couriers[3] to oak-cleaving thunderbolts,
Singe my white head! And thou, all-shaking thunder,

---

1. cocks—weathervanes.
2. thought-executing—killing as quick as thought.
3. Vaunt-couriers—forerunners.

Smite flat the thick rotundity o' th' world!
Crack nature's moulds, all germens[4] spill [5] at once,
That makes ingrateful man!

FOOL.   O nuncle, court holy-water[6] in a dry house is better
than this rain-water out o' door. Good nuncle, in, and ask thy
daughters' blessing. Here's a night pities neither wise man nor
fool.

LEAR.   Rumble thy bellyful! Spit, fire! Spout, rain!
Nor rain, wind, thunder, fire, are my daughters.
I tax[7] not you, you elements, with unkindness,
I never gave you kingdom, call'd you children;
You owe me no subscription: [8] then let fall
Your horrible pleasure. Here I stand, your slave,
A poor, infirm, weak, and despis'd old man;
But yet I call you servile ministers,[9]
That will with two pernicious daughters join
Your high-engender'd [10] battles 'gainst a head
So old and white as this. Oh! Oh! 't is foul!

FOOL.   He that has a house to put 's head in has a good head-
piece.

> The cod-piece that will house
>   Before the head has any,
> The head and he shall louse;
>   So beggars marry many.
> The man that makes his toe
>   What he his heart should make
> Shall of a corn cry woe,
>   And turn his sleep to wake.

For there was never yet fair woman but she made mouths[11] in a
glass.

Enter KENT.

LEAR.   No, I will be the pattern of all patience; I will say
nothing.

---

4. germens—seeds of life.   5. spill—destroy.
6. court holy-water—flattery.   7. tax—accuse.
8. subscription—obedience.   9. ministers—agents.
10. high-engender'd—begotten on high.
11. made mouths—grimaces.

KENT.   Who's there?

FOOL.   Marry, here's grace and a cod-piece; that's a wise man and a fool.

KENT.   Alas, sir, are you here? Things that love night
Love not such nights as these; the wrathful skies
Gallow[12] the very wanderers of the dark,
And make them keep their caves. Since I was man,
Such sheets of fire, such bursts of horrid thunder,
Such groans of roaring wind and rain, I never
Remember to have heard: man's nature cannot carry[13]
Th' affliction nor the fear.

LEAR.   Let the great gods,
That keep this dreadful pudder[14] o'er our heads,
Find out their enemies now. Tremble, thou wretch,
That hast within thee undivulged crimes,
Unwhipp'd of justice; hide thee, thou bloody hand;
Thou perjur'd, and thou simular[15] man of virtue
That art incestuous; caitiff, to pieces shake,
That under covert and convenient seeming[16]
Has practis'd on man's life; close pent-up guilts,
Rive[17] your concealing continents, and cry
These dreadful summoners grace.[18] I am a man
More sinn'd against than sinning.

KENT.   Alack, bare-headed!
Gracious my lord, hard by here is a hovel;
Some friendship will it lend you 'gainst the tempest.
Repose you there; whilst I to this hard house—
More harder than the stone whereof 't is rais'd;
Which even but now, demanding after[19] you,
Deni'd [20] me to come in—return, and force
Their scanted courtesy.

LEAR.   My wits begin to turn.
Come on, my boy. How dost, my boy? Art cold?
I am cold myself. Where is this straw, my fellow?

---

12. Gallow—terrify.   13. carry—endure.
14. pudder—turmoil.   15. simular—hypocritical.
16. convenient seeming—mask of conventional virtue.
17. Rive—break out of.   18. grace—for mercy.
19. demanding after—inquiring for.   20. Deni'd—forbade.

The art of our necessities[21] is strange,
That can make vile things precious. Come, your hovel.
Poor Fool and knave, I have one part in my heart
That's sorry yet for thee.

    FOOL.   [*Singing.*]

        He that has and a little tiny wit,—
           With heigh-ho, the wind and the rain,—
        Must make content with his fortunes fit,
           For the rain it raineth every day.

    LEAR.   True, boy. Come, bring us to this hovel.

                                Exeunt LEAR *and* KENT.

    FOOL.   This is a brave night to cool a courtezan.
I'll speak a prophecy[22] ere I go:
  When priests are more in word than matter;
  When brewers mar their malt with water;
  When nobles are their tailors' tutors;
  No heretics burn'd, but wenches' suitors;
  When every case in law is right;
  No squire in debt, nor no poor knight;
  When slanders do not live in tongues;
  Nor cutpurses come not to throngs;
  When usurers tell their gold i' th' field;
  And bawds and whores do churches build;
  Then shall the realm of Albion
  Come to great confusion.
  Then comes the time, who lives to see 't,
  That going shall be us'd with feet.
This prophecy Merlin shall make; for I live before his time.

                                     Exit.

---

21. art of our necessities—skill created by need.
22. prophecy—what follows is a familiar Elizabethan "gag": the Fool solemnly prophesies a number of absurd truisms.

[ACT III • 3] *Gloucester's castle.*

Enter GLOUCESTER *and* EDMUND.

    GLOUCESTER.   Alack, alack, Edmund, I like not this un-natural dealing. When I desired their leave that I might pity him, they took from me the use of mine own house; charged me, on pain of their perpetual displeasure, neither to speak of him, entreat for him, nor any way sustain[1] him.

EDMUND. Most savage and unnatural!

GLOUCESTER. Go to; say you nothing. There is division between the Dukes, and a worse matter than that. I have received a letter this night; 't is dangerous to be spoken; I have locked the letter in my closet. These injuries the King now bears will be revenged home; [2] there is part of a power already footed; [3] we must incline to the King. I will seek him, and privily relieve him. Go you and maintain talk with the Duke, that my charity be not of him perceived. If he ask for me, I am ill, and gone to bed. If I die for it, as no less is threatened me, the King my old master must be relieved. There is some strange thing toward, Edmund; pray you, be careful.   *Exit.*

EDMUND. This courtesy, forbid [4] thee, shall the Duke
Instantly know; and of that letter too.
This seems a fair deserving,[5] and must draw me
That which my father loses; no less than all.
The younger rises when the old doth fall.   *Exit.*

---

1. sustain—succour.   2. home—to the utmost.
3. footed—landed.   4. forbid—forbidden to.
5. deserving—action which will deserve reward.

[ACT III · 4] *The Heath. Before a hovel.*

Enter LEAR, KENT, *and* FOOL.

KENT.   Here is the place, my lord; good my lord, enter.
The tyranny of the open night's too rough
For nature to endure.   [*Storm still.*]

LEAR.   Let me alone.

KENT.   Good my lord, enter here.

LEAR.   Wilt break my heart?

KENT.   I had rather break mine own. Good my lord, enter.

LEAR.   Thou think'st 't is much that this contentious storm
Invades us to the skin; so 't is to thee;
But where the greater malady is fix'd,
The lesser is scarce felt. Thou 'dst shun a bear;

But if thy flight lay toward the roaring sea,
Thou 'dst meet the bear i' th' mouth. When the mind's free,[1]
The body's delicate;[2] the tempest in my mind
Doth from my senses take all feeling else
Save what beats there. Filial ingratitude!
Is it not as this mouth should tear this hand
For lifting food to 't? But I will punish home:
No, I will weep no more. In such a night
To shut me out! Pour on; I will endure.
In such a night as this! O Regan, Goneril!
Your old kind father, whose frank heart gave all,—
O, that way madness lies; let me shun that;
No more of that.

    KENT.   Good my lord, enter here.

    LEAR.   Prithee, go in thyself; seek thine own ease.
This tempest will not give me leave to ponder
On things would hurt me more. But I'll go in.
[*To the* FOOL.] In, boy; go first. You houseless poverty,[3]—
Nay, get thee in. I'll pray, and then I'll sleep.   *Exit* FOOL.
Poor naked wretches, wheresoe'er you are,
That bide the pelting of this pitiless storm,
How shall your houseless heads and unfed sides,
Your loop'd and window'd raggedness,[4] defend you
From seasons such as these? O, I have ta'en
Too little care of this! Take physic,[5] pomp;
Expose thyself to feel what wretches feel,
That thou mayst shake the superflux[6] to them,
And show the heavens more just.

    EDGAR.   [*Within.*] Fathom and half, fathom and half! Poor
Tom!   [*The* FOOL *runs out from the hovel.*]

    FOOL.   Come not in here, nuncle, here's a spirit. Help me,
help me!

    KENT.   Give me thy hand. Who's there?

    FOOL.   A spirit, a spirit! He says his name's poor Tom.

---

1. free—untroubled.   2. delicate—sensitive.
3. houseless poverty—homeless paupers.
4. loop'd and window'd raggedness—ragged clothing full of holes.
5. physic—medicine.
6. shake the superflux—give in charity what is superfluous.

KENT.   What art thou that dost grumble there i' th' straw?
Come forth.

Enter EDGAR, *disguised as a madman.*

EDGAR.   Away! the foul fiend follows me! "Through the sharp
hawthorn blow the winds." Hum! go to thy cold bed, and warm
thee.

LEAR.   Did'st thou give all to thy two daughters, and art thou
come to this?

EDGAR.   Who gives anything to poor Tom? whom the foul
fiend hath led through fire and through flame, and through ford
and whirlpool, o'er bog and quagmire; that hath laid knives under his pillow, and halters in his pew;[7] set ratsbane[8] by his porridge; made him proud of heart, to ride on a bay trotting-horse
over four-inched [9] bridges, to course[10] his own shadow for a
traitor. Bless thy five wits! Tom's a-cold,—O, do de, do de, do
de. Bless thee from whirlwinds, star-blasting, and taking! [11] Do
poor Tom some charity, whom the foul fiend vexes. There could
I have[12] him now, and there, and there again, and there.

                                                                [*Storm still.*]

LEAR.   What, his daughters brought him to this pass?
Couldst thou save nothing? Wouldst thou give 'em all?

FOOL.   Nay, he reserved a blanket, else we had been all
shamed.

LEAR.   Now, all the plagues that in the pendulous air
Hang fated o'er men's faults light on thy daughters!

KENT.   He hath no daughters, sir.

LEAR.   Death, traitor! nothing could have súbdu'd nature
To such a lowness but his únkind daughters.
Is it the fashion, that discarded fathers
Should have thus little mercy on their flesh?
Judicious punishment! 'T was this flesh begot
Those pelican[13] daughters.

EDGAR.   Pillicock[14] sat on Pillicock-hill.
Alow, alow, loo, loo!

---

7. pew—balcony.   8. ratsbane—poison.   9. four-inched—narrow.
10. course—chase.   11. taking—infection.   12. have—catch.
13. pelican—who feed on their mother's blood.
14. Pillicock, etc.—"pelican" reminds Poor Tom of an old nursery
rhyme.

FOOL.   This cold night will turn us all to fools and madmen.

EDGAR.   Take heed o' th' foul fiend. Obey thy parents; keep
thy word justly; swear not; commit not with man's sworn spouse;
set not thy sweet heart on proud array. Tom's a-cold.

LEAR.   What hast thou been?

EDGAR.   A serving-man, proud in heart and mind; that curled
my hair; wore gloves in my cap; served the lust of my mistress'
heart, and did the act of darkness with her; swore as many oaths
as I spake words, and broke them in the sweet face of heaven:
one that slept in the contriving of lust, and waked to do it. Wine
loved I deeply, dice dearly, and in woman out-paramoured the
Turk: [15] false of heart, light of ear, bloody of hand; hog in sloth,
fox in stealth, wolf in greediness, dog in madness, lion in prey.
Let not the creaking of shoes nor the rustling of silks betray[16]
thy poor heart to woman. Keep thy foot out of brothels, thy hand
out of plackets,[17] thy pen from lenders' books, and defy the foul
fiend. [*Sings.*] "Still through the hawthorn blows the cold wind."
Says suum, mun, nonny. Dolphin my boy, boy, sessa! let him trot
by.   [*Storm still.*]

LEAR.   Why, thou wert better in thy grave than to answer
with thy uncovered body this extremity of the skies. Is man no
more than this? Consider him well. Thou ow'st the worm no silk,
the beast no hide, the sheep no wool, the cat [18] no perfume. Ha!
here's three on 's are sophisticated! Thou art the thing itself; un-
accommodated man is no more but such a poor, bare, forked [19]
animal as thou art. Off, off, you lendings! [20] come, unbutton
here.   [*Tearing off his clothes.*]

Enter GLOUCESTER, *with a torch.*

FOOL.   Prithee, nuncle, be contented; 't is a naughty night to
swim in. Now a little fire in a wild field were like an old lecher's
heart; a small spark, all the rest on 's body cold. Look, here
comes a walking fire.

EDGAR.   This is the foul fiend Flibbertigibbet; he begins at
curfew, and walks till the first cock; [21] he gives the web and the

---

15. Turk—Sultan.   16. betray—tempt you to give.
17. plackets—openings in petticoats.   18. cat—civet-cat.
19. forked—two-legged.   20. lendings—clothes.
21. cock—cockcrow (midnight).

pin,[22] squints the eye, and makes the hare-lip; mildews the white wheat, and hurts the poor creature of earth.

> Swithold footed thrice the 'old; [23]
> He met the night-mare, and her ninefold; [24]
>> Bid her alight,
>> And her troth plight,
> And, aroint[25] thee, witch, aroint thee!

KENT.   How fares your Grace?

LEAR.   What's he?

KENT.   Who's there? What is 't you seek?

GLOUCESTER.   What are you there? Your names?

EDGAR.   Poor Tom, that eats the swimming frog, the toad, the tadpole, the wall-newt,[26] and the water; that in the fury of his heart, when the foul fiend rages, eats cow-dung for salads; swallows the old rat and the ditchdog; drinks the green mantle of the standing pool; who is whipp'd from tithing[27] to tithing, and stocked, punished, and imprisoned; who hath had three suits to his back, six shirts to his body,

> Horse to ride, and weapon to wear;
> But mice and rats, and such small deer,[28]
> Have been Tom's food for seven long year.

Beware my follower. Peace, Smulkin; peace, thou fiend!

GLOUCESTER.   What, hath your Grace no better company?

EDGAR.   The prince of darkness is a gentleman. Modo he's call'd, and Mahu.

GLOUCESTER.   Our flesh and blood, my lord, is grown so vile

That it doth hate what gets it.

EDGAR.   Poor Tom's a-cold.

GLOUCESTER.   Go in with me; my duty cannot suffer

T' obey in all your daughters' hard commands.

Though their injunction be to bar my doors

---

22. web and the pin—cataract of the eye.
23. 'old—wold, i.e., field.   24. ninefold—nine colts.
25. aroint—go away.   26. wall-newt—lizard.
27. tithing—district.   28. deer—game.

And let this tyrannous night take hold upon you,
Yet have I ventur'd to come seek you out,
And bring you where both fire and food is ready.

    LEAR. First let me talk with this philosopher.[29]
What is the cause of thunder?

    KENT. Good my lord, take his offer; go into the house.

    LEAR. I'll talk a word with this same learned Theban.
What is your study?

    EDGAR. How to prevent the fiend, and to kill vermin.

    LEAR. Let me ask you one word in private.

    KENT. Importune him once more to go, my lord;
His wits begin to unsettle.

    GLOUCESTER.   Canst thou blame him?

                                        [*Storm still.*]

His daughters seek his death. Ah, that good Kent!
He said it would be thus, poor banish'd man!
Thou say'st the King grows mad; I'll tell thee, friend,
I am almost mad myself. I had a son,
Now outlaw'd from my blood; 'a sought my life,
But lately, very late. I lov'd him, friend,
No father his son dearer; true to tell thee,
The grief hath craz'd my wits. What a night's this!
I do beseech your Grace,—

    LEAR.   O, cry you mercy, sir.
Noble philosopher, your company.

    EDGAR. Tom's a-cold.

    GLOUCESTER. In, fellow, there, into the hovel; keep thee
warm.

    LEAR. Come, let's in all.

    KENT.   This way, my lord.

    LEAR.   With him;
I will keep still with my philosopher.

    KENT. Good my lord, soothe him; let him take the fellow.

    GLOUCESTER. Take him you on.

    KENT. Sirrah, come on; go along with us.

    LEAR. Come, good Athenian.

---

29. philosopher—scientist.

GLOUCESTER.   No words, no words: hush.

EDGAR.

> Child [30] Rowland to the dark tower came;
> His word was still, Fie, foh, and fum,
>   I smell the blood of a British man.

Exeunt.

---

30. Child—candidate for knighthood.

[ACT III • 5] *Gloucester's castle.*

Enter CORNWALL *and* EDMUND.

CORNWALL.   I will have my revenge ere I depart his house.

EDMUND.   How, my lord, I may be censured that nature[1] thus gives way to loyalty, something fears me to think of.

CORNWALL.   I now perceive, it was not altogether your brother's evil disposition made him seek his death; but a provoking merit,[2] set a-work by a reproveable badness in himself.

EDMUND.   How malicious is my fortune, that I must repent to be just! This is the letter he spoke of, which approves[3] him an intelligent party[4] to the advantages of France. O heavens! that this treason were not, or not I the detector!

CORNWALL.   Go with me to the Duchess.

EDMUND.   If the matter of this paper be certain, you have mighty business in hand.

CORNWALL.   True or false, it hath made thee Earl of Gloucester. Seek out where thy father is, that he may be ready for our apprehension.[5]

EDMUND.   [*Aside.*] If I find him comforting the King, it will stuff his suspicion more fully.—I will perséver in my course of loyalty, though the conflict be sore between that and my blood.

CORNWALL.   I will lay trust upon thee; and thou shalt find a dearer father in my love.   *Exeunt.*

---

1. nature—natural affection.
2. provoking merit—a good quality that impelled him.
3. approves—reveals.
4. intelligent party—spy.
5. apprehension—arrest.

[ACT III • 6] *A building attached to Gloucester's castle.*

Enter KENT *and* GLOUCESTER.

GLOUCESTER.   Here is better than the open air; take it thankfully. I will piece out the comfort with what addition I can. I will not be long from you.

KENT.   All the power of his wits have given way to his impatience.[1] The gods reward your kindness!   *Exit* GLOUCESTER.

Enter LEAR, EDGAR, *and* FOOL.

EDGAR.   Frateretto calls me; and tells me Nero[2] is an angler in the lake of darkness.[3] Pray, innocent, and beware the foul fiend.

FOOL.   Prithee, nuncle, tell me whether a madman be a gentleman or a yeoman?

LEAR.   A king, a king!

FOOL.   No, he's a yeoman[4] that has a gentleman to his son; for he's a mad yeoman that sees his son a gentleman before him.

LEAR.   To have a thousand with red burning spits
Come hissing in upon 'em,—

EDGAR.   The foul fiend bites my back.

FOOL.   He's mad that trusts in the tameness of a wolf, a horse's health, a boy's love, or a whore's oath.

LEAR.   It shall be done; I will arraign them straight.[5]
[*To* EDGAR.] Come, sit thou here, most learned justicer;
[*To the* FOOL.] Thou, sapient sir, sit here. Now, you she foxes!

EDGAR.   Look, where he stands and glares!
Wantest thou eyes[6] at trial, madam?

Come o'er the bourn,[7] Bessy, to me,—

FOOL.   [*Sings.*]

Her boat hath a leak,
And she must not speak
Why she dares not come over to thee.

---

1. impatience—suffering.
2. Nero—the debauched emperor of Rome.   3. darkness—i.e., hell.
4. yeoman—property-holder.   5. straight—at once.
6. wantest thou eyes—do you wish spectators.   7. bourn—brook.

EDGAR.   The foul fiend haunts poor Tom in the voice of a
nightingale. Hoppedance cries in Tom's belly for two white
herring. Croak not, black angel; I have no food for thee.

KENT.   How do you, sir? Stand you not so amaz'd: [8]
Will you lie down and rest upon the cushion?

LEAR.   I'll see their trial first. Bring in their evidence.
[*To* EDGAR.] Thou robed man of justice, take thy place;
[*To the* FOOL.] And thou, his yoke-fellow of equity,
Bench by his side. [*To* KENT.] You are o' th' commission,[9]
Sit you too.

EDGAR.   Let us deal justly.

Sleepest or wakest thou, jolly shepherd?
    Thy sheep be in the corn;
And for one blast of thy minikin[10] mouth,
    Thy sheep shall take no harm.

Purr! the cat is grey.

LEAR.   Arraign her first; 't is Goneril. I here take my oath
before this honourable assembly, she kicked the poor king her
father.

FOOL.   Come hither, mistress. Is your name Goneril?

LEAR.   She cannot deny it.

FOOL.   Cry you mercy, I took you for a joint-stool.[11]

LEAR.   And here's another, whose warp'd looks proclaim
What store[12] her heart is made on. Stop her there!
Arms, arms, sword, fire! Corruption in the place!
False justicer, why hast thou let her scape?

EDGAR.   Bless thy five wits!

KENT.   O pity! Sir, where is the patience[13] now
That you so oft have boasted to retain?

EDGAR.   [*Aside.*] My tears begin to take his part so much,
They'll mar my counterfeiting.

LEAR.   The little dogs and all,
Tray, Blanch, and Sweetheart, see, they bark at me.

EDGAR.   Tom will throw his head at them. Avaunt, you curs!

---

8. amaz'd—astonished.
9. commission—commissioned as a justice.
10. minikin—dainty.   11. joint-stool—wooden stool.
12. store—material.   13. patience—self-control.

Be thy mouth or black or white,
Tooth that poisons if it bite;
Mastiff, greyhound, mongrel grim,
Hound or spaniel, brach or lym,[14]
Or bobtail tike or trundle-tail,[15]
Tom will make him weep and wail;
For, with throwing thus my head,
Dogs leapt the hatch,[16] and all fled.

Do de, de, de. Sessa! Come, march to wakes[17] and fairs and market-towns. Poor Tom, thy horn is dry.

LEAR.   Then let them anatomize[18] Regan; see what breeds about her heart. Is there any cause in nature that make these hard hearts? [*To* EDGAR.] You, sir, I entertain for one of my hundred; only I do not like the fashion of your garments. You will say they are Persian attire, but let them be changed.

Enter GLOUCESTER.

KENT.   Now, good my lord, lie here and rest a while.

LEAR.   Make no noise, make no noise; draw the curtains; so, so, so. We'll go to supper i' th' morning; so, so, so.

FOOL.   And I'll go to bed at noon.

GLOUCESTER.   Come hither, friend; where is the King my master?

KENT.   Here, sir; but trouble him not, his wits are gone.

GLOUCESTER.   Good friend, I prithee, take him in thy arms;
I have o'erheard a plot of death upon him.
There is a litter ready; lay him in 't,
And drive toward Dover, friend, where thou shalt meet
Both welcome and protection. Take up thy master.
If thou shouldst dally[19] half an hour, his life,
With thine, and all that offer to defend him,
Stand in assured loss. Take up, take up;
And follow me, that will to some provision
Give thee quick conduct.

---

14. brach or lym—bitch or bloodhound.
15. trundle-tail—drooping tail.
16. hatch—lower half of a divided door.
17. wakes—merrymakings.
18. anatomize—dissect.   19. dally—delay.

KENT.   Oppressed nature sleeps.
This rest might yet have balm'd [20] thy broken sinews,
Which, if convenience will not allow,
Stand in hard cure.[21] [*To the* FOOL.] Come, help to bear thy
    master;
Thou must not stay behind.
    GLOUCESTER.   Come, come, away.
                      Exeunt all but EDGAR.

    EDGAR.   When we our betters see bearing our woes,
We scarcely think our miseries our foes,
Who alone suffers,[22] suffers most i' th' mind,
Leaving free things and happy shows behind;
But then the mind much sufferance doth o'erskip,
When grief hath mates, and bearing fellowship.
How light and portable my pain seems now,
When that which makes me bend makes the King bow,
He childed as I fathered! Tom, away!
Mark the high noises; [23] and thyself bewray
When false opinion, whose wrong thoughts defile thee,
In thy just proof repeals and reconciles thee.
What will hap more to-night, safe scape the King!
Lurk, lurk.[24]   *Exit.*

---

20. balm'd—soothed.
21. stand in hard cure—will hardly be cured.
22. alone suffer—suffers by himself.
23. high noises—discord among the great.
24. Lurk, lurk—remain in hiding.

[ACT III • 7] *Gloucester's castle.*

Enter CORNWALL, REGAN, GONERIL, EDMUND, *and Servants.*

    CORNWALL.   [*To* GONERIL.] Post speedily to my lord your
husband; show him this letter. The army of France is landed.—
Seek out the traitor Gloucester.
                   Exeunt some of the Servants.
    REGAN.   Hang him instantly.
    GONERIL.   Pluck out his eyes.
    CORNWALL.   Leave him to my displeasure.—Edmund, keep
you our sister company; the revenges we are bound to take upon

your traitorous father are not fit for your beholding. Advise the
Duke, where you are going, to a most festinate¹ preparation; we
are bound to the like. Our posts shall be swift and intelligent
betwixt us. Farewell, dear sister; farewell, my lord of Gloucester.

Enter OSWALD.

How now! where's the King?
 OSWALD. My Lord of Gloucester hath convey'd him hence.
Some five or six and thirty of his knights,
Hot questrists² after him, met him at gate,
Who, with some other of the lords dependants,
Are gone with him towards Dover, where they boast
To have well-armed friends.
 CORNWALL.   Get horses for your mistress.
 GONERIL. Farewell, sweet lord, and sister.
 CORNWALL. Edmund, farewell.
          Exeunt GONERIL, EDMUND, *and* OSWALD.
         Go seek the traitor Gloucester,
Pinion him like a thief, bring him before us.
          Exeunt other Servants.
Though well we may not pass upon his life
Without the form of justice, yet our power
Shall do a courtesy to our wrath, which men
May blame, but not control.

Enter GLOUCESTER *brought in by two or three Servants.*

         Who's there? The traitor?
 REGAN. Ingrateful fox! 't is he.
 CORNWALL. Bind fast his corky³ arms.
 GLOUCESTER. What means your Graces? Good my friends,
  consider
You are my guests. Do me no foul play, friends.
 CORNWALL. Bind him, I say.   [*Servants bind him.*]
 REGAN.   Hard, hard. O filthy traitor!
 GLOUCESTER. Unmerciful lady as you are, I'm none.
 CORNWALL. To this chair bind him. Villain, thou shalt
  find—   [REGAN *plucks his beard.*]

---

1. festinate—speediest possible. 2. questrists—searchers.
3. corky—withered.

GLOUCESTER.   By the kind gods, 't is most ignobly done
To pluck me by the beard.

REGAN.   So white, and such a traitor!

GLOUCESTER.   Naughty lady,
These hairs, which thou dost ravish from my chin,
Will quicken,[4] and accuse thee. I am your host:
With robber's hands my hospitable favours
You should not ruffle[5] thus. What will you do?

CORNWALL.   Come, sir, what letters had you late from
    France?

REGAN.   Be simple-answer'd, for we know the truth.

CORNWALL.   And what confederacy have you with the
    traitors
Late footed in the kingdom?

REGAN.   To whose hands you have sent the lunatic king?
Speak.

GLOUCESTER.   I have a letter guessingly set down,
Which came from one that's of a neutral heart,
And not from one oppos'd.

CORNWALL.   Cunning.

REGAN.   And false.

CORNWALL.   Where hast thou sent the King?

GLOUCESTER.   To Dover.

REGAN.   Wherefore to Dover? Wast thou not charg'd at
    peril—

CORNWALL.   Wherefore to Dover? Let him answer that.

GLOUCESTER.   I am tied to th' stake, and I must stand the
    course.[6]

REGAN.   Wherefore to Dover?

GLOUCESTER.   Because I would not see thy cruel nails
Pluck out his poor old eyes; nor thy fierce sister
In his anointed flesh stick boarish fangs.
The sea, with such a storm as his bare head
In hell-black night endur'd, would have buoy'd [7] up
And quench'd the stelled fires; [8]
Yet, poor old heart, he holp[9] the heavens to rain.

---

4. quicken—come to life.   5. ruffle—violate.
6. course—attack.   7. buoy'd—swelled up.
8. stelled fires—light of the stars.   9. holp—helped.

If wolves had at thy gate howl'd that stern time,
Thou shouldst have said, "Good porter, turn the key."
All cruels else subscrib'd: [10] but I shall see
The winged vengeance overtake such children.

CORNWALL.   See 't shalt thou never. Fellows, hold the chair.
Upon these eyes of thine I'll set my foot.

GLOUCESTER.   He that will think to live till he be old,
Give me some help!—O cruel! O ye gods!

REGAN.   One side will mock another; th' other too.

CORNWALL.   If you see vengeance,—

FIRST SERVANT.   Hold your hand, my lord!
I have serv'd you ever since I was a child;
But better service have I never done you
Than now to bid you hold.

REGAN.   How now, you dog!

FIRST SERVANT.   If you did wear a beard upon your chin,
I'd shake it on this quarrel. What do you mean?

CORNWALL.   My villain! [11]   [*They draw and fight.*]

FIRST SERVANT.   Nay, then, come on, and take the chance of
anger.

REGAN.   Give me thy sword. A peasant stand up thus?
          [*She takes a sword, and runs at him behind.*]

FIRST SERVANT.   Oh, I am slain! My lord, you have one eye
left
To see some mischief on him. Oh!   [*Dies.*]

CORNWALL.   Lest it see more, prevent it. Out, vile jelly!
Where is thy lustre now?

GLOUCESTER.   All dark and comfortless. Where's my son
Edmund?
Edmund, enkindle all the sparks of nature,
To quit[12] this horrid act.

REGAN.   Out, treacherous villain!
Thou call'st on him that hates thee. It was he
That made the overture[13] of thy treason to us,
Who is too good to pity thee.

GLOUCESTER.   O my follies! then Edgar was abus'd [14]

---

10. cruels else subscribed—other cruel animals submitted.
11. villain—servant.   12. quit—requite.
13. overture—disclosure.   14. abus'd—wronged.

Kind gods, forgive me that, and prosper him!

REGAN.   Go thrust him out at gates, and let him smell
His way to Dover.   *Exit one with* GLOUCESTER.
        How is 't, my lord? How look you?

CORNWALL.   I have receiv'd a hurt; follow me, lady.
Turn out that eyeless villain; throw this slave
Upon the dunghill. Regan, I bleed apace;
Untimely comes this hurt. Give me your arm.
                              Exit CORNWALL, *led by* REGAN.

SECOND SERVANT.   I'll never care what wickedness I do,
If this man come to good.

THIRD SERVANT.   If she live long,
And in the end meet the old course[15] of death,
Women will all turn monsters.

SECOND SERVANT.   Let's follow the old earl, and get the
    Bedlam
To lead him where he would: his roguish madness
Allows itself to anything.

THIRD SERVANT.   Go thou: I'll fetch some flax and whites of
    eggs
To apply to his bleeding face. Now, Heaven help him!
                              Exeunt severally.

---

15. old course—natural death in old age.

[ACT IV • 1] *The open country near Gloucester's castle.*

Enter EDGAR.

EDGAR.   Yet better thus, and known to be contemn'd,[1]
Than, still contemn'd and flatter'd, to be worst.
The lowest and most dejected thing of fortune
Stands still in esperance,[2] lives not in fear.
The lamentable change is from the best;
The worst returns[3] to laughter. Welcome, then,
Thou unsubstantial air that I embrace!
The wretch that thou hast blown unto the worst
Owes nothing to thy blasts.

---

1. contemn'd—despised.   2. esperance—hope.
3. returns—can only change to.

Enter GLOUCESTER, *led by an* OLD MAN.

                              But who comes here?
My father, poorly led? World, world, O world!
But that thy strange mutations make us hate thee,
Life would not yield to age.[4]

OLD MAN.   O, my good lord, I have been your tenant, and
your father's tenant, these four-score years.

GLOUCESTER.   Away, get thee away! Good friend, be gone;
Thy comforts can do me no good at all;
Thee they may hurt.

OLD MAN.   Alack, sir, you cannot see your way.

GLOUCESTER.   I have no way, and therefore want no eyes;
I stumbled when I saw. Full oft 't is seen,
Our means secure[5] us, and our mere defects
Prove our commodities.[6] Ah! dear son Edgar,
The food [7] of thy abused father's wrath!
Might I but live to see thee in my touch,
I'd say I had eyes again!

OLD MAN.   How now! Who's there?

EDGAR.   [*Aside.*] O gods! Who is 't can say, "I am at the
    worst"?
I am worse than e'er I was.

OLD MAN.   'T is poor mad Tom.

EDGAR.   [*Aside.*] And worse I may be yet; the worst is not
So long as we can say, "This is the worst."

OLD MAN.   Fellow, where goest?

GLOUCESTER.   Is it a beggar-man?

OLD MAN.   Madman and beggar too.

GLOUCESTER.   He has some reason, else he could not beg.
I' th' last night's storm I such a fellow saw,
Which made me think a man a worm. My son
Came then into my mind, and yet my mind
Was then scarce friends with him. I have heard more since.
As flies to wanton[8] boys, are we to the gods,
They kill us for their sport.

---

4. yield to age—consent to live.   5. secure—make careless.
6. commodities—advantages.   7. food—object.
8. wanton—playful.

EDGAR.   [*Aside.*]   How should this be?
Bad is the trade that must play fool to sorrow,[9]
Ang'ring itself and others.—Bless thee, master!
GLOUCESTER.   Is that the naked fellow?
OLD MAN.   Ay, my lord.
GLOUCESTER.   Then, prithee, get thee gone. If, for my sake,
Thou wilt o'ertake us, hence a mile or twain
I' th' way toward Dover, do it for ancient love;
And bring some covering for this naked soul,
Who I'll entreat to lead me.
OLD MAN.   Alack, sir, he is mad.
GLOUCESTER.   'T is the time's plague,[10] when madmen lead
the blind.
Do as I bid thee, or rather do thy pleasure;
Above the rest, be gone.
OLD MAN.   I'll bring him the best 'parel that I have,
Come on 't what will.   *Exit.*
GLOUCESTER.   Sirrah, naked fellow,—
EDGAR.   Poor Tom's a-cold. [*Aside.*] I cannot daub[11] it
further—
GLOUCESTER.   Come hither, fellow.
EDGAR.   [*Aside.*] And yet I must.—Bless thy sweet eyes,
they bleed.
GLOUCESTER.   Know'st thou the way to Dover?
EDGAR.   Both stile and gate, horse-way and foot-path. Poor
Tom hath been scared out of his good wits. Bless thee, good
man's son, from the foul fiend! Five fiends have been in poor
Tom at once; of lust, as Obidicut; Hobbididence, prince of
dumbness; Mahu, of stealing; Modo, of murder; Flibbertigibbet,
of mopping and mowing,[12] who since possesses chambermaids
and waiting-women. So, bless thee, master!
GLOUCESTER.   Here, take this purse, thou whom the heavens'
plagues
Have humbled to all strokes: [13] that I am wretched
Makes thee the happier; heavens, deal so still!

---

9. sorrow—to one in sorrowful plight.
10. time's plague—a symbol of these bad times.
11. daub—pretend.   12. mopping and mowing—face making.
13. to all strokes—to be able to endure all misfortunes.

Let the superfluous and lust-dieted man,
That slaves[14] your ordinance,[15] that will not see
Because he does not feel, feel your power quickly;
So distribution should undo excess,
And each man have enough. Dost thou know Dover?
　　EDGAR.　Ay, master.
　　GLOUCESTER.　There is a cliff, whose high and bending head
Looks fearfully in the confined deep.
Bring me but to the very brim of it,
And I'll repair the misery thou dost bear
With something rich about me. From that place
I shall no leading need.
　　EDGAR.　　　　　　　Give me thy arm;
Poor Tom shall lead thee.　　　　　　　　*Exeunt.*

---

14. slaves—subordinates to his desires.　　15. ordinance—commands.

[ACT IV • 2] *Before the Duke of Albany's palace.*

Enter GONERIL, EDMUND, *and* OSWALD.

　　GONERIL.　Welcome, my lord! I marvel our mild husband
Not met us on the way.—Now, where's your master?
　　OSWALD.　Madam, within; but never man so chang'd.
I told him of the army that was landed;
He smil'd at it: I told him you were coming;
His answer was, "The worse:" of Gloucester's treachery,
And of the loyal service of his son,
When I inform'd him, then he call'd me sot,[1]
And told me I had turn'd the wrong side out.
What most he should dislike seems pleasant to him;
What like, offensive.
　　GONERIL.　[*To* EDMUND.] Then shall you go no further.
It is the cowish[2] terror of his spirit,
That dares not undertake; he'll not feel wrongs
Which tie[3] him to an answer. Our wishes on the way
May prove effects.[4] Back, Edmund, to my brother;
Hasten his musters and conduct his powers.

---

1. sot—fool.　　2. cowish—cowardly.
3. tie—force.　　4. prove effects—be fulfilled.

I must change arms at home, and give the distaff [5]
Into my husband's hands. This trusty servant
Shall pass between us. Ere long you are like to hear,
If you dare venture in your own behalf,
A mistress's command. Wear this; spare speech;
Decline your head. This kiss, if it durst speak,
Would stretch thy spirits up into the air.
Conceive,[6] and fare thee well.

    EDMUND.   Yours in the ranks of death.   *Exit.*
    GONERIL.   My most dear Gloucester!
O, the difference of man and man!
To thee a woman's services are due;
My Fool usurps my body.

    OSWALD.   Madam, here comes my lord.   *Exit.*

Enter the DUKE OF ALBANY.

    GONERIL.   I have been worth the whistle.
    ALBANY.   O Goneril!
You are not worth the dust which the rude wind
Blows in your face. I fear your disposition.
That nature which contemns its origin
Cannot be border'd certain[7] in itself.
She that herself will sliver and disbranch
From her material sap,[8] perforce must wither
And come to deadly use.[9]

    GONERIL.   No more; the text is foolish.

    ALBANY.   Wisdom and goodness to the vile seem vile;
Filths savour but themselves. What have you done?
Tigers, not daughters, what have you perform'd?
A father, and a gracious aged man,
Whose reverence even the head-lugg'd [10] bear would lick,
Most barbarous, most degenerate! have you madded.
Could my good brother suffer you to do it?
A man, a prince, by him so benefited!

---

5. distaff—spinning staff, i.e., symbol of woman's place.
6. Conceive—understand my meaning.
7. be border'd certain—have sure boundaries of conduct.
8. sap—i.e., trunk.   9. deadly use—destruction.
10. head-lugg'd—led by a leash.

If that the heavens do not their visible spirits
Send quickly down to tame[11] these vile offences,
It will come,
Humanity must perforce prey on itself,
Like monsters of the deep.

GONERIL.   Milk-liver'd man!
That bear'st a cheek for blows, a head for wrongs,
Who hast not in thy brows an eye discerning
Thine honour from thy suffering, that not know'st
Fools do those villains pity who are punish'd
Ere they have done their mischief; where's thy drum?
France spreads his banners in our noiseless[12] land,
With plumed helm thy state begins to threat;
Whiles thou, a moral fool, sits still, and criest,
"Alack, why does he so?"

ALBANY.   See thyself, devil!
Proper[13] deformity seems not in the fiend
So horrid as in woman.

GONERIL.   O vain fool!

ALBANY.   Thou changed and self-cover'd [14] thing, for shame!
Be-monster not thy feature. Were 't my fitness
To let these hands obey my blood,
They are apt enough to dislocate and tear
Thy flesh and bones; howe'er thou art a fiend,
A woman's shape doth shield thee.

GONERIL.   Marry, your manhood—Mew!

Enter a MESSENGER.

ALBANY.   What news?

MESSENGER.   O, my good lord, the Duke of Cornwall's dead;
Slain by his servant, going to put out
The other eye of Gloucester.

ALBANY.   Gloucester's eyes!

MESSENGER.   A servant that he bred, thrill'd with remorse,
Oppos'd against the act, bending his sword
To his great master; who, thereat enrag'd,

---

11. tame—put a stop to.   12. noiseless—passive.
13. Proper—natural to a friend.
14. self-covered—disguising your real nature.

Flew on him, and amongst them fell'd him dead;
But not without that harmful stroke, which since
Hath pluck'd him after.

ALBANY.   This shows you are above,
You justicers, that these our nether[15] crimes
So speedily can venge! But, O poor Gloucester!
Lost he his other eye?

MESSENGER.   Both, both, my lord.
This letter, madam, craves a speedy answer:
'T is from your sister.

GONERIL.   [*Aside*.] One way I like this well;
But being widow, and my Gloucester with her,
May all the building in my fancy[16] pluck[17]
Upon my hateful life: another way,
The news is not so tart. I'll read, and answer.   *Exit*.

ALBANY.   Where was his son when they did take his eyes?

MESSENGER.   Come with my lady hither.

ALBANY.   He is not here.

MESSENGER.   No, my good lord; I met him back again.

ALBANY.   Knows he the wickedness?

MESSENGER.   Ay, my good lord; 't was he inform'd against
  him;
And quit the house on purpose, that their punishment
Might have the freer course.

ALBANY.   Gloucester, I live
To thank thee for the love thou show'dst the King,
And to revenge thine eyes. Come hither, friend;
Tell me what more thou know'st.   *Exeunt*.

---

15. nether—in this world.
16. building in my fancy—castle in the air.
17. pluck—pull down.

[ACT IV · 3] *The French camp near Dover.*

Enter KENT *and a* GENTLEMAN.

KENT.   Why the King of France is so suddenly gone back,
know you no reason?

GENTLEMAN.   Something he left imperfect in the state,

which since his coming forth is thought of; which imports[1] to the kingdom so much fear and danger that his personal return was most required and necessary.

KENT.   Who hath he left behind him General?

GENTLEMAN.   The Marshal of France, Monsieur La Far.

KENT.   Did your letters pierce the Queen to any demonstration of grief?

GENTLEMAN.   Ay, sir; she took them, read them in my
    presence;
And now and then an ample tear trill'd down
Her delicate cheek. It seem'd she was a queen
Over her passion,[2] who, most rebel-like,
Sought to be king o'er her.

KENT.   O, then it mov'd her.

GENTLEMAN.   Not to a rage; patience and sorrow strove
Who should express her goodliest.[3] You have seen
Sunshine and rain at once: her smiles and tears
Were like a better way; those happy smilets
That play'd on her ripe lip seem'd not to know
What guests were in her eyes, which, parted thence,
As pearls from diamonds dropp'd. In brief,
Sorrow would be a rarity[4] most beloved,
If all could so become it.

KENT.   Made she no verbal question?

GENTLEMAN.   Faith, once or twice she heav'd the name of
    "father"
Pantingly forth, as if it press'd her heart;
Cried, "Sisters! sisters! Shame of ladies! sisters!
Kent! father! sisters! What, i' th' storm? i' th' night?
Let pity not be believ'd!" There she shook
The holy water from her heavenly eyes;
And clamour-moisten'd, then away she started
To deal with grief alone.

KENT.   It is the stars,
The stars above us, govern our conditions;

---

1. imports—threatens.
2. passion—sorrow.
3. express her goodliest—give her the more beautiful expression.
4. rarity—something precious.

Else one self mate and make⁵ could not beget
Such different issues.⁶ You spoke not with her since?
    GENTLEMAN.   No.
    KENT.   Was this before the King return'd?
    GENTLEMAN.   No, since.
    KENT.   Well, sir, the poor distressed Lear's i' th' town;
Who sometime, in his better tune, remembers
What we are come about, and by no means
Will yield to see his daughter.
    GENTLEMAN.   Why, good sir?
    KENT.   A sovereign shame so elbows⁷ him. His own unkind-
    ness,
That stripp'd her from his benediction, turn'd her
To foreign casualties,⁸ gave her dear rights
To his dog-hearted daughters,—these things sting
His mind so venomously, that burning shame
Detains him from Cordelia.
    GENTLEMAN.   Alack, poor gentleman!
    KENT.   Of Albany's and Cornwall's powers you heard not?
    GENT.   'T is so, they are afoot.
    KENT.   Well, sir, I'll bring you to our master Lear,
And leave you to attend him. Some dear cause
Will in concealment wrap me up a while;
When I am known aright, you shall not grieve
Lending⁹ me this acquaintance. I pray you, go
Along with me.   *Exeunt.*

---

5. self mate and make—same husband and wife.
6. issues—children.   7. elbows—stands at his side.
8. casualties—accidents.   9. Lending—affording.

[ACT IV • 4] *The same. A tent.*

*Enter, with drum and colours,*¹ CORDELIA, DOCTOR, *and Soldiers.*

    CORDELIA.   Alack, 't is he! Why, he was met even now
As mad as the vex'd sea, singing aloud,
Crown'd with rank fumiter² and furrow-weeds,

---

1. drum and colours—drummers and colour-bearers.
2. fumiter, etc.—the names of wild flowers and weeds.

With hardocks, hemlock, nettles, cuckoo-flowers,
Darnel, and all the idle weeds that grow
In our sustaining corn.[3] A century[4] send forth;
Search every acre in the high-grown field,
And bring him to our eye.   *Exit an Officer*.
          What can[5] man's wisdom[6]
In the restoring his bereaved sense?
He that helps him take all my outward worth.
     DOCTOR.   There is means, madam.
Our foster-nurse of nature is repose,
The which he lacks; that to provoke in him,
Are many simples[7] operative, whose power
Will close the eye of anguish.
     CORDELIA   All blest secrets,
All you unpublish'd virtues of the earth,
Spring with my tears! be aidant and remediate[8]
In the good man's distress! Seek, seek for him,
Lest his ungovern'd rage dissolve the life
That wants the means[9] to lead it.

Enter MESSENGER.

     MESSENGER.   News, madam!
The British powers are marching hitherward.
     CORDELIA.   'T is known before; our preparation stands
In expectation of them. O dear father,
It is thy business that I go about;
Therefore great France
My mourning and important[10] tears hath pitied.
No blown[11] ambition doth our arms incite,
But love, dear love, and our ag'd father's right.
Soon may I hear and see him!   *Exeunt*.

---

3. sustaining corn—wheat that supports life.
4. century—a company of soldiers.
5. What can—what power is in.
6. man's wisdom—science.
7. simples—medicinal herbs.
8. aidant and remediate—helpful remedies.
9. means—sense.
10. important—importunate.
11. blown—inflated.

[ACT IV • 5] *Gloucester's castle.*

Enter REGAN *and* OSWALD.

REGAN.   But are my brother's powers set forth?

OSWALD.   Ay, madam.

REGAN.   Himself in person there?

OSWALD.   Madam, with much ado.[1]
Your sister is the better soldier.

REGAN.   Lord Edmund spake not with your lord at home?

OSWALD.   No, madam.

REGAN.   What might import my sister's letter to him?

OSWALD.   I know not, lady.

REGAN.   Faith, he is posted [2] hence on serious matter.
It was great ignorance, Gloucester's eyes being out,
To let him live; where he arrives he moves
All hearts against us. Edmund, I think, is gone,
In pity of his misery, to dispatch
His nighted [3] life; moreover, to descry
The strength o' the enemy.

OSWALD.   I must needs after him, madam, with my letter.

REGAN.   Our troops set forth to-morrow, stay with us;
The ways are dangerous.

OSWALD.   I may not, madam:
My lady charg'd my duty in this business.

REGAN.   Why should she write to Edmund? Might not you
Transport her purposes by word? Belike
Some thing—I know not what. I'll love thee much,
Let me unseal the letter.

OSWALD.   Madam, I had rather—

REGAN.   I know your lady does not love her husband;
I am sure of that; and at her late being here
She gave strange eliads[4] and most speaking looks
To noble Edmund. I know you are of her bosom.[5]

OSWALD.   I, madam?

REGAN.   I speak in understanding; y' are, I know 't.
Therefore I do advise you, take this note: [6]

---

1. ado—effort.   2. posted—ridden.   3. nighted—blinded.
4. eliads—languishing looks.   5. of her bosom—in her confidence.
6. take this note—consider this.

My lord is dead; Edmund and I have talk'd;
And more convenient is he for my hand
Than for your lady's. You may gather more.
If you do find him, pray you, give him this;
And when your mistress hears thus much from you,
I pray, desire her call her wisdom to her:
So, fare you well.
If you do chance to hear of that blind traitor,
Preferment[7] falls on him that cuts him off.

OSWALD.   Would I could meet him, madam! I would show
What party I do follow.

REGAN.   Fare thee well.   *Exeunt.*

---

7. Preferment—promotion.

[ACT IV • 6] *The country near Dover.*

Enter GLOUCESTER, *and* EDGAR *dressed like a peasant.*

GLOUCESTER.   When shall we come to th' top of that same
   hill?

EDGAR.   You do climb up it now; look, how we labour.

GLOUCESTER.   Methinks the ground is even.

EDGAR.   Horrible steep.
Hark, do you hear the sea?

GLOUCESTER.   No, truly.

EDGAR.   Why, then, your other senses grow imperfect
By your eyes' anguish.

GLOUCESTER.   So may it be, indeed.
Methinks thy voice is alter'd, and thou speak'st
In better phrase and matter than thou didst.

EDGAR.   You're much deceiv'd. In nothing am I chang'd
But in my garments.

GLOUCESTER.   Methinks you're better spoken.

EDGAR.   Come on, sir, here's the place; stand still. How fear-
   ful
And dizzy 't is, to cast one's eyes so low!
The crows and choughs[1] that wing the midway air
Show scarce so gross[2] as beetles. Half way down

---

1. choughs—jackdaws.   2. gross—big.

Hangs one that gathers sampire,[3] dreadful trade!
Methinks he seems no bigger than his head.
The fishermen, that walk upon the beach,
Appear like mice; and yond tall anchoring bark,
Diminish'd to her cock,[4] her cock, a buoy
Almost too small for sight. The murmuring surge,
That on th' unnumber'd idle pebbles chafes,
Cannot be heard so high. I'll look no more,
Lest my brain turn, and the deficient sight[5]
Topple down headlong.
    GLOUCESTER.   Set me where you stand.
    EDGAR.   Give me your hand; you are now within a foot
Of th' éxtreme verge. For all beneath the moon
Would I not leap upright.
    GLOUCESTER.   Let go my hand.
Here, friend, 's another purse; in it a jewel
Well worth a poor man's taking. Fairies and gods
Prosper it with thee! Go thou further off;
Bid me farewell, and let me hear thee going.
    EDGAR.   Now fare you well, good sir.
    GLOUCESTER.   With all my heart.
    EDGAR.   Why I do trifle thus with his despair
Is done to cure it.
    GLOUCESTER.   [*Kneeling.*] O you mighty gods!
This world I do renounce, and in your sights
Shake patiently my great affliction off.
If I could bear it longer, and not fall
To quarrel with your great opposeless wills,
My snuff [6] and loathed part of nature should
Burn itself out. If Edgar live, O bless him!
Now, fellow, fare thee well.
    EDGAR.   Gone, sir; farewell!
—And yet I know not how conceit[7] may rob
The treasury of life, when life itself
Yields to the theft. [GLOUCESTER *throws himself forward and*
    falls on the stage floor.] Had he been where he thought,

---

3. sampire—aromatic plant, used as seasoning.
4. cock—cockboat.   5. deficient sight—failing sight.
6. snuff—useless remnant.   7. conceit—imagination.

By this had thought been past. Alive or dead?—
Ho, you sir! friend! Hear you, sir! speak!—
Thus might he pass[8] indeed; yet he revives.—
What are you, sir?
    GLOUCESTER.   Away, and let me die.
    EDGAR.   Hadst thou been aught but gossamer,[9] feathers, air,
So many fathom down precipitating,
Thou'dst shiver'd like an egg: but thou dost breathe;
Hast heavy substance; bleed'st not; speak'st; art sound.
Ten masts at each[10] make not the altitude
Which thou hast perpendicularly fell.
Thy life's a miracle. Speak yet again.
    GLOUCESTER.   But have I fall'n, or no?
    EDGAR.   From the dread summit of this chalky bourn.[11]
Look up a-height; the shrill-gorg'd [12] lark so far
Cannot be seen or head. Do but look up.
    GLOUCESTER.   Alack, I have no eyes.
Is wretchedness depriv'd that benefit,
To end itself by death? 'T was yet some comfort,
When misery could beguile[13] the tyrant's rage,
And frustrate his proud will.
    EDGAR.   Give me your arm.
Up: so; How is 't? Feel you your legs? You stand.
    GLOUCESTER.   Too well, too well.
    EDGAR.   This is above all strangeness.
Upon the crown o' th' cliff, what thing was that
Which parted from you?
    GLOUCESTER.   A poor unfortunate beggar.
    EDGAR.   As I stood here below, methought his eyes
Were two full moons; he had a thousand noses,
Horns whelk'd [14] and waved like the enridged sea.
It was some fiend; therefore, thou happy father,[15]
Think that the clearest gods, who make them honours
Of men's impossibilities,[16] have preserv'd thee.

---

8. pass—die.   9. gossamer—spider's webbing.
10. at each—laid end to end.   11. bourn—boundary.
12. gorg'd—throated.   13. beguile—elude.
14. whelk'd—twisted.   15. father—old man.
16. men's impossibilities—by doing things impossible to man.

GLOUCESTER.   I do remember now. Henceforth I'll bear
Affliction till it do cry out itself,
"Enough, enough," and die. That thing you speak of,
I took it for a man; often would it say,
"The fiend, the fiend:" He led me to that place.

EDGAR.   Bear free and patient thoughts.

Enter LEAR, *mad.*

But who comes here?
The safer sense[17] will ne'er accommodate[18]
His master thus.

LEAR.   No, they cannot touch me for coining; I am the King
himself.

EDGAR.   O thou side-piercing sight!

LEAR.   Nature's above art in that respect. There's your press-
money. That fellow handles his bow like a crow-keeper; draw me
a clothier's yard.[19] Look, look, a mouse! Peace, peace; this piece
of toasted cheese will do 't. There's my gauntlet; I'll prove it on a
giant. Bring up the brown bills.[20] O, well flown, bird! I' th'
clout,[21] i' th' clout! Hewgh! Give the word.[22]

EDGAR.   Sweet marjoram.

LEAR.   Pass.

GLOUCESTER.   I know that voice.

LEAR.   Ha! Goneril, with a white beard! They flattered me
like a dog, and told me I had white hairs in my beard ere the
black ones were there. To say "ay" and "no" to everything I
said! "Ay" and "no" too was no good divinity.[23] When the rain
came to wet me once, and the wind to make me chatter; when
the thunder would not peace at my bidding; there I found 'em,
there I smelt 'em out. Go to, they are not men o' their words:
they told me I was everything; 't is a lie, I am not agueproof.

GLOUCESTER.   The trick of that voice I do well remember.
Is 't not the King?

LEAR.   Ay, every inch a king!
When I do stare, see how the subject quakes.

---

17. safer sense—sane mind.   18. accommodate—dress up.
19. clothier's yard—the length of an arrow.
20. brown bills—halberds.   21. clout—bull's-eye.
22. word—password.   23. no good divinity—false doctrine.

I pardon that man's life. What was thy cause?[24]
Adultery?
Thou shalt not die. Die for adultery! No:
The wren goes to 't, and the small gilded fly
Does lecher in my sight.
Let copulation thrive; for Gloucester's bastard son
Was kinder to his father than my daughters
Got 'tween the lawful sheets.
To 't, luxury,[25] pell-mell! for I lack soldiers.
Behold yond simp'ring dame,
Whose face between her forks[26] presageth snow,[27]
That minces virtue, and does shake the head
To hear of pleasure's name,—
The fitchew,[28] nor the soiled horse, goes to 't
With a more riotous appetite.
Down from the waist they are Centaurs,[29]
Though women all above;
But to the girdle do the gods inherit,
Beneath is all the fiends';
There's hell, there's darkness, there's the sulphurous pit,
Burning, scalding, stench, consumption; fie, fie, fie! pah, pah!
Give me an ounce of civet, good apothecary, to sweeten my
imagination. There's money for thee.

GLOUCESTER.   O, let me kiss that hand!

LEAR.   Let me wipe it first; it smells of mortality.

GLOUCESTER.   O ruin'd piece of nature! This great world
Shall so wear out to nought. Dost thou know me?

LEAR.   I remember thine eyes well enough. Dost thou
squiny[30] at me? No, do thy worst, blind Cupid; I'll not love.
Read thou this challenge; mark but the penning of it.

GLOUCESTER.   Were all thy letters suns, I could not see one.

EDGAR.   [Aside.] I would not take[31] this from report. It is;
And my heart breaks at it.

LEAR.   Read.

---

24. cause—offense.   25. luxury—lasciviousness.
26. forks—part of the headdress.
27. snow—chastity.   28. fitchew—pole-cat.
29. Centaurs—mythical beasts, half-man, half-horse.
30. squiny—squint.   31. take—believe.

GLOUCESTER.   What, with the case[32] of eyes?

LEAR.   O, ho, are you there with me? No eyes in your head, nor no money in your purse? Your eyes are in a heavy case, your purse in a light; yet you see how this world goes.

GLOUCESTER.   I see it feelingly.

LEAR.   What, art mad? A man may see how this world goes with no eyes. Look with thine ears; see how yond justice rails upon yond simple thief. Hark, in thine ear: change places, and, handy-dandy,[33] which is the justice, which is the thief? Thou hast seen a farmer's dog bark at a beggar?

GLOUCESTER.   Ay, sir.

LEAR.   And the creature run from the cur? There thou mightst behold the great image of authority: a dog's obeyed in office.
Thou rascal beadle, hold thy bloody hand!
Why dost thou lash that whore? Strip thine own back;
Thou hotly lusts to use her in that kind [34]
For which thou whip'st her. The usurer hangs the cozener.[35]
Through tatter'd clothes small vices do appear;
Robes and furr'd gowns hides all. Plate sins with gold,
And the strong lance of justice hurtless breaks;
Arm it[36] in rags, a pigmy's straw does pierce it.
None does offend, none, I say, none; I'll able[37] 'em.
Take that of me, my friend, who have the power
To seal th' accuser's lips. Get thee glass eyes,
And, like a scurvy politician, seem
To see the things thou dost not. Now, now, now, now.
Pull off my boots; harder, harder: so.

EDGAR.   O, matter and impertinency[38] mix'd;
Reason in madness!

LEAR.   If thou wilt weep my fortune, take my eyes.
I know thee well enough; thy name is Gloucester.
Thou must be patient; we came crying hither.
Thou know'st, the first time that we smell the air,
We wawl and cry. I will preach to thee; mark.

GLOUCESTER.   Alack, alack the day!

---

32. case—sockets.   33. handy-dandy—formula in a child's game.
34. kind—manner.   35. cozener—petty cheat.
36. it—sin.   37. able—license.
38. impertinency—incoherent talk.

LEAR. When we are born, we cry that we are come
To this great stage of fools.—This a good block.[39]
It were a delicate stratagem, to shoe
A troop of horse with felt. I'll put 't in proof; [40]
And when I have stol'n upon these son-in-laws,
Then, kill, kill, kill, kill, kill, kill!

Enter a GENTLEMAN *with Attendants.*

GENTLEMAN. O, here he is! Lay hand upon him. Sir,
Your most dear daughter—
LEAR. No rescue? What, a prisoner? I am even
The natural fool [41] of fortune. Use me well;
You shall have ransom. Let me have a surgeon;
I am cut to th' brains.
GENTLEMAN.   You shall have anything.
LEAR. No seconds? [42] All myself?
Why, this would make a man a man of salt,
To use his eyes for garden water-pots,
Ay, and laying autumn's dust.
GENTLEMAN.   Good sir,—
LEAR. I will die bravely, like a smug bride groom. What!
I will be jovial. Come, come; I am a king,
My masters, know you that?
GENTLEMAN. You are a royal one, and we obey you.
LEAR. Then there's life in 't. Come, an you get it, you shall
get it by running. Sa, sa, sa, sa.
                    Exit running; Attendants follow.
GENTLEMAN. A sight most pitiful in the meanest wretch,
Past speaking of in a king! Thou hast one daughter
Who redeems Nature from the general curse
Which twain have brought her to.
EDGAR. Hail, gentle sir.
GENTLEMAN.   Sir, speed you: what's your will?
EDGAR. Do you hear aught, sir, of a battle toward? [43]

---

39. block—well-fashioned hat.
40. in proof—to trial.
41. natural fool—born to the sport of.
42. No seconds—no one to aid me.
43. toward—imminent.

GENTLEMAN.   Most sure and vulgar; [44] every one hears that,
That can distinguish sound.
EDGAR.   But, by your favour,
How near's the other army?
GENTLEMAN.   Near and on speedy foot; the main descry
Stands on the hourly thought.
EDGAR.   I thank you, sir; that's all.
GENTLEMAN.   Though that the Queen on special cause is
    here,
Her army is mov'd on.   *Exit.*
EDGAR.   I thank you, sir.
GLOUCESTER.   You ever-gentle gods, take my breath from
    me;
Let not my worser spirit tempt me again
To die before you please!
EDGAR.   Well pray you, father.
GLOUCESTER.   Now, good sir, what are you?
EDGAR.   A most poor man, made tame[45] to fortune's blows;
Who, by the art of known and feeling sorrows,
Am pregnant[46] to good pity. Give me your hand,
I'll lead you to some biding.[47]
GLOUCESTER.   Hearty thanks;
The bounty and the benison of Heaven
To boot, and boot!

Enter OSWALD.

OSWALD.   A próclaim'd prize! Most happy! [48]
That eyeless head of thine was first fram'd flesh
To raise my fortunes. Thou old unhappy traitor,
Briefly thyself remember; [49] the sword is out
That must destroy thee.
GLOUCESTER.   Now let thy friendly hand
Put strength enough to 't.   [EDGAR *interposes.*]
OSWALD.   Wherefore, bold peasant,
Dar'st thou support a publish'd traitor? Hence;

---

44. vulgar—commonly known.   45. tame—submissive.
46. pregnant—susceptible.   47. biding—refuge.
48. happy—opportune.
49. thyself remember—prepare thy conscience for death.

Lest that th' infection of his fortune take
Like hold on thee. Let go his arm.

    EDGAR.   'Chill [50] not let go, zir, without vurther 'casion.

    OSWALD.   Let go, slave, or thou diest!

    EDGAR.   Good gentleman, go your gait, and let poor volk
pass. An 'chud ha' bin zwaggered out of my life, 't would not
ha' bin zo long as 't is by a vortnight. Nay, come not near th' old
man; keep out, 'che vor[51] ye, or Ise try whether your costard [52]
or my ballow[53] be the harder. 'Chill be plain with you.

    OSWALD.   Out, dunghill!

    EDGAR.   'Chill pick your teeth, zir. Come, no matter vor your
foins.[54]   [*They fight, and* EDGAR *knocks him down.*]

    OSWALD.   Slave, thou hast slain me. Villain, take my purse.
If ever thou wilt thrive, bury my body;
And give the letters which thou find'st about me
To Edmund Earl of Gloucester; seek him out
Upon the English party. O, untimely death!
Death!   [*Dies.*]

    EDGAR.   I know thee well; a serviceable villain,
As duteous to the vices of thy mistress
As badness would desire.

    GLOUCESTER.   What, is he dead?

    EDGAR.   Sit you down, father; rest you.
Let's see these pockets; the letters that he speaks of
May be my friends. He's dead; I am only sorry
He had no other death's-man.[55] Let us see.
Leave, gentle wax; and, manners, blame us not.
To know our enemies' minds, we'd rip their hearts;
Their papers, is more lawful. [*Reads the letter.*]

    Let our reciprocal vows be remembered. You have many oppor-
tunities to cut him off; if your will want not, time and place will be
fruitfully offered. There is nothing done, if he return the conqueror; then am I the prisoner, and his bed my jail; from the loathed
warmth whereof deliver me, and supply the place for your labour.

               Your—wife, so I would say—

                     Affectionate servant,

                                GONERIL.

---

50. 'Chill—I will. (Edgar assumes a peasant dialect).
51. vor—warn.   52. costard—head.   53. ballow—cudgel.
54. foins—thrusts.   55. death's-man—executioner.

O indistinguish'd [56] space of woman's will!
A plot upon her virtuous husband's life;
And the exchange my brother! Here, in the sands,
Thee I'll rake up,[57] the post unsanctified
Of murderous lechers; and in the mature time
With this ungracious paper strike the sight
Of the death-practis'd [58] duke. For him 't is well
That of thy death and business I can tell.

   GLOUCESTER.   The King is mad; how stiff is my vile sense
That I stand up and have ingenious[59] feeling
Of my huge sorrows! Better I were distract;
So should my thoughts be sever'd from my griefs,

                                [Drum afar off.]

And woes by wrong imaginations lose
The knowledge of themselves.

   EDGAR.   Give me your hand.
Far off, methinks, I hear the beaten drum.
Come, father, I'll bestow you with a friend.   *Exeunt.*

---

56. indistinguish'd—infinite.   57. rake up—bury.
58. death-practis'd—whose death is plotted.   59. ingenious—acute.

[ACT IV • 7] *A tent in the French camp.*

Enter CORDELIA, KENT, *and* DOCTOR, *and Gentleman.*

   CORDELIA.   O thou good Kent, how shall I live and work
To match thy goodness? My life will be too short,
And every measure fail me.

   KENT.   To be acknowledg'd, madam, is o'erpaid.
All my reports go with[1] the modest truth;
Nor more nor clipp'd, but so.

   CORDELIA.   Be better suited; [2]
These weeds are memories of those worser hours.
I prithee, put them off.

   KENT.   Pardon, dear madam;
Yet to be known shortens[3] my made intent.
My boon I make it, that you know me not
Till time and I think meet.

---

1. go with—correspond to.   2. suited—clothed.
3. shortens—cuts short.

CORDELIA. Then be 't so, my good lord. [*To the* DOCTOR.]
How does the King?

DOCTOR. Madam, sleeps still.

CORDELIA. O you kind gods,
Cure this great breach in his abused nature!
Th' untun'd and jarring senses, O, wind up
Of this child-changed father!

DOCTOR.   So please your Majesty
That we may wake the King? He hath slept long.

CORDELIA. Be govern'd by your knowledge, and proceed
I' th' sway of your own will.

Enter LEAR *in a chair carried by Servants.*

       Is he array'd?

DOCTOR. Ay, madam; in the heaviness of sleep
We put fresh garments on him.

GENTLEMAN. Good madam, be by, when we do awake him;
I doubt not of his temperance.[4]   [*Music.*]

CORDELIA.   Very well.

DOCTOR. Please you, draw near.—Louder the music there!

CORDELIA. O my dear father! Restoration hang
Thy medicine on my lips; and let this kiss
Repair those violent harms that my two sisters
Have in thy reverence made!

KENT.   Kind and dear princess!

CORDELIA. Had you not been their father, these white flakes[5]
Did challenge pity of them. Was this a face
To be oppos'd against the warring winds?
To stand against the deep dread-bolted thunder?
In the most terrible and nimble stroke
Of quick, cross lightning? to watch—poor pérdu![6]—
With this thin helm? Mine enemy's dog,
Though he had bit me, should have stood that night
Against my fire; and wast thou fain,[7] poor father,
To hovel thee with swine and rogues forlorn
In short and musty straw? Alack, alack!

---

4. temperance—sanity. 5. flakes—hairs.
6. pérdu—isolated sentry. 7. fain—glad.

'T is wonder that thy life and wits at once
Had not concluded all. He wakes; speak to him.

DOCTOR.   Madam, do you; 't is fittest.

CORDELIA.   How does my royal lord? How fares your Majesty?

LEAR.   You do me wrong to take me out o' th' grave.
Thou art a soul in bliss; [8] but I am bound
Upon a wheel of fire, that mine own tears
Do scald like molten lead.

CORDELIA.   Sir, do you know me?

LEAR.   You are a spirit, I know; when did you die?

CORDELIA.   Still, still, far wide! [9]

DOCTOR.   He's scarce awake; let him alone a while.

LEAR.   Where have I been? Where am I? Fair daylight?
I am mightily abus'd. I should even die with pity,
To see another thus. I know not what to say.
I will not swear these are my hands. Let's see;
I feel this pin prick. Would I were assur'd
Of my condition!

CORDELIA.   O, look upon me, sir,
And hold your hand in benediction o'er me.
No, sir, you must not kneel.

LEAR.   Pray, do not mock me.
I am a very foolish fond old man.
Fourscore and upward, not an hour more nor less;
And, to deal plainly,
I fear I am not in my perfect mind.
Methinks I should know you, and know this man;
Yet I am doubtful; for I am mainly[10] ignorant
What place this is, and all the skill I have
Remembers not these garments; nor I know not
Where I did lodge last night. Do not laugh at me;
For, as I am a man, I think this lady
To be my child Cordelia.

CORDELIA.   And so I am, I am.

LEAR.   Be your tears wet? Yes, faith. I pray, weep not.
If you have poison for me, I will drink it.

---

8. bliss—Heaven.   9. wide—astray (in his wits).
10. mainly—completely.

I know you do not love me; for your sisters
Have, as I do remember, done me wrong:
You have some cause, they have not.

CORDELIA.　　　　　　　　　　　No cause, no cause.

LEAR.　Am I in France?

KENT.　　　　　　　　　In your own kingdom, sir.

LEAR.　Do not abuse me.

DOCTOR.　Be comforted, good madam; the great rage,
You see, is kill'd in him: and yet it is danger
To make him even o'er[11] the time he has lost.
Desire him to go in; trouble him no more
Till further settling.

CORDELIA.　Will 't please your Highness walk?

LEAR.　　　　　　　　　　　You must bear with me.
Pray you now, forget and forgive; I am old and foolish.

Exeunt all but KENT *and* GENTLEMAN.

GENTLEMAN.　Holds it true, sir, that the Duke of Cornwall
was so slain?

KENT.　Most certain, sir.

GENTLEMAN.　Who is conductor of his people?

KENT.　As 't is said, the bastard son of Gloucester.

GENTLEMAN.　They say Edgar, his banished son, is with the
Earl of Kent in Germany.

KENT.　Report is changeable.[12] 'T is time to look about; the
powers of the kingdom approach apace.

GENTLEMAN.　The arbitrement[13] is like to be bloody. Fare
you well, sir.　　　　　　　　　　　　　　　　*Exit.*

KENT.　My point[14] and period will be throughly wrought,
Or well or ill, as this day's battle's fought.　　　　*Exit.*

---

11. even o'er—recall past events.
12. Report is changeable—rumors are not reliable.
13. arbitrement—decision.　　14. point—full stop.

[ACT V • 1] *The British camp, near Dover.*

Enter, with drum and colours, EDMUND, REGAN, *Gentlemen,
and Soldiers.*

EDMUND.　Know of the Duke if his last purpose hold,
Or whether since he is advis'd by aught

To change the course. He's full of alteration
And self-reproving; bring his constant pleasure.[1]

> [*To a Gentleman, who goes out.*]

REGAN.   Our sister's man is certainly miscarried.[2]

EDMUND.   'T is to be doubted,[3] madam.

REGAN.   Now, sweet lord,
You know the goodness I intend upon you.
Tell me—but truly—but then speak the truth,
Do you not love my sister?

EDMUND.   In honour'd love.

REGAN.   But have you never found my brother's way
To the forfended [4] place?

EDMUND.   That thought abuses you.

REGAN.   I am doubtful that you have been conjunct
And bosom'd [5] with her,—as far as we call hers.[6]

EDMUND.   No, by mine honour, madam.

REGAN.   I never shall endure her. Dear my lord,
Be not familiar with her.

EDMUND.   Fear me not.
She and the Duke her husband!

Enter, with drum and colours, ALBANY, GONERIL, *and Soldiers.*

GONERIL.   [*Aside.*] I had rather lose the battle than that sister
Should loosen him and me.

ALBANY.   Our very loving sister, well be-met.
Sir, this I heard: the King is come to his daughter,
With others whom the rigour of our state[7]
Forc'd to cry out. Where I could not be honest,
I never yet was valiant. For this business,
It toucheth us, as France invades our land,
Not bolds[8] the King, with others, whom, I fear,
Most just and heavy causes make oppose.[9]

EDMUND.   Sir, you speak nobly.

---

1. constant pleasure—final determination.
2. miscarried—come to harm.   3. doubted—feared.
4. forfended—forbidden.   5. conjunct and bosom'd—intimate.
6. as far as we call hers—in every way.
7. rigour of our state—our harsh government.
8. Not bolds—not as it encourages.
9. make oppose—make them oppose us.

REGAN.   Why is this reason'd?

GONERIL.   Combine together 'gainst the enemy;
For these domestic and particular broils
Are not the question here.

ALBANY.   Let's then determine
With the ancient[10] of war on our proceeding.

EDMUND.   I shall attend you presently at your tent.

REGAN.   Sister, you'll go with us?

GONERIL.   No.

REGAN.   'T is most convenient; pray you, go with us.

GONERIL.   [*Aside.*] O, ho, I know the riddle. I will go.

Exeunt both the armies.

As they are going out, enter EDGAR *disguised.*

EDGAR.   If e'er your Grace had speech with man so poor,
Hear me one word.   [ALBANY *remains.*]

ALBANY.   I'll overtake you.—Speak.

EDGAR.   Before you fight the battle, ope this letter.
If you have victory, let the trumpet sound
For him that brought it. Wretched though I seem,
I can produce a champion that will prove
What is avouched there. If you miscarry,
Your business of the world hath so an end,
And machination ceases. Fortune love you!

ALBANY.   Stay till I have read the letter.

EDGAR.   I was forbid it.
When time shall serve, let but the herald cry,
And I'll appear again.   *Exit.*

ALBANY.   Why, fare thee well; I will o'erlook thy paper.

Re-enter EDMUND.

EDMUND.   The enemy's in view; draw up your powers.
Here is the guess of their true strength and forces
By diligent discovery;[11] but your haste
Is now urg'd on you.

ALBANY.   We will greet the time.   *Exit.*

EDMUND.   To both these sisters have I sworn my love;

---

10. ancient—veteran leaders.   11. discovery—scouting.

Each jealous[12] of the other, as the stung
Are of the adder. Which of them shall I take?
Both? one? or neither? Neither can be enjoy'd,
If both remain alive. To take the widow
Exasperates, makes mad her sister Goneril;
And hardly shall I carry out my side,
Her husband being alive. Now then we'll use
His countenance for the battle; which being done,
Let her that would be rid of him devise
His speedy taking off. As for the mercy
Which he intends to Lear and to Cordelia,
The battle done, and they within our power,
Shall never see his pardon; for my state
Stands on[13] me to defend, not to debate.   *Exit.*

---

12. jealous—suspicious.
13. Stands on—requires.

[ACT V • 2] *A field between the two camps.*

Alarum[1] within. Enter, with drum and colours, LEAR, CORDELIA,
and Soldiers, marching over the stage; and exeunt.
Enter EDGAR *and* GLOUCESTER.

EDGAR.   Here, father, take the shadow of this tree
For your good host; pray that the right may thrive.
If ever I return to you again,
I'll bring you comfort.
GLOUCESTER.   Grace go with you, sir! *Exit* EDGAR.

Alarum and retreat sounded within. Re-enter EDGAR.

EDGAR.   Away, old man; give me thy hand; away!
King Lear hath lost, he and his daughter ta'en.
Give me thy hand; come on.
GLOUCESTER.   No further, sir; a man may rot even here.
EDGAR.   What, in ill thoughts again? Men must endure
Their going hence, even as their coming hither;
Ripeness is all. Come on.
GLOUCESTER.   And that's true too.   *Exeunt.*

---

1. Alarum—summons to battle.

[ACT V • 3] *The British camp near Dover.*

Enter in conquest, with drum and colours, EDMUND; LEAR *and*
        CORDELIA *as prisoners;* CAPTAIN, *Soldiers, etc.*

EDMUND.   Some officers take them away. Good guard,
Until their greater pleasures first be known
That are to censure[1] them.

CORDELIA.   We are not the first
Who, with best meaning, have incurr'd the worst.
For thee, oppressed king, am I cast down;
Myself could else out-frown false Fortune's frown.
Shall we not see these daughters and these sisters?

LEAR.   No, no, no, no! Come, let's away to prison;
We two alone will sing like birds i' th' cage.
When thou dost ask me blessing, I'll kneel down
And ask of thee forgiveness. So we'll live,
And pray, and sing, and tell old tales, and laugh
At gilded butterflies, and hear poor rogues
Talk of court news; and we'll talk with them too,
Who loses and who wins; who's in, who's out;
And take upon's[2] the mystery of things
As if we were gods' spies; [3] and we'll wear out,
In a wall'd prison, packs and sects of great ones,
That ebb and flow by the moon.

EDMUND.   Take them away.

LEAR.   Upon such sacrifices, my Cordelia,
The gods themselves throw incense. Have I caught thee?
He that parts us shall bring a brand from heaven,
And fire us[4] hence like foxes. Wipe thine eyes;
The good-years[5] shall devour them, flesh and fell,
Ere they shall make us weep. We'll see 'em starve first.
Come.   *Exeunt* LEAR *and* CORDELIA, *guarded.*

EDMUND.   Come hither, captain; hark.
Take thou this note; [*Giving a paper.*] go follow them to prison.
One step I have advanc'd thee; if thou dost
As this instructs thee, thou dost make thy way

---

1. censure—judge.   2. take upon's—pretend to understand,
3. God's spies—angels.   4. fire us—drive us out by fire.
5. good-years—pestilence.

To noble fortunes. Know thou this, that men
Are as the time is; to be tender-minded
Does not become a sword. Thy great employment
Will not bear question; either say thou 'lt do 't,
Or thrive by other means.

    CAPTAIN.   I'll do 't, my lord.

    EDMUND.   About it; and write happy when thou hast done.
Mark, I say, instantly; and carry[6] it so
As I have set it down.

    CAPTAIN.   I cannot draw a cart, nor eat dried oats;
If it be man's work, I'll do 't.   *Exit.*

Flourish. Enter ALBANY, GONERIL, REGAN, *another* CAPTAIN, *and
Soldiers.*

    ALBANY.   Sir, you have show'd to-day your valiant strain,
And fortune led you well. You have the captives
Who were the opposites[7] of this day's strife;
I do require them of you, so to use them
As we shall find their merits and our safety
May equally determine.

    EDMUND.   Sir, I thought it fit
To send the old and miserable king
To some retention and appointed guard;
Whose age has charms in it, whose title more,
To pluck the common bosom[8] on his side,
And turn our impress'd lances[9] in our eyes
Which do command them. With him I sent the Queen,
My reason all the same; and they are ready
To-morrow, or at further space, t' appear
Where you shall hold your session. At this time
We sweat and bleed: the friend hath lost his friend;
And the best quarrels, in the heat, are curs'd
By those that feel their sharpness:
The question of Cordelia and her father
Requires a fitter place.

    ALBANY.   Sir, by your patience,

---

6. carry—execute.   7. opposites—opponents.
8. common bosom—the affections of the people.
9. impress'd lances—weapons of our soldiers.

I hold you but a subject[10] of this war,
Not as a brother.
　　REGAN.　　　　　　That's as we list to grace him.
Methinks our pleasure might have been demanded,
Ere you had spoke so far. He led our powers,
Bore the commission of my place and person;
The which immediacy[11] may well stand up,
And call itself your brother.
　　GONERIL.　　　　　　　　Not so hot.
In his own grace he doth exalt himself,
More than in your addition.
　　REGAN.　　　　　　　In my rights,
By me invested, he compeers[12] the best.
　　ALBANY.　That were the most, if he should husband you.
　　REGAN.　Jesters do oft prove prophets.
　　GONERIL.　　　　　　　　　Holla, holla!
That eye that told you so look'd but a-squint.
　　REGAN.　Lady, I am not well; else I should answer
From a full-flowing[13] stomach. General,
Take thou my soldiers, prisoners, patrimony;
Dispose of them, of me; the walls are thine.
Witness the world, that I create thee here
My lord and master.
　　GONERIL.　　　　　Mean you to enjoy him then?
　　ALBANY.　The let-alone[14] lies not in your good will.
　　EDMUND.　Nor in thine, lord.
　　ALBANY.　　　　　　　　　Half-blooded [15] fellow, yes.
　　REGAN.　[_To_ EDMUND.] Let the drum strike, and prove my
　　　title thine.
　　ALBANY.　Stay yet; hear reason. Edmund, I arrest thee
On capital treason; and, in thine attaint,[16]
This gilded serpent. [_Pointing to_ GONERIL.] For your claim, fair
　　sister,
I bar it in the interest of my wife.

---

10. subject—subordinate officer.
11. The which immediacy—he, as my immediate representative.
12. compeers—equals.　　13. full-flowing—angry.
14. let-alone—prohibition.　　15. Half-blooded—bastard.
16. in thine attaint—accused with you.

'T is she is sub-contracted to this lord,
And I, her husband, contradict your bans.
If you will marry, make your loves to me,
My lady is bespoke.

GONERIL.   An interlude! [17]

ALBANY.   Thou art armed, Gloucester; let the trumpet sound.
If none appear to prove upon thy person
Thy heinous, manifest, and many treasons,
There is my pledge   [*Throwing down a glove.*]
      I'll prove it on thy heart,
Ere I taste bread, thou art in nothing less
Than I have here proclaim'd thee.

REGAN.   Sick, O sick!

GONERIL.   [*Aside.*] If not, I'll ne'er trust medicine.

EDMUND.   There's my exchange. [*Throwing down a glove.*]
      What in the world he is
That names me traitor, villain-like he lies.
Call by the trumpet;—he that dares approach,
On him, on you, who not? I will maintain
My truth and honour firmly.

ALBANY.   A herald, ho!

EDMUND.   A herald, ho, a herald!

ALBANY.   Trust to thy single virtue; [18] for thy soldiers,
All levied in my name, have in my name
Took their discharge.

REGAN.   My sickness grows upon me.

ALBANY.   She is not well; convey her to my tent.

                                        Exit REGAN, *led.*

Enter a HERALD.

Come hither, herald,—Let the trumpet sound—
And read out this.

CAPTAIN.   Sound, trumpet!   [*A trumpet sounds.*]

HERALD.   [*Reads.*]

If any man of quality or degree within the lists of the army will
maintain upon Edmund, supposed Earl of Gloucester, that he is a
manifold traitor, let him appear by the third sound of the trumpet.
He is bold in his defence.

---

17. An interlude—what a farce.   18. virtue—strength.

EDMUND.   Sound!   [*First trumpet.*]
HERALD.   Again!   [*Second trumpet.*]
HERALD.   Again!   [*Third trumpet.*]
                    [*Trumpet answers within.*]

Enter EDGAR, *at the third sound, armed with a trumpet before
him.*

ALBANY.   Ask him his purposes, why he appears
Upon this call o' th' trumpet.
HERALD.   What are you?
Your name, your quality? and why you answer
This present summons?
EDGAR.   Know, my name is lost,
By treason's tooth bare-gnawn and canker-bit; [19]
Yet am I noble as the adversary
I come to cope.
ALBANY.   Which is that adversary?
EDGAR.   What's he that speaks for Edmund Earl of
    Gloucester?
EDMUND.   Himself; what say'st thou to him?
EDGAR.   Draw thy sword,
That, if my speech offend a noble heart,
Thy arm may do thee justice; here is mine.
Behold, it is the privilege of mine honours,
My oath, and my profession. I protest,
Maugre[20] thy strength, youth, place, and eminence,
Despite thy victor-sword and fire-new fortune,
Thy valour, and thy heart, thou art a traitor;
False to thy gods, thy brother, and thy father;
Conspirant 'gainst this high illustrious prince;
And from th' extremest upward of thy head
To the descent and dust beneath thy foot,
A most toad-spotted traitor. Say thou "No,"
This sword, this arm, and my best spirits are bent
To prove upon thy heart, whereto I speak,
Thou liest.
EDMUND.   In wisdom I should ask thy name;
But, since thy outside looks so fair and warlike,

19. canker-bit—worm eaten.   20. Maugre—despite.

And that thy tongue some 'say[21] of breeding breathes,
What safe and nicely I might well delay,
By rule of knighthood, I disdain and spurn.
Back do I toss these treasons to thy head,
With the hell-hated lie o'erwhelm thy heart,
Which, for they yet glance by and scarcely bruise,
This sword of mine shall give them instant way,
Where they shall rest for ever. Trumpets, speak!

> [*Alarums. They fight.* EDMUND *falls.*]

ALBANY.   Save him, save him!

GONERIL.   This is mere practice,[22] Gloucester.
By the law of arms thou wast not bound to answer
An unknown opposite: thou art not vanquish'd,
But cozen'd and beguil'd.

ALBANY.   Shut your mouth, dame,
Or with this paper shall I stop it. Hold, sir.—
Thou worse than any name, read thine own evil.
No tearing, lady; I perceive you know it.

GONERIL.   Say, if I do, the laws are mine, not thine,
Who can arraign me for 't?

ALBANY.   Most monstrous! oh!—
Know'st thou this paper?

GONERIL.   Ask me not what I know.   *Exit.*

ALBANY.   Go after her; she's desperate; govern[23] her.

EDMUND.   What you have charg'd me with, that have I done;
And more, much more; the time will bring it out.
'T is past, and so am I. But what art thou
That has this fortune on me? If thou 'rt noble,
I do forgive thee.

EDGAR.   Let's exchange charity.
I am no less in blood than thou art, Edmund;
If more, the more thou 'st wrong'd me.
My name is Edgar, and thy father's son.
The gods are just, and of our pleasant vices
Make instruments to plague us.
The dark and vicious place where thee he got
Cost him his eyes.

---

21. 'say—trace.   22. practice—trickery.
23. govern—restrain.

EDMUND.   Thou 'st spoken right, 't is true.
The wheel is come full circle; I am here.
    ALBANY.   Methought thy very gait did prophesy
A royal nobleness. I must embrace thee.
Let sorrow split my heart, if ever I
Did hate thee or thy father!
    EDGAR.   Worthy prince, I know 't.
    ALBANY.   Where have you hid yourself?
How have you known the miseries of your father?
    EDGAR.   By nursing them, my lord. List a brief tale;
And when 't is told, oh, that my heart would burst!
The bloody proclamation to escape,
That follow'd me so near,—oh, our lives' sweetness!
That we the pain of death would hourly die
Rather than die at once!—taught me to shift
Into a madman's rags, t' assume a semblance
That very dogs disdain'd; and in this habit
Met I my father with his bleeding rings,
Their precious stones new lost; became his guide,
Led him, begg'd for him, sav'd him from despair;
Never,—O fault!—reveal'd myself unto him,
Until some half-hour past, when I was arm'd.
Not sure, though hoping, of this good success,
I ask'd his blessing, and from first to last
Told him my pilgrimage; but his flaw'd heart,
Alack, too weak the conflict to support!
'Twixt two extremes of passion, joy and grief,
Burst smilingly.
    EDMUND.   This speech of yours hath mov'd me,
And shall perchance do good. But speak you on;
You look as you had something more to say.
    ALBANY.   If there be more, more woeful, hold it in;
For I am almost ready to dissolve,
Hearing of this.
    EDGAR.   This would have seem'd a period [24]
To such as love not sorrow; but another,
To amplify too much, would make much more,
And top extremity.[25]

---

24. period—end.   25. top extremity—pass all limits.

Whilst I was big in clamour came there in a man,
Who, having seen me in my worst estate,
Shunn'd my abhorr'd society; but then, finding
Who 't was that so endur'd, with his strong arms
He fasten'd on my neck, and bellow'd out
As he'd burst heaven; threw him on my father;
Told the most piteous tale of Lear and him
That ever ear received; which in recounting,
His grief grew puissant,[26] and the strings of life
Began to crack. Twice then the trumpets sounded,
And there I left him tranc'd.[27]

ALBANY.   But who was this?
EDGAR.   Kent, sir, the banish'd Kent; who in disguise
Follow'd his enemy[28] king, and did him service
Improper for[29] a slave.

Enter a GENTLEMAN *with a bloody knife.*

GENTLEMAN.   Help, help, O, help!
EDGAR.   What kind of help?
ALBANY.   Speak, man.
EDGAR.   What means this bloody knife?
GENTLEMAN.   'T is hot, it smokes;
It came even from the heart of—O, she's dead!
ALBANY.   Who dead? Speak, man.
GENTLEMAN.   Your lady, sir, your lady; and her sister
By her is poison'd; she confesses it.
EDMUND.   I was contracted to them both. All three
Now marry in an instant.
EDGAR.   Here comes Kent.

Enter KENT.

ALBANY.   Produce the bodies, be they alive or dead.
This judgement of the heavens, that makes us tremble,
Touches us not with pity.   *Exit* GENTLEMAN.
                    —O, is this he?

---

26. puissant—powerful.   27. tranc'd—unconscious.
28. enemy—who had declared him an enemy.
29. Improper for—more than would be demanded of.

The time will not allow the compliment[30]
Which very manners urges.

    KENT.   I am come
To bid my king and master aye good-night.
Is he not here?

    ALBANY.   Great thing of us forgot!
Speak, Edmund, where's the King? and where's Cordelia?

           [*The bodies of* GONERIL *and* REGAN *are brought in.*]
See'st thou this object, Kent?

    KENT.   Alack, why thus?

    EDMUND.   Yet Edmund was belov'd!
The one the other poison'd for my sake,
And after slew herself.

    ALBANY.   Even so. Cover their faces.

    EDMUND.   I pant for life. Some good I mean to do,
Despite of mine own nature. Quickly send,
Be brief in it, to the castle; for my writ
Is on the life of Lear and on Cordelia.
Nay, send in time.

    ALBANY.   Run, run, O, run!

    EDGAR.   To who, my lord? Who has the office? Send
Thy token of reprieve.

    EDMUND.   Well thought on. Take my sword,
Give it the captain.

    EDGAR.   Haste thee, for thy life.

                        Exit GENTLEMAN.

    EDMUND.   He hath commission from thy wife and me
To hang Cordelia in the prison, and
To lay the blame upon her own despair,
That she fordid [31] herself.

    ALBANY.   The gods defend her! Bear him hence a while.

                       [EDMUND *is borne off.*]

Enter LEAR *with* CORDELIA *in his arms,* GENTLEMAN *following.*

    LEAR.   Howl, howl, howl! O, you are men of stones!
Had I your tongues and eyes, I'd use them so
That heaven's vault should crack. She's gone for ever!
I know when one is dead, and when one lives;

---

30. compliment—ceremony.   31. fordid—destroyed.

She's dead as earth. Lend me a looking-glass;
If that her breath will mist or stain the stone,[32]
Why, then she lives.

    KENT.   Is this the promis'd end? [33]

    EDGAR.   Or image of that horror?

    ALBANY.   Fall, and cease!

    LEAR.   This feather stirs; she lives! If it be so,
It is a chance which does redeem all sorrows
That ever I have felt.

    KENT.   [*Kneeling.*] O my good master!

    LEAR.   Prithee, away.

    EDGAR.   'T is noble Kent, your friend.

    LEAR.   A plague upon you, murderous traitors all!
I might have sav'd her; now she's gone for ever!
Cordelia, Cordelia! stay a little. Ha!
What is 't thou say'st? Her voice was ever soft,
Gentle, and low; an excellent thing in woman.
I kill'd the slave that was a-hanging thee.

    GENTLEMAN.   'T is true, my lords, he did.

    LEAR.   Did I not, fellow?
I have seen the day, with my good biting falchion[34]
I would have made them skip. I am old now,
And these same crosses[35] spoil me. Who are you?
Mine eyes are not o' th' best. I'll tell you straight.

    KENT.   If Fortune brag of two she lov'd and hated,[36]
One of them we behold.

    LEAR.   This is a dull sight. Are you not Kent?

    KENT.   The same,
Your servant Kent. Where is your servant Caius?

    LEAR.   He's a good fellow, I can tell you that;
He'll strike and quickly too. He's dead and rotten.

    KENT.   No, my good lord; I am the very man,—

    LEAR.   I'll see that straight.

    KENT.   —That, from your first of difference[37] and decay,
Have follow'd your sad steps.

---

32. stone—glass, mirror.   33. promis'd end—Day of Judgement.
34. falchion—sword.   35. crosses—sufferings.
36. lov'd and hated—i.e., at the same time.
37. first of difference—beginning of the change in your fortunes.

LEAR.   You're welcome hither.

KENT.   Nor no man else; all's cheerless, dark, and deadly.
Your eldest daughters have fordone themselves,
And desperately are dead.

LEAR.   Ay, so I think.

ALBANY.   He knows not what he says; and vain is it
That we present us to him.

Enter a MESSENGER.

EDGAR.   Very bootless.

MESSENGER.   Edmund is dead, my lord.

ALBANY.   That's but a trifle here,—
You lords and noble friends, know our intent.
What comfort to this great decay[38] may come
Shall be appli'd. For us, we will resign,
During the life of this old majesty,
To him our absolute power; [*To* EDGAR *and* KENT.] you, to your
    rights,
With boot, and such addition as your honours
Have more than merited. All friends shall taste
The wages of their virtue, and all foes
The cup of their deservings. O, see, see!

LEAR.   And my poor fool [39] is hang'd! No, no, no life!
Why should a dog, a horse, a rat, have life,
And thou no breath at all? Thou 'lt come no more,
Never, never, never, never, never!
Pray you, undo this button. Thank you, sir.
Do you see this? Look on her, look, her lips,
Look there, look there!   [*Dies.*]

EDGAR.   He faints! My lord, my lord!

KENT.   Break, heart; I prithee, break!

EDGAR.   Look up, my lord.

KENT.   Vex not his ghost; O, let him pass! He hates him
That would upon the rack[40] of this tough world
Stretch him out longer.

EDGAR.   He is gone, indeed.

---

38. decay—fallen man.
39. poor fool—i.e., Cordelia.
40. rack—instrument of torture.

KENT.   The wonder is he hath endur'd so long;
He but usurp'd his life.

ALBANY.   Bear them from hence. Our present business
Is general woe. [*To* KENT *and* EDGAR.] Friends of my soul, you
    twain
Rule in this realm, and the gor'd [41] state sustain.

KENT.   I have a journey, sir, shortly to go:
My master calls me, I must not say no.

EDGAR.   The weight of this sad time we must obey;
Speak what we feel, not what we ought to say.
The oldest hath borne most; we that are young
Shall never see so much, nor live so long.

                      Exeunt, with a dead march.

---

41. gor'd—wounded.

THE TEMPEST

ALONSO, *King of Naples.*
SEBASTIAN, *his brother.*
PROSPERO, *the right Duke
  of Milan.*
ANTONIO, *his brother, the
  usurping Duke of Milan.*
FERDINAND, *son to the
  King of Naples.*
GONZALO, *an honest old
  counsellor.*
ADRIAN,
FRANCISCO, } *Lords.*
CALIBAN, *a savage and
  deformed slave.*

TRINCULO, *a jester.*
STEPHANO, *a drunken butler.*
MASTER OF A SHIP, BOAT-
  SWAIN, MARINERS.
MIRANDA, *daughter to* PROS-
  PERO.
ARIEL, *an airy spirit.*

IRIS,
CERES,
JUNO, } *Spirits.*
NYMPHS,
REAPERS,

Other Spirits attending on *Prospero.*

SCENE: *On board a ship at sea; afterwards an uninhabited
island.*

[ACT I · 1] *On board a ship at sea.*

A tempestuous noise of thunder and lightning heard. Enter a
SHIPMASTER *and a* BOATSWAIN.

SHIPMASTER. Boatswain!
BOATSWAIN. Here, master; what cheer?
SHIPMASTER. Good;[1] speak to the mariners: fall to 't,
yarely,[2] or we run ourselves aground; bestir, bestir.   *Exit.*

Enter MARINERS.

BOATSWAIN. Heigh, my hearts! Cheerly, cheerly, my hearts!

---

1. Good—good fellow.
2. yarely—promptly.

Yare, yare! Take in the topsail. Tend to th' master's whistle.—
Blow till thou burst thy wind, if room[3] enough!

Enter ALONSO, SEBASTIAN, ANTONIO, FERDINAND, GONZALO, *and others.*

ALONSO.   Good boatswain, have care. Where's the master?
Play the men.

BOATSWAIN.   I pray now, keep below.

ANTONIO.   Where is the master, boatswain?

BOATSWAIN.   Do you not hear him? You mar our labour.
Keep your cabins; you do assist the storm.

GONZALO.   Nay, good, be patient.

BOATSWAIN.   When the sea is. Hence! What cares these
roarers for the name of king? To cabin! Silence! Trouble us not.

GONZALO.   Good, yet remember whom thou hast aboard.

BOATSWAIN.   None that I more love than myself. You are a
counsellor; if you can command these elements to silence, and
work the peace of the present, we will not hand a rope more;
use your authority. If you cannot, give thanks you have lived so
long, and make yourself ready in your cabin for the mischance
of the hour, if it so hap.—Cheerly, good hearts!—Out of our
way, I say.   *Exit.*

GONZALO.   I have great comfort from this fellow. Methinks
he hath no drowning mark upon him; his complexion is perfect
gallows.[4] Stand fast, good Fate, to his hanging; make the rope of
his destiny our cable, for our own doth little advantage.[5] If he be
not born to be hanged, our case is miserable.   *Exeunt.*

Re-enter BOATSWAIN.

BOATSWAIN.   Down with the topmast! Yare! Lower, lower!
Bring her to try wi' the maincourse.[6] [*A cry within.*] A plague
upon this howling! They are louder than the weather or our
office.[7]

---

3. room—open sea.
4. complexion is perfect gallows—looks born to be hanged.
5. advantage—help.
6. main course—mainsail.
7. our office—the performance of our duties.

Enter SEBASTIAN, ANTONIO, *and* GONZALO.

Yet again! What do you here? Shall we give o'er and drown?
Have you a mind to sink?

SEBASTIAN.   A pox o' your throat, you bawling, blasphemous,
incharitable dog!

BOATSWAIN.   Work you, then.

ANTONIO.   Hang, cur! hang, you whoreson, insolent noise-
maker! We are less afraid to be drowned than thou art.

GONZALO.   I'll warrant him for[8] drowning though the ship
were no stronger than a nutshell and as leaky as an unstanched
wench.

BOATSWAIN.   Lay her a-hold, a-hold! Set her two courses off
to sea again; lay her off.

Enter MARINERS, *wet.*

MARINERS.   All lost! To prayers, to prayers! All lost!

BOATSWAIN.   What, must our mouths be cold?

GONZALO.   The King and Prince at prayers! Let's assist them,
For our case is as theirs.

SEBASTIAN.   I'm out of patience.

ANTONIO.   We are merely cheated of our lives by drunkards.
This wide-chopp'd [9] rascal—would thou mightst lie drowning
The washing of ten tides!

GONZALO.   He'll be hang'd yet,
Though every drop of water swear against it
And gape at wid'st to glut[10] him.

                    [*A confused noise within:* Mercy on us!]
We split, we split! Farewell, my wife and children!
Farewell, brother! We split, we split, we split!

ANTONIO.   Let's all sink wi' th' King.

SEBASTIAN.   Let's take leave of him.   *Exit.*

GONZALO.   Now would I give a thousand furlongs of sea for
an acre of barren ground, long heath, brown furze, anything.
The wills above be done! but I would fain die a dry death.

                                                    Exeunt.

---

8. for—against.
9. wide-chopp'd—bawling.
10. glut—swallow.

[ACT I • 2] *The island. Before Prospero's cell.*

Enter PROSPERO *and* MIRANDA.

MIRANDA.   If by your art, my dearest father, you have
Put the wild waters in this roar, allay them.
The sky, it seems, would pour down stinking pitch,
But that the sea, mounting to th' welkin's[1] cheek,
Dashes the fire out. O, I have suffered
With those that I saw suffer! a brave[2] vessel
(Who had, no doubt, some noble creature in her)
Dash'd all to pieces! O, the cry did knock
Against my very heart. Poor souls, they perish'd.
Had I been any god of power, I would
Have sunk the sea within the earth or ere[3]
It should the good ship so have swallow'd and
The fraughting[4] souls within her.
PROSPERO.   Be collected;
No more amazement. Tell your piteous heart
There's no harm done.
MIRANDA.   O, woe the day!
PROSPERO.   No harm.
I have done nothing but in care of thee,
Of thee, my dear one, thee my daughter, who
Art ignorant of what thou art, naught knowing
Of whence I am, nor that I am more better[5]
Than Prospero, master of a full poor cell,
And thy no greater father.
MIRANDA   More to know
Did never meddle[6] with my thoughts.
PROSPERO.   'T is time
I should inform thee farther. Lend thy hand,
And pluck my magic garment from me. So,

[*Lays down his mantle.*]

Lie there, my art. Wipe thou thine eyes; have comfort.
The direful spectacle of the wreck, which touch'd
The very virtue of compassion in thee,

---

1. welkin—sky.   2. brave—gallant.
3. or ere—before.   4. fraughting—making up the cargo.
5. more better—anything more than.   6. meddle—form a part of.

I have with such provision[7] in mine art
So safely ordered that there is no soul—
No, not so much perdition[8] as an hair
Betid to any creature in the vessel
Which thou heard'st cry, which thou saw'st sink. Sit down;
For thou must now know farther.

MIRANDA.   You have often
Begun to tell me what I am; but stopp'd
And left me to a bootless inquisition,[9]
Concluding, "Stay, not yet."

PROSPERO.   The hour's now come;
The very minute bids thee ope thine ear.
Obey and be attentive. Canst thou remember
A time before we came unto this cell?
I do not think thou canst, for then thou wast not
Out[10] three years old.

MIRANDA.   Certainly, sir, I can.

PROSPERO.   By what? By any other house or person?
Of anything the image tell me, that
Hath kept with thy remembrance.

MIRANDA.   'T is far off
And rather like a dream than an assurance[11]
That my remembrance warrants. Had I not
Four or five women once that tended me?

PROSPERO.   Thou hadst, and more, Miranda. But how is it
That this lives in thy mind? What seest thou else
In the dark backward [12] and abysm of time?
If thou rememb'rest aught ere thou cam'st here,
How thou cam'st here thou may'st.

MIRANDA.   But that I do not.

PROSPERO.   Twelve year since, Miranda, twelve year since,
Thy father was the Duke of Milan and
A prince of power.

MIRANDA.   Sir, are not you my father?

PROSPERO.   Thy mother was a piece of virtue, and
She said thou wast my daughter; and thy father

---

7. provision—foresight.   8. perdition—loss.
9. bootless inquisition—fruitless inquiry.   10. Out—quite.
11. assurance—actual recollection.   12. backward—past.

Was Duke of Milan, and his only heir
And princess no worse issued.

MIRANDA. O the heavens!
What foul play had we, that we came from thence?
Or blessed was 't we did?

PROSPERO. Both, both, my girl.
By foul play, as thou say'st, were we heav'd thence,
But blessedly holp[13] hither.

MIRANDA. O, my heart bleeds
To think o' th' teen[14] that I have turn'd you to,[15]
Which is from my remembrance! Please you, farther.

PROSPERO. My brother and thy uncle, call'd Antonio—
I pray thee, mark me—that a brother should
Be so perfidious!—he whom next thyself
Of all the world I lov'd, and to him put
The manage of my state; as at that time
Through all the signories[16] it was the first,
And Prospero the prime duke, being so reputed
In dignity, and for the liberal arts[17]
Without a parallel; those being all my study,
The government I cast upon my brother
And to my state grew stranger, being transported
And rapt in secret studies. Thy false uncle—
Dost thou attend me?

MIRANDA. Sir, most heedfully.

PROSPERO. Being once perfected [18] how to grant suits,
How to deny them, who t' advance and who
To trash for overtopping,[19] new created
The creatures that were mine, I say, or chang'd 'em,
Or else new form'd 'em; having both the key
Of officer and office, set all hearts i' th' state
To what tune pleas'd his ear; that now he was
The ivy which had hid my princely trunk,
And suck'd my verdure out on 't. Thou attend'st not.

---

13. holp—helped.   14. teen—sorrow.
15. turn'd you to—caused you to remember.
16. signories—dukedoms (of Italy).
17. the liberal arts—scholarship.   18. perfected—expert.
19. trash for overtopping—trim back those who grow too great.

MIRANDA. O, good sir, I do.

PROSPERO.   I pray thee, mark me.
I, thus neglecting worldly ends, all dedicated
To closeness[20] and the bettering of my mind
With that which, but by being so retir'd,
O'er-priz'd all popular rate,[21] in my false brother
Awak'd an evil nature; and my trust,
Like a good parent, did beget of him
A falsehood, in its contrary as great[22]
As my trust was; which had indeed no limit,
A confidence sans[23] bound. He being thus lorded,
Not only with what my revénue yielded,
But what my power might else exact,—like one
Who having into truth, by telling of it,
Made such a sinner of his memory
To credit his own lie,—he did believe
He was indeed the Duke: out o' th' substitution,
And executing[24] the outward face of royalty,
With all prerogative, hence his ambition growing—
Dost thou hear?

MIRANDA. Your tale, sir, would cure deafness.

PROSPERO. To have no screen[25] between this part he play'd
And him he play'd it for, he needs will be
Absolute Milan.[26] Me, poor man!—my library
Was dukedom large enough—of temporal royalties
He thinks me now incapable; confederates[27]—
So dry he was for sway—wi' th' King of Naples
To give him annual tribute, do him homage,
Subject his coronet to his crown, and bend
The dukedom yet unbow'd [28]—alas, poor Milan!—
To most ignoble stooping.

---

20. closeness—private study.
21. O'er-priz'd all popular rate—was more valuable than is commonly recognized.
22. in its contrary as great—as great in contrast to my trust.
23. sans—without.   24. executing—acting with.
25. screen—distinction.
26. Absolute Milan—Duke of Milan in actuality.
27. confederates—makes a bargain.
28. yet unbow'd—which had never before yielded.

MIRANDA.   O the heavens!

PROSPERO.   Mark his condition and th' event,[29] then tell me
If this might be a brother.

MIRANDA.   I should sin
To think but nobly of my grandmother.
Good wombs have borne bad sons.

PROSPERO.   Now the condition.
This King of Naples, being an enemy
To me inveterate, hearkens my brother's suit;
Which was, that he, in lieu o' th' premises,[30]
Of homage and I know not how much tribute,
Should presently extirpate[31] me and mine
Out of the dukedom, and confer fair Milan
With all the honours on my brother; whereon,
A treacherous army levied, one midnight
Fated to th' purpose did Antonio open
The gates of Milan; and i' th' dead of darkness,
The ministers[32] for the purpose hurried thence
Me and thy crying self.

MIRANDA.   Alack, for pity!
I, not rememb'ring how I cried out then,
Will cry it o'er again: it is a hint[33]
That wrings mine eyes to 't.

PROSPERO.   Hear a little further,
And then I'll bring thee to the present business
Which now's upon's, without the which this story
Were most impertinent.[34]

MIRANDA.   Wherefore did they not
That hour destroy us?

PROSPERO.   Well demanded, wench;
My tale provokes that question. Dear, they durst not,
(So dear the love my people bore me) nor set
A mark so bloody on the business; but
With colours fairer painted their foul ends.

---

29. event—sequel.
30. in lieu o' th' premises—in return for these considerations.
31. extirpate—banish.   32. ministers—agents.
33. hint—occasion.
34. impertinent—pointless.

In few,[35] they hurried us aboard a bark,
Bore us some leagues to sea; where they prepared
A rotten carcass of a butt,[36] not rigg'd,
Nor tackle, sail, nor mast; the very rats
Instinctively have quit it. There they hoist us,
To cry to th' sea that roar'd to us, to sigh
To the winds whose pity, sighing back again,
Did us but loving wrong.

    MIRANDA.   Alack, what trouble
Was I then to you!

    PROSPERO.   O, a cherubin
Thou wast that did preserve me. Thou didst smile,
Infused [37] with a fortitude from heaven,
When I have deck'd the sea with drops full salt,
Under my burden groan'd; which rais'd in me
An undergoing stomach,[38] to bear up
Against what should ensue.

    MIRANDA.   How came we ashore?

    PROSPERO.   By Providence divine.
Some food we had and some fresh water that
A noble Neapolitan, Gonzalo,
Out of his charity, who being then appointed
Master of this design, did give us, with
Rich garments, linens, stuffs, and necessaries,
Which since have steaded [39] much; so, of his gentleness,
Knowing I lov'd my books, he furnish'd me
From mine own library with volumes that
I prize above my dukedom.

    MIRANDA.   Would I might
But ever see that man!

    PROSPERO.   Now I arise.   [*Puts on his robe.*]
Sit still, and hear the last of our sea-sorrow.
Here in this island we arriv'd; and here
Have I, thy schoolmaster, made thee more profit[40]
Than other princess can that have more time
For vainer hours, and tutors not so careful.

---

35. In few—briefly.   36. butt—clumsy boat.   37. Infused—filled.
38. undergoing stomach—spirit of endurance.
39. steaded—been of service.   40. profit—proficient.

MIRANDA.   Heavens thank you for 't! And now, I pray you,
  sir,
For still 't is beating in my mind, your reason
For raising this sea-storm?
  PROSPERO.   Know thus far forth.
By accident most strange, bountiful Fortune,
Now my dear lady,[41] hath mine enemies
Brought to this shore; and by my prescience
I find my zenith[42] doth depend upon
A most auspicious star, whose influence
If now I court not but omit, my fortunes
Will ever after droop. Here cease more questions.
Thou art inclin'd to sleep; 't is a good dulness,
And give it way. I know thou canst not choose.

                                [MIRANDA *sleeps.*]

Come away, servant, come; I am ready now.
Approach, my Ariel; come.

Enter ARIEL.

  ARIEL.   All hail, great master! grave sir, hail! I come
To answer thy best pleasure, be 't to fly,
To swim, to dive into the fire, to ride
On the curl'd clouds. To thy strong bidding task[43]
Ariel and all his quality.[44]
  PROSPERO.   Hast thou, spirit,
Perform'd to point the tempest that I bade thee?
  ARIEL.   To every article.
I boarded the king's ship; now on the beak,
Now in the waist, the deck, in every cabin,
I flam'd amazement. Sometime I'd divide,
And burn in many places: on the topmast,
The yards and bowsprit, would I flame distinctly,
Then meet and join. Jove's[45] lightning, the precursors
O' th' dreadful thunder-claps, more momentary
And sight-outrunning were not; the fire and cracks

---

41. dear lady—kind benefactress.
42. zenith—height of fortunes.   43. task—impose a task on.
44. quality—abilities.   45. Jove—chief of the gods.

Of sulphurous roaring the most mighty Neptune[46]
Seem to besiege, and make his bold waves tremble,
Yea, his dread trident shake.

PROSPERO.   My brave spirit!
Who was so firm, so constant, that this coil [47]
Would not infect his reason?

ARIEL.   Not a soul
But felt a fever of the mad, and play'd
Some tricks of desperation. All but mariners
Plung'd in the foaming brine and quit the vessel,
Then all afire with me. The King's son, Ferdinand,
With hair up-staring,[48]—then like reeds, not hair,—
Was the first man that leap'd; cried, "Hell is empty,
And all the devils are here."

PROSPERO.   Why, that's my spirit!
But was not this nigh shore?

ARIEL.   Close by, my master.

PROSPERO. But are they, Ariel, safe?

ARIEL.   Not a hair perish'd;
On their sustaining[49] garments not a blemish,
But fresher than before; and, as thou bad'st me,
In troops[50] I have dispers'd them 'bout the isle.
The King's son have I landed by himself,
Whom I left cooling of the air with sighs
In an odd angle[51] of the isle, and sitting,
His arms in this sad knot.

PROSPERO.   Of the King's ship
The mariners say how thou hast dispos'd,
And all the rest o' th' fleet.

ARIEL.   Safely in harbour
Is the King's ship; in the deep nook, where once
Thou call'dst me up at midnight to fetch dew
From the still-vex'd Bermoothes,[52] there she's hid;

---

46. Neptune—god of the sea.   47. coil—turmoil.
48. up-staring—standing on end.
49. sustaining—which kept them afloat.
50. troops—groups.
51. odd angle—out-of-the-way corner.
52. still-vex'd Bermoothes—ever-stormy Bermudas.

The mariners all under hatches[53] stow'd,
Who, with a charm join'd to their suffer'd labour,
I have left asleep; and for the rest o' th' fleet,
Which I dispers'd, they all have met again,
And are upon the Mediterranean float
Bound sadly home for Naples,
Supposing that they saw the King's ship wreck'd
And his great person perish.

PROSPERO.   Ariel, thy charge
Exactly is perform'd; but there's more work.
What is the time o' th' day?

ARIEL.   Past the mid season.

PROSPERO.   At least two glasses.[54] The time 'twixt six and
   now
Must by us both be spent most preciously.

ARIEL.   Is there more toil? Since thou dost give me pains,
Let me remember thee what thou hast promis'd,
Which is not yet perform'd me.

PROSPERO.   How now? moody?
What is 't thou canst demand?

ARIEL.   My liberty.

PROSPERO.   Before the time be out? No more!

ARIEL.   I prithee,
Remember I have done thee worthy service,
Told thee no lies, made thee no mistakings, serv'd
Without or grudge or grumblings. Thou did promise
To bate[55] me a full year.

PROSPERO.   Dost thou forget
From what a torment I did free thee?

ARIEL.   No.

PROSPERO.   Thou dost, and think'st it much to tread the ooze
Of the salt deep,
To run upon the sharp wind of the north,
To do me business in the veins o' th' earth
When it is bak'd with frost.

ARIEL.   I do not, sir.

PROSPERO.   Thou liest, malignant thing! Hast thou forgot

---

53. under hatches—below.   54. glasses—hours.
55. bate—reduce my term of service.

The foul witch Sycorax, who with age and envy
Was grown into a hoop? [56] Hast thou forgot her?
   ARIEL.   No, sir.
   PROSPERO.   Thou hast. Where was she born? Speak; tell me.
   ARIEL.   Sir, in Argier.[57]
   PROSPERO.   O, was she so? I must
Once a month recount what thou hast been,
Which thou forget'st. This damn'd witch Sycorax,
For mischiefs manifold and sorceries terrible
To enter human hearing, from Argier,
Thou know'st, was banish'd; for one thing she did
They would not take her life. Is not this true?
   ARIEL.   Ay, sir.
   PROSPERO.   This blue-ey'd [58] hag was hither brought with
     child,
And here was left by th' sailors. Thou, my slave,
As thou report'st thyself, was then her servant;
And, for thou wast a spirit too delicate
To act her earthy and abhorr'd commands,
Refusing her grand hests,[59] she did confine thee,
By help of her more potent ministers
And in her most unmitigable rage,
Into a cloven pine; within which rift
Imprison'd thou didst painfully remain
A dozen years; within which space she died
And left thee there, where thou didst vent[60] thy groans
As fast as mill-wheels strike. Then was this island—
Save for the son that she did litter here,
A freckl'd whelp, hag-born,[61]—not honour'd with
A human shape.
   ARIEL.   Yes, Caliban her son.
   PROSPERO.   Dull thing, I say so; he, that Caliban
Whom now I keep in service. Thou best know'st
What torment I did find thee in; thy groans
Did make wolves howl, and penetrate the breasts

---

56. grown into a hoop—bent double.   57. Argier—Algiers.
58. blue-ey'd—with dark rings around her eyes.
59. grand hests—most important orders.
60. vent—utter.   61. hag-born—witch's offspring.

Of ever-angry bears. It was a torment
To lay upon the damn'd, which Sycorax
Could not again undo. It was mine art,
When I arriv'd and heard thee, that made gape
The pine, and let thee out.
    ARIEL.   I thank thee, master.
    PROSPERO.   If thou more murmur'st, I will rend an oak
And peg thee in his knotty entrails till
Thou hast howl'd away twelve winters.
    ARIEL.   Pardon, master;
I will be correspondent[62] to command
And do my spriting gently.
    PROSPERO.   Do so, and after two days
I will discharge thee.
    ARIEL.   That's my noble master!
What shall I do? say what. What shall I do?
    PROSPERO.   Go make thyself like a nymph o' th' sea; be subject
To no sight but thine and mine, invisible
To every eyeball else. Go take this shape
And hither come in 't. Go, hence with diligence!   *Exit* ARIEL.
Awake, dear heart, awake! Thou hast slept well;
Awake!
    MIRANDA.   The strangeness of your story put
Heaviness in me.
    PROSPERO.   Shake it off. Come on,
We'll visit Caliban my slave, who never
Yields us kind answer.
    MIRANDA.   'T is a villain, sir,
I do not love to look on.
    PROSPERO.   But, as 't is,
We cannot miss[63] him: he does make our fire,
Fetch in our wood, and serves in offices
That profit us. What, ho! slave! Caliban!
Thou earth, thou! speak.
    CALIBAN.   [*Within.*] There's wood enough within.

---

62. correspondent—submissive.
63. miss—do without.

PROSPERO.   Come forth, I say! there's other business for
   thee.
Come, thou tortoise! when? [64]

Re-enter ARIEL *like a water-nymph.*

Fine apparition! My quaint Ariel,
Hark in thine ear. [*Whispers.*]
   ARIEL.   My lord, it shall be done.   *Exit.*
   PROSPERO.   Thou poisonous slave, got by the devil himself
Upon thy wicked dam,[65] come forth!

Enter CALIBAN.

   CALIBAN.   As wicked [66] dew as e'er my mother brush'd
With raven's feather from unwholesome fen
Drop on you both! A south-west[67] blow on ye
And blister you all o'er!
   PROSPERO.   For this, be sure, to-night thou shalt have
   cramps,
Side-stitches that shall pen thy breath up; urchins[68]
Shall, for that vast[69] of night that they may work,
All exercise on thee; thou shalt be pinch'd
As thick as honeycomb, each pinch more stinging
Than bees that made 'em.
   CALIBAN.   I must eat my dinner.
This island's mine, by Sycorax my mother,
Which thou tak'st from me. When thou cam'st first,
Thou strok'st me and made much of me, wouldst give me
Water with berries in 't, and teach me how
To name the bigger light, and how the less,
That burn by day and night; and then I lov'd thee
And show'd thee all the qualities[70] o' th' isle,
The fresh springs, brine-pits, barren place and fertile.
Curs'd be I that did so! All the charms
Of Sycorax, toads, beetles, bats, light on you!
For I am all the subjects that you have,

---

64. when—exclamation of impatience.
65. dam—mother.   66. wicked—poisonous.
67. south-west—unhealthy wind.   68. urchins—goblins.
69. vast—great void.   70. qualities—resources.

Which first was mine own king; and here you sty[71] me
In this hard rock, whiles you do keep from me
The rest o' th' island.

PROSPERO.   Thou most lying slave,
Whom stripes[72] may move, not kindness! I have us'd thee,
Filth as thou art, with human care, and lodg'd thee
In mine own cell, till thou didst seek to violate
The honour of my child.

CALIBAN.   O ho, O ho! would 't had been done!
Thou didst prevent me; I had peopl'd else
This isle with Calibans.

PROSPERO.   Abhorred slave,
Which any print[73] of goodness wilt not take,
Being capable of all ill! I pitied thee,
Took pains to make thee speak, taught thee each hour
One thing or other: when thou didst not, savage,
Know thine own meaning, but wouldst gabble like
A thing most brutish, I endow'd thy purposes
With words that made them known. But thy vile race,[74]
Though thou didst learn, had that in 't which good natures
Could not abide to be with; therefore wast thou
Deservedly confin'd into this rock, who hadst
Deserv'd more than a prison.

CALIBAN.   You taught me language; and my profit on 't
Is, I know how to curse. The red [75] plague rid [76] you
For learning me your language!

PROSPERO.   Hag-seed,[77] hence!
Fetch us in fuel; and be quick, thou'rt best,
To answer other business. Shrug'st thou, malice?
If thou neglect'st or dost unwillingly
What I command, I'll rack[78] thee with old cramps,
Fill all thy bones with aches, make thee roar
That beasts shall tremble at thy din.

CALIBAN.   No, pray thee.
[*Aside.*] I must obey. His art is of such power

---

71. sty—pen me up.   72. stripes—blows.
73. print—impression.   74. race—nature.
75. red—bubonic.   76. rid—destroy.
77. Hag-seed—son of a witch.   78. rack—torture.

It would control my dam's god, Setebos,[79]
And make a vassal [80] of him.

    PROSPERO.   So, slave; hence! *Exit* CALIBAN.

Enter FERDINAND; *and* ARIEL, *invisible, playing and singing.*

ARIEL'S SONG

Come unto these yellow sands,
    And then take hands.[81]
Curtsied when you have, and kiss'd
    The wild waves whist,[82]
Foot it featly[83] here and there,
And, sweet sprites, bear
    The burthen.[84]

BURTHEN *dispersedly*[85]

    Hark, hark! bow-wow,
    The watch dogs bark! Bow-wow!

ARIEL.

    Hark, Hark! I hear
    The strain of strutting chanticleer[86]
    Cry, "Cock-a-diddle-dow."

    FERDINAND.   Where should this music be? I' th'
    air or th' earth?
It sounds no more; and, sure, it waits upon
Some god o' th' island. Sitting on a bank,
Weeping again the King my father's wreck,
This music crept by me upon the waters,
Allaying both their fury and my passion[87]
With its sweet air; thence I have follow'd it,
Or it hath drawn me rather. But 't is gone.
No, it begins again.

---

79. Setebos—a Patagonian deity, hence, a devil.
80. vassal—slave.   81. take hands—i.e., for dancing.
82. whist—silenced.   83. featly—nimbly.
84. burthen—refrain.
85. dispersedly—coming from various parts of the stage.
86. chanticleer—rooster.
87. passion—grief.

ARIEL'S SONG

Full fathom five thy father lies;
  Of his bones are coral made;
Those are pearls that were his eyes:
  Nothing of him that doth fade
But doth suffer a sea-change
Into something rich and strange.
Sea-nymphs hourly ring his knell:

BURTHEN. Ding-dong.

ARIEL. Hark! now I hear them,—ding-dong, bell.

FERDINAND.   The ditty does remember[88] my drown'd father.
This is no mortal business, nor no sound
That the earth owes.[89] I hear it now above me.

PROSPERO.   The fringed curtains of thine eye advance[90]
And say what thou seest yond.

MIRANDA.   What is 't? A spirit?
Lord, how it looks about! Believe me, sir,
It carries a brave form. But 't is a spirit.

PROSPERO.   No, wench; it eats and sleeps and hath such
   senses
As we have, such. This gallant which thou seest
Was in the wreck; and, but he's something stain'd
With grief, that's beauty's canker,[91] thou mightst call him
A goodly person. He hath lost his fellows
And strays about to find 'em.

MIRANDA.   I might call him
A thing divine; for nothing natural
I ever saw so noble.

PROSPERO.   [Aside.] It goes on, I see,
As my soul prompts it. Spirit, fine spirit! I'll free thee
Within two days for this.

FERDINAND.   Most sure, the goddess
On whom these airs attend! Vouchsafe my prayer
May know if you remain[92] upon this island,
And that you will some good instruction give

---

88. remember—call to mind.   89. owes—owns.
90. advance—raise.   91. canker—worm that eats away (beauty).
92. remain—reside.

How I may bear me here: my prime request,
Which I do last pronounce, is, O you wonder!
If you be maid or no? [93]

MIRANDA.   No wonder, sir,
But certainly a maid.

FERDINAND.   My language! heavens!
I am the best of them that speak this speech,
Were I but where 't is spoken.

PROSPERO.   How? the best?
What wert thou, if the King of Naples heard thee?

FERDINAND.   A single[94] thing, as I am now, that wonders
To hear thee speak of Naples. He does hear me;
And that he does I weep. Myself am Naples,[95]
Who with mine eyes, never since at ebb,[96] beheld
The King my father wreck'd.

MIRANDA.   Alack, for mercy!

FERDINAND.   Yes, faith, and all his lords; the Duke of Milan
And his brave son being twain.

PROSPERO.   [*Aside*.] The Duke of Milan
And his more braver daughter could control [97] thee,
If now 't were fit to do 't. At the first sight
They have chang'd eyes.[98] Delicate Ariel,
I'll set thee free for this. [*To* FERDINAND.] A word, good sir;
I fear you have done yourself some wrong; [99] a word.

MIRANDA.   Why speaks my father so ungently? This
Is the third man that e'er I saw, the first
That e'er I sigh'd for. Pity move my father
To be inclin'd my way!

FERDINAND.   O, if a virgin,
And your affection not gone forth, I'll make you
The Queen of Naples.

PROSPERO.   Soft, sir! one word more.
[*Aside*.] They are both in either's powers; but this swift business

---

93. maid or no—mortal maid or goddess.
94. single—lone, helpless.   95. Naples—king of Naples.
96. Never since at ebb—which have been weeping ever since.
97. control—disprove your words.
98. chang'd eyes—have eyes only for one another.
99. done yourself some wrong—not told the whole truth.

I must uneasy make, lest too light winning
Make the prize light.——One word more; I charge thee
That thou attend me. Thou dost here usurp
The name thou ow'st not; and hast put thyself
Upon this island as a spy, to win it
From me, the lord on 't.

FERDINAND.   No, as I am a man.

MIRANDA.   There's nothing ill can dwell in such a temple.
If the ill spirit have so fair a house,
Good things will strive to dwell with 't.

PROSPERO.   Follow me.
Speak not you for him; he's a traitor. Come.
I'll manacle thy neck and feet together.
Sea-water shalt thou drink; thy food shall be
The fresh-brook mussels, wither'd roots and husks
Wherein the acorn cradled. Follow.

FERDINAND.   No;
I will resist such entertainment till
Mine enemy has more power.

                     [He draws, but is charmed from moving.]

MIRANDA.   O dear father,
Make not too rash a trial of him, for
He's gentle and not fearful.[100]

PROSPERO.   What! I say;
My foot[101] my tutor? Put thy sword up, traitor,
Who mak'st a show but dar'st not strike, thy conscience
Is so possess'd with guilt. Come from thy ward,[102]
For I can here disarm thee with this stick
And make thy weapon drop.

MIRANDA.   Beseech you, father.

PROSPERO.   Hence! hang not on my garments.

MIRANDA.   Sir, have pity;
I'll be his surety.

PROSPERO.   Silence! one word more
Shall make me chide thee, if not hate thee. What!
An advocate for an impostor! hush!
Thou think'st there is no more such shapes as he,

---

100. fearful—dangerous.   101. foot—subordinate.
102. ward—posture of defence.

Having seen but him and Caliban. Foolish wench!
To th' most of men this is a Caliban,
And they to him are angels.

    MIRANDA.   My affections
Are then most humble; I have no ambition
To see a goodlier man.

    PROSPERO.   Come on; obey.
Thy nerves[103] are in their infancy again
And have no vigour in them.

    FERDINAND.   So they are.
My spirits, as in a dream, are all bound up.
My father's loss, the weakness which I feel,
The wreck of all my friends, nor this man's threats,
To whom I am subdu'd, are but light to me,
Might I but through my prison once a day
Behold this maid: all corners else o' th' earth
Let liberty make use of; space enough
Have I in such a prison.

    PROSPERO.   [*Aside.*] It works. [*To* FERDINAND.]
      Come on.
—Thou hast done well, fine Ariel!—Follow me.
[*To* ARIEL.] Hark what thou else shalt do me.

    MIRANDA.   Be of comfort;
My father's of a better nature, sir,
Than he appears by speech. This is unwonted [104]
Which now came from him.

    PROSPERO.   [*To* ARIEL.] Thou shalt be as free
As mountain winds; but then exactly do
All points of my command.

    ARIEL.   To th' syllable.

    PROSPERO.   Come, follow.—
      Speak not for him.   *Exeunt.*

---

103. nerves—sinews.
104. unwonted—unusual.

[ACT II • 1] *Another part of the island.*

Enter ALONSO, SEBASTIAN, ANTONIO, GONZALO, ADRIAN, FRAN-
CISCO, *and others.*

GONZALO.　Beseech you, sir, be merry; you have cause,
So have we all, of joy; for our escape
Is much beyond our loss. Our hint[1] of woe
Is common; every day some sailor's wife,
The masters of some merchant, and the merchant
Have just our theme of woe; but for the miracle,
I mean our preservation, few in millions
Can speak like us. Then wisely, good sir, weigh
Our sorrow with our comfort.

ALONSO.　　　　　　　　　　　Prithee, peace.

SEBASTIAN.　He receives comfort like cold porridge.

ANTONIO.　The visitor[2] will not give him o'er so.[3]

SEBASTIAN.　Look, he's winding up the watch of his wit; by
and by it will strike.

GONZALO.　Sir,—

SEBASTIAN.　One. Tell.[4]

GONZALO.　When every grief is entertain'd [5] that's offer'd,
Comes to the entertainer—

SEBASTIAN.　A dollar.

GONZALO.　Dolour[6] comes to him, indeed; you have spoken
truer than you purposed.

SEBASTIAN.　You have taken it wiselier than I meant you
should.

GONZALO.　Therefore my lord,—

ANTONIO.　Fie, what a spendthrift is he of his tongue!

ALONSO.　I prithee, spare.

GONZALO.　Well, I have done. But yet,—

SEBASTIAN.　He will be talking.

ANTONIO.　Which, of he or Adrian, for a good wager, first
begins to crow?

SEBASTIAN.　The old cock.

---

1. hint—occasion.　　2. visitor—priest.
3. give him o'er so—let him off with so little preaching.
4. Tell—count (the number of strokes).
5. entertain'd—received passively.　　6. Dolour—grief.

ANTONIO. The cockerel.[7]

SEBASTIAN. Done. The wager?

ANTONIO. A laughter.[8]

SEBASTIAN. A match!

ADRIAN. Though this island seem to be desert,—

SEBASTIAN. Ha, ha, ha! Antonio! So you're paid.

ADRIAN. Uninhabitable and almost inaccessible,—

SEBASTIAN. Yet,—

ADRIAN. Yet,—

ANTONIO. He could not miss 't.

ADRIAN. It must needs be of subtle, tender, and delicate temperance.[9]

ANTONIO. Temperance was a delicate wench.

SEBASTIAN. Ay, and a subtle; as he most learnedly delivered.

ADRIAN. The air breathes upon us here most sweetly.

SEBASTIAN. As if it had lungs and rotten ones.

ANTONIO. Or as 't were perfumed by a fen.

GONZALO. Here is everything advantageous to life.

ANTONIO. True; save means to live.

SEBASTIAN. Of that there's none, or little.

GONZALO. How lush and lusty the grass looks! How green!

ANTONIO. The ground indeed is tawny.

SEBASTIAN. With an eye of green in 't.

ANTONIO. He misses not much.

SEBASTIAN. No; he doth but mistake the truth totally.

GONZALO. But the rarity of it is,—which is indeed almost beyond credit[10]—

SEBASTIAN. As many vouched[11] rarities are.

GONZALO. That our garments, being, as they were, drenched in the sea, hold notwithstanding their freshness and glosses, being rather new-dyed than stained with salt water.

ANTONIO. If but one of his pockets could speak, would it not say he lies?

SEBASTIAN. Ay, or very falsely pocket up his report.

GONZALO. Methinks our garments are now as fresh as when

---

7. cockerel—the young cock (Adrian).
8. laughter—the winner laughs at the loser.
9. temperance—temperature.   10. credit—belief.
11. vouched—guaranteed.

we put them on first in Afric, at the marriage of the King's fair daughter Claribel to the King of Tunis.

SEBASTIAN.   'T was a sweet marriage, and we prosper well in our return.

ADRIAN.   Tunis was never graced before with such a paragon to their queen.

GONZALO.   Not since widow Dido's[12] time.

ANTONIO.   Widow! a pox o' that! How came that widow in? Widow Dido!

SEBASTION.   What if he had said "widower Aeneas" too? Good Lord, how you take it!

ADRIAN.   "Widow Dido" said you? You make me study of that. She was of Carthage, not of Tunis.

GONZALO.   This Tunis, sir, was Carthage.

ADRIAN.   Carthage?

GONZALO.   I assure you, Carthage.

ANTONIO.   His word is more than the miraculous harp.[13]

SEBASTIAN.   He hath raised the wall and houses too.

ANTONIO.   What impossible matter will he make easy next?

SEBASTIAN.   I think he will carry this island home in his pocket and give it his son for an apple.

ANTONIO.   And, sowing the kernels of it in the sea, bring forth more islands.

GONZALO.   Ay.

ANTONIO.   Why, in good time.

GONZALO.   Sir, we were talking that our garments seem now as fresh as when we were at Tunis at the marriage of your daughter, who is now Queen.

ANTONIO.   And the rarest that e'er came there.

SEBASTIAN.   Bate,[14] I beseech you, widow Dido.

ANTONIO.   O, widow Dido! ay, widow Dido.

GONZALO.   Is not, sir, my doublet[15] as fresh as the first day I wore it? I mean, in a sort.[16]

ANTONIO.   That "sort" was well fished for.

---

12. Dido—queen of Carthage who fell in love with Aeneas on his flight from the ruins of Troy.
13. miraculous harp—Amphion's harp, which magically raised the walls of Thebes.   14. Bate—except.
15. doublet—jacket.   16. in a sort—after a fashion.

GONZALO.   When I wore it at your daughter's marriage?

ALONSO.   You cram these words into mine ears against
The stomach of my sense. Would I had never
Married my daughter there! for, coming thence,
My son is lost and, in my rate,[17] she too,
Who is so far from Italy removed
I ne'er again shall see her. O thou mine heir
Of Naples and of Milan, what strange fish
Hath made his meal on thee?

FRANCISCO.   Sir, he may live.
I saw him beat the surges[18] under him,
And ride upon their backs: he trod the water,
Whose enmity he flung aside, and breasted
The surge most swoln that met him: his bold head
'Bove the contentious waves he kept, and oared
Himself with his good arms in lusty stroke
To th' shore, that o'er his wave-worn basis[19] bowed,
As stooping to relieve him: I not doubt
He came alive to land.

ALONSO.   No, no, he's gone.

SEBASTIAN.   Sir, you may thank yourself for this great loss,
That would not bless our Europe with your daughter,
But rather loose her to an African;
Where she at least is banish'd from your eye,
Who hath cause to wet[20] the grief on 't.

ALONSO.   Prithee, peace.

SEBASTIAN.   You were kneel'd to and impórtun'd otherwise
By all of us, and the fair soul herself
Weigh'd [21] between loathness and obedience, at
Which end o' th' beam[22] should bow. We have lost your son,
I fear, for ever: Milan and Naples have
Moe[23] widows in them of this business' making
Than we bring men to comfort them.
The fault's your own.

---

17. rate—estimation.   18. surges—waves.
19. o'er his wave-worn basis—over its wave-swept base.
20. wet—weep for.   21. Weigh'd—hesitates.
22. at Which end o' th' beam—to which side of the scale.
23. Moe—more.

ALONSO.   So is the dear'st[24] o' th' loss.

GONZALO.   My lord Sebastian,
The truth you speak doth lack some gentleness
And time[25] to speak it in. You rub the sore,
When you should bring the plaster.

SEBASTIAN.   Very well.

ANTONIO.   And most chirurgeonly.[26]

GONZALO.   It is foul weather in us all, good sir,
When you are cloudy.

SEBASTIAN.   Foul weather?

ANTONIO.   Very foul.

GONZALO.   Had I plantation[27] of this isle, my lord,—

ANTONIO.   He'd sow 't with nettle-seed.

SEBASTIAN.   Or docks, or mallows.

GONZALO.   And were the king on 't, what would I do?

SEBASTIAN.   Scape being drunk for want of wine.

GONZALO.   I' th' commonwealth I would by contraries[28]
Execute all things; for no kind of traffic[29]
Would I admit; no name of magistrate;
Letters should not be known; riches, poverty,
And use of service, none; contract, succession,
Bourn, bound of land, tilth, vineyard, none;
No use of metal, corn, or wine, or oil;
No occupation; all men idle, all;
And women too, but innocent and pure;
No sovereignty;—

SEBASTIAN.   Yet he would be king on 't.

ANTONIO.   The latter end of his commonwealth forgets the
beginning.

GONZALO.   All things in common nature should produce
Without sweat or endeavour: treason, felony,
Sword, pike, knife, gun, or need of any engine,[30]
Would I not have; but nature should bring forth,
Of it own kind, all foison,[31] all abundance,
To feed my innocent people.

---

24. dear'st—bitterest.   25. time—proper time.
26. chirurgeonly—like a surgeon.   27. plantation—colonization.
28. contraries—contrary to custom.   29. traffic—commerce.
30. engine—machinery of war.   31. foison—plenty.

SEBASTIAN.   No marrying 'mong his subjects?

ANTONIO.   None, man; all idle; whores and knaves.

GONZALO.   I would with such perfection govern, sir,
T' excel the golden age.[32]

SEBASTIAN.   Save his Majesty!

ANTONIO.   Long live Gonzalo!

GONZALO.   And,—do you mark me, sir?

ALONSO.   Prithee, no more; thou dost talk nothing to me.

GONZALO.   I do well believe your Highness; and did it to
minister occasion[33] to these gentlemen, who are of such sensible[34] and nimble lungs that they always use to laugh at nothing.

ANTONIO.   'T was you we laughed at.

GONZALO.   Who in this kind of merry fooling am nothing to
you: so you may continue and laugh at nothing still.

ANTONIO.   What a blow was there given!

SEBASTIAN.   An[35] it had not fallen flatlong.[36]

GONZALO.   You are gentlemen of brave mettle; you would
lift the moon out of her sphere,[37] if she would [38] continue in it
five weeks without changing.

Enter ARIEL *invisible,*[39] *playing solemn music.*

SEBASTIAN.   We would so, and then go a bat-fowling.

ANTONIO.   Nay, good my lord, be not angry.

GONZALO.   No, I warrant you; I will not adventure my discretion so weakly. Will you laugh me asleep, for I am very
heavy?

ANTONIO.   Go sleep, and hear us.

          [*All sleep except* ALONSO, SEBASTIAN, *and* ANTONIO.]

ALONSO.   What, all so soon asleep! I wish mine eyes
Would, with themselves, shut up my thoughts. I find
They are inclin'd to do so.

SEBASTIAN.   Please you, sir.
Do not omit[40] the heavy offer of it.

---

32. golden age—the age of innocence after the creation of the world.
33. minister occasion—give cues.   34. sensible—sensitive.
35. An—if.   36. flatlong—with the flat of the sword.
37. sphere—course.   38. would—showed a desire to.
39. invisible—wearing a special cloak which was the conventional
stage symbol of invisibility.   40. omit—reject.

It seldom visits sorrow; when it doth,
It is a comforter.

ANTONIO. We two, my lord,
Will guard your person while you take your rest,
And watch your safety.

ALONSO. Thank you. Wondrous heavy.

[ALONSO *sleeps.*] *Exit* ARIEL.

SEBASTIAN. What a strange drowsiness possesses them!

ANTONIO. It is the quality o' th' climate.

SEBASTIAN. Why
Doth it not then our eyelids sink? I find not
Myself dispos'd to sleep.

ANTONIO. Nor I; my spirits are nimble.
They fell together all, as by consent;
They dropp'd, as by a thunder-stroke. What might,
Worthy Sebastian, O, what might—? No more:—
And yet methinks I see it in thy face,
What thou shouldst be: the occasion speaks[41] thee, and
My strong imagination sees a crown
Dropping upon thy head.

SEBASTIAN. What, art thou waking?

ANTONIO. Do you not hear me speak?

SEBASTIAN. I do; and surely
It is a sleepy[42] language, and thou speak'st
Out of thy sleep. What is it thou didst say?
This is a strange repose, to be asleep
With eyes wide open; standing, speaking, moving,
And yet so fast asleep.

ANTONIO. Noble Sebastian,
Thou let'st thy fortune sleep—die, rather; wink'st[43]
Whiles thou art waking.

SEBASTIAN. Thou dost snore distinctly;
There's meaning in thy snores.

ANTONIO. I am more serious than my custom; you
Must be so too, if heed me; which to do
Trebles thee o'er.[44]

---

41. occasion speaks—opportunity summons.
42. sleepy—i.e., of a dream.   43. wink'st—shut your eyes.
44. Trebles thee o'er—makes you three times the man you are.

SEBASTIAN.   Well, I am standing[45] water.
ANTONIO.   I'll teach you how to flow.
SEBASTIAN.   Do so. To ebb
Hereditary sloth instructs me.
ANTONIO.   O,
If you but knew how you the purpose cherish
Whiles thus you mock it! how, in stripping it
You more invest[46] it! Ebbing men, indeed,
Most often do so near the bottom run
By their own fear or sloth.
SEBASTIAN.   Prithee, say on.
The setting[47] of thine eye and cheek proclaim
A matter from thee, and a birth indeed
Which throes[48] thee much to yield.
ANTONIO.   Thus, sir:
Although this lord [49] of weak remembrance, this,
Who shall be of as little memory
When he is earth'd, hath here almost persuaded—
For he's a spirit of persuasion, only
Professes[50] to persuade—the King his son's alive,
'T is as impossible that he's undrown'd
As he that sleeps here swims.
SEBASTIAN.   I have no hope
That he's undrown'd.
ANTONIO.   O, out of that no hope
What great hope have you! No hope that way is
Another way so high a hope that even
Ambition cannot pierce a wink[51] beyond,
But doubt discovery[52] there. Will you grant with me
That Ferdinand is drown'd?
SEBASTIAN.   He's gone.
ANTONIO.   Then, tell me,
Who's the next heir of Naples?

---

45. standing—i.e., between ebb and flow.
46. more invest—give it more glorious robes.
47. setting—earnest expression.   48. throes—pains.
49. this lord—i.e., Francisco.
50. only Professes—his sole profession is.
51. wink—jot.   52. discovery—what it sees.

SEBASTIAN.   Claribel.
ANTÓNIO.   She that is Queen of Tunis; she that dwells
Ten leagues beyond man's life; she that from Naples
Can have no note, unless the sun were post—
The man i' th' moon's too slow—till newborn chins
Be rough and razorable; she that—from[53] whom
We all were sea-swallow'd, though some cast[54] again,
And by that destiny to perform an act
Whereof what's past is prologue, what to come
In yours and my discharge.[55]

SEBASTIAN.   What stuff is this! How say you?
'T is true, my brother's daughter's Queen of Tunis;
So is she heir of Naples; 'twixt which regions
There is some space.

ANTONIO.   A space whose every cubit
Seems to cry out, "How shall that Claribel
Measure us[56] back to Naples? Keep[57] in Tunis,
And let Sebastian wake." [58] Say, this were death
That now hath seiz'd them; why, they were no worse
Than now they are. There be that can rule Naples
As well as he that sleeps; lords that can prate
As amply and unnecessarily
As this Gonzalo; I myself could make
A chough[59] of as deep chat. O, that you bore
The mind that I do! what a sleep were this
For your advancement! Do you understand me?

SEBASTIAN.   Methinks I do.

ANTONIO.   And how does your content
Tender[60] your own good fortune?

SEBASTIAN.   I remember
You did supplant your brother Prospero.

ANTONIO.   True.
And look how well my garments sit upon me;

---

53. from—coming from.
54. cast—cast up; also, cast in roles.
55. discharge—act to be done.   56. Measure us—travel over us.
57. Keep—let her stay.   58. wake—i.e., to his fortune.
59. make A chough—teach a jackdaw.
60. Tender—regard.

Much feater[61] than before: my brother's servants
Were then my fellows; now they are my men.
    SEBASTIAN.   But, for your conscience?
    ANTONIO.   Ay, sir, where lies that? If 't were a kibe,[62]
'T would put me to my slipper; but I feel not
This deity in my bosom. Twenty consciences,
That stand 'twixt me and Milan, candied [63] be they
And melt ere they molest! Here lies your brother,
No better than the earth he lies upon
If he were that which now he's like, that's dead;
Whom I, with this obedient steel, three inches of it,
Can lay to bed for ever; whiles you, doing thus,
To the perpetual wink for aye might put
This ancient morsel, this Sir Prudence, who
Should not upbraid our course. For all the rest,
They'll take suggestion[64] as a cat laps milk;
They'll tell the clock to[65] any business that
We say befits the hour.
    SEBASTIAN.   Thy case, dear friend,
Shall be my precedent; as thou got'st Milan,
I'll come by Naples. Draw thy sword. One stroke
Shall free thee from the tribute which thou payest,
And I the King shall love thee.
    ANTONIO.   Draw together;
And when I rear my hand, do you the like,
To fall it on Gonzalo.
    SEBASTIAN.   O, but one word. [*They talk apart.*]

Re-enter ARIEL *invisible, with music and song.*

    ARIEL.   My master through his art foresees the danger
That you, his friend, are in; and sends me forth—
For else his project dies—to keep them living.
                      [*Sings in* GONZALO'S *ear.*]

        While you here do snoring lie,
        Open-ey'd Conspiracy

---

61. feater—more becomingly.   62. kibe—chilblain.
63. candied—frozen.   64. suggestion—temptation.
65. tell the clock to—will say the hour is come for.

His time⁶⁶ doth take.
If of life you keep a care,
Shake off slumber, and beware;
Awake, awake!

ANTONIO.   Then let us both be sudden.

GONZALO.   Now, good angels
Preserve the King.   [*Wakes* ALONSO.]

ALONSO.   Why, how now? Ho, awake! Why are you drawn?
Wherefore this ghastly looking?

GONZALO.   What's the matter?

SEBASTIAN.   Whiles we stood here securing your repose,
Even now, we heard a hollow burst of bellowing
Like bulls, or rather lions; did 't not wake you?
It struck mine ear most terribly.

ALONSO.   I heard nothing.

ANTONIO.   O, 't was a din to fright a monster's ear,
To make an earthquake! Sure, it was the roar
Of a whole herd of lions.

ALONSO.   Heard you this, Gonzalo?

GONZALO.   Upon mine honour, sir, I heard a humming,
And that a strange one too, which did awake me.
I shak'd you, sir, and cried: as mine eyes open'd,
I saw their weapons drawn: there was a noise,
That's verily.⁶⁷ 'T is best we stand upon our guard,
Or that we quit this place. Let's draw our weapons.

ALONSO.   Lead off this ground; and let's make further search
For my poor son.

GONZALO.   Heavens keep him from these beasts!
For he is, sure, i' th' island.

ALONSO.   Lead away.

ARIEL.   Prospero my lord shall know what I have done.
So, King, go safely on to seek thy son.   *Exeunt.*

---

66. time—opportunity.
67. verily—truth.

[ACT II • 2] *Another part of the island.*

Enter CALIBAN *with a burden of wood. A noise of thunder heard.*

CALIBAN.   All the infections that the sun sucks up,
From bogs, fens, flats, on Prosper fall and make him
By inch-meal [1] a disease! His spirits hear me
And yet I needs must curse. But they'll nor pinch,
Fright me with urchin-shows, pitch me i' th' mire,
Nor lead me, like[2] a firebrand, in the dark
Out of my way, unless he bid 'em; but
For every trifle are they set upon me,
Sometime like apes that mow[3] and chatter at me
And after bite me, then like hedgehogs which
Lie tumbling in my barefoot way and mount
Their pricks at my footfall; sometime am I
All wound with adders who with cloven tongues
Do hiss me into madness.

Enter TRINCULO.
                    Lo, now lo!
Here comes a spirit of his, and to torment me
For bringing wood in slowly. I'll fall flat;
Perchance he will not mind me.

TRINCULO.   Here's neither bush nor shrub, to bear off any
weather at all, and another storm brewing; I hear it sing i' th'
wind: yond same black cloud, yond huge one, looks like a
foul bombard [4] that would shed his liquor. If it should thunder
as it did before, I know not where to hide my head; yond same
cloud cannot choose but fall by pailfuls. What have we here? A
man or a fish? Dead or alive? A fish; he smells like a fish; a very
ancient and fish-like smell; a kind of not-of-the-newest Poor-
John.[5] A strange fish! Were I in England now, as once I was, and
had but this fish painted,[6] not a holiday fool there but would
give a piece of silver: there would this monster make a man; [7]
any strange beast there makes a man: when they will not give a

---

1. inch-meal—inch by inch.   2. like—in the shape of.
3. mow—grimace.   4. bombard—tankard.
5. Poor-John—salted fish.
6. painted—i.e., on a banner displayed outside a booth at a fair.
7. a man—i.e., a man's fortune.

doit[8] to relieve a lame beggar, they will lay out ten to see a dead
Indian. Legged like a man! and his fins like arms! Warm o' my
troth! I do now let loose my opinion, hold it no longer: this is
no fish, but an islander, that hath lately suffered by a thunderbolt. [*Thunder.*] Alas, the storm is come again! My best way is
to creep under his gaberdine; [9] there is no other shelter here-
about: misery acquaints a man with strange bedfellows. I will
here shroud till the dregs of the storm be past.

Enter STEPHANO, *singing: a bottle in his hand.*

STEPHANO.

> I shall no more to sea, to sea,
> Here shall I die ashore—

This is a very scurvy tune to sing at a man's funeral. Well, here's
my comfort.   [*Drinks. Sings.*]

> The master, the swabber, the boatswain, and I,
>   The gunner and his mate
> Lov'd Moll, Meg, and Marian, and Margery,
>   But none of us car'd for Kate;
>   For she had a tongue with a tang,
>   Would cry to a sailor, Go hang!
> She lov'd not the savour of tar nor of pitch,
> Yet a tailor might scratch her where'er she did itch;
>   Then to sea, boys, and let her go hang!

This is a scurvy tune too; but here's my comfort.   [*Drinks.*]

CALIBAN.   Do not torment me! Oh!

STEPHANO.   What's the matter? Have we devils here? Do
you put tricks upon 's with savages and men of Ind,[10] ha? I have
not scaped drowning to be afeard now of your four legs; for it
hath been said, "As proper a man as ever went on four legs cannot make him give ground"; and it shall be said so again while
Stephano breathes at nostrils.

CALIBAN.   The spirit torments me! Oh!

STEPHANO.   This is some monster of the isle with four legs
who hath got, as I take it, an ague.[11] Where the devil should he
learn our language? I will give him some relief, if it be but for

---

8. doit—the smallest coin.   9. gaberdine—long cloak.
10. Ind—India.   11. ague—fever, causing him to shiver.

that. If I can recover him and keep him tame and get to Naples with him, he's a present for any emperor that ever trod on neat's-leather.[12]

CALIBAN.   Do not torment me, prithee; I'll bring my wood home faster.

STEPHANO.   He's in his fit now and does not talk after the wisest. He shall taste of my bottle; if he have never drunk wine afore, it will go near to remove his fit. If I can recover him and keep him tame, I will not take too much[13] for him; he shall pay for him that hath him, and that soundly.

CALIBAN.   Thou dost me yet but little hurt; thou wilt anon,[14] I know it by thy trembling. Now Prosper works upon thee.

STEPHANO.   Come on your ways: open your mouth; here is that which will give language to you, cat: open your mouth; this will shake your shaking, I can tell you, and that soundly: you cannot tell who's your friend: open your chops[15] again.

TRINCULO.   I should know that voice; it should be—but he is drowned; and these are devils. O defend me!

STEPHANO.   Four legs and two voices; a most delicate monster! His forward voice now is to speak well of his friend; his backward voice is to utter foul speeches and to detract. If all the wine in my bottle will recover him, I will help his ague. Come. Amen! I will pour some in thy other mouth.

TRINCULO.   Stephano!

STEPHANO.   Doth thy other mouth call me? Mercy, mercy! This is a devil, and no monster. I will leave him; I have no long spoon.[16]

TRINCULO.   Stephano! If thou beest Stephano, touch me and speak to me; for I am Trinculo,—be not afeard—thy good friend Trinculo.

STEPHANO.   If thou beest Trinculo, come forth. I'll pull thee by the lesser legs. If any be Trinculo's legs, these are they. Thou art very Trinculo indeed! How cam'st thou to be the siege[17] of this moon-calf?[18] Can he vent Trinculos?

---

12. neat's-leather—cow-hide.
13. not take too much—no price shall be too excessive.
14. anon—in a moment.   15. chops—jaws.
16. spoon—cf. the proverb, "He that would eat with the devil must have a long spoon."   17. siege—excrement.   18. moon-calf—monster.

TRINCULO.   I took him to be killed with a thunder-stroke. But art thou not drowned, Stephano? I hope now thou art not drowned. Is the storm over-blown? I hid me under the dead moon-calf's gaberdine for fear of the storm. And art thou living, Stephano? O Stephano, two Neapolitans scaped!

STEPHANO.   Prithee, do not turn me about; my stomach is not constant.[19]

CALIBAN.   [*Aside.*] These be fine things, an if they be not sprites.
That's a brave god and bears celestial liquor.
I will kneel to him.

STEPHANO.   How didst thou scape? How cam'st thou hither? Swear by this bottle how thou cam'st hither,—I escaped upon a butt of sack[20] which the sailors heaved o'erboard—by this bottle, which I made of the bark of a tree with mine own hands since I was cast ashore.

CALIBAN.   I'll swear upon that bottle to be thy true subject; for the liquor is not earthly.

STEPHANO.   Here; swear then how thou escap'dst.

TRINCULO.   Swam ashore, man, like a duck. I can swim like a duck, I'll be sworn.

STEPHANO.   Here, kiss the book.[21] Though thou canst swim like a duck, thou art made like a goose.

TRINCULO.   O Stephano, hast any more of this?

STEPHANO.   The whole butt, man: my cellar is in a rock by th' seaside where my wine is hid. How now, moon-calf! how does thine ague?

CALIBAN.   Hast thou not dropp'd from heaven?

STEPHANO.   Out o' th' moon, I do assure thee. I was the man i' th' moon when time was.[22]

CALIBAN.   I have seen thee in her and I do adore thee.
My mistress show'd me thee and thy dog and thy bush.[23]

STEPHANO.   Come, swear to that, kiss the book: I will furnish it anon with new contents. Swear.

---

19. constant—settled.   20. butt of sack—barrel of sherry.
21. book—i.e., the bottle.
22. when time was—once upon a time.
23. bush—the man in the moon was represented as having a dog and a thornbush with him.

TRINCULO.   By this good light, this is a very shallow monster!
I afeard of him! A very weak monster! The man i' th' moon! A
most poor credulous monster! Well drawn,[24] monster, in good
sooth!

CALIBAN.   I'll show thee every fertile inch o' th' island;
And I will kiss thy foot. I prithee, be my god.

TRINCULO.   By this light, a most perfidious and drunken
monster! When 's god's asleep, he'll rob his bottle.

CALIBAN.   I'll kiss thy foot. I'll swear myself thy subject.

STEPHANO.   Come on then; down, and swear.

TRINCULO.   I shall laugh myself to death at this puppy-
headed monster. A most scurvy monster! I could find in my heart
to beat him—

STEPHANO.   Come, kiss.

TRINCULO.   But that the poor monster's in drink. An abominable monster!

CALIBAN.   I'll show thee the best springs; I'll pluck thee
    berries;
I'll fish for thee and get thee wood enough.
A plague upon the tyrant that I serve!
I'll bear him no more sticks, but follow thee,
Thou wondrous man.

TRINCULO.   A most ridiculous monster, to make a wonder
of a poor drunkard!

CALIBAN.   I prithee, let me bring thee where crabs[25] grow;
And I with my long nails will dig thee pignuts;
Show thee a jay's nest and instruct thee how
To snare the nimble marmoset. I'll bring thee
To clust'ring filberts and sometimes I'll get thee
Young scamels[26] from the rock. Wilt thou go with me?

STEPHANO.   I prithee now, lead the way without any more
talking. Trinculo, the King and all our company else being
drowned, we will inherit here. Here! bear my bottle. Fellow
Trinculo, we'll fill him by and by again.

                                    [CALIBAN *sings drunkenly:*]
    Farewell, master; farewell, farewell!

---

24. drawn—drunk.   25. crabs—crab apples.
26. scamels—seabirds (gulls?).

TRINCULO.   A howling monster; a drunken monster!
CALIBAN.   [*Sings.*]

> No more dams I'll make for fish;
>> Nor fetch in firing[27]
>> At requiring;
> Nor scrape trenchering,[28] nor wash dish.
>> 'Ban, 'Ban, Ca—Caliban
> Has a new master, get a new man.

Freedom, hey-day! hey-day, freedom! freedom, hey-dey, free-dom!

STEPHANO.   O brave monster! Lead the way.   *Exeunt.*

---

27. firing—firewood.   28. trenchering—wooden platters.

[ACT III • 1] *Before Prospero's cell.*

Enter FERDINAND, *bearing a log.*

FERDINAND.   There be some sports are painful, and their
    labour
Delight in them sets off; [1] some kinds of baseness
Are nobly undergone, and most poor matters
Point to rich ends. This my mean task
Would be as heavy to me as odious, but
The mistress which I serve quickens[2] what's dead
And makes my labours pleasures. O, she is
Ten times more gentle than her father's crabbed,
And he's compos'd of harshness. I must remove
Some thousands of these logs and pile them up,
Upon a sore injunction.[3] My sweet mistress
Weeps when she sees me work, and says such baseness[4]
Had never like executor.[5] I forget;
But these sweet thoughts do even refresh my labours,
Most busiest when I do it.[6]

---

1. sets off—cancels.   2. quickens—puts life into.
3. upon a sore injunction—under a severe penalty.
4. baseness—low work.
5. like executor—such a workman.
6. Most busiest when I do it—when I work at my task most busily.

Enter MIRANDA; *and* PROSPERO *at a distance, unseen.*

MIRANDA.   Alas, now, pray you,
Work not so hard. I would the lightning had
Burnt up those logs that you are enjoin'd to pile!
Pray, set it down and rest you. When this burns,
'T will weep for having wearied you. My father
Is hard at study; pray now, rest yourself;
He's safe for these three hours.
  FERDINAND.   O most dear mistress,
The sun will set before I shall discharge
What I must strive to do.
  MIRANDA.   If you'll sit down,
I'll bear your logs the while: pray, give me that;
I'll carry it to the pile.
  FERDINAND.   No, precious creature;
I had rather crack my sinews, break my back,
Than you should such dishonour undergo,
While I sit lazy by.
  MIRANDA.   It would become me
As well as it does you; and I should do it
With much more ease, for my good will is to it,
And yours it is against.
  PROSPERO.   Poor worm, thou art infected!
This visitation shows it.
  MIRANDA.   You look wearily.
  FERDINAND.   No, noble mistress; 't is fresh morning with
  me
When you are by at night. I do beseech you—
Chiefly that I might set it in my prayers—
What is your name?
  MIRANDA.   Miranda.—O my father,
I have broke your hest to say so!
  FERDINAND.   Admir'd [7] Miranda!
Indeed the top of admiration! worth
What's dearest to the world! Full many a lady
I have ey'd with best regard, and many a time
Th' harmony of their tongues hath into bondage

---

7. Admir'd—admirable (translating the name, Miranda).

Brought my too diligent ear; for several virtues
Have I lik'd several women, never any
With so full soul, but some defect in her
Did quarrel with the noblest grace she ow'd
And put it to the foil; [8] but you, O you,
So perfect and so peerless, are created
Of every creature's best!

MIRANDA.   I do not know
One of my sex; no woman's face remember,
Save, from my glass,[9] mine own; nor have I seen
More that I may call men than you, good friend,
And my dear father: how features are abroad,[10]
I am skilless[11] of; but, by my modesty,
The jewel in my dower, I would not wish
Any companion in the world but you;
Nor can imagination form a shape,
Besides yourself, to like of. But I prattle
Something too wildly, and my father's precepts
I therein do forget.

FERDINAND.   I am in my condition
A prince, Miranda; I do think, a king;
I would, not so!—and would no more endure
This wooden slavery[12] than to suffer
The flesh-fly blow my mouth. Hear my soul speak.
The very instant that I saw you, did
My heart fly to your service; there resides,
To make me slave to it; and for your sake
Am I this patient log-man.

MIRANDA.   Do you love me?

FERDINAND.   O heaven, O earth, bear witness to this sound,
And crown what I profess with kind event[13]
If I speak true! if hollowly, invert
What best is boded [14] me to mischief! I
Beyond all limit of what else i' th' world
Do love, prize, honour you.

---

8. put it to the foil—defeated it.   9. glass—mirror.
10. abroad—elsewhere.   11. skilless—ignorant.
12. wooden slavery—slavery to the woodpile.
13. event—outcome.   14. boded—fated.

MIRANDA.   I am a fool
To weep at what I am glad of.
PROSPERO.   [*Apart.*]   Fair encounter
Of two most rare affections! Heavens rain grace
On that which breeds between 'em!
FERDINAND.   Wherefore weep you?
MIRANDA.   At mine unworthiness, that dare not offer
What I desire to give, and much less take
What I shall die to want.[15] But this is trifling;
And all the more it seeks to hide itself,
The bigger bulk it shows. Hence, bashful cunning!
And prompt me, plain and holy innocence!
I am your wife, if you will marry me;
If not, I'll die your maid: [16] to be your fellow[17]
You may deny me; but I'll be your servant,
Whether you will or no.
FERDINAND.   My mistress,[18] dearest;
And I thus humble ever.
MIRANDA.   My husband, then?
FERDINAND.   Ay, with a heart as willing
As bondage e'er of freedom: here's my hand.
MIRANDA.   And mine, with my heart in 't: and now farewell
Till half an hour hence.
FERDINAND.   A thousand thousand!
                    Exeunt FERDINAND *and* MIRANDA *severally.*
PROSPERO.   So glad of this as they I cannot be,
Who[19] are surpris'd withal; [20] but my rejoicing
At nothing can be more. I'll to my book,
For yet ere supper-time must I perform
Much business appertaining.   *Exit.*

---

15. to want—if I lack.
16. maid—maidservant.
17. fellow—wife.
18. mistress—sovereign lady.
19. Who—i.e., Ferdinand and Miranda.
20. withal—with it.

[ACT III · 2] *Another part of the island.*

Enter CALIBAN, STEPHANO, *and* TRINCULO.

STEPHANO.   Tell not me: when the butt is out,[1] we will drink water; not a drop before; therefore bear up, and board 'em. Servant-monster, drink to me.

TRINCULO.   Servant-monster! the folly of this island! They say there's but five upon this isle: we are three of them; if th' other two be brained like us, the state totters.

STEPHANO.   Drink, servant-monster, when I bid thee. Thy eyes are almost set[2] in thy head.

TRINCULO.   Where should they be set else? He were a brave monster indeed, if they were set in his tail.

STEPHANO.   My man-monster hath drowned his tongue in sack: for my part, the sea cannot drown me; I swam, ere I could recover the shore, five and thirty leagues off and on. By this light, thou shalt be my lieutenant, monster, or my standard.[3]

TRINCULO.   Your lieutenant, if you list; he's no standard.[4]

STEPHANO.   We'll not run, Monsieur Monster.

TRINCULO.   Nor go[5] neither; but you'll lie like dogs and yet say nothing neither.

STEPHANO.   Moon-calf, speak once in thy life, if thou beest a good moon-calf.

CALIBAN.   How does thy honour? Let me lick thy shoe. I'll not serve him; he is not valiant.

TRINCULO.   Thou liest, most ignorant monster! I am in case[6] to justle a constable. Why, thou deboshed[7] fish, thou, was there ever man a coward that hath drunk so much sack as I to-day? Wilt thou tell a monstrous lie, being but half a fish and half a monster?

CALIBAN.   Lo, how he mocks me! Wilt thou let him, my lord?

TRINCULO.   "Lord" quoth he! That a monster should be such a natural![8]

CALIBAN.   Lo, lo, again! Bite him to death, I prithee.

---

1. out—empty.   2. set—closed from drink.
3. standard—junior officer.
4. standard—punning on Caliban's drunken unsteadiness.
5. go—walk.   6. case—condition.
7. deboshed—debauched.   8. natural—idiot.

STEPHANO.   Trinculo, keep a good tongue in your head. If you prove a mutineer,—the next tree! The poor monster's my subject and he shall not suffer indignity.

CALIBAN.   I thank my noble lord. Wilt thou be pleas'd
To hearken once again to the suit I made to thee?

STEPHANO.   Marry, will I; kneel and repeat it. I will stand, and so shall Trinculo.

Enter ARIEL, *invisible.*

CALIBAN.   As I told thee before, I am subject to a tyrant, a sorcerer, that by his cunning hath cheated me of the island.

ARIEL.   Thou liest.

CALIBAN.   Thou liest, thou jesting monkey, thou.
I would my valiant master would destroy thee!
I do not lie.

STEPHANO.   Trinculo, if you trouble him any more in 's tale, by this hand, I will supplant⁹ some of your teeth.

TRINCULO.   Why, I said nothing.

STEPHANO.   Mum, then, and no more. Proceed.

CALIBAN.   I say, by sorcery he got this isle;
From me he got it. If thy greatness will
Revenge it on him,—for I know thou dar'st,
But this thing dare not,—

STEPHANO.   That's most certain.

CALIBAN.   Thou shalt be lord of it and I'll serve thee.

STEPHANO.   How now shall this be compassed? ¹⁰
Canst thou bring me to the party?

CALIBAN.   Yea, yea, my lord. I'll yield him thee asleep,
Where thou mayst knock a nail into his head.

ARIEL.   Thou liest; thou canst not.

CALIBAN.   What a pied ninny¹¹ 's this! Thou scurvy patch! ¹²
I do beseech thy greatness, give him blows
And take his bottle from him. When that's gone
He shall drink nought but brine; for I'll not show him
Where the quick freshes¹³ are.

STEPHANO.   Trinculo, run into no further danger. Interrupt

---

9. supplant—knock out.   10. compassed—effected.
11. pied ninny—particolored fool.   12. patch—fool.
13. quick freshes—fresh springs.

the monster one word further, and, by this hand, I'll turn my mercy out o' doors and make a stock-fish[14] of thee.

TRINCULO. Why, what did I? I did nothing. I'll go farther off.

STEPHANO. Didst thou not say he lied?

ARIEL. Thou liest.

STEPHANO. Do I so? Take thou that. [*Beats him.*] As you like this, give me the lie another time.

TRINCULO. I did not give the lie. Out o' your wits and hearing too? A pox o' your bottle! this can sack and drinking do. A murrain[15] on your monster, and the devil take your fingers!

CALIBAN. Ha, ha, ha!

STEPHANO. Now, forward with your tale. Prithee, stand farther off.

CALIBAN. Beat him enough: after a little time I'll beat him too.

STEPHANO. Stand farther. Come, proceed.

CALIBAN. Why, as I told thee, 't is a custom with him,
I' th' afternoon to sleep. There thou mayst brain him,
Having first seiz'd his books, or with a log
Batter his skull, or paunch[16] him with a stake,
Or cut his wezand [17] with thy knife. Remember
First to possess his books; for without them
He's but a sot, as I am, nor hath not
One spirit to command: they all do hate him
As rootedly as I. Burn but his books.
He has brave utensils,[18]—for so he calls them,—
Which, when he has a house, he'll deck withal.
And that most deeply to consider is
The beauty of his daughter: he himself
Calls her a nonpareil: [19] I never saw a woman
But only Sycorax my dam and she;
But she as far surpasseth Sycorax
As great'st does least.

STEPHANO. Is it so brave a lass?

---

14. stock-fish—dried cod, beaten before cooking.
15. murrain—plague.   16. paunch—disembowel.
17. wezand—throat.   18. brave utensils—fine furnishings.
19. nonpareil—without a rival.

CALIBAN.   Ay, lord; she will become thy bed, I warrant,
And bring thee forth brave brood.

STEPHANO.   Monster, I will kill this man: his daughter and
I will be king and queen,—save our Graces!—and Trinculo
and thyself shall be viceroys. Dost thou like the plot, Trinculo?

TRINCULO.   Excellent.

STEPHANO.   Give me thy hand: I am sorry I beat thee; but,
while thou liv'st, keep a good tongue in thy head.

CALIBAN.   Within this half hour will he be asleep.
Wilt thou destroy him then?

STEPHANO.   Ay, on mine honour.

ARIEL.   This will I tell my master.

CALIBAN.   Thou mak'st me merry; I am full of pleasure.
Let us be jocund. Will you troll the catch[20]
You taught me but while-ere?

STEPHANO.   At thy request, monster, I will do reason, any
reason. Come on, Trinculo, let us sing.   [*Sings.*]

> Flout 'em and scout 'em
> And scout 'em and flout 'em;
> Thought is free.

CALIBAN.   That's not the tune.

              [ARIEL *plays the tune on a tabor*[21] *and pipe.*]

STEPHANO.   What is this same?

TRINCULO.   This is the tune of our catch, played by the
picture of Nobody.[22]

STEPHANO.   If thou beest a man, show thyself in thy likeness.
If thou beest a devil, take 't as thou list.

TRINCULO.   O, forgive me my sins!

STEPHANO.   He that dies pays all debts. I defy thee. Mercy
upon us!

CALIBAN.   Art thou afeard?

STEPHANO.   No, monster, not I.

CALIBAN.   Be not afeard. The isle is full of noises,
Sounds and sweet airs, that give delight and hurt not.
Sometimes a thousand twangling instruments
Will hum about mine ears, and sometime voices

---

20. troll the catch—sing the round.   21. tabor—small drum.
22. picture of Nobody—an invisible musician.

That, if I then had wak'd after long sleep,
Will make me sleep again; and then, in dreaming,
The clouds methought would open and show riches
Ready to drop upon me, that, when I wak'd,
I cried to dream again.

STEPHANO. This will prove a brave kingdom to me, where I shall have my music for nothing.

CALIBAN. When Prospero is destroyed.

STEPHANO. That shall be by and by. I remember the story.

TRINCULO. The sound is going away. Let's follow it, and after do our work.

STEPHANO. Lead, monster; we'll follow. I would I could see this taborer; he lays it on.

TRINCULO. Wilt come? I'll follow Stephano.   *Exeunt.*

[ACT III • 3] *Another part of the island.*

Enter ALONSO, SEBASTIAN, ANTONIO, GONZALO, ADRIAN, FRANCISCO, *etc.*

GONZALO. By 'r lakin,[1] I can go no further, sir;
My old bones aches. Here's a maze trod indeed
Through forth-rights[2] and meanders! By your patience,
I needs must rest me.

ALONSO.   Old lord, I cannot blame thee,
Who am myself attach'd [3] with weariness
To th' dulling of my spirits. Sit down, and rest.
Even here I will put off [4] my hope and keep it
No longer for my flatterer: he is drown'd
Whom thus we stray to find, and the sea mocks
Our frustrate search on land. Well, let him go.

ANTONIO. [*Aside to* SEBASTIAN.] I am right glad that he's
    so out of hope.
Do not, for one repulse, forego the purpose
That you resolv'd t' effect.

SEBASTIAN. [*Aside to* ANTONIO.] The next advantage[5]
Will we take throughly.

---

1. By'r lakin—by the Virgin Mary.
2. forth-rights—straight paths.   3. attach'd—overcome.
4. put off—abandon.   5. advantage—opportunity.

ANTONIO.   [*Aside to* SEBASTIAN.] Let it be to-night;
For, now they are oppress'd with travel, they
Will not, nor cannot, use such vigilance
As when they are fresh.
SEBASTIAN.   [*Aside to* ANTONIO.] I say, to-night. No more.

Solemn and strange music; and PROSPERO *on the top[6] invisible.*
Enter several strange shapes, bringing in a banquet; [7] *and dance*
about it with gentle actions of salutation; and, inviting the King,
etc., to eat, they depart.

ALONSO.   What harmony is this? My good friends, hark!
GONZALO.   Marvellous sweet music!
ALONSO.   Give us kind keepers, heavens! What were these?
SEBASTIAN.   A living drollery.[8] Now I will believe
That there are unicorns,[9] that in Arabia
There is one tree, the phoenix' throne, one phoenix[10]
At this hour reigning there.
ANTONIO.   I'll believe both;
And what does else want credit,[11] come to me,
And I'll be sworn 't is true. Travellers ne'er did lie,
Though fools at home condemn 'em.
GONZALO.   If in Naples
I should report this now, would they believe me?
If I should say, I saw such islanders—
For, certes,[12] these are people of the island—
Who, though they are of monstrous shape, yet, note,
Their manners are more gentle-kind, than of
Our human generation you shall find
Many, nay, almost any.
PROSPERO.   [*Aside.*] Honest lord,
Thou hast said well; for some of you there present
Are worse than devils.
ALONSO.   I cannot too much muse[13]

---

6. on the top—on the upper stage.
7. banquet—a light supper of pastry, etc.
8. drollery—puppet show.
9. unicorns—mythical horses with horns on their heads.
10. phoenix—mythical bird, of which only one was alive at a time.
11. want credit—is not believed.
12. certes—surely.   13. muse—wonder at.

Such shapes, such gesture, and such sound, expressing,
Although they want the use of tongue, a kind
Of excellent dumb discourse.

PROSPERO.   [*Aside*.] Praise in departing.[14]

FRANCISCO.   They vanish'd strangely.

SEBASTIAN.   No matter, since
They have left their viands behind, for we have stomachs.
Will 't please you taste of what is here?

ALONSO.   Not I.

GONZALO.   Faith, sir, you need not fear. When we were boys,
Who would believe that there were mountaineers
Dew-lapp'd like bulls, whose throats had hanging at 'em
Wallets of flesh? or that there were such men
Whose heads stood in their breasts? which now we find
Each putter-out of five for one[15] will bring us
Good warrant of.

ALONSO.   I will stand to and feed,
Although my last: no matter, since I feel
The best is past. Brother, my lord the Duke,
Stand to and do as we.

Thunder and lightning. Enter ARIEL, *like a harpy;* [16] *claps his
wings upon the table; and, with a quaint device,*[17] *the banquet
vanishes.*

ARIEL.   You are three men of sin, whom Destiny,
That hath to instrument[18] this lower world
And what is in 't, the never-surfeited [19] sea
Hath caus'd to belch up you; and on this island
Where man doth not inhabit; you 'mongst men
Being most unfit to live. I have made you mad;
And even with such-like valour men hang and drown
Their proper[20] selves.   [ALONSO, SEBASTIAN, *etc., draw.*]
                        You fools! I and my fellows

---

14. Praise in departing—a proverb, save your applause till you see how
it ends.
15. putter-out of five for one—traveler to strange countries.
16. harpy—mythical creature, half-hawk, half-woman.
17. a quaint device—stage mechanism.
18. to instrument—as its instrument.
19. never-surfeited—always hungry.   20. proper—own.

Are ministers of Fate: the elements,
Of whom your swords are temper'd,[21] may as well
Wound the loud winds, or with bemock'd-at stabs
Kill the still-closing waters, as diminish
One dowle[22] that's in my plume: my fellow-ministers
Are like invulnerable. If you could hurt,
Your swords are now too massy[23] for your strengths
And will not be uplifted. But remember—
For that's my business to you—that you three
From Milan did supplant[24] good Prospero;
Expos'd unto the sea, which hath requit it,[25]
Him and his innocent child; for which foul deed
The powers, delaying, not forgetting, have
Incens'd the seas and shores, yea, all the creatures,
Against your peace. Thee of thy son, Alonso,
They have bereft; and do pronounce by me
Ling'ring perdition, worse than any death
Can be at once, shall step by step attend
You and your ways; whose wraths to guard you from—
Which here, in this most desolate isle, else falls
Upon your heads—is nothing but heart's sorrow[26]
And a clear life ensuing.
[*He vanishes in thunder; then, to soft music, enter the shapes
again, and dance, with mocks and mows, and carrying out the
table.*]
   PROSPERO.   Bravely the figure of this harpy hast thou
Perform'd, my Ariel; a grace it had, devouring.
Of my instruction hast thou nothing bated
In what thou hadst to say; so, with good life[27]
And observation strange,[28] my meaner ministers
Their several kinds have done. My high charms work,
And these mine enemies are all knit up
In their distractions: they now are in my power;
And in these fits I leave them, while I visit

---

21. temper'd—composed.   22. dowle—bit of down.
23. massy—heavy.   24. supplant—expel.
25. requit it—repaid you.   26. heart's sorrow—repentance.
27. with good life—realistically.
28. observation strange—remarkable obedience.

Young Ferdinand, whom they suppose is drown'd,
And his and mine lov'd darling.   *Exit.*

GONZALO.   I' th' name of something holy, sir, why stand you
In this strange stare?

ALONSO.   O, it is monstrous, monstrous!
Methought the billows spoke and told me of it;
The winds did sing it to me, and the thunder,
That deep and dreadful organ-pipe, pronounc'd
The name of Prosper; it did bass [29] my trespass.[30]
Therefore my son i' th' ooze is bedded, and
I'll seek him deeper than e'er plummet sounded
And with him there lie mudded.   *Exit.*

SEBASTIAN.   But one fiend at a time,
I'll fight their legions o'er.

ANTONIO.   I'll be thy second.
                    Exeunt SEBASTIAN *and* ANTONIO.

GONZALO.   All three of them are desperate: their great guilt,
Like poison given to work a great time after,
Now gins to bite the spirits. I do beseech you
That are of suppler joints, follow them swiftly
And hinder them from what this ecstasy[31]
May now provoke them to.

ADRIAN.   Follow, I pray you.
                    Exeunt omnes.

---

29. bass—in deep tones speak.   30. my trespass—of my sin.
31. ecstasy—madness.

[ACT IV • 1] *Before Prospero's cell.*

Enter PROSPERO, FERDINAND, *and* MIRANDA.

PROSPERO.   If I have too austerely punish'd you,
Your compensation makes amends, for I
Have given you here a third of mine own life,
Or that for which I live; who once again
I tender to thy hand. All thy vexations
Were but my trials of thy love, and thou
Hast strangely[1] stood the test. Here, afore Heaven,

---

1. Strangely—remarkably well.

I ratify this my rich gift. O Ferdinand,
Do not smile at me that I boast her off,[2]
For thou shalt find she will outstrip all praise
And make it halt[3] behind her.
  FERDINAND.   I do believe it
Against an oracle.[4]
  PROSPERO. Then, as my gift and thine own acquisition
Worthily purchas'd, take my daughter: but
If thou dost break her virgin-knot before
All sanctimonious ceremonies may
With full and holy rite be minister'd,
No sweet aspersion[5] shall the heavens let fall
To make this contract grow; but barren Hate,
Sour-eyed Disdain and Discord shall bestrew
The union of your bed with weeds so loathly
That you shall hate it both. Therefore take heed,
As Hymen's[6] lamps shall light you.
  FERDINAND.   As I hope
For quiet days, fair issue, and long life,
With such love as 't is now, the murkiest den,
The most opportune place, the strong'st suggestion[7]
Our worser genius can,[8] shall never melt
Mine honour into lust, to take away
The edge of that day's celebration
When I shall think or Phoebus' steeds are founder'd [9]
Or Night kept chain'd below.
  PROSPERO.   Fairly spoke.
Sit then and talk with her; she is thine own.
What, Ariel! my industrious servant, Ariel!

Enter ARIEL.

  ARIEL. What would my potent master? Here I am.
  PROSPERO. Thou and thy meaner fellows your last service
Did worthily perform; and I must use you

2. boast her off—praise her so highly. 3. halt—limp.
4. Against an oracle—even if a god declared otherwise.
5. aspersion—dew. 6. Hymen—god of marriage.
7. suggestion—temptation.
8. worser genius can—evil nature is capable of.
9. Phoebus' steeds are foundered—the horses of the sun are lamed.

In such another trick. Go bring the rabble,
O'er whom I give thee power, here to this place.
Incite them to quick motion; for I must
Bestow upon the eyes of this young couple
Some vanity[10] of mine art. It is my promise,
And they expect it from me.

ARIEL.   Presently? [11]

PROSPERO.   Ay, with a twink.[12]

ARIEL.

          Before you can say "come" and "go."
          And breathe twice and cry "so, so,"
          Each one, tripping on his toe,
          Will be here with mop[13] and mow.
          Do you love me, master? No?

PROSPERO.   Dearly, my delicate Ariel. Do not approach
Till thou dost hear me call.

ARIEL.   Well, I conceive.[14]   *Exit.*

PROSPERO.   Look thou be true; do not give dalliance[15]
Too much the rein: the strongest oaths are straw
To the fire i' th' blood. Be more abstemious,
Or else, good night your vow!

FERDINAND.   I warrant you, sir;
The white cold virgin snow upon my heart
Abates the ardour of my liver.[16]

PROSPERO.   Well.
Now come, my Ariel! bring a corollary,[17]
Rather than want a spirit. Appear and pertly! [18]
No tongue! all eyes! Be silent.   [*Soft music.*]

Enter IRIS.[19]

IRIS.   Ceres,[20] most bounteous lady, thy rich leas[21]
Of wheat, rye, barley, vetches, oats, and pease;

---

10. vanity—trifling exhibition.   11. Presently—at once.
12. with a twink—in the twinkling of an eye.   13. mop—grin.
14. conceive—understand.   15. dalliance—love-making.
16. liver—believed to be the seat of the passion of love.
17. corollary—more spirits than are necessary.
18. pertly—promptly.
19. Iris—the rainbow, female messenger of the gods.
20. Ceres—goddess of harvest.   21. leas—meadows.

Thy turfy mountains, where live nibbling sheep,
And flat meads thatch'd with stover,[22] them to keep;
Thy banks with pioned and twilled [23] brims,
Which spongy April at thy hest betrims
To make cold nymphs chaste crowns; and thy broom-groves,
Whose shadow the dismissed bachelor[24] loves,
Being lass-lorn; thy pole-clipp'd vineyard;
And thy sea-marge, sterile and rocky-hard,
Where thou thyself dost air;—the queen o' th' sky,
Whose watery arch and messenger am I,
Bids thee leave these, and with her sovereign grace,
Here on this grass-plot, in this very place,
To come and sport; her peacocks fly amain.[25]
Approach, rich Ceres, her to entertain.

Enter CERES.

   CERES.   Hail, many-coloured messenger, that ne'er
Dost disobey the wife of Jupiter;
Who with thy saffron wings upon my flowers
Diffusest honey-drops, refreshing showers,
And with each end of thy blue bow dost crown
My bosky[26] acres and my unshrubb'd down,[27]
Rich scarf to my proud earth; why hath thy queen
Summon'd me hither, to this short-grass'd green?
   IRIS.   A contract of true love to celebrate;
And some donation freely to estate[28]
On the blest lovers.
   CERES.   Tell me, heavenly bow,
If Venus or her son,[29] as thou dost know,
Do now attend the Queen? Since they did plot
The means that dusky Dis[30] my daughter got,
Her and her blind boy's scandal'd [31] company
I have forsworn.

---

22. stover—fodder.
23. pioned and twilled—channeled and indented.
24. dismissed bachelor—rejected lover.   25. amain—quickly.
26. bosky—wooded.   27. down—upland.
28. estate—bestow.   29. son—i.e., blind Cupid.
30. Dis—Pluto, who made Ceres' daughter queen of Hades.
31. scandal'd—disgraced.

IRIS.   Of her society
Be not afraid: I met her deity
Cutting the clouds towards Paphos,[32] and her son
Dove-drawn with her. Here thought they to have done
Some wanton charm upon this man and maid,
Whose vows are, that no bed-right shall be paid
Till Hymen's torch be lighted; but in vain.
Mars's hot minion[33] is return'd again;
Her waspish-headed son has broke his arrows,
Swears he will shoot no more, but play with sparrows
And be a boy right out.   [JUNO *descends.*]
   CERES.   Highest queen of state,
Great Juno, comes; I know her by her gait.
   JUNO.   How does my bounteous sister? Go with me
To bless this twain, that they may prosperous be
And honour'd in their issue.
   JUNO.   [*Sings.*]

         Honour, riches, marriage-blessing,
         Long continuance, and increasing,
         Hourly joys be still upon you!
         Juno sings her blessings on you.

   CERES.   [*Sings.*]

         Earth's increase foison plenty,
         Barns and garners never empty,
         Vines with clustering bunches growing,
         Plants with goodly burden bowing.
         Spring come to you at the farthest
         In the very end of harvest!
         Scarcity and want shall shun you;
         Ceres' blessing so is on you.

   FERDINAND.   This is a most majestic vision, and
Harmonious charmingly. May I be bold
To think these spirits?
   PROSPERO.   Spirits, which by mine art
I have from their confines call'd to enact
My present fancies.

---

32. Paphos—the holy city of Venus.
33. Mars's hot minion—i.e., Venus, mistress of the war god.

FERDINAND.   Let me live here ever;
So rare a wonder'd father and a wise
Makes this place Paradise.
  PROSPERO.   Sweet, now, silence!
Juno and Ceres whisper seriously.
There's something else to do; hush, and be mute,
Or else our spell is marr'd.
    [JUNO *and* CERES *whisper, and send* IRIS *on employment.*]
  IRIS. You nymphs, call'd Naiads, of the wandring brooks,
With your sedg'd crowns³⁴ and ever-harmless looks,
Leave your crisp³⁵ channels, and on this green land
Answer your summons; Juno does command.
Come, temperate nymphs, and help to celebrate
A contract of true love; be not too late.

Enter certain NYMPHS.

You sunburnt sicklemen,³⁶ of August weary,
Come hither from the furrow and be merry.
Make holiday; your rye-straw hats put on
And these fresh nymphs encounter every one
In country footing.³⁷

Enter certain REAPERS, *properly habited: they join with the*
NYMPHS *in a graceful dance; towards the end whereof* PROSPERO
    starts suddenly, and speaks.

  PROSPERO. [*Aside.*] I had forgot that foul conspiracy
Of the beast Caliban and his confederates
Against my life. The minute of their plot
Is almost come. [*To the Spirits.*] Well done! avoid; no more!
    [*To a strange hollow and confused noise, they heavily*³⁸
    vanish.]
  FERDINAND. This is strange. Your father's in some passion
That works him strongly.
  MIRANDA.   Never till this day
Saw I him touch'd with anger, so distemper'd.
  PROSPERO. You do look, my son, in a mov'd sort,

---

34. sedg'd crowns—garlands of water grass.
35. crisp—rippling. 36. sicklemen—harvesters.
37. in country footing—in a country dance. 38. heavily—slowly.

As if you were dismay'd: be cheerful, sir,
Our revels now are ended. These our actors,
As I foretold you, were all spirits, and
Are melted into air, into thin air;
And, like the baseless fabric of this vision,
The cloud-capp'd towers, the gorgeous palaces,
The solemn temples, the great globe itself,
Yea, all which it inherit,[39] shall dissolve
And, like this insubstantial pageant faded,
Leave not a rack[40] behind. We are such stuff
As dreams are made on, and our little life
Is rounded [41] with a sleep. Sir, I am vex'd,—
Bear with my weakness—my old brain is troubled.
Be not disturb'd with my infirmity.
If you be pleas'd, retire into my cell
And there repose: a turn or two I'll walk,
To still my beating mind.

FERDINAND. MIRANDA.   We wish your peace   *Exeunt.*
PROSPERO.   Come with a thought. I thank thee, Ariel; come.

Enter ARIEL.

ARIEL.   Thy thoughts I cleave to. What's thy pleasure?
PROSPERO.   Spirit,
We must prepare to meet with Caliban.
ARIEL.   Ay, my commander. When I presented [42] Ceres,
I thought to have told thee of it, but I fear'd
Lest I might anger thee.
PROSPERO.   Say again, where didst thou leave these varlets?
ARIEL.   I told you, sir, they were red-hot with drinking;
So full of valour that they smote the air
For breathing in their faces; beat the ground
For kissing of their feet; yet always bending[43]
Towards their project. Then I beat my tabor;
At which, like unback'd [44] colts, they prick'd their ears,
Advanc'd their eyelids, lifted up their noses
As they smelt music. So I charm'd their ears

---

39. inherit—inhabit.   40. rack—cloud.
41. rounded—encompassed.   42. presented—enacted.
43. bending—directing their steps.   44. unback'd—unbroken.

That calf-like they my lowing follow'd through
Tooth'd briers, sharp furzes, pricking gorse, and thorns,
Which enter'd their frail shins. At last I left them
I' th' filthy-mantled [45] pool beyond your cell,
There dancing up to th' chins, that the foul lake
O'erstunk their feet.

PROSPERO.   This was well done, my bird.
Thy shape invisible retain thou still.
The trumpery[46] in my house, go bring it hither,
For stale[47] to catch these thieves.

ARIEL.   I go, I go.   *Exit.*

PROSPERO.   A devil, a born devil, on whose nature
Nurture[48] can never stick; on whom my pains,
Humanely taken, all, all lost, quite lost;
And as with age his body uglier grows,
So his mind cankers.[49] I will plague them all,
Even to roaring.

Re-enter ARIEL, *loaden with glittering apparel,*[50] *etc.*

                Come, hang them on this line.[51]

PROSPERO *and* ARIEL *remain, invisible. Enter* CALIBAN, STEPH-
ANO, *and* TRINCULO, *all wet.*

CALIBAN.   Pray you, tread softly, that the blind mole may
   not
Hear a foot fall; we now are near his cell.

STEPHANO.   Monster, your fairy, which you say is a harmless fairy, has done little better than played the Jack[52] with us.

TRINCULO.   Monster, I do smell all horse-piss, at which my
nose is in great indignation.

STEPHANO.   So is mine. Do you hear, monster? If I should
take a displeasure against you, look you,—

TRINCULO.   Thou wert but a lost monster.

CALIBAN.   Good my lord, give me thy favour still.

---

45. filthy-mantl'd—scum-covered.
46. trumpery—cheap, glittering clothes.   47. stale—bait.
48. Nurture—education.   49. cankers—grows malignant.
50. glittering apparel—the "trumpery."
51. line—linden tree.   52. Jack—knave.

Be patient, for the prize I'll bring thee to
Shall hoodwink[53] this mischance; therefore speak softly.
All's hush'd as midnight yet.

TRINCULO.   Ay, but to lose our bottles in the pool,—

STEPHANO.   There is not only disgrace and dishonour in
that, monster, but an infinite loss.

TRINCULO.   That's more to me than my wetting; yet this is
your harmless fairy, monster!

STEPHANO.   I will fetch off [54] my bottle, though I be o'er
ears for my labour.

CALIBAN.   Prithee, my king, be quiet. See'st thou here,
This is the mouth o' th' cell. No noise, and enter.
Do that good mischief [55] which may make this island
Thine own for ever, and I, thy Caliban,
For aye thy foot-licker.

STEPHANO.   Give me thy hand. I do begin to have bloody
thoughts.

TRINCULO.   O King Stephano! O peer! O worthy Stephano!
look what a wardrobe here is for thee!

CALIBAN.   Let it alone, thou fool; it is but trash.

TRINCULO.   O, ho, monster! we know what belongs to a
frippery.[56] O King Stephano!

STEPHANO.   Put off that gown, Trinculo; by this hand, I'll
have that gown.

TRINCULO.   Thy Grace shall have it.

CALIBAN.   The dropsy drown[57] this fool! what do you mean
To dote thus on such luggage? [58] Let 't alone
And do the murder first. If he awake,
From toe to crown he'll fill our skins with pinches,
Make us strange stuff.

STEPHANO.   Be you quiet, monster. Mistress line, is not this
my jerkin? [59] Now is the jerkin under the line: now, jerkin, you
are like to lose your hair[60] and prove a bald jerkin.

---

53. hoodwink—make you forget.   54. fetch off—recover.
55. mischief—i.e., the murder of Prospero.
56. frippery—an old-clothes shop.   57. drown—choke.
58. luggage—cumbersome stuff.
59. jerkin—jacket, in this instance, trimmed with fur.
60. lose your hair—from a tropical fever; a lame jest depending on
the two meanings of *line: tree* and *equator.*

TRINCULO.   Do, do; we steal by line and level,[61] an 't like your Grace.

STEPHANO.   I thank thee for that jest; here's a garment for 't. Wit shall not go unrewarded while I am king of this country. "Steal by line and level" is an excellent pass of pate; [62] there's another garment for 't.

TRINCULO.   Monster, come, put some lime upon your fingers, and away with the rest.

CALIBAN.   I will have none on 't. We shall lose our time, And all be turn'd to barnacles,[63] or to apes With foreheads villanous low.

STEPHANO.   Monster, lay-to your fingers. Help to bear this away where my hogshead of wine is, or I'll turn you out of my kingdom. Go-to, carry this.

TRINCULO.   And this.

STEPHANO.   Ay, and this.

A noise of hunters heard. Enter divers Spirits, in shape of dogs and hounds, hunting them about, PROSPERO *and* ARIEL *setting them on.*

PROSPERO.   Hey, Mountain,[64] hey!

ARIEL.   Silver! there it goes, Silver!

PROSPERO.   Fury, Fury! there, Tyrant, there! hark! hark!

[CALIBAN, STEPHANO, *and* TRINCULO *are driven out.*]

Go charge my goblins that they grind their joints
With dry convulsions, shorten up their sinews
With aged cramps, and more pinch-spotted make them
Than pard [65] or cat o' mountain.[66]

ARIEL.   Hark, they roar!

PROSPERO.   Let them be hunted soundly. At this hour
Lies at my mercy all mine enemies.
Shortly shall all my labours end, and thou
Shalt have the air at freedom. For a little
Follow, and do me service.   *Exeunt.*

---

61. line and level—plumb line and carpenter's level.
62. pass of pate—head work.
63. barnacles—wild geese.
64. Mountain, etc.—names of hounds.
65. pard—leopard.
66. cat o' mountain—lynx.

[ACT V • 1] *Before Prospero's cell.*

Enter PROSPERO *in his magic robes, and* ARIEL.

PROSPERO.   Now does my project gather to a head.
My charms crack not; my spirits obey; and Time
Goes upright[1] with his carriage.[2] How's the day?
ARIEL.   On the sixth hour; at which time, my lord,
You said our work should cease.
PROSPERO.   I did say so,
When first I rais'd the tempest. Say, my spirit,
How fares the King and 's followers?
ARIEL.   Confin'd together
In the same fashion as you gave in charge,
Just as you left them; all prisoners, sir,
In the line-grove which weather-fends[3] your cell;
They cannot budge till your release. The King,
His brother, and yours, abide all three distracted,
And the remainder mourning over them,
Brimful of sorrow and dismay; but chiefly
Him that you term'd, sir, "The good old lord Gonzalo,"
His tears runs down his beard, like winter's drops
From eaves of reeds.[4] Your charm so strongly works 'em
That if you now beheld them, your affections
Would become tender.
PROSPERO.   Dost thou think so, spirit?
ARIEL.   Mine would, sir, were I human.
PROSPERO.   And mine shall.
Hast thou, which art but air, a touch, a feeling
Of their afflictions, and shall not myself,
One of their kind, that relish all as sharply[5]
Passion[6] as they, be kindlier mov'd than thou art?
Though with their high wrongs I am struck to the quick,
Yet with my nobler reason 'gainst my fury

---

1. Time Goes upright—everything is proceeding on schedule.
2. carriage—burden.
3. weather-fends—protects against the weather.
4. reeds—a thatched roof.
5. relish all as sharply—am as keenly sensitive to.
6. Passion—suffering.

Do I take part: the rarer[7] action is
In virtue[8] than in vengeance: they being penitent,
The sole drift[9] of my purpose doth extend
Not a frown further. Go release them, Ariel.
My charms I'll break, their senses I'll restore,
And they shall be themselves.

    ARIEL.   I'll fetch them, sir.   *Exit.*

    PROSPERO.   Ye elves of hills, brooks, standing lakes, and
       groves,
And ye that on the sands with printless foot
Do chase the ebbing Neptune,[10] and do fly him
When he comes back; you demi-puppets[11] that
By moonshine do the green sour ringlets[12] make,
Whereof the ewe not bites; and you whose pastime
Is to make midnight mushrooms, that rejoice
To hear the solemn curfew; by whose aid,
Weak masters though ye be, I have bedimm'd
The noontide sun, call'd forth the mutinous winds,
And 'twixt the green sea and the azur'd vault[13]
Set roaring war; to the dread rattling thunder
Have I given fire, and rifted [14] Jove's stout oak
With his own bolt; the strong-bas'd promontory
Have I made shake, and by the spurs[15] pluck'd up
The pine and cedar; graves at my command
Have wak'd their sleepers, op'd, and let 'em forth
By my so potent art. But this rough magic
I here abjure, and, when I have requir'd [16]
Some heavenly music, which even now I do,
To work mine end upon their senses that
This airy charm is for, I'll break my staff,
Bury it certain fathoms in the earth,
And deeper than did ever plummet sound
I'll drown my book.[17]   *[Solemn music]*

---

7. rarer—nobler.   8. virtue—self-control.
9. sole drift—tendency.   10. Neptune—sea-tide..
11. demi-puppets—tiny creatures.
12. green sour ringlets—"fairy rings."   13. azur'd vault—blue sky.
14. rifted—split.   15. spurs—roots.
16. requir'd—requested.   17. book—i.e., of magic spells.

Here enters ARIEL *before: then* ALONSO, *with a frantic gesture,*[18]
attended by GONZALO; SEBASTIAN *and* ANTONIO *in like manner,*
attended by ADRIAN *and* FRANCISCO. *They all enter the circle*
which PROSPERO *had made, and there stand charmed; which*
PROSPERO *observing, speaks.*

A solemn air[19] and the best comforter
To an unsettled fancy cure thy brains,
Now useless, boil'd within thy skull! There stand,
For you are spell-stopp'd.
Holy Gonzalo, honourable man,
Mine eyes, ev'n sociable[20] to the show of thine,
Fall fellowly drops. The charm dissolves apace,
And as the morning steals upon the night,
Melting the darkness, so their rising senses
Begin to chase the ignorant fumes that mantle[21]
Their clearer reason. O good Gonzalo,
My true preserver, and a loyal sir
To him thou follow'st! I will pay thy graces
Home[22] both in word and deed. Most cruelly
Did thou, Alonso, use me and my daughter.
Thy brother was a furtherer in the act.
Thou art pinch'd for 't now, Sebastian. Flesh and blood,
You, brother mine, that entertain'd ambition,
Expell'd remorse[23] and nature, whom, with Sebastian,
Whose inward pinches therefore are most strong,
Would here have kill'd your king, I do forgive thee,
Unnatural though thou art. Their understanding
Begins to swell, and the approaching tide
Will shortly fill the reasonable shore[24]
That now lie foul and muddy. Not one of them
That yet looks on me, or would know me! Ariel,
Fetch me the hat and rapier in my cell;
I will discase me,[25] and myself present

---

18. gesture—bearing.   19. air—melody.
20. sociable—sympathetic.   21. mantle—muffle up.
22. Home—thoroughly.   23. remorse—pity.
24. reasonable shore—shore of reason.
25. discase me—remove my magician's robe.

As I was sometime Milan: [26] quickly, spirit;
Thou shalt ere long be free.

     [ARIEL *sings and helps to attire him.*]

ARIEL.

     Where the bee sucks, there suck I.
     In a cowslip's bell I lie;
     There I couch when owls do cry.
     On the bat's back I do fly
     After summer merrily.
    Merrily, merrily shall I live now
    Under the blossom that hangs on the bough.

 PROSPERO. Why, that's my dainty Ariel! I shall miss thee;
But yet thou shalt have freedom. So, so, so.
To the King's ship, invisible as thou art;
There shalt thou find the mariners asleep
Under the hatches. The master and the boatswain
Being awake, enforce them to this place,
And presently, I prithee.
 ARIEL. I drink the air before me, and return
Or ere your pulse twice beat.   *Exit.*
 GONZALO. All torment, trouble, wonder, and amazement
Inhabits here. Some heavenly power guide us
Out of this fearful country!
 PROSPERO.   Behold, sir King,
The wronged Duke of Milan, Prospero.
For more assurance that a living prince
Does now speak to thee, I embrace thy body;
And to thee and thy company I bid
A hearty welcome.
 ALONSO.   Whe'er thou be'st he or no,
Or some enchanted trifle[27] to abuse me,
As late I have been, I not know. Thy pulse
Beats as of flesh and blood; and, since I saw thee,
Th' affliction of my mind amends, with which,
I fear, a madness held me: this must crave,
An if [28] this be at all, a most strange story.
Thy dukedom I resign and do entreat

---

26. Milan—duke of Milan. 27. trifle—apparition.
28. An if—if.

Thou pardon me my wrongs. But how should Prospero
Be living and be here?

PROSPERO.   First, noble friend,
Let me embrace thine age, whose honour cannot
Be measur'd or confin'd.

GONZALO.   Whether this be
Or be not, I'll not swear.

PROSPERO.   You do yet taste[29]
Some subtleties[30] o' the isle, that will not let you
Believe things certain. Welcome, my friends all!
[*Aside to* SEBASTIAN *and* ANTONIO.] But you, my brace of lords,
     were I so minded,
I here could pluck his Highness' frown upon you
And justify[31] you traitors. At this time
I will tell no tales.

SEBASTIAN.   [*Aside.*] The devil speaks in him.

PROSPERO.   No.
For you, most wicked sir, whom to call brother
Would even infect my mouth, I do forgive
Thy rankest fault; all of them; and require[32]
My dukedom of thee, which perforce, I know,
Thou must restore.

ALONSO.   If thou be'st Prospero,
Give us particulars of thy preservation,
How thou hast met us here, whom three hours since
Were wreck'd upon this shore, where I have lost—
How sharp the point of this remembrance is!—
My dear son Ferdinand.

PROSPERO.   I am woe for 't, sir.

ALONSO.   Irreparable is the loss, and Patience
Says it is past her cure.

PROSPERO.   I rather think
You have not sought her help, of whose soft grace
For the like loss I have her sovereign[33] aid
And rest myself content.

ALONSO.   You the like loss!

---

29. taste—experience.   30. subtleties—magic qualities.
31. justify—prove.   32. require—request.
33. sovereign—all-powerful.

PROSPERO.   As great to me as late;[34] and, súpportable
To make the dear loss, have I means much weaker
Than you may call to comfort you, for I
Have lost my daughter.

ALONSO.   A daughter?
O heavens, that they were living both in Naples,
The King and Queen there! That they were, I wish
Myself were muddled in that oozy bed
Where my son lies. When did you lose your daughter?

PROSPERO.   In this last tempest. I perceive, these lords
At this encounter do so much admire[35]
That they devour their reason and scarce think
Their eyes do offices of truth,[36] their words
Are natural breath; but, howsoe'er you have
Been justled from your senses, know for certain
That I am Prospero and that very duke
Which was thrust forth of Milan, who most strangely
Upon this shore, where you were wreck'd, was landed,
To be the lord on 't. No more yet of this;
For 't is a chronicle of day by day,
Not a relation for a breakfast nor
Befitting this first meeting. Welcome, sir;
This cell's my court. Here have I few attendants,
And subjects none abroad: [37] pray you, look in.
My dukedom since you have given me again,
I will requite[38] you with as good a thing;
At least bring forth a wonder, to content ye
As much as me my dukedom.

[*Here* PROSPERO *discovers*[39] FERDINAND *and* MIRANDA *playing
at chess.*]

MIRANDA.   Sweet lord, you play me false.

FERDINAND.   No, my dearest love,
I would not for the world.

---

34. late—recent.   35. admire—wonder.
36. do offices of truth—perform their duty truly.
37. abroad—away from home.
38. requite—repay.
39. discovers—reveals (perhaps by drawing the curtain of the inner
stage, exposing the interior of his "cell").

MIRANDA.　Yes, for a score of kingdoms you should wrangle,
And I would call it fair play.

ALONSO.　　　　　　　　　If this prove
A vision[40] of the island, one dear son
Shall I twice lose.

SEBASTIAN.　　　A most high miracle!

FERDINAND.　Though the seas threaten, they are merciful;
I have curs'd them without cause.　　　　　[*Kneels.*]

ALONSO.　　　　　　　　Now all the blessings
Of a glad father compass thee about!
Arise, and say how thou cam'st here.

MIRANDA.　　　　　　　　O, wonder!
How many goodly creatures are there here!
How beauteous mankind is! O brave new world,
That has such people in 't!

PROSPERO.　　　　　'T is new to thee.

ALONSO.　What is this maid with whom thou wast at play?
Your eld'st[41] acquaintance cannot be three hours.
Is she the goddess that hath sever'd us,
And brought us thus together?

FERDINAND.　　　　　　Sir, she is mortal,
But by immortal Providence she's mine.
I chose her when I could not ask my father
For his advice, nor thought I had one. She
Is daughter to this famous Duke of Milan,
Of whom so often I have heard renown,
But never saw before; of whom I have
Receiv'd a second life; and second father
This lady makes him to me.

ALONSO.　　　　　　　I am hers.
But, O, how oddly will it sound that I
Must ask my child [42] forgiveness!

PROSPERO.　　　　　There, sir, stop.
Let us not burden our remembrances with
A heaviness[43] that's gone.

GONZALO.　　　　I have inly[44] wept,

---

40. vision—mirage.　　41. eld'st—at the very longest.
42. child—i.e., daughter-in-law.　　43. heaviness—bitter experience.
44. inly—inwardly.

Or should have spoke ere this. Look down, you gods,
And on this couple drop a blessed crown!
For it is you that have chalk'd forth the way
Which brought us hither.
    ALONSO.   I say, Amen, Gonzalo!
    GONZALO.   Was Milan thrust from Milan, that his issue
Should become Kings of Naples? O, rejoice
Beyond a common joy, and set it down
With gold on lasting pillars: in one voyage
Did Claribel her husband find at Tunis,
And Ferdinand, her brother, found a wife
Where he himself was lost, Prospero his dukedom
In a poor isle, and all of us ourselves
When no man was his own.[45]
    ALONSO.   [*To* FERDINAND *and* MIRANDA.] Give me your
        hands.
Let grief and sorrow still embrace his heart
That doth not wish you joy!
    GONZALO.   Be it so! Amen!

Re-enter ARIEL, *with the Master and Boatswain amazedly
following.*

O, look, sir, look, sir! here is more of us.
I prophesied, if a gallows were on land,
This fellow could not drown. Now, blasphemy,[46]
That swear'st grace o'erboard, not an oath on shore?
Hast thou no mouth by land? What is the news?
    BOATSWAIN.   The best news is, that we have safely found
Our king and company; the next, our ship—
Which, but three glasses since, we gave out split—
Is tight and yare[47] and bravely rigg'd as when
We first put out to sea.
    ARIEL.   [*Aside to* PROSPERO.] Sir, all this service
Have I done since I went.
    PROSPERO.   [*Aside to* ARIEL.] My tricksy spirit!
    ALONSO.   These are not natural events; they strengthen
From strange to stranger. Say, how came you hither?

---

45. his own—in possession of his senses.
46. blasphemy—blasphemous fellow.   47. yare—ready.

BOATSWAIN.   If I did think, sir, I were well awake,
I'd strive to tell you. We were dead of sleep,
And—how we know not—all clapp'd ⁴⁸ under hatches;
Where but even now with strange and several ⁴⁹ noises
Of roaring, shrieking, howling, jingling chains,
And moe diversity of sounds, all horrible,
We were awak'd; straightway, at liberty;
Where we, in all our trim,⁵⁰ freshly beheld
Our royal, good, and gallant ship, our master
Cap'ring⁵¹ to eye her. On a trice,⁵² so please you,
Even in a dream, were we divided from them
And were brought moping⁵³ hither.
    ARIEL.   [*Aside to* PROSPERO.] Was 't well done?
    PROSPERO.   [*Aside to* ARIEL.] Bravely, my diligence. Thou
        shalt be free.
    ALONSO.   This is as strange a maze as e'er men trod;
And there is in this business more than nature⁵⁴
Was ever conduct⁵⁵ of: some oracle
Must rectify⁵⁶ our knowledge.
    PROSPERO.   Sir, my liege,
Do not infest⁵⁷ your mind with beating on
The strangeness of this business: at pick'd leisure,
Which shall be shortly, single⁵⁸ I'll resolve you,
Which to you shall seem probable, of every
These happen'd accidents; till when, be cheerful
And think of each thing well. [*Aside to* ARIEL.] Come hither,
        spirit.
Set Caliban and his companions free;
Untie the spell. [*Exit* ARIEL.] How fares my gracious sir?
There are yet missing of your company
Some few odd lads that you remember not.

---

48. clapp'd—shut.
49. several—particular.
50. trim—rigging and equipment.
51. Cap'ring—dancing for joy.
52. On a trice—in a moment.
53. moping—dazed.
54. nature—natural causes.
55. conduct—director.   56. rectify—verify.
57. infest—worry.   58. single—by myself.

Re-enter ARIEL, *driving in* CALIBAN, STEPHANO, *and* TRINCULO, *in their stolen apparel.*

STEPHANO.   Every man shift for all the rest, and let no man take care for himself; for all is but fortune. Coragio,[59] bully monster, coragio!

TRINCULO.   If these be true spies[60] which I wear in my head here's a goodly sight.

CALIBAN.   O Setebos, these be brave spirits indeed!
How fine my master is! I am afraid
He will chastise me.

SEBASTIAN.   Ha, ha!
What things are these, my lord Antonio?
Will money buy 'em?

ANTONIO.   Very like; one of them
Is a plain fish, and, no doubt, marketable.

PROSPERO.   Mark but the badges[61] of these men, my lords,
Then say if they be true. This mis-shapen knave,
His mother was a witch, and one so strong
That could control the moon, make flows and ebbs,
And deal in her command without her[62] power.
These three have robb'd me; and this demi-devil—
For he's a bastard one—had plotted with them
To take my life. Two of these fellows you
Must know and own; this thing of darkness I
Acknowledge mine.

CALIBAN.   I shall be pinch'd to death.

ALONSO.   Is not this Stephano, my drunken butler?

SEBASTIAN.   He is drunk now. Where had he wine?

ALONSO.   And Trinculo is reeling ripe. Where should they
Find this grand liquor that hath gilded [63] 'em?
How cam'st thou in this pickle?

TRINCULO.   I have been in such a pickle since I saw you last that, I fear me, will never out of my bones. I shall not fear fly-blowing.

SEBASTIAN.   Why, how now, Stephano!

---

59. Coragio—courage.   60. spies—eyes.
61. badges—livery; here, stolen garments.
62. without her—beyond the moon's.   63. gilded—intoxicated.

STEPHANO.   O, touch me not; I am not Stephano, but a
   cramp.

PROSPERO.   You'd be king o' the isle, sirrah?

STEPHANO.   I should have been a sore one then.

ALONSO.   This is a strange thing as e'er I look'd on.

[Pointing to CALIBAN.]

PROSPERO.   He is as disproportion'd in his manners
As in his shape. Go, sirrah, to my cell;
Take with you your companions: as you look
To have my pardon, trim it[64] handsomely.

CALIBAN.   Ay, that I will; and I'll be wise hereafter
And seek for grace. What a thrice-double ass
Was I, to take this drunkard for a god
And worship this dull fool!

PROSPERO.   Go to; away!

ALONSO.   Hence, and bestow your luggage[65] where you found
   it.

SEBASTIAN.   Or stole it, rather.

PROSPERO.   Sir, I invite your Highness and your train
To my poor cell, where you shall take your rest
For this one night; which, part of it, I'll waste
With such discourse as, I not doubt, shall make it
Go quick away,—the story of my life
And the particular accidents gone by
Since I came to this isle: and in the morn
I'll bring you to your ship and so to Naples,
Where I have hope to see the nuptial
Of these our dear-belov'd solémnized;
And thence retire me to my Milan, where
Every third thought shall be my grave.

ALONSO.   I long
To hear the story of your life, which must
Take[66] the ear strangely.

PROSPERO.   I'll deliver all;
And promise you calm seas, auspicious gales,
And sail so expeditious that shall catch
Your royal fleet far off. [<i>Aside to</i> ARIEL.] My Ariel, chick,

---

64. trim it—set it to rights.   65. luggage—the stolen garments.
66. Take—bewitch.

That is thy charge. Then to the elements
Be free, and fare thou well! Please you, draw near.

Exeunt omnes.

EPILOGUE[67]

Spoken by PROSPERO

Now my charms are all o'erthrown,
And what strength I have 's mine own,
Which is most faint: now, 't is true,
I must be here confin'd by you,
Or sent to Naples. Let me not,
Since I have my dukedom got
And pardon'd the deceiver, dwell
In this bare island by your spell;
But release me from my bands
With the help of your good hands.
Gentle breath of yours my sails
Must fill, or else my project fails,
Which was to please. Now I want
Spirits to enforce, art to enchant,
And my ending is despair,
Unless I be reliev'd by prayer,
Which pierces so that it assaults
Mercy itself and frees all faults.
    As you from crimes would pardon'd be.
    Let your indulgence set me free.   *Exit.*

67. Epilogue—a conventional feature of the older drama. A member
of the cast requests the audience to forgive the shortcomings of the
play and bestow applause on the actors.

Rinehart Editions